FLY FISHING
MONTANA

JOHN HOLT

Photographs by Ginny Holt

Guilford, Connecticut

An imprint of Rowman & Littlefield

Distributed by NATIONAL BOOK NETWORK

British Library Cataloguing-in-Publication Information available

Library of Congress Cataloging-in-Publication Data available

ISBN 978-0-7627-9682-3 (paperback)

∞™ The paper used in this publication meets the minimum requirements of American National Standard for Information Sciences—Permanence of Paper for Printed Library Materials, ANSI/NISO Z39.48-1992.

For Francis "Red" Weldon—one of the good guys

Moral: Humility and open-mindedness sometimes catch
far more fish than all the wise guys.

—ROBERT TRAVER
Anatomy of a Fisherman

TABLE OF CONTENTS

Introduction   vii

DRAINAGES WEST OF THE
   CONTINENTAL DIVIDE   1
Bitterroot Blackfoot   3
Blackfoot River   21
Upper Clark Fork   37
Lower Clark Fork   61
Flathead   81
Glacier National Park   121
Kootenai   133
Swan   151

DRAINAGES EAST OF THE
   CONTINENTAL DIVIDE   161
Beaverhead River   163
Big Hole River   181
Blackfeet Reservation   193
Clarks Fork of the
   Yellowstone   203
Gallatin River   211
Jefferson River   221
Madison River   229
Marias River   243

Milk River   249
Missouri River   255
   Upper Missouri   263
   Lower Missouri   272
Musselshell River   281
Red Rock River   287
Smith River   291
Stillwater River   299
Yellowstone River   305

Travel in Montana   327
Additional Indian
   Reservations   328
Real and Perceived Dangers   329
Suggested Gear   331
Stream Etiquette   333
Whirling Disease   335
Stream Access   339

Hatch Charts   345
Further Information   362
Index   363
About the Author and
   Photographer   374

Unlike rainbows, browns, and brook trout, Yellowstone cutthroats are native to Montana.

INTRODUCTION

When my editor Allen Jones at Lyons Press first approached me about doing an updated and distilled version of my original *Montana Fly-Fishing Guides, East and West,* I was somewhat reluctant, to say the least, but the more I thought about the opportunity to fine-tune the two books and condense them into one volume, the more I warmed to the idea. When Allen mentioned that he wanted to replace all of the original black-and-white photographs with color shots by my wife, Ginny, I finally said an enthusiastic "Yes." Her work makes this a vibrant and better book.

Also gone are the photos and related material for fly patterns. Flies to use on given waters are still discussed, but the rivers and lakes themselves are more in focus. I also eliminated the countless tiny, minor, and/or lesser waters listed at the end of each river section in the original guides. All of the information was updated and condensed. My selection of rivers was admittedly subjective and arbitrary but based on nearly fifty years of roaming back roads, two-tracks, and mountain trails in search of fun and unique fishing. The distillation of all of the information contained in the original volumes helped create a more functional, easier-to-use volume. There are enough rivers, streams, and lakes to occupy several lifetimes of determined fishing. I'm pleased to have had the opportunity to make these needed changes in books that were written nearly twenty years ago.

We spent late March through October traveling, photographing, fishing, and camping in the beautiful landscape that is Montana, the land we love. What I found surprised me. Of the many waters I fished, all of them were as least as good as, if not better than, when I originally researched the two guidebooks. This tells me that we as fly fishers and conservationists, along with groups like Montana Trout Unlimited and the Montana Department of Fish, Wildlife & Parks (FWP), have been doing our jobs in this area, ensuring that we have good country to spend time in, fishing and just enjoying the serenity of largely pristine lands.

The biggest change since the original guides were published is the closure of all fishing to bull trout due to falling numbers of the species in the state. If one is caught while fishing for other species, it must be released immediately. The fish are mentioned throughout the book only to give an indication of the type and quality of the specific water being discussed. Hopefully this glorious and ferocious native will return to catchable numbers sometime down the road. There is limited angling for bull trout as stated by FWP in its regulations: "Bull Trout Catch Card—A FWP bull trout permit on your fishing license and a separate catch card are required and must be in possession while intentionally fishing for bull trout in the main stem South Fork Flathead River upstream from Hungry Horse Reservoir and Lake Koocanusa. A catch card is not required for bull trout fishing on Swan Lake. Catch cards will provide FWP with critical management information." Better than nothing, I guess.

With so much water out there to fish, the need for a guide written strictly for fly fishers becomes clear. Other guides are available, many giving much sound information and advice. Concise, accurate information for fly fishers dedicated to catching trout 99 percent of the time (chasing bass with deer-hair poppers or northern pike with saltwater patterns has a certain, esoteric appeal occasionally) helps in this pursuit. For out-of-state visitors, where to start can itself be a frustrating, mind-numbing dilemma.

I am one of the fortunate ones who live in Montana and have the opportunity to fish a hundred-plus days a season. Each river, stream, creek, lake, pond, reservoir, and ditch mentioned in previous volumes of this guide has been cross-checked with the latest data available from the Montana Department of Fish, Wildlife & Parks. Additionally, dozens of guides, fly shop owners, fisheries biologists, and hard-core anglers have been interviewed about the current state of trout-chasing affairs.

What the reader will find in here are listings and descriptions of hundreds of waters worthy of an angler's effort. Divided into sections by drainages, major rivers are described in detail at the opening of each section. Tributaries and lakes that provide quality angling are then covered (in varying degree) in alphabetical order in each drainage section. Information includes the type of water, species present, abundance and size range of the fish, any fly patterns that are locally important, and other pertinent facts. Specific insect hatches may also be discussed.

One of the best ways to navigate in unfamiliar territory is by using United States Geological Survey (USGS) topographical maps. These show in detail important features, including rivers, tiny creeks, lakes, ponds, mountains, forests, dams, swamps, buildings, roads, etc. Anyone who can read a highway map can read a topo. They are an inexpensive means to finding waters discussed in this guide.

Because there are literally hundreds of topo maps for Montana alone, it would be cumbersome and costly to own them all. By checking online (web addresses are listed at the end of the book) you can decide which maps to order with little effort, or if you are hopelessly addicted to maps and the treasures they reveal like I am, kiss an evening good-bye. Larger-scale maps are also listed.

And because every river or lake can be destroyed in the course of a season by logging, development, agriculture (especially irrigation drawdown), mining, or simply overuse by anglers, environmental problems affecting specific waters will also be mentioned. The fly-fishing community absolutely must become involved with preserving and even enhancing the world-class trout habitat of Montana. If we do not, it all truly will be gone in the future. Personal commitment is needed. To me that is one of the possible benefits of the guide—some new people will be introduced to what Montana has to offer fly fishers. Those that would destroy these fine waters in service of the almighty twisted dollar only listen to the heat generated by the outraged aggregation of an angry mob—in this case one clutching fly rods and wearing waders. I would much rather work a stream with an angler who shares my love of rivers and fish than watch helplessly as chain saws and D9s rip the guts out of both water and trout.

The environmental comments are not a declaration of doom. They are a call to join in these battles. The good news is that although some of those battles are temporarily lost, more are being won. Not only are waters being protected, but many damaged fisheries are rebounding in water quality, aesthetics, and productivity. The fact is that fly fishing for trout in Montana is as good or better in the majority of waters mentioned in this book. With the help of people inside and outside who care about this state, it will be true twenty years from now.

Even with the swelling of our dedicated ranks, there is still a lot of lightly or rarely fished water. And fishing on crowded waters like the Madison, Bighorn, or Bitterroot is still superb. The action would be even better if everyone exercised the maximum degree of courtesy and common sense. Learning to share the resource will be a valuable skill in the future.

Admittedly some lakes, especially those with brook trout, are overpopulated and produce stunted fish. Keeping a few of these for a campfire dinner may actually improve the health of the system. But for anyone to keep a trophy brown from the Beaverhead or a trophy rainbow from the Missouri is both selfish and destructive. Catch-and-release with barbless hooks is the only way to travel most of our waters anymore.

Finally, there are dozens of fly patterns mentioned in this book and I've had success with all of them, but for me I've learned that less is more. Over the past five seasons I've used nine patterns—in various sizes and shadings—to the near exclusion of all others They are: Cree-hackled, brown-bodied Woolly Bugger, Humpy, Biggs Special/Sheep Creek Nymph, Gold-Ribbed Hare's Ear Nymph, Partridge and Orange Soft Hackle, Joe's Hopper, BWO Olive Thorax, Elk Hair Caddis, and my current favorite, the Hendrickson. I am able to take fish in nearly every type of water under most conditions. Use as few or as many as you like—whatever works, and most importantly is fun for you.

The bottom line with fly fishing is the feeling of a large fish running for freedom as the rod bends double and the reel's drag buzzes toward mechanical breakdown. That's all this book is really about . . . the water, the trout, and the angler.

DRAINAGES WEST OF THE CONTINENTAL DIVIDE

A favorite among fly fishers, brown trout are elusive, aggressive, and strong.

Bitterroot Blackfoot

The Bitterroot has gained a loyal following of serious fly fishers over the years. Anglers from around the country come to cast over the river's rainbow, brown, cutthroat, and brook trout (this is roughly their order of importance). A good day on the water means catching twenty to forty trout, most of them under 15 inches, but with the occasional brute up to 4 or 5 pounds.

The quality of the fishing—numbers of fish, scenic beauty, challenging water—has led to an explosion of floaters. Recently a friend and I put on the water at dawn. Our shuttle rig was the only one at the takeout. At the end of the float there were several dozen outfits jammed into the parking area. Our early start ensured that we had a glorious day's fishing all to ourselves. To beat the crowds start early, very early.

The river has its beginnings in the Bitterroot Mountains on the west and the Sapphires on the east. From the confluence of the East and West Forks near Connor, the river falls a little over 800 feet during its leisurely 85-mile journey to the Clark Fork at Missoula. There are some fast runs, tricky bends, and a few nasty irrigation dams, but for the most part the river is easy going.

If you float the river from the West Fork down through Connor, past Sleeping Child, by Victor, on to Stevensville, through Lolo, and down to Missoula, you can experience every type of trout fishing a Rocky Mountain river can offer. From shallow riffles near the headwaters to gravel-banked runs and on into deep pools and glides, past thick piles of downed trees, and over slow-moving flats, the Bitterroot has all the faces.

CONNOR TO HAMILTON

The first section, from the confluence of the East and West Forks just below Conner down to Hamilton, qualifies as a small river most of the year. Flows range from less than 100 cubic feet per second (cfs) in February to over 2,000 cfs during the June-July runoff. The Bitterroot twists enough to dig holes and slots, but there are plenty of long, gentle riffles. The water from the Old Darby Bridge down to Wally Crawford Access is an easy, short float, with no diversion dams—perfect for the visitor rowing his own boat. The fishing is consistent throughout the summer, mostly for smaller trout.

Bitterroot Blackfoot

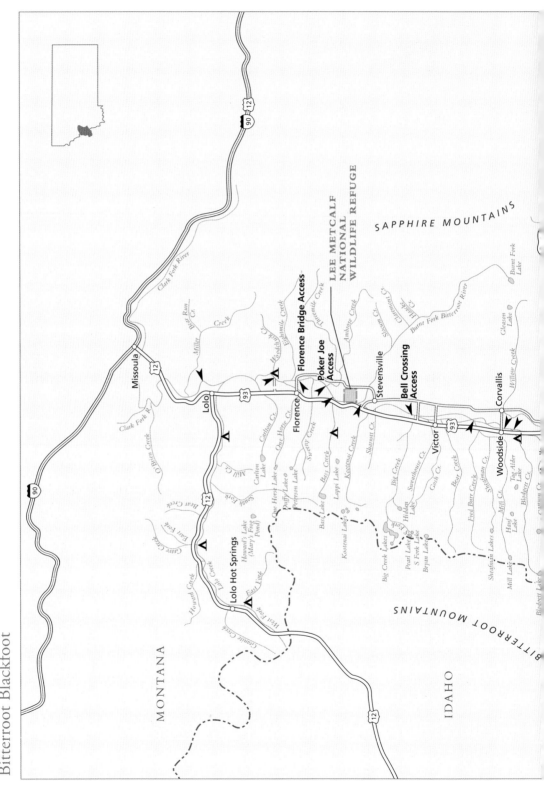

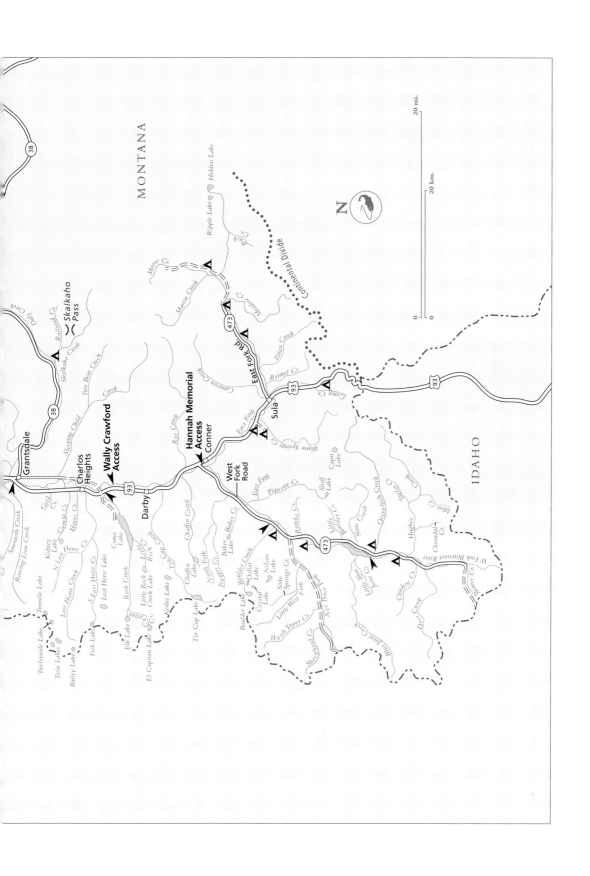

The Bitterroot is a fine floating-and-wading river best fished in the early morning and late in the day to avoid the crowds.

HAMILTON TO VICTOR

The second section, from Hamilton to Victor, still suffers in areas from channel destabilization. The river braids, creating numerous islands, and digs away at the unsecured banks. This part of the Bitterroot also gets hit harder by irrigation drawdown during the summer. The fishing, especially in the upper half, is still very good and, in the opinion of local veteran angler Woody Emrich, "If we can win a few more battles, this is going to be the best piece of the Bitterroot."

Maybe every fly fisher's fantasy is to have a private trout stream. On the Bitterroot, from this section down, even if he can't get a deed to it, it's not hard for the angler to find a piece of water to call his own. There are side channels and oxbows with independent current from groundwater or irrigation seepage. The heads of these cutoffs go dry or get low during the summer, so no boat traffic enters the channel. The angler can discover these "short pieces" by walking the shore a few miles. Many of them, with their sipping fish, look just like spring creeks.

VICTOR TO FLORENCE
The third section, from Victor to Florence, is slower water (none of this river is steep gradient anyway). There are deeper holes and longer flats. The trout feed steadily and fussily on the hatches. The river passes the Lee Metcalf National Wildlife Refuge, which covers 1,700 acres and stretches along 4.5 miles of one bank. The fishing in this section slumps during midsummer in hot years, but it is a classic piece of dry-fly water during the other three seasons.

FLORENCE TO THE CONFLUENCE WITH THE CLARK FORK
An interesting opportunity exists on the lower end of the Bitterroot. In the sloughs off the main channel between Florence and the mouth of the river, there are good numbers of pike and largemouth bass. At the peak fishing times, from July through September, surface disturbers (size 1/0 plastic Sliders for the pike and size 6 deer-hair bugs for the bass) produce fine topwater fishing. A major food item in this section of the Bitterroot is crayfish, and in the slower, deep flats of the main channel, a crayfish pattern catches not only bass but some really large trout.

Stoneflies begin showing up on the river in March. The skwala hatch is a time of high excitement for many anglers. Skwalas differ from their salmon fly relatives. Their hatching is not marked by wild, blizzard-like flurries that move steadily upriver day by day. Instead, the skwala comes off in smaller numbers, hatching on a localized basis throughout the stream course in pretty much the same spots year after year. So once the angler turns up a spot or two, he can return each spring and, with a little looking, wade into some good action. Rainbows will provide most of the fishing, with a few browns and maybe a cutthroat or two tossed into the mix.

The first flush of water from a combination of rain and snowmelt actually improves the fishing, but once the runoff begins, forget about fishing the main river. Millions of acre-feet of snowmelt pour out of the mountains and wash through the valley. Things often don't return to normal until July. Side channels and the mouths of feeder streams are the best locations at this time (tarpon fishing in Florida is not a bad idea either).

The important hatches include (besides the skwala): chironomid midges, bringing up trout all winter; the grannom caddis, coming off heavily during the first weeks of May, especially on the upper stretch; the salmon fly, beginning in mid-June; the golden stone, a flurry in late June (John Foust, local angler, says that they are great one in three years); the green drake and the brown drake, also starting near the end of June; the spotted sedge and the little sister sedge, dominating the evening activity starting in late June; the western leadwing, beginning in late June (this is not an important dry-fly insect, but the nymphs might explain the popularity of the Prince Nymph and the Leadwing Coachman wet fly on the river); the pale morning dun, starting in early July; the gray drake, the spinners important in early July (this mayfly seems to flourish wherever there are slow, weedy canals around the river); the trico, appearing over the flats in August, especially on the lower river; the blue-winged red quill, emerging mid-day from late August through mid-September; the giant orange sedge, appearing in early September; and the blue-winged olive, starting in mid-September and hatching the heaviest on overcast days.

If there is a "don't miss" event on the Bitterroot, it is the combined blitz of the green drake and the brown drake. The spectacular flush of duns equals the hatch on any western river. Oddly, the larger green drake outnumbers the smaller brown drake (it's usually the other way around). On the prime stretches, like the loop around Hamilton (the float stretch from Angler's Roost to the Silver Bridge), rising trout and whitefish churn the surface all afternoon.

For the streamer fisherman there is an important difference between the upper and the lower stretches. In the upper river sculpins and suckers are the main forage species, and the best imitations and tactics mimic these bottom-clinging baitfish. But in the lower river squawfish and redside shiners dominate. The shiners, 3 to 4 inches long at maturity, become important during their spawning period in late June and early July, when male shiners turn especially bright, and red or even purple swimming streamers can be incredibly effective for large trout.

For mayflies the parachute-style imitations dominate on the river. That preference extends even to general searchers, the size 12 to 20 Parachute Adams, the most popular all-around pattern. Comparaduns, in appropriate color schemes (specially the slate-olive for the blue-winged olives), effectively match the smaller insects.

One local pattern that has achieved national recognition, the Ugly Rudamus, serves as a general caddis/stonefly imitation. The standard, popular flies, such as the

IMPORTANT HATCHES

Blue-Winged Olive	Green Drake
Blue-Winged Red Quill	Little Sister Sedge
Brown Drake	Pale Morning Dun
Chironomid Midges	Salmon Fly
Giant Orange Sedge	Skwala
Golden Stone	Spotted Sedge
Grannom Caddis	Trico
Gray Drake	Western Leadwing

POPULAR FLIES

Chernobyl Ant

Gold-Ribbed Hare's Ear

Humpy—red, yellow, tan,
   Adams

Joe's Hopper

Madam X

Matt's Stone

Parachute Adams

Peeking Caddis

Pheasant Tail

Prince Nymph

Ugly Rudamus

Woolly Bugger

Elk Hair Caddis and the Emergent Sparkle Pupa, are often altered to match the various caddis hatches (both are tied with a dark wing and an orange body in size 8 for the giant orange sedge).

The Bitterroot is a good river for popping a dry-fly attractor on the riffles. The Madam X, a down-wing, rubber-legged fly born in this area, ranks with the Renegades, H & L Variants, Trudes, Humpies, and Wulffs in popularity. All of these patterns work consistently from sizes 18 to 8, with the smaller ones better in midsummer.

The most common nymphs for the Bitterroot are the Bomber Nymph (especially in a green drake version), Gray Nymph, Gold-Ribbed Hare's Ear, Red Squirrel Nymph, Woolly Worm, Prince Nymph, Peeking Caddis, Matt's Stone, and Pheasant Tail. Most people fish medium sizes, 8 to 16.

You can get on the Bitterroot along its entire length at a number of bridges crossing the river and through various parcels of public land. There are also several clearly marked state fishing accesses along the river. Be aware of weirs and diversions. They can be deadly.

FISHING WATERS IN THE BITTERROOT DRAINAGE

Baker Lake: To get to this alpine lake just under Trapper Peak, drive to the trailhead up the West Fork Highway and then take the gravel road at Pierce Creek. The hike in is an easy 2.5 miles, making Baker a popular spot. It is often good for cutthroats that are measured in inches, not pounds.

Bass Creek: The outlet stream for Bass Lake tumbles over a bed of nutrient-poor igneous rocks, never scouring holes deep enough to shelter large fish. It comes into the Bitterroot a few miles north of Stevensville. This is typical of many west-side streams that look wonderful but tend to yield small fish. There are plenty of small cutthroat, rainbow, and brook trout to fill a day on the wilderness section. The lower few miles are dewatered for irrigation. This is a common problem for not only west-side but east-side streams as well. Irrigation damages both the resident fishery and the spawning runs out of the Bitterroot.

Bass Lake: This deep lake in the Selway-Bitterroot Wilderness is 100 acres when full. Bass Lake is one of the old, man-made water-storage projects in the region. Reached by a tough 7-mile hike, it has a number of fat 10- to 20-inch rainbows, remnants from previous airdrops. The lake is not rich in nutrients, with insect samplings showing low populations of mayflies, caddisflies, and damselflies. Midge larvae and pupae are the main food source, with a healthy portion of terrestrials—beetles, grasshoppers, and ants—thrown in. Wind is a common companion up here, so take a 6-weight outfit. Wet patterns such as the Hare's Ear, Pheasant Tail, and Twist Nymph in olive (always a good lake color) work well. Flying Ants, Foam Beetles, Gartside Hoppers, and the Deer Hair Hornet are deadly on flat, calm water.

Big Creek: This classic mountain stream begins way back in the Bitterroots and flows quickly from Big Creek Lakes down to the river near Victor. The lower reaches are sucked dry for irrigation. The upper runs, followed by trail, are easy fishing for brooks and cutts that love Wulffs, Humpies, Trudes—all the sophisticated stuff. In the canyon, 4 to 5 miles below the lakes, the trail skirts the stream and hikers stare down into green pools so deep that the bottom isn't visible. This is a good spot for the fly fisher to get specific, drifting nymphs that naturally sink fast, such as bead-heads or teardrops, for the cutthroats, or even swimming small streamers, such as a Baby Cutthroat or a Muddler.

Big Creek Lakes: In high country, these glacial-cirque waters are at the head of Big Creek in a basin edged with pine and talus slopes. At high water these lakes are actually one body of water totaling close to 250 acres and maybe 100 feet deep. Plenty of 8- to 14-inch westslope cutthroats and rainbows swim here (the larger cutthroats stay around the inlet cover at the upper end). As in most high-country lakes of size, there are also a few picky trout in the 3- to 4-pound range. And as always, a nymph like the Gold-Ribbed Hare's Ear, cast well ahead of the cruising fish and then moved ever so slightly, produces consistently. Time your strike to the flash of white jaws.

Montanans use their wilderness areas. Even though it's an 11-mile trek into this area, on a normal July weekend a troop of thirty Boy Scouts, a horse outfitter with a half-dozen clients, and eight other pairs or groups of backpackers camped around the lake.

Bitterroot Irrigation Ditch: On the east side the Ditch is fishable mainly during the growing season when ranchers need water. The artificial flow is paralleled for its 80-mile length by two-lane road. Some very big rainbows, brooks, and browns, recruited in the spring from the river, are caught in this thing each season. It's a strange fishing spot that sometimes resembles a spring creek and at other times looks like the Los Angeles River. Light tippets and precisely matching patterns, especially during the heavy hatches of trico, gray drake, and blue-winged olive mayflies, fool these trout. Hopper and beetle imitations also work in the heat of the summer. Creeping tactics are required for these spooky fish. The whole place is short on aesthetics, but a 5-pound trout is a 5-pound trout.

The secret is knowing precisely where to fish along the canal. The irrigators periodically kill the weeds with chemicals, wiping out insects and fish in the process. Some stretches of the ditch run barren for weeks after this cleanup, and any angler casting the water blind may very well be wasting time. Your best bet is to walk and hunt for risers.

Blodgett Creek: Entering the river near Hamilton, Blodgett has cutthroats, brooks, and the raging bulls of autumn. The lower section is dewatered. A campground sits at the end of the road. Blodgett is ridiculously fast fishing for 6- to 10-inch fish once you get a half-mile up the grail. Seven miles up, past old logjams and sheer cliffs, there are beaver dams where you can get a 16-inch cutthroat. Two patterns, a Light Caddis Variant and a Hare's Ear Trude, cover just about any situation, but this is also the perfect spot to try the odd flies that never work anywhere else.

Marshall Bloom, a volunteer worker on a fry-loss study on Blodgett Creek led by Fish, Wildlife & Parks biologist Chris Clancy, provided the following data: Trout fry, hatched in the creek, drifted down toward the river from mid-June to mid-July. They only drifted for three to four hours each night, probably to avoid predators, and spent the days in the shallow stream margins.

Workers set drift nets at three sites—above an irrigation diversion, in the irrigation canal, and below the irrigation diversion. Above the canal 900 fry were collected in one session, over 500 immature trout were captured in the canal itself, and only 200 fry were recovered below the canal.

Blodgett Lake: You can see hints of the cirque country that holds this water as you drive along US 93. Even if it weren't full of healthy cutthroats, the lake would be worth a long walk, especially in early autumn. The top three flies recommended for Blodgett are the Twitch-Pause Nymph, Otter Shrimp, and Zug Bug.

Blue Joint Creek: A fine little stream that pours into Painted Rocks Lake, Blue Joint is easily fished along the 20-mile trail for some nice cutthroats up to 14 inches, as well as lesser numbers of other species. The trout here take either the Royal Humpy, with its red-and-white color scheme, or the Coachman Trude, with its green-and-white color scheme, preferring one over the other at any given moment.

Boulder Creek: A typical Bitterroot mountain stream (and like many, it gets better as you go up a way), the Boulder joins the West Fork of the Bitterroot several miles upstream from the confluence of the West and East Forks. Four miles up the trail, through aspen groves and huckleberry patches, there's a waterfall with a large pool at the bottom. That hole has the greatest variety of trout species, with the biggest specimens of each (for example, cutts up to 14 inches instead of 8 inches).

Boulder Lake: This glacial cirque lake has a few cutthroats to 18 inches that are finicky feeders. Bring long leaders and small nymphs (preferably something matching a midge—a size 18 Serendipity is a good choice). Reached by 10 miles of relatively easy trail from the end of the Boulder Creek Road, Boulder Lake is dammed at the outlet and holds 20 acres at full pool.

Burnt Fork Bitterroot River: Located in the Stevensville area, this is a nice, easy-to-fish stream pouring out of the Sapphire Mountains that is followed by dirt and gravel road and then trail to Burnt Fork Lake. The lower reaches dry up from irrigation, but the upper reaches vary from open meadowland pools and runs to forested stretches filled with brushy banks and logjams. An Elk Hair Caddis and an Adams are as fancy as you normally need to be on this creek. It has good numbers of cutthroats and brookies, some over a foot.

Burnt Fork Lake: Reached by several trails, the most obvious being the one at the end of Burnt Fork Road, this lake is excellent right after the ice goes out. Relatively nutrient-rich due to the surrounding limestone formations, the lake is drawn down quite a bit for irrigation but it is 30 acres when full and good fishing for bull, cutthroat, and rainbow trout averaging less than a foot. Damselfly nymphs and Woolly Worms—bigger flies than are usually successful in these high-mountain fisheries—handle the subsurface action. Caddis, mayfly, midge, and terrestrial imitations work on top.

Camas Lakes: Way up the Camas Creek drainage, getting to Camas Lakes is a hell of a hike. You can't get a horse into them. There's a stretch where you have to climb over, jump over, and squeeze between boulders ranging from car-size to house-size. The upper lake is better than the lower lake. There are still a lot of small cutthroats there, but at least on this one you have the chance to hook a big fish.

Cameron Creek: This 7 miles of good small-water fishing unfortunately is mostly on private, posted land. It enters the East Fork near Sula. This is a brook, bull, cutthroat, and rainbow stream.

Carlton Lake: Reached by the Carlton Lake Road south of Lolo, this lake, at 7,700 feet, sits exposed in scrub timber just below Lolo Peak. The wind always blows; any air coming off the snow is chilling. Carlton is 40 acres when full, but during summer drawdown it is an ugly 20-acre bowl. There are small cutthroats, rainbows, and hybrids, all of which do a neat disappearing act at times.

In spite of all this, Carlton is a popular day trip with hikers and four-wheelers, probably because it is so close to Missoula. Anyone who makes the trip up here should visit the truly spectacular waterfall a few hundred yards below the outlet.

Como Lake: Fifteen miles southwest of Hamilton on Rock Creek and easily reached by country road, Como is over 1,000 acres when not drawn down for irrigation. There is a public campground, and this place is well known and overrun with happy visitors as long as the weather remains warm. Water-skiers hatch here in the summer. It's a beautiful lake when full and irrigation-ditch ugly when sucked down 50 feet or so. Como is planted with thousands of 8- to 10-inch Arlee rainbows, along with some tired brood stock from the hatchery. Working the north shoreline away from the crowds is the best bet, especially around the mouths or tributaries. A float tube or canoe helps. There is currently a project under way to expand the storage capacity on Como Lake to provide more water for irrigation and instream flows.

Daly Creek: Seventeen miles up the gravel Skalkaho Highway east of Hamilton, this swiftly flowing water is ice-cold, clear, and small, but fun fishing for small cutts and rainbows. For years Daly was closed to all fishing because deposits of the mineral cinnabar, in a disturbed area, were poisoning the stream with mercury. Don't drink the water.

East Fork Bitterroot River: Forested in the upper reaches and open in the lower reaches, this stream runs for 37 miles to Sula and under US 93 to join the West Fork. Irrigation really does a number on the lower section and some of the middle section. In the northwest part of the state, the streams are silted up from logging. Down here they just suck the life out of them. The hell with the fish.

All the same, there are cutthroats and rainbows in entertaining numbers to maybe a touch over 12 inches, plus minor concentrations of brown and brook trout. In the spring, rainbows finished with spawning hang around long enough for the salmon fly hatch in the second week of June. The stream usually runs clear during the hatch, making it good water for large dry flies (an Evazote Salmon Fly, buoyant and flush-floating, is a good pattern). There are no dams on this fork to pump up the summer flow and it gets low, sending the fishing into a funk after July. In the winter, the mountain whitefish love nymphs if you get a serious case of cabin fever.

The East Fork used to have a healthy population of cutthroats up to 16 inches, natives adapted to the river. Now it has mostly small rainbows. Without some protection from the crowds, it remains just another roadside fishery that doesn't live up to its potential.

El Capitan Lake: A very popular backcountry lake above Como Lake, El Capitan sees both backpacking and horse traffic, but still has decent action for foot-long-or-so cutthroats in its 15 acres of dark water. Small Woolly Worms, sizes 12 and 14, tied with fluorescent chenille, work especially well here, as do Biggs Specials.

Gleason Lake: Go up Willow Creek Road, then walk the last mile in the Sapphire Mountains to this nutrient-rich water. It has plenty of healthy westslope cutthroats that love leech patterns and damsel nymphs. Try fishing a Purple Bunny Leech over the weed beds with a sinking line (this tactic took trout after trout here one afternoon).

Hidden Lake: At nearly 7,000 feet in the Big Creek drainage, Hidden Lake is managed for cutthroats (planted with 1,000 4-to-6-inchers yearly) that do well due in large part to the lack of fishing pressure. Easy to fish—remember they are, after all, cutthroats.

Hughes Creek: In the West Fork drainage, this small stream is followed by gravel road and trail for nearly 20 miles. Plenty of simple pleasure here for 7-inch cutthroats and brookies amid the pine forests. A size 16 Hare's Ear Nymph or a Red Humpy works well.

Kootenai Creek: Entering the river near Stevensville, Kootenai is dewatered below (of course), a good mountain stream above. The way it tumbles, in a pool-and-fall sequence, makes buoyant dry flies, maybe a deer-hair Irresistible, especially efficient for the hordes of pan-size cutthroats. This is worth the walk just to fish under the "hanging canyons," those walls extending out over the stream.

Kootenai Lakes: Three lakes lie at the upper end of the Kootenai drainage. Middle Lake was planted with goldens many years ago, but they're history. North Lake has some nice rainbows, and South Lake is packed with stunted brookies. Almost all high-country lakes now are managed for cutthroats, so look for rainbow-cutthroat hybrids (or even golden-rainbow hybrids). In lakes stuffed with small brookies, any fly will catch fish (except for the Stu Apte Tarpon pattern). Catch a bunch for a lakeside meal and do the lake (and the trout) a favor.

Little Rock Creek: One of the numerous pretty and productive mountains streams that run into Como Lake, a set of waterfalls just up from the mouth stops any spawning run coming out of the lake, but there are resident cutthroats up to 10 inches living in the small pools and pockets. For some reason the ticks (more dangerous than a lot of better-known terrors of the woods) are especially bad here in the spring.

Lolo Creek: Lolo flows alongside the Lewis and Clark Highway (US 12) for 30 miles to the town of Lolo and is accessible for much of its length from the road. There is a famous hot springs here, with a resort where a tired angler can soak in a pool after a hard day of flogging. The stream is heavily hit by both residents and travelers who cannot resist the look of the water. In the upper section Lolo runs through dense pine forests. In the middle it flows through open meadow, including a lot of former pasture land now getting chopped up into homesites. There is a little bit of everything in the drainage, most commonly brookies, cutts, and rainbows, but with browns moving up from the river in the fall.

Eastern fly fishermen especially like the lower section, from a mile above the Lolo Bridge down to the Bitterroot, because the stream reminds them of home waters. Cottonwoods nearly join in a canopy over the pools and runs. The water digs deeper, providing hiding spots for nicer fish. The stream rewards the angler who casts accurately, giving up only small trout, mostly brookies, from the open areas but much nicer fish from the dark, shaded holds.

Lolo isn't a stream where the angler can always ignore the hatches. It's rich enough in this lower stretch to get not only well-known mayflies and caddisflies, but also strong numbers of some real oddities. A professional entomologist should collect this water—there are undoubtedly significant populations of "relict species" because of the springs flowing into it. In early November there is a surprising hatch of one large, stunning mayfly, the gray-flecked duns riding like little sailboats. And this insect doesn't fit any of the descriptions in any of the angling entomologies. Trout relish these mayflies, feeding on them any day the weather is decent.

Good hatches include the spotted sedge, coming out in good numbers through June, and the ginger quill, appearing in early July. These are both big enough insects, popping in enough quantity, to get the larger trout looking at the surface.

Lost Horse Lake: Nearly 70 acres, Lost Horse is typical of many of the backcountry lakes (like Twin, Tenmile, and Twelvemile Lakes) in the Bitterroots. There are boggy sections along the shoreline with clumps of rock rising above the water. It is managed for native cutthroats that do well in this environment. The fishing is often easy for trout averaging 12 inches and on rare occasions reaching a pound or two. Warm valley winds often curl along the slopes, carrying grasshoppers, ants, and beetles out onto these lakes in the afternoon. The trout have keyed to this phenomenon, so take a selection of terrestrial patterns on trips to this alpine country.

Martin Creek: The huge fire that swept through this area of the East Fork in the early 1960s decreased both the size and number of trout in this mountain stream, but the drainage is healing itself. There are enough small cutthroats in the riffles, pools, and pockets, all ready to flash to a size 16 Trude or Adams, to make this fun fishing.

Nez Perce Fork: Followed by road for 20 miles from the West Fork to the headwaters, Nez Perce Fork offers very good fishing for cutthroats and brookies, along with some browns. There are little yellow sally stoneflies fluttering around all summer, enough to make a size 16 Yellow Trude a main fly.

Painted Rocks Lake: This reservoir provides 4 miles of waterskiing bliss in wooded country along the west side of the West Fork Highway. It's hard to say which hurts the fishing more in the summer, the irrigation drawdown or the passing speedboats (put up a warning flag if you're bobbing around in a float tube). Generally there are plenty of better places to cast a fly in the Bitterroot Valley, but there are enough cutthroats to make this lake worth a visit early in the season when the lake is full, the boaters are still in winter shock, and the fish cruise the shorelines in the cold water.

Peterson Lake: Go up Sweeney Creek Road south of Florence, then on logging road to reach Peterson Lake at the head of the North Fork. The lake offers good fishing for small rainbows, cutthroats, and hybrids. There is usually a strong inverse correlation on these high-mountain lakes between the size of the trout and the pace of the fishing action.

Ripple Lake: Some big trout swim here that are not often caught. The small lake lies up the East Fork in the Anaconda-Pintler Wilderness and has both cutthroats and rainbows.

Roaring Lion Creek: This small canyon stream washes out of the Bitterroots south of Hamilton, home to good numbers of small cutthroats. Don't fish any of these mountain creeks too early—the water out of the snowfields is just too cold for good fly fishing— but they come into their own in the summer.

Rock Creek: A real pretty, forested mountain stream, not far from Darby, Rock Creek flows swiftly over smooth shelves and short drops. The lower stretch is ruined by irrigation, but some fair-size brookies, cutthroats, and rainbows hold out in the upper sections.

Sheafman Lakes: Seven miles of trail, starting at the mouth of Sheafman Canyon north of Woodside and twisting into the Bitterroots in rugged, timbered, and steep-walled country, take you to these high-mountain waters. The lower 6-acre lake is managed for cutthroat trout that do not grow large but are fairly abundant. The upper lake is barren.

Shelf Lake: Hike 6 miles of trail from the lower end of Painted Rocks Lake to reach this 7,600-foot-high lake that offers average fishing for 12-inch cutthroats.

Skalkaho Creek: Pretty name—it means "place of the beaver." This is one of the last unspoiled drainages in this part of the country, flowing clear and swift toward the Bitterroot near Hamilton. Plans to clear-cut much of this drainage would spell disaster for the excellent numbers of medium-size cutthroats (beautiful, oddly colored fish with dark, purplish-brown backs) and the occasional brown and brook trout. Forested mountains stretch off in all directions. The water runs over a golden, coppery-colored streambed. Fishing is easy.

Sleeping Child Creek: This stream joins the Bitterroot south of Hamilton and is heavily fished for various salmonid species which, except for the transient spawners, never reach great size. In the lower reaches, however, those spawners turn this creek into a wonder. For some reason the browns in the fall really use Sleeping Child, starting their upstream push as soon as there is enough water. A favorite tactic is to fish a hopper as a dry indicator and a heavily weighted Hare's Ear Nymph working the deeper runs and pools. The whole exercise of reading the water changes, and you should look for spawners in holding areas.

In the upper reaches the stream is followed by a good trail to its mountainous head-waters on the east side of the valley. The water is so clear that you have trouble judging the depth. The flies have to be fished in and under the wood snags, but at the same time a fine leader, at least a 5X, increases the number of strikes. You will get broken off in Sleeping Child by some of the spring and fall spawners that linger even in this tumbling section.

South Fork Lolo Creek: Mainly a cutthroat stream, this creek crosses private land in the lower reaches but is decent angling in the upper runs.

South Fork Skalkaho Creek: A downsized version of the main creek, the South Fork has cutthroats. It is reached from the Skalkaho Highway some 20 minutes (and 10,000 hairpin, blind curves) above Hamilton.

Threemile Creek: Threemile joins the Bitterroot just north of the Lee Metcalf Wildlife Refuge. There must be hundreds of creeks like this that come wandering down out of the hills and then cut their narrow way through pasture and meadowland to main rivers. There are usually some small cutthroats up above and some bigger brooks or rainbows in the middle sections. All too often these streams are hurt by grazing and irrigation in the bottom reaches.

These little buggers often aren't worth fishing, but the kid in me makes passing them up impossible. Dapping nothing but the leader while lying on my belly, the sight of a little trout sucking in a size 20 Adams is as much fun as anything. The mind of a child at work here, thankfully. On Threemile, at least, this creep-and-crawl fishing is safe for the moment. There is a major riparian restoration project going on in the lower few miles of the creek.

Tin Cup Creek: This creek reaches the river just north of Darby. The glaciated geology of this drainage blesses Tin Cup with a variety of terrains. There are spread-out bog reaches, meandering meadow stretches, and tumbling runs, all inhabited by excellent numbers of slightly larger-than-average cutthroats and brookies.

Tin Cup Lake: Why one high-mountain lake in an area is richer than its neighbors is always a mystery. Tin Cup, fairly fertile despite its 9,000-foot-plus elevation and seasonal irrigation drawdowns, has lots of stunted westslope cutthroats—the kind with moray eel–shaped heads and rattlesnake bodies—that will hit anything. But at the inlet, especially off the shallow shelf on the southwest side, there are 16- to 20-inch fish. These bigger trout don't hit just anything. As a matter of fact, they can get downright uppity, cruising along the edge picking something from the bottom. They won't do more than glance at a Woolly Worm or a baitfish imitation, but they will take a small nymph, a size 18 Pheasant Tail or size 14 Biggs Special, if it is sitting right in front of their noses.

Warm Springs Creek: Near the Idaho border, upstream from Connor, this little stream is in country so nice that it reminds you of what western Montana was like fifty years ago. There are cutthroat, rainbow, and brook trout, with some of the better ones hanging in the big, sandy holes. Attractor patterns and small streamers do the trick.

West Fork Bitterroot River: This fork heads along the southwestern border of Montana, flowing through Painted Rocks Reservoir to join the East Fork near Connor. Above Painted Rocks the water holds fair numbers of brook, cutthroat, and rainbow trout. Below the lake you will find a smaller-scale version of the upper Bitterroot, open and rocky banks alternating with brushy shores. This is excellent dry-fly water for browns, rainbows, and cutthroats. It fishes very well through the summer because of the cool releases from the dam.

Private land blocks much of the water, but roads and Forest Service land provide adequate access for non-floaters. This stretch is floatable, but it is a tight squeeze in spots and big logjams appear suddenly around corners—this stream is dangerous enough to discourage the inexperienced boatman.

The West Fork has roughly the same insects as the main river, but the timing is a little different for the hatches. The water, with the dam moderating runoff in early summer and adding flow in midsummer, also fishes better than the main river for some hatches.

Fishing Warm Springs Creek, look for holding water at the bottom of riffle runs and along the foliage-shadowed banks.

One special midsummer terrestrial to look for on the West Fork is the spruce moth. Some streams get infestations and some don't. The West Fork has the right forest composition for this insect. The spruce moth has a long cycle, building up over the years to peak abundance.

The angler can drift popular attractors, such as the Kolzer Orange and H & L Variant, or popular searchers, such as the Caddis Variant and Hare's Ear Parachute, all summer on the West Fork and catch cutthroats and rainbows to 15 inches steadily. Again, Humpies in all colors and sizes work well, too.

Willow (Fool or Sage Hen) Lake: Located in Skalkaho country, Willow is at the end of a poorly maintained trail (which discourages visitors). There are plenty of average rainbows and a few very big ones. Willow Lake is surrounded by meadows, which makes the lake shallower and richer than most mountain lakes, with an abundance of aquatic plants. The weeds change the fly selection, making imitations of damsel nymphs, mayfly nymphs, and caddis larvae more important. The trout cruise and take whatever is along the bottom instead of rushing up to grab any speck of food.

With its serpentine, shaded mysteries, the Blackfoot River is one of my favorite fisheries.
Stephen Beaumont/Shutterstock.com

Blackfoot River

The Norman Maclean novella *A River Runs Through It*, with the Blackfoot River as its setting, begins with the best-known sentence in angling literature: "In our family, there was no clear line between religion and fly fishing." While the whole "river runs through it" routine has been done to death through various media forms, the quote does capture my feeling for this river.

That book mirrors what the Blackfoot was in the first half of this century. The development of mining, logging, and ranching in the drainage finally overwhelmed the ability of the river to heal itself (biologists call these "cumulative impacts"). In 1992 the respected watchdog group American Rivers put the Blackfoot on its list of Top Ten Endangered Rivers. The river was so different from the picture painted by Norman Maclean that the movie, produced by Robert Redford, of *A River Runs Through It* was filmed mostly on the Gallatin.

For many reasons, including the devoted attentions of anglers and conservation groups, the river is improved in 2013 from twenty years ago. The future seems mildly optimistic for the Blackfoot.

Of those Four Horsemen of the Trout Stream Apocalypse—mining, ranching, logging, and subdivision development—there is no doubt about the prime culprit on the Blackfoot. Logging of the forests on private lands in the basin and ranching, with the gross overgrazing of national forest lands in the Alice Creek drainage, exacerbated the sedimentation problems, but as bad as they are, they cannot approach the damage caused by mining. Abandoned workings in the headwaters ooze a brew so acid, so laden with heavy metals, that it wipes out life as it slowly creeps downstream year after year.

The worst mines are the Mike Horse and the Paymaster in the Heddleston Mining District. The current owners refused for years to do anything at all about these sites. Finally the Montana Department of Health and Environmental Sciences (DHES) coaxed them to look at the problem. As of this writing, they have made some minor overtures at cleanup, but the jury is still out on whether DHES has the will to insist on a complete and lasting restoration of these headwater areas.

A proposed mine of huge dimensions is in the works for the upper Blackfoot River 8 miles northeast of the small town of Lincoln, but seems to have gone away for now. If ever completed, the mine, originally planned by the Phelps Dodge Corporation, would have devastating effects on both Lincoln and the river itself. The gold deposit—possibly as much as 5.2 million ounces with a potential value of $2 billion—is one of the largest

Blackfoot River

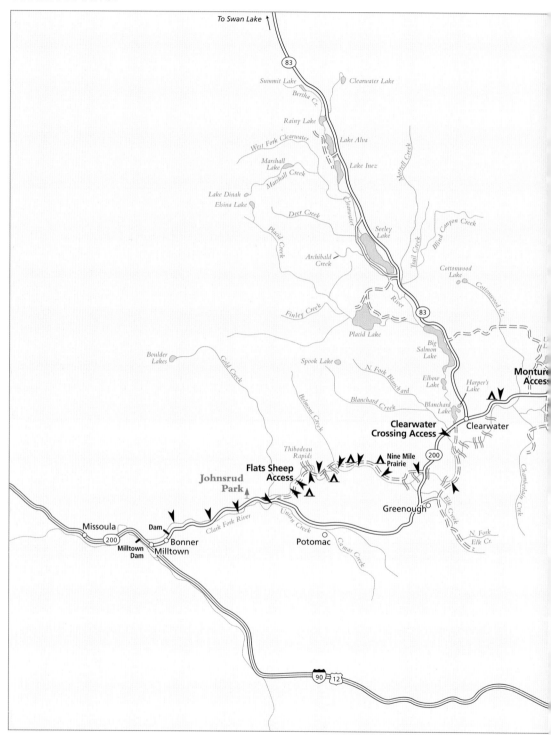

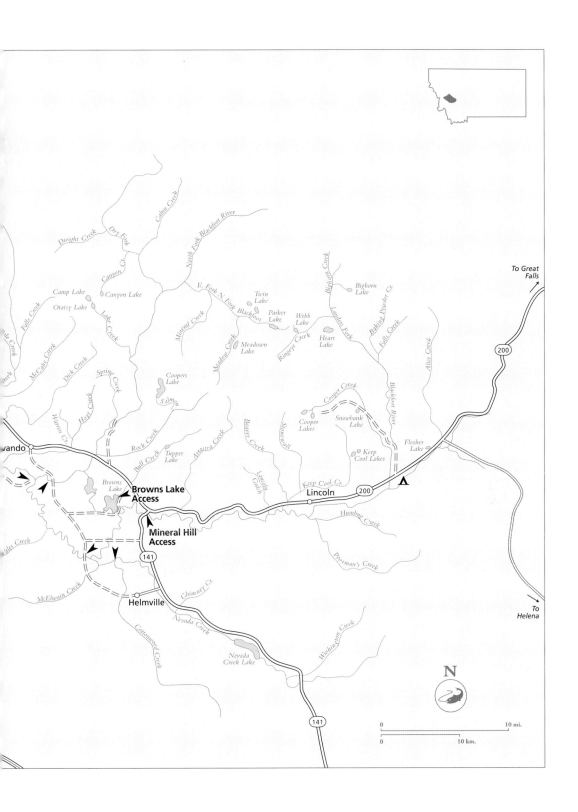

in the country. The giant cyanide heap–leaching gold extraction process could pollute both groundwater and the river, killing off a number of species of trout and char now residing in the main river and its tributaries. In addition, the influx of nearly 400 hard-rock miners into the area would change its character for decades, at least.

Led by the Big Blackfoot Chapter of Trout Unlimited, efforts to restore the Blackfoot began in the late 1980s and by 1992 the trout were rebounding from River Junction, at the mouth of the North Fork of the Blackfoot, down to Bonner. The improvement continues to this day, though at a more gradual pace.

Outside of spring runoff, when the river rages with a vengeance from late April into early July (much to the consternation of salmon fly devotees everywhere), the Blackfoot flows very clear and deep emerald green. The structure and the trout themselves are frequently visible through several feet of water.

The river drains the Garnet Range to the southeast, a good piece of the Scapegoat Wilderness rising to the northwest, and numerous drainages pouring out of the timbered mountains rolling on either side of the water.

THE HEADWATERS TO LINCOLN

The Blackfoot is pretty but somewhat sterile above Lincoln. Parts of it dry up completely in the winter, and the poison of the Mike Horse and Paymaster mines enters the river east of Lincoln, just below Rogers Pass. The contaminated mine sediments are creeping downstream at a rate of 0.6 mile per year.

LINCOLN TO THE HELMVILLE BRIDGE

From Lincoln to the Helmville Bridge, the river looks like designer brown trout water, with thick brush and trees lining undercut banks. Brown trout are by far the dominant species in this section, in part because of their ability to survive in tougher conditions than other trout. The few cutthroats, brookies, and rainbows hold around the mouths of tributaries that add clean flow. The current picks up, oxygenating the water and cleaning the streambed somewhat. This stretch is not difficult to wade, except for climbing over, under, and around logjams. Those obstructions make floating very tough, even dangerous, but it is possible for those who do not mind dragging their craft over downed trees. This section fishes best from the end of June into early July.

This is prime streamer water. The numbers of trout might not be high, but there are good fish in the holes and runs. Woolly Buggers, Spruce Streamers, and Muddlers (Yellow Marabou Muddlers are a great variation for browns), blasted bank-tight then danced and shimmied in the current, pull trout out from cover. In this smaller water, floating lines and weighted flies give a better action than sinking or sink-tip lines. The opposite is true on the bigger, faster water of the lower river. Watching a 24-inch brown chase your streamer like an out-of-control ski-jet is exhilarating. Maintaining enough self-control to keep from jerking the fly out of the water is another matter.

HELMVILLE BRIDGE TO THE MOUTH OF THE NORTH FORK

For roughly two-thirds of the distance from the Helmville Bridge to the mouth of the North Fork of the Blackfoot, the river slows down. The terrain is scenic enough, but floating this section borders on boring. This is due not just to the lack of pace, but to the twisting nature of the river.

There are adequate numbers of browns, some of fair size, hanging beneath the brushy, undercut banks and bends of the river. One great spot, which always holds a number of larger fish, is the mouth of Nevada Creek. This is good hopper water at midday, but in the morning and the evening trout line up in the bankside runs and sip mayfly duns and spinners.

One thing that makes these fish so tough is the lack of fishing pressure. They haven't habituated to the human presence. They are not used to humans flogging away with fly rods. A sloppy cast (the kind that comes so naturally to so many of us) usually puts the browns down fast.

MOUTH OF THE NORTH FORK TO CLEARWATER JUNCTION

From the confluence of the North Fork of the Blackfoot down to the junction with the Clearwater, the main river changes into beautiful rainbow trout water, with some nice browns and cutthroats thrown in for good measure. There are long riffles, runs, and deep glides; below Sperry Grade Access there is a spectacular canyon stretch. The big three—mayflies, caddisflies, and stoneflies—are present in healthy numbers in the cold, well-oxygenated water. This is a beautiful float, especially through the looming cliffs of 5-mile-long Box Canyon, but there's a dangerous rapid at the bottom of the canyon that inexperienced boatmen should portage around.

The dry-fly fishing settles into a midsummer pattern. During the middle of the day, large attractors, sizes 4 to 10, floated on seams and slots out in the river, take the best fish. The drifts have to be long and drag-free. The fly, oddly enough, has a much better chance if it's green. Productive patterns included the H & L Variant, Lime Trude, Olive Stimulator, Picket Pin, Lime Double Wing, Renegade, and Green Humpy—and the only thing in common with this assortment is the color.

Grasshoppers, reaching plague numbers in this valley some summers, plop onto the water in abundance. A good grasshopper imitation (green-bodied, of course—and this advice came separately from Forrest Schaeffer, an area expert in the matter) makes even the old, cautious browns rush up to the surface. The fly should be drifted away from the bank. The rule of thumb during the day seems to be that the water should be at least 2 feet deep.

Early in the morning or late in the afternoon, the angler can match the hatch and work the shallows. Bigger trout move close to the shore to feed with the lower light, sipping whatever insects happen to be kicking around. The fish don't get real fussy about the imitation, maybe because there aren't many heavy hatches, just a smattering of everything, but the presentation still has to be drag-free.

With the pine forests so green, and the water so clear and cold, the westslope cutthroat fishing on the Upper Blackfoot reminds me of casting in the Bob Marshall Wilderness.

This piece is such fun water to cover. The rainbows and the whitefish can often be seen, their tails and sides flashing as they nose the substrate for nymphs. Walking the riffles on a hot July afternoon, drifting a Zug Bug, qualifies as world-class decadence.

CLEARWATER JUNCTION TO JOHNSRUD PARK

From Clearwater Bridge down to Johnsrud Park, a section entirely within the 26-mile-long Blackfoot River Recreation Corridor, the river flows swiftly, studded with boulders that make floating challenging. This is a very popular whitewater area, the canoes, rafts, driftboats, kayaks, and inner tubes going by like an unending parade on a warm day

The fishing is typically in deep pocket water in and around the large rocks. There is not much time here for trout to decide on what to eat, and the calories-expended to calories-gained ratio is instantly factored in by the fish. Large nymphs and wets underneath or bushy caddisfly and stonefly drys on the surface will draw more strikes than the size 20 Pheasant Tail Nymphs or Olive Comparaduns in this fast-paced environment. Goddard Caddis and Parachute Caddis, buoyant and visible flies, fish well in the rough water.

Wading this stretch is difficult, but working to get to the good water is often the most important part of the presentation. The fly drifts a lot better if you don't have to mend continually to avoid a belly in the line. The trout are opportunistic but not foolish.

Johnsrud Park to Bonner

From Johnsrud down to the diversion dam above Bonner, the river is a series of long runs, boulder-strewn whitewater, and deep holes. The dry flies need to be big and bushy. In the pools try pulling a buoyant pattern, such as a Deer Hair Woolly, under and then letting it pop back to the top. Sometimes it takes a "trigger" movement like that to make these trout come to the surface.

Here is where the "down and dirty" fly fisherman does as well. Probing the deep pools takes at least a 10-foot, sink-tip line and often some lead above the nymph. The fly itself is weighted. It is tough to keep track of the pattern and to control the inevitable belly in the line. You have to use enough weight to get the fly to the bottom, without draping on so much that the nymph drags along like a doorknob. You'll lose flies if you're doing this right.

The fall is always Woolly Bugger time. The big trout, browns in particular, cannot resist a black or olive Bugger cast bank-tight, snaked and danced through the rocks and boulders, and then zipped into the clear water. Pause occasionally in your retrieve and let the Bugger drift a bit.

The Blackfoot never developed a nationally famous series of original patterns. In the 1930s the flies created in Missoula were fished on all the surrounding rivers. Franz Pott's woven-hair flies, Norman Means's balsa bugs, and Jack Boehme's hair-winged flies were popular, but even they never supplanted the older, classic wet flies. These Missoula patterns were thick-bodied and heavily hackled.

In his angling shop, actually a corner of the Turf Bar in Missoula, Jack Boehme left a handwritten list of the "flies for the Blackfoot." They included the Mosquito, Black Gnat, Gray Hackle Peacock, and Red Ant (which looked nothing like an ant), the samples in his fly case running from sizes 6 to 12.

Maybe this lack of legacy stems from the generous nature of the river. It is seldom necessary to exactly match any hatch. There are lots of aquatic insects, but rarely a blizzard of any one species. The blue-winged olive, both in the spring (March) and in the

POPULAR FLIES

Deer Hair Woolly	Olive Stimulator
Goddard Caddis	Parachute Caddis
Green Humpy	Renegade
H & L Variant	Spruce Streamer
Lime Double Wing	Woolly Bugger
Lime Trude	Yellow Marabou Muddler

fall (September), emerges in good numbers, especially on the lower water around Johnsrud Park. During the salmon fly hatch the heavy runoff, with its brown flood, wipes out any surface fishing four years out of five. There are still a few straggling salmon flies during a normal year just as the water drops, and a good adult imitation, like the locally popular Maki Salmon Fly, catches fish.

The golden stones, coming at the end of the runoff and after the salmon flies, might be the single most important hatch on the river. A flush imitation, like a size 6 to 10 Elk Hair Golden Stone, works better than a high-riding pattern on the Blackfoot. There are pale morning duns and tricos during the summer. The little olive stoneflies hang around the river. Caddisflies, especially the green sedge, a fast-water fly, flutter in small swarms on summer evenings. A sparse hatch of the giant orange sedge shows up in September, and trout always seem to notice this big insect.

Of course, you can always collect specimens and perfectly match whatever happens to be hatching in size, color, and shape. You can pick out the newest creation, a CDC Caddis or a Duck Butt Dun, and catch trout. There is no law against this, even if such fussiness seems a little out of place on the river. Hatch-matching is one of those rights (implied if not specifically mentioned) that is guaranteed in the Constitution. It is just that an exact imitation is usually not critical for catching trout on the Big Blackfoot.

State fishing access sites dot the river from Johnsrud Park up to Browns Lake, and reaching the river from MT 200 is not difficult. There is a good gravel road that runs through the recreation corridor, skirting the river, from Johnsrud Park to the Roundup Bar (the bar burned in the early 1990s, but the name lives on) access.

The Blackfoot does not have the reputation of many other rivers in Montana, but if this stream was located in, say, Wisconsin or Pennsylvania, it would be nationally famous. Such is the quality of fly fishing in Montana. The river is a fine fishery that is slowly improving—a challenging, diverse piece of water to cast a fly over.

FISHING WATERS IN THE BLACKFOOT DRAINAGE

Alice Creek: Alice begins below Rogers Pass, flowing out of the Alice Mountains south to MT 200. It is a small stream, with not a lot of water to begin with, and years of drought in the late 1980s have shrunk it even further. The trout are still there, mostly cutthroats from 6 to 10 inches, but Alice is fished quite a bit and, as a result, it is an average creek at best. To escape the crowds, and find slightly bigger trout, go into the canyon stretch, about 5 miles above the highway.

Arrastra Creek: This stream contains westslope cutthroat and is an important spawning stream and tributary of the Blackfoot. There are also a few large browns lower down in autumn and brook trout scattered about. The fish are spooky in this clear water. Fine tippets of 5X or 6X and size 16 to 20 attractor drys like a Royal Coachman or Red Humpy often work, as does a Humpy Adams or Goddard Caddis.

Bighorn (Sheep) Lake: As with most mountain lakes in the area, this one now receives periodic plantings of westslope cutthroats instead of rainbows and Yellowstone cutthroats. But there are still a few old—and large—rainbows hanging on in Bighorn. It's hard to get to these fish. A poorly maintained 2-mile spur off the Bighorn Creek Trail goes nearly to the Continental Divide. The last part of the trek is a steep, ankle-busting drop down to this 10-acre, bowl-shaped lake.

Browns Lake: Five hundred acres in open, often windy country, it's about 15 minutes by good gravel road from Ovando. There are boat ramps, public toilets, and camping sites. This is not a wilderness experience. There's no truth to the rumor that the trout have seen so many bait fishermen that they feed selectively on corn and marshmallows.

Is this any place for a self-respecting fly fisher? It is if he wants to catch trout up to 10 pounds. The state stocks Browns Lake with both Arlee and Kamloop strain rainbows. The Arlee plantings get taken out fast both summer and winter (a very popular lake for ice fishing), but any survivors quickly balloon to 2 to 4 pounds. The Kamloop planters are not so easy to catch. The Kamloops don't swell to the "stuffed" appearance of the Arlees in their early years, but live and grow much longer, reaching the double-digit weights occasionally. Trollers take a greater toll on the Kamloops than the bait fishermen (and this should tell the fly fishermen something).

Brown's fishes best early in the season, before the weeds bloom and the picnickers sprout in profusion. The inlet and outlet (both Bull Creek) are shallow and inconsistent fishing. The best place for a fly fisher in a float tube or a boat is the center basin, about 20 feet deep but with humps as shallow as 10 feet. Those humps hold concentrations of fish. The nymph or streamer fisherman with a sinking line and a lot of patience can pick up trout all day.

The best time for the angler limited to bank fishing is during the June and July damsel hatches. He is in the right position, pulling his fly back toward the shore, to mimic the incoming swimming naturals. The peak of this migration usually happens early in the morning—a good time to beat the regular crowds to the water.

Camp Lake: It's nearly 10 miles above Coopers Lake, up the Lake Creek Trail, and has rainbows and cutthroats. The trout grow well, nice and plump, until about 15 inches, and then they start to get skinny between 16 and 20 inches. This is a clue that food forms are small, probably a good base of midges, but there aren't enough larger insects or forage fish. The best flies are small, too. The pressure is pretty intense on Camp for a backcountry lake.

Clearwater Lake: Over 100 acres and 40 feet deep, Clearwater is only a few miles by a good trail off a logging road east of MT 83. Maybe it's those steep drop-offs that intimidate fly fishermen, but many of my friends who haunt the high-mountain lakes all summer avoid this one, even though they all know that it has big, 2- to 4-pound cutthroats. The trout are here, and I've taken a number of them using a Biggs Special/ Sheep Creek (my favorite subsurface lake pattern) allowed to sink for several seconds and then twitched slightly. The take is often savage and break-offs happen.

Clearwater River: In its upper reaches this is an easily worked stream for cutthroats, brookies, and rainbows. There are lots of logjams, riffles, and small pools. Plenty of people hit this water as it flows through Rainy, Alva, Inez, and Seeley Lakes.

Between Seeley and Salmon Lakes the river winds and twists through thick tag alder. There are plenty of deep gravely pools and runs, a good bit of which is visible from MT 83. This is very difficult water to wade and cast to properly, but there is a transient population of browns in the fall and in the spring. The fun comes with the hook-up because there's not a lot of room to play a good fish.

The fly fisher who uses normal dry-fly and nymph tactics isn't going to hit the bonanza on the Clearwater. The browns move into the river from the lakes (natural, glacially formed waters) and spawn in the fall. These fish stay in the river over the winter and into the spring, until it warms up too much, usually in late June, and then they migrate back into the lakes. These big trout eat minnows. Size 6 brown, Cree-hackled Woolly Buggers weighted and twitched or even dead-drifted like a nymph will always turn big heads.

The water between Salmon and the confluence with the Blackfoot is good in the spring, too. It get rainbows up from the main river. There are stonefly hatches, especially the goldens, that bring trout to the surface. Smaller streamers work in this section.

Cooper Creek: Cooper Creek has some average fishing for cutthroats in the upper reaches; below it is followed by a good road that equates to good access and heavy pressure. This stream is not the outlet of Coopers Lake, but rather a tributary of the Landers Fork.

Coopers Lake: Nearly 200 acres, this lake is deep and not very fertile. It is 18 miles from Ovando on a good road that skirts and then crosses Rock Creek. It is planted regularly with cutthroats that are hit hard and rarely last long enough to reach any size. The ones that do are shell-shocked and skittish.

Copper Creek: This is fished more than it deserves by people driving up to Snowbank Lake. Fifty years ago there were 18- and 20-pound bull trout caught out of this little stream. The logging and the road building dumped sediment into it, hurting the native species. There are still cutthroat in Copper.

Cottonwood Creek: Cottonwood flows through open meadowland to the Blackfoot not far above Sperry Grade. Two miles of it wander through the Blackfoot-Clearwater Game Range. The water does not look like much here, and it's often muddy and difficult to wade, but for the quiet, accurate caster there are brown, brook, and rainbow trout. Seven-foot rods and stooped postures are called for. There is brush and undercut banks, and you could work this stretch of water for days. This one is fun, tough, and frustrating at times.

Cottonwood Lakes: These lakes are a 9-mile drive from the Seeley Lake Campground up the Cottonwood Creek Road. Their waters have cutthroat, rainbow, and some brook trout that grow nicely in the fertile water. Of course, the bigger ones, up to 4 pounds, are not the village dummies. They cruise the shoreline, nosing for insects (try matching the Callibaetis nymph with a size 12 Gold-Ribbed Hare's Ear). The large trout seldom rise, even when there are insects on the surface, but they gently take slowly retrieved nymphs.

Dry Fork of the North Fork of the Blackfoot River: Go up the North Fork Trail, then up past the lower 3 miles that go dry every summer. The upper reaches, 12 miles of classic water, are full of 10- to 15-inch cutthroats. The fish are easy, the country is scenic, and a little walking gets you away from civilization. A small box of dry flies—a few Wulffs, Double Wings, and Humpies, rough attractors that cover the three main situations, upwing, downwing, and just plain fat insects—is all you'll need here if the water is warm enough. Sometimes, with the river running from 40 to 50 degrees Fahrenheit, nymphs near the bottom are necessary.

East Fork of the North Fork of the Blackfoot River: This one is up a trail that starts at the North Fork Guard Station. The East Fork is somewhat similar to the Dry Fork, except for an abundance of beaver dams and ponds. Some of these are well past their prime and silted up. Others are not bad for smallish cutthroats. The country is forest and moist meadow, and the creek is followed by good trail (popular with horse packers).

Harper's Lake: Harper's is a strange place to my way of thinking. There are some fat cutthroats in this 18-acre, 28-foot-deep pond sitting out in the open south of MT 83, just a mile or so up from Clearwater Junction. Rainbows, including big, old, sluggish brook stock, are dumped here every year.

Match the crayfish. The water is full of them (and you can catch enough to have your own shellfish extravaganza). A Clouser Crawfish or a Bug Skin Crawfish, retrieved with a stop and run-run-run strip (a "run" lasting 5 feet with short pauses in between) over the bottom, isn't going to pick up the small stockers, but who cares? The big fly can get a half-dozen 15-inch-and-up trout on Harper's in a day.

Heart Lake: Up the trail at the end of the Landers Fork Road, Heart is just jammed with beautiful 8- to 16-inch grayling that are easy to catch. There are trout here, too, often the kind measured in pounds instead of inches, but they are the rare treat. Depending on the snowpack, this country is not usually fishable before July, but the lake is prime if you can get into it as soon as possible.

Keep Cool Creek: After joining with Stonewall Creek, Keep Cool enters the river just below Lincoln. Here is a shining example of good management. The riparian habitat is in great shape. The stream, often running below 10 cfs during the summer, meanders in a deep channel through meadow cover. The fishing for rainbows, brookies, and cutthroats with migratory bull and brown trout in the fall, most in the 8- to 10-inch range, is excellent.

Keep Cool Lakes: Managed on a yearly basis for Eagle Lake rainbows that grow well, this locally popular reservoir is right up Keep Cool Creek, not far from Lincoln.

Lake Alva: Three hundred thirty acres, Alva is just upstream from Inez in the Clearwater River chain of lakes next to MT 83. It is plagued by hordes of small yellow perch (unless you're one of the people who know how delicious perch are—and then it's blessed with them). The trout, cutthroat and bull, compete badly. There are largemouth bass in some of the coves, but this is not a great bass lake either.

Lake Inez: A summer-home lake just downstream from Lake Alva, Inez has lots of boat traffic and a public campground. It is also overrun with yellow perch, but there are some cutthroat trout and kokanee salmon.

Landers Fork of the Blackfoot River: Upriver from Lincoln, the lower water on this one is not much. It is scoured, all the cover washed out. The stream gradually improves for small brook, bull, and cutthroat trout as you move upstream. The riparian habitat is recovering and the fishing is getting better. It is still not great.

Meadow Creek: A tributary of the East Fork, Meadow Creek gets hit hard at the bottom, in large part due to two campgrounds, but there are 8 miles of fine fishing along the trail for rainbows and cutthroats.

Monture Creek: Like many waters, Monture is named after a person, French-Canadian fur trader Nicholas Monteur. Since he did something of note—traveling in Blackfoot Indian territory long before most white men would risk it—he at least deserves the honor.

Monture is crossed by MT 200, the Blackfoot Highway, 2 miles south of Ovando, and enters the Big Blackfoot just above Scotty Brown Bridge. The stream is large enough, especially early in the season, to float from the highway down to the river in a small craft. The distance is only a couple of miles, but a boat gets you away from convenient access points and into better trout water. In this lower section the stream twists and digs through glacial gravels, creating one deep hole after another, every pool seemingly holding its share of rainbow, cutthroat, and brown trout.

Early in the season, until at least July, Monture, like other mountain streams, runs cold. Dry flies do not pull fish up from the bottom well, so unless the trout are already looking up at a hatch of insects, the best choice is usually a nymph. Later in the summer both the winding water below the highway and the tumbling water above it get plenty of grasshoppers. A good hopper imitation does well for any angler brave enough to slam the fly into the darker patches under logs and brush. The trout still aren't big, averaging 10 inches on a good day, but they rush the fly courageously.

The angler can follow Monture upstream on 12 miles of gravel road and then 18 miles of good (and well-used) trail to the headwaters. There is a maintained camping area, Monture Creek Campground, just below the Blackfoot Highway crossing. It is a nice place to base for the entire Blackfoot drainage.

Morrell Creek: This creek flows past the Double Arrow development up into the southern reaches of the Swan Range. Water levels drop quite low and the fishing in the lower sections is slow to nonexistent for cutthroats and brookies. There may be a brown or two and some kokanees in the autumn up from the Clearwater River. The wild reaches above the falls are barren.

Nevada Creek: On the Helmville cutoff from MT 200, this small stream has plenty of sweeping bends, grassy and brushy undercut banks, and, despite siltation, dewatering, and overheating, some good browns. The stream is followed by the highway here and there to the reservoir. Try dry flies in the evening and maybe a Woolly Bugger or two against the banks for good measure. The upper reaches are followed by an old logging road and hold small cutthroats and rainbows. With restoration of the riparian area, this stream could be a lot better.

Nevada Creek Lake: Ten miles south of Helmville on the Nevada Creek Road, this 100-acre reservoir is drawn down several feet much of the year. The water, clouded by blooms of algae, contains rainbows (numbers depend on the stockings and fishing pressure at any given moment). Aesthetically this lake stinks, but some fat fish cruise the weeds. To me not worth bothering with, but it's your choice.

North Fork of the Blackfoot River: If wilderness areas ever need a symbol to justify their existence, the North Fork can be that reminder. Imagine the alternative: the trees strip-logged from the edges, banks pounded down by cattle, the flow a summertime trickle after dewatering, water sterilized by the weeping discharge of a few abandoned mines. In this drainage all of these things would not be a probability—they'd be a certainty.

The North Fork has its own gateway above Ovando, the Harry Morgan Access. The stream flows lazily in open meadow in the lower stretches. Above the falls this is primarily a cutthroat stream. The water flows over clean, light-colored gravels, digging slots against banks and tumbling into deep riffles. There are insects hatching all summer, but never enough to get the backcountry cuts in a fussy mood. Generally buggy-looking flies, the ones that represent a whole group of insects, are effective if they match the predominant form in size.

The river is just as easy to fish with nymphs as it is with dry flies. Little stonefly patterns, in sizes 14 through 10, match an important insect and catch a lot of trout in the North Fork. Good patterns include the Golden Stone Nymph and Ted's Stonefly Nymph.

It is really important to release all fish on the North Fork. It gets enough pressure, enough trout killed for camp meals, that the average size of the cutthroats is down to 13 or 14 inches. Old records show that the population levels out at 16 or 17 inches with minimal human harvest.

Otatsy Lake: Swampy on the north and timbered the rest of the way around, Otatsy sits in a cluster with other good backcountry lakes (Camp, Canyon, Heart, Parker, and Webb) and as a result it is on a popular circuit. It's filled with 9- to 13-inch cutthroats and rainbows.

Placid Lake: Not a direct link in the Clearwater lake chain, it is only a few miles off the chain, up Owl Creek by good road. This is a summer-home madhouse that looks like it escaped from a Chevy Chase movie. Lots of 4-inch rainbows are planted here each year. There are also trash fish, some largemouth bass, kokanee salmon, and several species of trout (unfortunately, in declining numbers). It's not worth bothering with.

Rainy Lake: A good lake for cutthroats that average less than a foot, Rainy is on MT 83 north of Seeley Lake. It's about 70 acres and best fished from a float tube or a boat. Trout seem to rise continuously on it.

Salmon Lake: Right next to MT 83 south of Seeley Lake, Salmon is an attractive piece of water (except for the huge log monument to a local resident's ego on one of the islands). All kinds of trout live here, including cutthroats, rainbows, bulls, and browns, along with kokanee salmon and various warmwater species. The best trout water is along the south shore, and the best largemouth bass water is near the marshes at the inlet. There is serious boat traffic on the lake in the summer.

Seeley Lake: Seeley is a true madhouse in the summer with boats, water-skiers, and float planes. It is over 1,000 acres and reached by roads all over the place. The resort town of Seeley Lake is on the east shore. Despite all the recreational craziness, there is some good fishing for cutthroat and rainbow trout. The north shoreline, where the Clearwater dumps in, is the best place to work streamers (rainbows especially are a good play in the spring here), but give any loons (the bird, not the boaters) a wide berth. They nest on the north side of the lake in the spring.

Snowbank Lake: Up a road near the Copper Creek Campground and planted with cutthroats that grow *slowly*, this lake is worth a visit for anyone interested in geology—a classic glacial kettle.

Summit Lake: This is a beautiful lake right next to MT 83. The view into the Mission Mountains is spectacular. Tag alders and willows surround the swampy shoreline. You need a float tube to cast dry flies to the free-rising cutthroats that run from 10 to 12 inches. No one fishes here much except for a few loons like myself. For some reason I love this place.

Twin Lakes: These are in the East Fork Drainage in the Scapegoat Wilderness. Upper Twin is planted with cutthroats. It is only 6 acres, but the trout grow big. Lower Twin is 16 acres and is managed for rainbows that don't grow nearly as large. Nice country— worthwhile fishing.

Upsata Lake: An open-country, pothole lake near Ovando that is 85 acres and up to 40 feet deep, Upsata is popular with area residents for good numbers of rainbows that sometimes hit 20 inches, largemouth bass up to a couple of pounds or so, and some perch. It's best in the spring right after ice-out. The angler can work from a float tube, throwing bright weighted streamers into the shore and quickly retrieving them along the bottom. The trout are in there busting the heck out of rough-fish fry.

Warren Creek: Flowing to the Blackfoot not far from Ovando, Warren Creek is not bad fishing for cutthroats and rainbows. The landowners, in cooperation with the Big Blackfoot Chapter of Trout Unlimited, are doing extensive work on the riparian zone of Warren.

A number of small streams near Ovando are good fishing, some of them for brook trout up to a couple of pounds. They are crossed here and there by dirt and gravel roads, allowing limited access. When in doubt, though, check around and ask for permission. Trespassers really nailed some of this fine water in the seventies and a few of the aged property owners are still mad as hell forty years later. Nymphs down deep take the brookies, cutthroats, and rainbows under the brushy banks. There are even a few browns of size in these little creeks.

West Fork Clearwater River: Tumbling out of the mountains through very thick forest, this is a small stream with some nice fish such as westslope cutthroat to a couple of pounds. Spotty fishing, large drys like Humpies and Wulffs and soft hackles that include the Partridge and Orange size 14, and maybe a Woolly Bugger size 8, work well.

The upper river sees sizable numbers of browns 18 inches and up.

Upper Clark Fork

To many fly fishers viewing the upper Clark Fork while buzzing along I-90, the mile upon mile of brushy undercut banks, wide gravel riffles, and deep runs look like ideal big-fish habitat. From Warm Springs down to Milltown, the nearly 100-mile drive can take on the trappings of Chinese water torture for those who love to fish, but who must race on to meet other commitments. The angler just knows that there are hundreds, no thousands, of big browns under those banks or up on the rocky shelves sucking in insects. Not to wet a line is cruel—life at its harshest.

It is good water to dream about. No other river in Montana is a better example of the fate that awaits all of our streams if avarice and neglect dominate in this state. But no other river demonstrates the ability of our waters to bounce back from past abuse.

Montana is nicknamed the Treasure State because of its mining past, personified by Butte's Berkeley Pit. Copper, silver, and gold were dug, hammered, and blasted from the earth in staggering quantities. The wastes from this hard-rock labor were flushed untreated into Silver Bow Creek, the headwater tributary of the Clark Fork, the tailings accumulating in the riparian corridor of the river. There are millions upon millions of tons of the stuff, extending all the way to Milltown Dam, and the sediments are loaded with deadly concentrations of heavy metals. From before the turn of the century until the 1950s, mining waste turned the water red, destroying all life (even stopping the growth of algae). The smelter in Anaconda also dumped toxins into the drainage.

This situation changed with the creation of a waste treatment system. The most important element in the plan was a series of "settling ponds," shallow potholes where the tainted water from Silver Bow Creek was treated with lime salts to precipitate out the heavy metals. This left the flow at the outlet of the ponds, the official starting point of the Clark Fork, clean enough to support trout.

And support trout it does—in incredible numbers. In the 5-mile special management section, beginning at Warm Springs, brown trout in the 12- to 16-inch range, with a few weighing several pounds or more, swim in good health. Biologists' surveys indicate a population of catchable-size brown trout between 1,900 to 2,400 per mile, an astounding figure considering the hammering the water still takes from a quality standpoint.

The Clark Fork, in this upper stretch, is not a large river (a decent long jumper could leap across it). This makes the 2,400-trout-per-mile figure truly astonishing. The Madison, with ten times the water volume, has 4,500 catchable-size trout per mile; the

Missouri, with twenty times the water volume, ranges from 2,000 to 4,000 catchable-size trout per mile.

So is everything perfect on the Clark Fork? Hardly. This drainage, all the way from Butte to Milltown, has been declared the nation's largest Superfund site by the Environmental Protection Agency (EPA). The massive task of removing or capping the tailings deposited for nearly a hundred years in the floodplain is just beginning.

In the meantime, every few years a heavy rainstorm washes deposits from surrounding areas into the Clark Fork. The sudden flush of heavy metals kills thousands of trout. The carnage is this gruesome simply because even in a short stretch there are so many browns to kill. Such incidents are localized and do not destroy the river, but they are symptoms of a lingering disease in the watershed.

The Clark Fork's past was one of incredible destruction. The present, however, is surprisingly good. The upper river really is one of the richest trout streams in the state.

Fishing access sites, county roads, and several bridges provide access all along the upper Clark Fork. Many ranchers along this section will grant access also, if you ask permission politely.

Butte to Warm Springs

This section of the river, known as Silver Bow Creek, is still unable to support trout. Maybe, after the Superfund cleanup, the water will rebound, but the best estimates are that this won't happen for thirty years.

Anaconda Settling Ponds (at Warm Springs) to Deer Lodge

The first 5 miles of the Clark Fork are under special regulations (artificial lures and flies only). The river is naturally rich, sitting on the bed of limestone that underlies the entire Deer Lodge Valley, and in true spring-creek fashion it meanders tortuously. It cuts and digs between willow-and-alder-choked banks, creating the fabulous habitat that harbors such a high population of brown trout.

The trout grow very quickly to the 15- to 18-inch range and the average-size catchable fish is a healthy 14 inches, but they don't have the food base to get much larger than this. The exceptions are a few big cannibalistic browns. There are no sculpins and very few whitefish for the trout to eat. The upper Clark Fork is, as FWP biologist Wayne Hadley calls it, "a caddisfly economy."

The major caddisflies are two net-spinning genera, the spotted sedge and the little sister sedge. As larvae they are filter-feeders, capturing food from the current in their nets. The populations of these insects are incredible, over 2,000 larvae per square yard in the river, and when they emerge, peaking from late May through July, there are evening blizzards that trigger a trout feeding frenzy.

It would seem that this early summer period should be easy fishing with this combination of wall-to-wall trout and heavy hatches. The truth is that the only trout in the upper river are browns (no other species can survive the concentrations of heavy metals), and browns are seldom easy.

There are often complex hatches with more than one species coming off at one time. The browns will key to one, and if you are not catching fish, you'd better rethink your strategy. This section of the Clark Fork was the birthplace of some important caddisfly imitations. Gary LaFontaine developed the Deep Sparkle Pupa and the Emergent Sparkle Pupa to fool the hypercritical trout of the river.

During the heavy caddis hatches, the choice is simple. When the browns are rolling on the surface, taking pupae struggling in the film, the Emergent in matching size and color catches fish. The best variations are a size 14 Brown and Yellow for the spotted sedge, and a size 16 or 18 Ginger for the little sister sedge. Grease the fly with floatant so that it rides half in and half out of the surface film, and fish it either dead-drift or with twitches over rising trout.

So much emphasis (and dogma) has been placed on drag-free drifts that a good deal of quality action is missed when it comes to caddis. The insect is now known for taking sedate, stately rides downstream as though on a regal tour of its riverine world. But when emerging and egg-laying, the bugs bounce and sputter all over the place. Giving the fly a little action or even using the dreaded "drag" judiciously will many times outperform the accepted methods.

There are other insects in the upper river. The Clark Fork rivals the Beaverhead as prime cranefly habitat. The cranefly larvae, semiaquatic insects that burrow in the damp muck of the banks, get washed into the river with the first flush of snowmelt in April and trout gorge on these chunks of food (matched by a size 8 Cranefly Larva Nymph). Also important to anglers are the midsummer flights of adult craneflies. So many insects hover over and dip onto the flats at dawn in July and August that the river surface is an orange haze. Trout leap and slash at the dancing insects (matched by a size 12 Orange Skating Spider).

There are also blue-winged olive mayflies, the early season (March and April) and late season (September and October) broods of Baetis making the trout rise. Tricos appear in August, but the spinner flights aren't heavy enough to get the bigger fish working. There are some stoneflies, both salmon flies and goldens, hatching sporadically in early summer. All of these hatches seem to be getting better as the water quality improves.

Grasshoppers are important during midsummer. There are a lot of hopper patterns out there, but my favorite is still the old Joe's Hopper. The more chewed up the thing gets, the better it works, especially dragged in or just below the surface film. Gartside's, Jacklin's, Dave's, Jay's, and Juanita's hoppers also work well.

The river has its seasonal moods. It fishes best for rising trout right before and right after runoff. By midsummer it gets warm and low (irrigators hit it hard), and unless the area receives early rains, the river slips into a funk. It's still possible to catch trout, but the best times are from 1 a.m. until 6 a.m. There is a dedicated group of night fishermen who slap size 8 White Deer Hair Moths on or swim size 4 Muddlers through the deep pools. Autumn, when the browns are moving and aggressive, is really streamer time. They especially like yellow-and-brown or orange-and-brown patterns, such as the Marabou Muddler, Golden Demon, Mansfield, and Dark Edson Tiger, but since the average-size trout far outnumber the behemoths, a smaller fly, a size 4 to 10, does much better than a tarpon pattern.

The trout populations start declining below the 5-mile special regulation section. The banks are more open, cattle graze and trample the riparian vegetation, and diversion dams pull off the water needed to dilute the heavy metals and moderate the temperatures. By the time the river reaches Deer Lodge, the trout numbers are down to 300 catchable-size trout per mile. This sounds dismal, especially when compared to the numbers of fish in the upper water, but this is still a small river and there are enough trout to make it a good fishery. It's not unusual during prime months to catch twenty browns on an afternoon right in the middle of Deer Lodge.

DEER LODGE TO DRUMMOND

The trout numbers, mostly browns but with a few rainbows and cutthroats around the mouths of the tributaries, are good, not great, all the way to Drummond. Guides begin floating the Clark Fork at the confluence with the Little Blackfoot, especially right after the tributary's runoff. There are probably more large trout in this part of the river, and it's not unusual to catch a number over 18 inches on a good day.

This is a good stretch to dead-drift larger nymphs, sizes 6 to 10, tight to the brush piles and undercut banks. Girdle Bugs, Bitch Creeks, Woolly Buggers, Deep Sparkle Pupas, and Prince Nymphs are proven flies on this stretch. At the end of the drift, it's always wise to allow the nymph to wiggle in the current for a few seconds and then, with a slow-steady retrieve, make it swim right up past the obstruction. Even discerning browns have their weak spots.

Biologist Wayne Hadley comments on this section, "People think that below every tributary there are more trout. I've found that there is no truth to this in my samplings, and that includes below the Little Blackfoot River. Yes, way downstream, below Rock Creek, there is a noticeable improvement in fish populations, but otherwise there is no difference below the tributaries. The new water coming in does not seem to make much, if any, difference. The trout are spread out.

"There are some dead stretches because the tailing problem is handled in Band-Aid fashion with berms down to Drummond. If the cleanup is done correctly, there will be a noticeable improvement in numbers throughout this part of the upper river."

DRUMMOND TO THE MOUTH OF ROCK CREEK

This stretch quickly deteriorates into dead water. The populations around Beavertail in midsummer are thirty trout per mile (and these aren't big trout). The river is hurt

Removal of Milltown Dam

One of the biggest and most positive changes on the river in recent years has been the removal of the Milltown Dam several miles upriver from Missoula. Heavy metal accumulations from past decades of upstream mining will eventually be flushed away, and species like browns and westslope cutthroats will begin moving back and forth along the upper reaches in a more historically natural fashion.

The western end point of the upper Clark Fork's Superfund complex is the Milltown Dam area. For a hundred years the dam plugged the river just 8 miles upstream of Missoula at the confluence of the Clark Fork and Blackfoot Rivers. The 180-acre reservoir behind Milltown Dam was full of contaminated sediment—6.6 million cubic yards of it—that washed down from Butte's copper mines during the record flood of 1908 and stacked up behind the dam. The contaminated sediment, laden with arsenic and copper, poisoned local wells for years and also killed off fish and other aquatic life during high flows and ice jams.

On August 2, 2005—after twenty-two strenuous years of investigating the site, developing a cleanup plan, and negotiating who pays for what—officials from four federal and state agencies, the Confederated Salish and Kootenai Tribes, ARCO, and Northwest Energy signed an agreement to remove Milltown Dam and the most contaminated sediments piled up behind it. The dam came out of the river one-half at a time between spring 2008 and spring 2009, and sediment excavation—a two-year project—lasted until 2010. Restoration efforts are now under way at the free-flowing confluence of the Clark Fork and Blackfoot.

According to the website of the Clark Fork Coalition, a group that has tirelessly spearhead improvement and protection of the river's drainage: "By removing Milltown Dam and the contaminated sediments, we are doing the right thing for our environment, our health, our economy, and the future of our communities. It will eliminate the damaging environmental impacts of the dam and sediments. Yes, there were some metals impacts to the river in the short run, but as the project nears completion, we're seeing these risks disappear forever.

"Fish of all species have migrated unhindered past the former dam site since the first breach, and their upstream and downstream populations are on the increase. The arsenic contamination in groundwater will dissipate within a decade, perhaps as quickly as four years, according to models. The risk of downstream releases of metals is now permanently eliminated, and there will be no risk of dam failure that would send millions of tons of contaminated sediment downstream.

"The return of the confluence of the Clark Fork and Blackfoot rivers to a free-flowing state will revitalize the area's economy and create a significant community asset, providing fishing, boating, and other types of river recreation that are in high demand in western Montana."

in part by numerous hot-water springs emptying into the river, but if the flow wasn't sucked down for irrigation, there would be enough volume to moderate those high temperatures.

In the fall, with cooler weather, browns and rainbows run upstream into the lower few miles of this water. These trout hold here over the winter, until the river heats up again the following summer, and at least as far up as Beavertail the fishing can be good in the spring.

MOUTH OF ROCK CREEK TO MILLTOWN DAM

The Clark Fork comes alive again at the mouth of Rock Creek. This tributary, pouring out of the high mountains and running most of the way undefiled through US Forest Service land, more than doubles the midsummer flow of the main river. Suddenly there are more rainbows and cutthroats mixed into the trout population, and suddenly there is a full spectrum of insect hatches.

On the upper Clark Fork it is possible to do well with matching flies in the longer flats and in the side channels. This section gets the same sequence of hatches as the lower Clark Fork (below Milltown Dam), but the main river is such a splendid series of deep holes and runs that the bigger trout in the heavy current don't rise much during most hatches.

The exceptions to this general indifference are the big insects. Area expert Paul Koller says, "There is typically a three-day spurt of salmon fly activity between Clinton and Turah. It doesn't move upstream in any pattern. Instead it just pops throughout that section. Trout key on it quickly. It happens two weeks before the hatch starts on Rock Creek, usually in the last week of May."

In late June, right after runoff, there is a good, mixed hatch (probably the best on the whole Clark Fork) of green drakes, brown drakes, golden stones, and a number of other species ranging from size 6 to size 12 that are abundant and important. These bugs are meaty enough to get big trout feeding regularly on top.

POPULAR FLIES

Bitch Creek	Orange Skating Spider
Cranefly Larva Nymph	Prince Nymph
Girdle Bug	White Deer Hair Moth
Joe's Hopper	Woolly Bugger
Mansfield	Yellow Humpy
Marabou Muddler	

Normal dry flies, even big bushy attractors, are usually less than spectacular on this part of the Clark Fork. A floating pattern must have inherent buoyancy from balsa or foam, or it will get sucked down by the undertow.

One problem in midsummer, during the irrigation season on this stretch, is that the returning water often flushes loose large concentrations of green algae. The gunk floats downstream, tangling your fly. The fishing is borderline impossible, but some big trout are turned on because plenty of food also is freed. One tactic that works (and is work) is to use a weighted Yellow Marabou Muddler and strip the thing quickly through the crud. You will be constantly cleaning the fly, but the browns love yellow and you will take fish if you exercise diligence.

FISHING WATERS IN THE UPPER CLARK FORK DRAINAGE

Albicaulis Lake: You'll find this 17-acre lake nearly 8,000 feet above sea level up the Racetrack Creek drainage. It's about an 8-mile jeep-track drive from the campground to good fishing for rainbows and rainbow-cutthroat hybrids, especially around submerged logs near the shore. The wind usually blows up here, and thank goodness it does. When the lake's surface is calm, these are the spookiest trout around. Flat water means 16-foot, 6X leaders and long casts.

Alder Creek: This small, rapidly flowing tributary of Rock Creek enters the river from the west, near Bitterroot Flat Campground. Followed by trail, Alder has plenty of small cutthroats that don't receive much pressure. Dapping a small Madam X in the pockets and riffles will net you a thousand trout in a day. As with most Rock Creek tributaries, spawning rainbow and bull trout use the lower reaches.

Anaconda Settling Ponds: Located on the west side of I-90 near Warm Springs and just west of the Mill-Willow Bypass, these ponds have some truly huge trout in them—browns up to 14 pounds and rainbows up to 11 pounds. The Settling Ponds have attracted a national cadre of devotees to large trout. Four-pound fish are common, and skilled anglers may catch a dozen of these and larger in a day's fishing (the key word here is *skilled*).

What lends a sense of the absurd to this fishing is the fact that the structures were built to settle wastes out of mining discharges. The inflow was (and still is) treated with lye salts to precipitate out the heavy metals. Sediments containing these mine leachings fortunately get covered by thick beds of aquatic weeds, the overlay of vegetation providing ideal habitat for insects, leeches, snails, and scuds.

Because of their origin and appearance, no one comes here for aesthetic reasons. The area is an ugly, scarred moonscape, mounds of dirt and rock covered with thistle and spurge. Patches of copper tailings, so toxic even weeds can't grow in them, pockmark the area. Skeleton forests of dead trees litter the skyline. Anglers come here to catch and release (strictly enforced with artificial lures only) large browns and rainbows—not to drink in the scenery.

Taking trout is a matter of matching the food. Anyone flogging away with general attractors is usually in for a long day. The water fishes best early or late in the season or during prolonged spells of cool weather. The ponds become too warm in the dog days of summer, and the trout take an extended siesta. Like many fertile, stillwater fisheries, the ponds are on one moment and off the next. Patience, observation, and then a careful presentation are the keys to success. Use whatever rod and line combination allows you to make consistently long, accurate, and quiet casts. Leaders over 12 feet long don't hurt either.

The only fly fishermen who catch a lot of trout (and "a lot" means between six and twelve a day) are the stalkers. They crouch behind a bush, staring into the water for cruising fish. These trout are usually 18- to 21-inch rainbows, but browns occasionally hunt the weed edges, too. The fish don't move for a fly. The imitation has to cross right in front of them. And the pattern has to be a great stillwater fly to get consistent strikes—a good one won't do.

Catching the really large trout is a time-consuming game. Try working a big leech pattern—size 2 isn't too big—in the deepest holes over the weed beds. Vary your retrieves, as much to fight boredom as to entice trout, and cast time after time in search of a behemoth in the mood to eat something.

All ponds and canals are open to fishing from August 15 to September 30, with the exception of Hog Hole Pond and Pond 3, which are open May 25 to September 30. Catch-and-release with artificial lures only; no motorized boats allowed. All of these waters are subject to specific regulations that may change from year to year, so checking the current regs is a must.

Big Pozega (Deep) Lake: Fifty-two dammed acres lying in the Modesty Creek drainage, you get to Big Pozega on a four-wheel-drive road. There are cutthroats and cutthroat-rainbow hybrids that survive the severe water fluctuations caused by irrigation demands. It is an interesting lake to fish because the trout don't look like they're stamped out of a cookie cutter. They are a range of sizes, averaging 10 to 12 inches, with bigger fish cruising the edges of the downed timber.

Bohn Lake: Located in a glacial cirque in the Dempsey Creek headwaters, this 25-acre lake at 7,100 feet elevation is fertile, growing plenty of cutthroats in the 16- to 20-inch class. You can motor right to it with a four-wheel-drive rig. The fish are fed well enough to demand the more sophisticated tactics and flies of the rich ponds in the valley—the Rollover Scud and the Floating Damsel Nymph are effective patterns here, too.

Boulder Lakes: These three small lakes in the Boulder Creek drainage (no kidding?) have been planted with westslope cutthroats in the past and now provide average fishing for average cutthroats. The lowest lake, the biggest, is the best.

Brewster Creek: A tributary of Rock Creek with good access from a Forest Service road, it's brushy and small, but offers fast fishing. Every species of trout that exists in the Rock Creek drainage is in Brewster, including a few that outgrow their 6- to 9-inch brethren.

Burns Slough: Lots of swampy water and acres of cattails lie on both sides of the railroad tracks up past Bearmouth. There are largemouth bass here, and the water is planted with Arlee rainbows. The bass aren't big, but they're eager (locals call this area "Bass-a-Matic"). Fishing beneath the power lines is a hair-raising experience.

Carruthers Lake: Hike to this pretty mountain lake on 3 miles of trail west of Bohn Creek up the Dempsey drainage. There are good numbers of small cutthroats here. A 9-incher is a brute and even he will be skinny. The fishing here is typically monotonously repetitive and fast. A few trout kept for an evening meal wouldn't hurt the situation too much—it almost qualifies as mercy killing.

Copper Creek: This easy-to-fish stream drops out of the Anaconda-Pintler Wilderness to the Middle Fork of Rock Creek. Cutthroats and a few brookies take small attractors, Wulffs and the like, especially in the middle reaches where the banks have some cover. The stream is followed by a good trail to the headwaters.

Cottonwood Creek: Flowing into the Clark Fork at Deer Lodge, Cottonwood is followed by road and then trail for 12 miles to its headwaters. This one could be a little gem, but in town it has been straightened and walled in for flood protection. Storm drains empty directly into it. Houses crowd alongside it. Garbage is dumped into it. In spite of all this, the spring creek runs over thick beds of aquatic vegetation. Brook trout up to 10 inches and the occasional brown up to 14 inches hang in the holes right in town. Instead of being a tribute, protected in a park setting, to the city of Deer Lodge it is just another tragedy—and the people of the area are not even aware enough to be ashamed.

Because the main river once ran thick with mining sludge, most of the tributaries in the valley are drained to meet irrigation demands for valley farms and ranches, particularly for hay crops. Natural flows have often been altered by dams in the mountains that store spring runoff and then dribble out the resource during the summer. Still, some of the streams dry up in sections during years of poor snowpack and rainfall.

On many Deer Lodge Valley creeks (and those in similar areas), the best way to locate quality fishing is to follow them upstream, above the agrarian flat lands where the water is withdrawn. There are pools, riffles, and pocket water in the foothills even higher up. During the summer, when the valley ponds and the main river warm to the point where fishing hits the skids, the little, cold, sparkling streams offer entertaining action for cutthroat, rainbow, and brook trout.

Dead Man's (Dead) Lake: A small cirque lake just down the hill from Albicaulis, Dead Man's has some decent cutthroats up to 16 inches. This is beautiful, high-mountain country and that alone makes it worth the visit.

Dolus Lakes: From the trailhead at Rock Creek Lake, hike in to these alpine cirque lakes northwest of Deer Lodge. Dolus Lakes have mainly cutthroats, some hybrids, and a few browns. Located in a tight chain, between 7,800 and 8,000 feet in elevation, it's easy to fish all four of them in a day. They offer good fishing for trout up to 15 inches.

Dutchman Creek: This little flow runs between Warm Springs Creek and Lost Creek. The stream itself is small, but there is a diked pond for water storage that has brown trout to 8 pounds (every puddle in the valley floor gives up fish like this).

East Fork Reservoir: In the Rock Creek drainage about 10 minutes by road from Georgetown Lake, the reservoir covers 500 acres and is 75 feet deep when not drawn down. Brook trout and rainbow trout with delusions of grandeur are taken along the drop-offs with streamers. This lake fishes well early in the season, before irrigation demands.

East Fork Rock Creek: This small water flows into the East Fork Reservoir and is followed by MT 38 and then trail to the headwaters. It is an easy stream to fish, except for the willows and tag alders that guard the banks much of the way. Grasshoppers are thick up here, as is the smell of sage after a warm rain. The cutthroats and even crazed brookies, 8- to 12-inch fish with more ambition than intelligence, slash and race after a hopper pattern spinning in the current. This stream is a lot of fun over cold beer and casual conversation.

Echo Lake: This 75-acre summer-resort lake, not far from Georgetown Lake, is replete with a public campground, vacation homes, domestic disputes, and water-skiers. Lots of 4- to 6-inch rainbows are dumped in here each year, and as they mature they are fools for leech patterns and damselfly nymphs. There are wild brook trout in the lake, and they react the same way to these patterns.

Flint Creek: This classic, small brown-trout stream winds through mostly private land, though the landowners have been kind enough to grant access to those who ask. There

A fine small brown-trout stream not far from Drummond, Flint Creek holds fair numbers of fish over 14 inches.

are also cutthroats, brooks, rainbows, and whitefish. Parts of the stream are accessible from MT 1. Some lower sections go dry during drought years, so the visiting angler, lacking local knowledge, should drive up to Philipsburg and work that area.

On a recent warm September day, I waded a stretch that wound through grassy meadows through alder and willow, taking brown after brown to 15 inches on first size 14 Yellow Humpies and then size 10 Joe's Hoppers. When this stream is right, it's a glorious experience.

Wading carefully (read: crouched and quiet) along the willow-and-grass-lined banks, a Gartside's Hopper during the day and a Goddard Caddis in the evening (brown trout like flies that "plop") work all summer. In the fall the mouth of the stream (just go to the city park in Drummond and walk the quarter mile up the Clark Fork) gets a great run of browns from the river. The first mile of Flint Creek, and the first pool in the Clark Fork itself, get crammed with spawners. Streamers (yes, this means Woolly Buggers at ten paces), swept under the banks and through the runs as soon as the days noticeably shorten and cool, is what fly fishing is all about at this time.

Four Mile Basin Lakes: Not many (if any) beautiful little golden trout remain here, and they are tough to catch. When they head for the spawning inlets, a weighted

Muddler worked across their noses a few times often does the trick. The big male goldens look like sunsets on a planet from another star system. The females are emerald and blood red. These are fantastic fish, but then, so are all the trout. These lakes lie over the hill west of Twin Lakes, a couple of miles by trail from the end of the Twin Lakes Creek jeep road.

Georgetown Lake: Almost 3,000 surface acres lie right next to MT 1 with summer homes, resorts, public access, boat launches, waterskiing, and campgrounds. So what? Georgetown in the early season and again in the fall has some of the nicest brook trout in the state, along with a lot of fat rainbows. The brookies take Olive Zonkers and damselfly nymphs fished with sink-tips along the eastern shore (there are spring holes here). A fly has to get right down to the tops of the thick weed growth before the fish will pay attention to it. Float tubes work best, but there'll be company from boaters bait fishing for the trout.

Georgetown stands right now as an unabashed success story. In the 1940s this was one of the finest trophy trout lakes in the country, the fish averaging over 4 pounds. But, incredibly, Montana Department of Fish, Wildlife & Parks stocking policies turned this rich, relatively shallow (maximum depth of 38 feet) water into a put-and-take fishery. Bait fishermen from nearby cities would come up to take limits of 9- to 12-inch hatchery rainbows, the gullible Arlee strain, on worms, corn, and marshmallows. This was often a family activity, a fine way to spend a day with children, but it was silly to ruin the finest lake in the state when there were many beautiful, but infertile, waters nearby that would be perfect for hatchery-truck, dump stocking.

There are hatches on Georgetown that qualify as fly-fishing events. In June (exact time depending on the weather) the damselfly nymphs start migrating en masse toward the shallows. The trout don't even have to cruise. They sit in the open lanes in the weeds and capture the nymphs coming toward them. A matching, size 6 or 8 olive fly has to swim the same direction as the natural, toward the bank, to be completely effective. On a windy day, on the leeward side of the lake, it's also possible to match the freshly emerged adult insects, still internally "soft" and a pewter gray color (it takes an hour or so for them to change to the bright blue body of the adult). The weak, clumsy insects get blown back onto the water by any breeze.

By July the large Limnephilidae caddisflies start emerging on Georgetown. The adults, size 6 and 8 insects, don't fly off the water after hatching. These "travelers" run over the surface. A trout keys on the wake an adult leaves, swimming up behind the insect and exploding on it. A good dry-fly imitation, such as the Devil Bug, has to leave the same V-shaped disturbance when it is brought in with a steady retrieve.

Georgetown gets a spinner fall of tricos, but not a massive number of insects. The most important mayfly is the Callibaetis. The hatches start in August, and during the morning trout cruise the surface hunting for the duns and spinners resting on the water. The fish move in a pattern, and you have to put your fly, such as a size 14 CDC Callibaetis Dun or size 14 Gray Clear Wing Spinner, in a feeding path.

Goat Mountain Lakes: These half-dozen little waters dotting the side of Goat Mountain are accessible by a poor road and a good trail up the Rock Creek drainage. All of them are full of small cutthroats that love dry flies. A Foam Beetle or a Foam Ant does nicely. This is wonderful country to visit for a few days.

Gold Creek: This pretty stream still hurts from the mining tailings left on its banks decades ago. It is followed by a gravel road off the Gold Creek exit on I-90. There is fishing for rainbows and cutthroats in the meadows, and for cutthroats in the forested reaches up above. Some real nice browns, including a 30-inch fish caught on a Marabou Single Egg in 1990, come up from the Clark Fork in the fall.

Gold Creek Dredge Ponds: There are two of them, one on each side of the Gold Creek Road about 7 miles up from I-90. The ponds are, for the most part, very deep, the dredging operations in the first half of the twentieth century having used large machinery to scoop out tons of gravel. There are brown and cutthroat trout in both waters.

At times you would swear that these ponds are barren, but that's only because the trout go down 30 or more feet and hold on the steep slopes. At other times, rare occasions when a large number of insects fall on the surface, these waters suddenly come alive with rising fish.

Green Canyon Lake: On the west side of the Copper Creek drainage, this lake is managed for cutthroats, with maybe a few rainbow-cutthroat hybrids remaining from earlier plantings. It is a deep lake and 10- to 16-inch fish cruise close to the edge, along the shallow rim, looking for food.

Hearst Lake: Lying above 8,000 feet in a glacial cirque north of Mount Haggin and southwest of downtown Anaconda, you can hike to Hearst by steep trail. It has a nice population of 12-inch-or-better cutthroats. An unweighted nymph, allowed to sink ever so slowly, brings cruising trout a long way.

Hidden Lakes: In the Rock Creek drainage (not *the* Rock Creek, but the one that empties into the Clark Fork near Garrison), these five small lakes sit between 8,000 and 9,500 feet, all with hordes of small brookies and cutthroats that make good eating. The fish are overpopulated here. A little thinning would help the remaining stock.

Job Corps (Duck) Ponds: The ponds lie right along I-90 near Warm Springs. To get there, take the Warm Springs exit and drive down the gravel road that parallels the interstate. There is a series of ponds, side by side, dug on the flats. They are all shallow (13 feet maximum), weedy, and full of trout. The fish—mostly rainbows but with brooks, browns, and cutts, too—don't run as big as the ones in the close-by Settling Ponds, but there are a lot of trout in the 15- to 20-inch range.

The ponds were built in the 1980s as a training project by the Anaconda Job Corps. The main purpose was to provide waterfowl habitat, not trout habitat, and the fishing season was set accordingly to protect the nesting birds.

The ponds open on August 15 and close on September 30. By the time they open the Callibaetis hatch is going strong, and on windless days the fish pock the surface with crossing necklaces of rise forms. None of these trout seem particularly hard to catch, probably because they don't see anglers for most of the year, and even a general match, like a size 14 Parachute Adams, is accepted gratefully. On windy days an imitation of the Callibaetis nymph, a size 14 Soft Hackle March Brown, works consistently. A float tube or kick boat helps an angler maneuver, but trees haven't grown up around the ponds yet and it's easy enough to cast from the bank on any of them.

Little Blackfoot River: Crossed and followed by US 12 and county roads from Garrison (where it enters the Clark Fork) up beyond Elliston, this little stream is quite resilient, despite the best efforts of local ranchers to dewater and channelize sections of it. Prime stretches of the river have been straightened and ruined as trout habitat in unsuccessful attempts at flood control, but in the undisturbed riffle and pool habitat, the water kept cooler than 62 degrees Fahrenheit even during the hottest summer days by numerous small springs, a healthy population of feisty browns holds out for almost the full length of the river. Up above Elliston the brookies and cutthroats finally take over.

I remember one late summer afternoon working my way upstream well above Avon, taking nice browns on a size 10 Joe's Hopper, when I came upon a young lass sunbathing in the nude along a gravel bank. She sat up, turned my way, smiled and said "Howdy," then rolled over with her back to me. I proceeded fishing upstream none the worse for wear. Gotta love this stream.

After the runoff the river enters a two- to three-week "golden" period. The stream is still bank full but clear. Many different species of mayflies, caddisflies, and stoneflies are hatching, and the trout are rising joyfully and indiscriminately to the potpourri of surface items. Near the end of this glorious period, in early or mid-July, there is a heavy emergence of pale evening duns, and on this hatch the fish get a bit fussy. A size 14 Light Cahill not only matches this insect but also serves as a good, all-around dry fly for this time frame.

During the summer the Little Blackfoot turns into the perfect grasshopper stream. The water stays cool, especially for browns, and the trout feed actively through the middle of the day. The grass and brush, growing right to the edge of the stream, is full of grasshoppers. You shouldn't just peck around the open water with your flies—slam them back into and under the deadfalls and brush. The difference may be 10- to 12-inch browns caught in the open water or 14- to 16-inch browns back in the trash (the farther in, the better). The best hopper pattern for this fishing is the most aerodynamic one that you can cast accurately with a fast, tight loop. For this reason, a good choice on the Little Blackfoot is the Henry's Fork Hopper. Alternative flies for this bank crashing, useful when a fish refuses a hopper and demands something a bit more subtle, are a size 16 Mohawk for midday, or a size 14 Elk Hair Caddis or size 14 Brown and Yellow Emergent Sparkle Pupa for the evening.

The same grasshopper tactics work in the fall, but now suddenly the brown trout run bigger. These fish were in the stream all summer, but they were buried so deep in the best cover that nothing would bring them out. In the fall they start to move to spawning areas and they are a little more vulnerable to the good caster (or at least the courageous one). Streamers, especially the Little Brown Trout pattern, are exceptionally effective in the fall, right up into November. The lower miles of the Little Blackfoot get a run of browns up from the Clark Fork.

This river, known affectionately to fly fishers as the Little B, deserves special protection. It is a popular trout fishery for the anglers of a major city, Helena (right over the Continental Divide), local residents, and tourists driving US 12. Concerned individuals, conservation organizations, and the state should work at protecting the riparian habitat and the stream flow. The Little Blackfoot is just small enough to be fragile.

Lost Creek: This stream has two distinct personalities. It comes out of the Flint Creek Range, tumbling down a steep canyon and passing through Lost Creek State Park near Anaconda. In these upper reaches it is pure, cold cutthroat and brook trout water, good fishing for anyone skilled with short-line nymph or dry-fly tactics.

When Lost Creek hits the limestone floor of the valley and takes on the characteristics of a spring creek, it changes into a brown trout stream. In autumn most of the tributaries in this valley get a run of spawning browns from the Clark Fork. From mid-September through November, the streams have more water because irrigation demands have dwindled. As far up as the trout can migrate, from the flats to the mountains, the water often is filled with fish (2,000 per mile in Lost Creek). Once an angler finds the spawning trout, any yellow-and-brown streamer (or any nymph for that matter) drifted in front of them will usually provoke a strike. Territorial behavior is at its peak. But take it easy on these fish: They do have a few things on their diminutive minds.

Lower (Little) Barker Lake: Even though this one lies at nearly 8,000 feet, it is reachable by rough road off MT 1 (the Georgetown Highway). It is good fishing for rainbows and cutthroats, most around 10 inches but with some up to 16 inches.

Lower Willow Creek Reservoir: Take the Drummond exit off I-90 and go to Hall. This reservoir is reached by 9 miles of county road. It's 170 acres deep (when it is not drawn down to dust for irrigation) with some nice, wild cutthroats that come in from the creek. These fish should be left alone when they are vulnerable in excessively low water.

Meadow Lakes: To get to these six lakes in the Racetrack Creek headwaters, hike 6 miles on the trail from the end of the Racetrack Creek Road. They range in altitude from 7,650 to 8,650 feet and vary in size from 4 to 25 acres. There are fish in the four largest lakes. The two small, mud-bottomed ones are barren. They are all rich in aquatic life, but for some reason only number three grows monsters, up to 30 inches.

When summer storms wail through this barren country, you will feel the crack and sizzle of the lightning and smell the ozone when it blasts the gray rock. Originally managed for rainbows, like most alpine waters, Meadow Lakes are now getting cutthroat plants on a periodic basis.

Medicine Lake: In the upper Rock Creek drainage, Medicine Lake is managed for westslope cutthroats that do well in the fertile aquatic environment. Even at 7,000 feet, damsels are found. Nymphs are the best bet, but splatting an electric-blue dry on the surface, letting the thing sit, and then creating a commotion is interesting. One minute the bug is there; the next minute there is a big hole in the water. The action can be slow, but then you're not in the mountains to punch a clock. You can hike in a couple of miles from the end of Sand Basin Road (south of the West Fork of Rock Creek) or take 4.5 miles of jeep road from the junction of Elk Creek and the South Fork of Rock Creek.

Middle Fork Rock Creek: This 25 miles of shallow, easily fished water holds fair numbers of rainbows, cutthroats, and whitefish that might reach 10 inches.

Mud Lake: North of Big Racetrack Lake, you can drive to Mud Lake on a four-wheel-drive road. There is some on-again, off-again fishing for 10- to 16-inch cutthroats.

Phyllis Lakes: These two 10-acre lakes in the Anaconda-Pintler Wilderness are home to cutthroat trout. Upper Phyliss has some 12-inchers. Lower Phyliss receives some plantings on occasion by a devoted fisheries biologist, and there are slightly better numbers and sizes in this one. Take the trail about 2 miles southwest of Johnson Lake to get there.

Racetrack Creek: There are over 12 miles of good small-stream fishing through the middle and upper stretches of Racetrack Creek. The entire way up to Racetrack Lake is accessible by county road, jeep road, and trail. The upper portion above the campground is rough, tumbling water where you move from pool to pool. Below the campground the runs dig through glacial gravel with a good carpet of aquatic weeds. There are cutthroats from 8 to 13 inches, along with lesser numbers of brook, brown, and rainbow trout.

As with most mountain streams, on opening day (the third Saturday in May) the stream is normally bank-full and difficult to work. When the stream begins to lower sometime in mid-June through July (depending on the snowpack and weather), the trout go on a feeding spree for a couple of weeks. With ample flows, the fish are spread throughout the creek. A wet fly, such as the classic Leadwing Coachman or a woven-bodied Sandy Mite, covers a lot of water. A dry fly like a Royal Trude or a Lady Heather drums up the fish. Late in the season, through summer and fall, the trout hold in the deeper pools and slots. The fishing is challenging and you have to study each spot, figuring the angle of approach and the best method of presentation.

The lower alluvial flats of the creek are sucked low for irrigation, not completely destroying but hurting what could be an excellent brown trout fishery. Somehow, in this puddle-jump water of summer, a population of 15- to 20-inch fish survive (probably because of springs). The stream also plays host to an autumn run of nice browns, but then I've never met a bad brown.

Racetrack Lake: Reached by jeep road, this dammed, 35-acre, deep lake suffers from irrigation drawdown, but it is still good fishing for 8- to 13-inch cutthroats, rainbows, and hybrids. When in doubt, work the rocky points with small streamers, stripping the fly fast (a method that only works consistently in lakes with eager fish).

Rainbow Lake: In the headwaters of Gold Creek, you can drive to Rainbow Lake by jeep road above the dismantled ghost town of Pioneer. About 20 acres, it is fertile with good numbers of 16- to 20-inch cutthroats and few big rainbows, up to 30 inches, that are fussy but can be taken with a little stealth and patience.

One food item Rainbow has in abundance is leeches, and these leeches are the 3- to 4-inch variety. That is what the large, cruising trout are hunting for along the edges. The fish rush toward any puff of silt off the bottom. A fly tied on an upside-down keel hook, the Bristle Leech, lies on the bottom without snagging and kicks up a cloud with the first strip of the retrieve. It is a deadly pattern in Rainbow Lake.

Ranch Creek: A tributary of Rock Creek, with Grizzly Campground on the lower end, Ranch is real good small-creek fishing for all the species in the main stream. It's no secret that the mouth of every tributary on Rock Creek gets great in the fall.

Rock Creek (Garrison): This creek drains a bunch of alpine lakes (nearly twenty) and passes through rugged, timbered canyons to Rock Creek Lake. Below the lake is good fishing for small cutthroats, rainbows, browns, and brookies. The lower portions,

Fall fishing farther up Rock Creek is always productive for medium-size trout.

before the stream reaches the Clark Fork about 3 miles from Garrison, get dried up during the summer. This is also not *the* Rock Creek.

Rock Creek: Don't believe the "creek" part—this is a small river. It is also one of the most famous fly-fishing waters in Montana, designated Blue Ribbon by the state. It is hit heavily not only by the people from Missoula (an urban area of 70,000-plus), but also by a good number of tourists. Fortunately, all of these anglers can spread out on 50 miles of prime trout water. Yes, this is *the* Rock Creek.

There are two ways to reach Rock Creek. To fish the upper end, you can take the Drummond exit off I-90, drive to Philipsburg on MT 1, turn right on MT 38, and go to Gillies Bridge. At that point you hit both the stream and the Rock Creek Road.

Rock Creek Road, finished in 1926 by the Forest Service, is paved only on the bottom 11 miles. For most of its length, it is rough gravel (and that's the way local conservationists fight to keep it). You can take the Rock Creek exit and follow the road all the way to the top, but it is quicker and a lot less dusty to reach the upper end by way of Philipsburg. The Rock Creek exit off I-90, 20 miles east of Missoula, is the best way to reach the lower sections of the stream.

Rock Creek starts at the confluence of the East Fork and the West Fork. The stream wanders through a wide valley, a collection of pools, pockets, and riffles, and it is easy fishing for 8- to 12-inch cutthroats, rainbows, and brooks. Any spot deep enough to hold a larger trout usually does, however, and that's the place to throw a bigger streamer, nymph, or dry fly. Moose love to roam and munch the rich grasses here, so be on the lookout for them. I've had more trouble with moose than grizzlies over the years.

About a mile above Gillies Bridge, the canyon—craggy, orange and red walls of sedimentary rock—squeezes in and the stream starts to dig better holding spots. Suddenly, this isn't small-fish water anymore. There are still plenty of 8- to 12-inch trout here, especially up any side channel, but the fly fisher who knows how to work rough western water catches 15- to 22-inch rainbows and cutthroats.

Remember: On this water, larger drys take larger fish.

Nymphs work on this section, but bouncing a weighted fly over the bottom gets you three or four whitefish for every trout. A streamer, on the other hand, doesn't catch as many fish as other types of flies, but it brings out the bigger trout. For real nostalgia you can bounce a Sandy Mite or a Lady Mite, old Pott-style, woven wet flies that are still sold in the area and are still very effective.

The composition of the fish population in Rock Creek changes from top to bottom. Above Gillies Bridge the predominant trout are cutthroats, cutthroat-rainbow hybrids, and rainbows, with a scattering of brook and brown trout. The pure rainbows start to dominate below Hogback Creek, making up 60 percent of the population and averaging 12 to 14 inches, but under the strict catch-and-release regulations in effect from the Hogback down to Butte Cabin Creek, cutthroats are rebounding in numbers, now amounting to 20 percent of the total. Bull trout are not the main species anywhere in Rock Creek, but the stream has one of the finest populations of this species in the state. Bull trout reach their greatest abundance in the upper and middle reaches.

The section around the Dalles is a strange, hard-to-master piece of river. The fish are there, browns becoming more and more prevalent, but the water, flowing around house-size boulders and into huge holes, is so deep that it is hard to catch the decent trout. Some anglers swear that it is impossible. Ordinary tactics only work here when a great hatch of salmon flies coincides with clearer and lower than normal runoff. Then the brutes feed along the edges on nymphs and adults.

The other two choices around the Dalles are depth bombing and night fishing. It takes a high-density sinking line and a weighted fly, either a nymph or a streamer, to get anywhere near the bottom in some of those holes. At night, at least, you can throw an unweighted or lightly weighted fly, even if it is a big one. Either method produces trout over 20 inches for the skilled practitioner.

In the lower section of Rock Creek, brown trout take over, making up 80 percent of the population. The water from Ranch Creek (the end of the paved road) down to the mouth is the most heavily hit part of the stream. These cottonwood bottoms are also where many fly fishers get skunked, probably due to three reasons: Most of the trout are browns, holding in deeper cover and demanding better presentations when they're not feeding, putting them out of reach most of the time. The heavy hatches, combined with better-defined pools and flats, let the trout feed selectively. And the trout get fished over so much that they get especially wary when they feel the presence of an angler.

This bottom water receives a great run of spawning browns from the Clark Fork in the fall. These fish move from spot to spot, so preoccupied that they're not nearly as skittish as the resident trout. A good streamer fisherman, pounding out a fly with those brown and yellow colors that bother big browns, takes fish up to 5 pounds, especially early or late in the day, or on overcast days.

Rock Creek is a very rich river (anyone skating on the algae-slick boulders can attest to that). The big hatch of the year, from the bottom all the way to the top, is the salmon fly. The emergence starts in early June, during the high-water runoff, creating a trout feeding frenzy and fly fisher madness. The hatch moves upstream 3 to 5 miles a day, and many anglers attempt to keep just ahead of the action.

While large dry flies, such as Sofa Pillows, Orange Stimulators, Orange Fluttering Stones, and Elk Hair Salmon Flies, bring up some rainbows, browns, and cutthroats, most anglers ignore the surface fishing and go to nymph imitations. Rock Creek runs high and turbid during normal years, which slows the action on top significantly in the lower sections. If you are willing to work weighted size 2 and 4 nymphs, often with sink-tip lines, quartering upstream and then crawled (not easy in the fast current of spring runoff) toward the bouldery bank, some fine angling awaits you. The retrieve mimics the actions of the stonefly nymphs crawling to shore to dry on the sun-warmed rocks. Seven-weight, 9-foot rods make casting, working the drift, and then picking up the heavy rig much easier. Short leaders, down to 4 feet, with 2X or 3X tippets work well.

Anyone whose heart is set on fishing dry flies during the hatch should find it at the upper end, above the Hogback. The water still runs high, but it's clear and trout smash the big adults and matching floaters. There are larger trout up here early in the season, too. The 16- to 22-inch rainbows from below, after spawning, stay in the upper section until the water levels start to drop in late June and early July.

Rock Creek is swollen enough during runoff to float (allowed only until June 30 each year). Once the water returns to normal, steady hatches of caddisflies, mayflies, and stoneflies come off well into the fall. Noteworthy hatches include the great gray spotted sedge, all through June; the golden stone, from late June through July; the spotted sedge, peaking in early July; the green sedge, in July and August; and the giant orange sedge, in early September (the lower 10 miles of Rock Creek have the best hatch of this insect of any river in the western part of the state). There are plenty of small mayflies—tricos, pale morning duns, and blue-winged olives—but they're more important in the pools of the bottom section than in the rougher currents about Harry's Flat.

Major terrestrials—grasshoppers, ants, and beetles—are important all summer, but the real event is the spruce moth flights. When these insects come off the evergreen trees in August and get trapped on the water by the thousands, they push the trout into a slop-feeding frenzy. The trick, since these are local infestations popping up in

Rock Creek in autumn is as pretty as it gets, and the fishing is good, too.

different places in different years, is finding the heaviest concentration, and that takes a little bit of "road hunting," driving from noon to 4 p.m. looking for moths in the air. They can be anywhere evergreen forests line the stream.

Too many anglers end up discouraged by the August fishing on Rock Creek. Just remember that the bottom section receives by far the most angling pressure. The trout may average 14 inches, with a good mix of sizes, but even the smaller ones are extremely wary by midsummer. The big boys are buried in the gravel, hiding from the thundering herd of neoprene-clad anglers. They have seen every pattern known to man by now.

So here's a tip for anyone determined to fish the lower, and even the middle, stretches in the summer. There's a myth of gigantic proportions, a silly one, that says "You don't have to get up early to fish Montana rivers." The truth is that trout everywhere feed heavily at dawn because nymphs and larvae, in the phenomena known as behavioral drift, are washing downstream free in the currents. This usually isn't a great dry-fly time, but the angler who can present a Prince Nymph, Peeking Caddis, or Montana Stone naturally is going to catch a lot of trout, with an inordinate share of large ones, and probably never see another angler from dawn to 7 a.m.

Ninety percent of the land bordering Rock Creek is owned by the US Forest Service. Access is abundant, at pullouts along the road and in conveniently spaced public campgrounds. With tighter restrictions on kill limits, this popular fishery continues to improve, mainly with larger trout, each season.

Ross Fork Rock Creek: Much of this stream is on private and posted land. The open stretches are small pocket water holding little cutthroats, brookies, and some small (for this species) whitefish moving upstream late in the season.

Schwartz Creek: Small, flowing out of timbered mountains near Clinton, Schwartz has some decent brookies and cutthroats, and a few spawner rainbows and browns. There's not a lot of casting water, but this is a pretty little stream.

Spring Creek: Filled with rainbows, small brookies, and cutthroats in the upper reaches, the best water flows through the Handley Ranch and permission is required. There are ponds, actually the remains of an old fish hatchery, on the lower end that are good early in the season before weeding up, but the fish are ever so spooky in these shallow waters. The Rock Creek Road crosses the lower reaches several miles up from I-90. Classic, pretty, and oh-so-clear water that is small but fertile.

Stewart Lake: Regularly planted with rainbows, this 20-acre lake is reached by road a few miles northeast of Philipsburg. The fish get hit with a good deal of angling pressure, so they never reach any great size.

Storm Lake: In the Anaconda-Pintler Range, Storm covers 55 acres at nearly 9,000 feet. The water is aquatically fecund, growing fat cutthroats and rainbows to 20 inches or so. The staple food in the lake is scuds. To get to Storm take scenic MT 1 west of Anaconda, then turn south on the road that parallels Storm Lake Creek.

Thornton Lake: Thirty acres in the headwaters of Racetrack Creek, you can hike to Thornton by an easy, 1-mile trail (which makes it a popular destination). It is fair fishing for rainbows that may top out at 12 inches.

Trask Lake: Part of the Hidden Lakes group, Trask is the largest of the bunch at an overwhelming 10 acres. It has small (as in stunted) brookies and cutthroats.

Twin Lakes: Go to the Spring Hill Campground, on MT 1 above Anaconda, and from there drive up the jeep road for 8 miles and walk up the trail for 1 mile. Neither lake is very large or very deep, but both waters support good populations of 12-inch cutthroats. These lakes receive regular plantings.

Wallace Reservoir: Short on aesthetics, especially after drawdown for irrigation, this lake north of I-90 near Clinton still has some fat cutthroat trout, up to 15 inches, that feed on the abundant aquatic insects and some small, dark green frogs that tend to get careless on occasion. Dig out the bass poppers.

Warm Spring Creek (Warm Springs): You can begin working this water inside the city limits of Anaconda. Above town this is a small stream that is both productive and lightly fished, since most people whiz by on their way to Georgetown Lake. The gradient is modest from Washoe Park up to the Job Corps Center, with the channel running behind houses on the left side of MT 1 The best fishing in this stretch is in the early season for cutthroats and rainbows.

As you head upstream, the creek passes under the road, changing into a mountain stream. The water is rich with insects and forage fish, and rainbows and cutthroats to over 15 inches feed on them. Eight- to 12-inch trout are the norm here, though. Getting the trout requires small-stream tactics, like picking the pockets with an upstream dry, bouncing the bottom with a short-line nymph, and swimming the edges with a downstream wet or streamer. Most of us choose a short rod when working this type of water with a dry fly—7 feet or less. When nymphing, an 8½-foot rod works much better, allowing you to reach out to those prime runs and little pockets where the big trout hide. The typical pattern selection for this type of water would include attractors (Gray Wulff and Royal Trude), general caddis simulations (Elk Hair Caddis and Emergent Sparkle Pupa), and general mayfly simulations (Adams and March Brown). Nymphs such as the Bead-Head Hare's Ear and Bright Green Caddis Larva are deadly. A Girdle Bug and a small Woolhead Sculpin are nice swimming flies.

The lower stretches still suffer from the deleterious effects of mining and irrigation drawdown. Despite this, some hefty browns can be caught here.

West Fork Rock Creek: This small stream dances and cascades over jumbles of flat, dark rock and between mossy banks. Small logjams add to the habitat that holds little cutthroat and brook trout, along with some whitefish.

The lower Clark Fork is big water with eddies, riffles, and corner pockets that often need big flies to draw the attention of big fish.

Lower Clark Fork

The Yellowstone, the Missouri, and the Kootenai come to mind when thinking of the big waters of Montana. These are large streams, but they are all considerably smaller than the lower Clark Fork River. Before the Clark Fork enters Idaho, on its way to joining the Columbia, it receives the waters of the Blackfoot, Bitterroot, Thompson, and St. Regis Rivers, along with the entire Flathead drainage, and it grows into the largest flow in the state. Even at St. Regis, before the Flathead enters, the gauging station records stream flows of 25,000 cfs on the Clark Fork during the peak May runoff.

A river of this dimension can intimidate even the most experienced fly fishers. Where does one start? How do you bring the trout up to the surface or drop the fly down to the fish? What is the most productive water?

MOUTH OF THE BLACKFOOT RIVER TO KELLY ISLAND

The Blackfoot, clear and pure compared to the highly enriched Clark Fork, is actually the bigger of the two rivers, doubling the flow at Milltown Dam. The stretch from the dam to Missoula is known as the "urban float." You can put a boat in below the dam (far below the churning water of the spillway) and reach the city limits in a few hours. The trout species in this section, in order of abundance, are browns, rainbows, and cutthroats.

The river is a mix of short riffles with long, smooth runs and flats. Hit the banks with a big fly, maybe a greased Muddler on top or a Woolly Bugger under the surface, and try to pull the browns out of the brush. At the flats, if fish are rising, you can wade and stalk individual trout, but if there are no insects on the water, these areas are usually dead. In the deep, swift runs you either have to pull trout up with a big attractor, maybe a size 6 or 4 Outlaw Hopper, or find fish below with a large nymph, maybe a size 8 or 6 Casual Dress.

KELLY ISLAND (THE MOUTH OF THE BITTERROOT) TO PETTY CREEK

This section below Missoula is a mystery even to the fish and game biologists. It is big, rich water, but there are only about 500 trout per mile in this part of the Clark Fork. No one really knows the reason for the low populations. Lack of spawning areas (with little recruitment from dewatered tributaries)? Not enough holding structure?

Lower Clark Fork

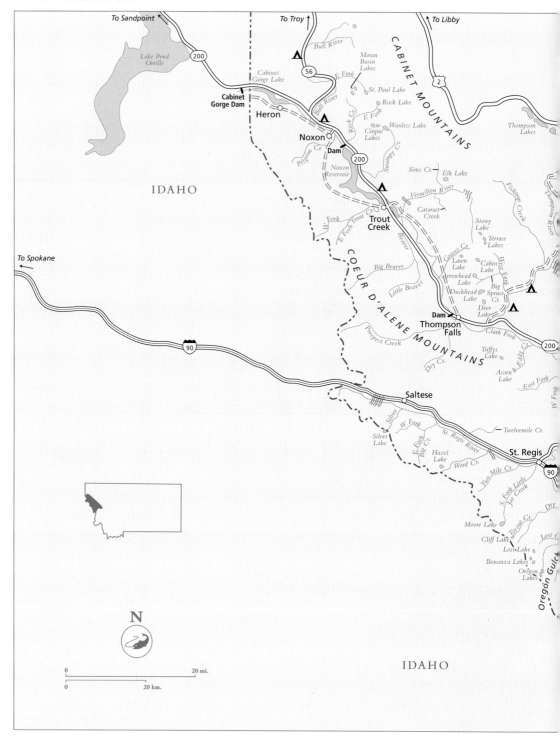

To Sandpoint

To Troy

To Libby

CABINET MOUNTAINS

Bull River

Lake Pend Oreille

200

56

Cabinet Gorge Lake

2

Moran Basin Lakes

E Fork

St. Paul Lake

Cabinet Gorge Dam

Bull River

Rock Lake

E Fork

Thompson Lakes

Heron

Rock Cr.

E Fork

Wanless Lake

Noxon

Cirque Lakes

Dam

Swampy Cr.

200

IDAHO

Pilgrim Cr.

Noxon Reservoir

Sims Cr.

Elk Lake

Fishtrap Creek

Thompson River

Vermilion River

Cataract Creek

Stony Lake

W Fork

E Fork

Trout Cr.

Trout Creek

Beaver

Graves Cr.

Lawn Lake

Terrace Lakes

Cabin Lake

West Fork

To Spokane

Big Beaver

Arrowhead Lake

Big Spruce Cr.

COEUR D'ALENE MOUNTAINS

Little Beaver

Duckhead Lake

Deer Lake

Dam

Thompson Falls

Clark Fork

90

Prospect Creek

Tuffys Lake

Eddy Cr.

200

Dry Cr.

Acorn Lake

East Fork

Saltese

W Fork

W Fork

Twelvemile Cr.

St. Regis River

St. Regis

Silver

90

Silver Lake

E Fork

Big Cr.

Hazel Lake

Ward Cr.

Two Mile Cr.

S Fork Little Joe Creek

Dry

Lost C

Moore Lake

Toyne Cr.

Oregon Gulch

Cliff Lake

Lost Lake

Bonanza Lakes

Oregon Lakes

N

0   20 mi.

0   20 km.

IDAHO

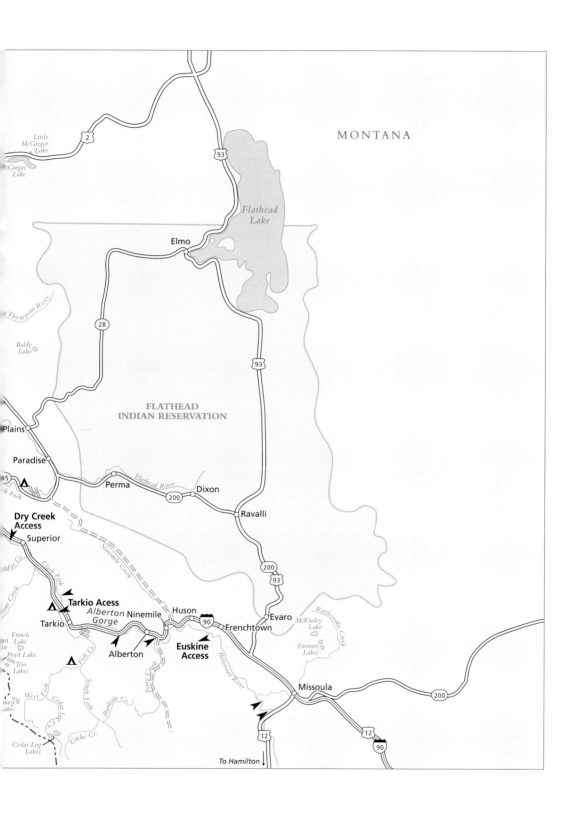

Residual pollution? Too much competition from rough fish? One thing is for certain, the problems have nothing to do with the food supply. The insect hatches are predictable and spectacular, and there is a great forage base of crawfish and minnows.

Five hundred trout per mile in a large river sounds dismal, but actually there are plenty of fish to cast to on a normal day. The rainbows and cutthroats, the predominant species down here, gather into pods. Pockets of feeding activity are scattered throughout the river. Thirty fish gulping here; 300 yards of lifeless water there. Then forty fat, 12- to 18-inch rainbows dimpling the surface below that gravel bar over along the far bank. And so on.

On a recent late-September day, I spent some time fishing a large riffle and the pool it fed into about 15 miles above St. Regis. It was near dusk and large rainbows to 20 inches rose to size 12 Hendricksons cast in the slower seams on the inside edge of the broken water and at the top of the pool. This fly has a universal appeal on Montana rivers, much like the Adams. I did not expect such success or consistent action, but will make a point to fish similar water on the lower Clark Fork and comparable rivers at this time of the year.

Many productive-looking pieces of water are poor fishing, while similar areas just downstream are filled with trout. Finding working fish is as much a part of the challenge as making quality presentations with effective flies. Many local anglers cruise the roads looking for rising fish before rigging up.

It helps immensely to know the hatches on this water. Often there'll be two or three major insects present at the same time and the fish will get real fussy. Typically the important species in this part of the river will also be important above Kelly Island and below Petty Creek.

There are midge hatches all winter, and on nice days the pods gather on the slower flats and sip drifting pupae or adults. It takes small flies and fine tippets to consistently fool trout. The most practical approach is a "two-fly" method. Try a big, visible dry fly, like a Royal Wulff, combined with a size 18 or smaller matching pattern, a Griffith Gnat or a Halo Midge Pupa, on 18 inches of leader tied directly to the eye of the bigger fly.

Mid-March brings two fine stonefly hatches. The skwala, better known on the Bitterroot River, is present in good numbers on the Clark Fork, too. There is an even more abundant hatch, the nemoura stone. The emergence of this grayish-brown-bodied stonefly moves upstream 4 or 5 miles each day, and the fishing is best in areas of peak abundance. The fickle spring weather can rain, snow, or blow out the fishing anytime, but local anglers wait for those warm but overcast days ideal for dry-fly fishing.

Some early mayflies and caddisflies also trigger good rises of trout in the pre-runoff period. One abundant hatch is the early red quill mayfly, matched with a size 14 Red Quill or a Red Quill Parachute, the activity stretching out over parts of April and May. By mid-May the blue-winged olive mayfly and the grannom caddis bust out in great numbers, and if the river doesn't rise and is muddy with runoff, the surface activity is wonderful.

There are a lot of little quirks on this tough river that are worth knowing about. Streamer fishing? From late June through July the redside shiners spawn, the males of this minnow developing a bright band of red, and a red streamer outfishes any other color during this period. Best searching dry fly? The streamside willows on the Clark Fork get infested with small black beetles, the insects turning the leaves into lacework, and enough of these terrestrials fall into the river to make the trout responsive to a beetle imitation, such as a size 18 or 20 Crowe Beetle or Black Mohawk.

All of this water is easy floating. There are no dangerous stretches before the Petty Creek Access. A stiff upstream wind can make a long day of floating, stopping a boat dead on the slow-moving flats. That's when you have to row downstream.

Petty Creek to Forest Grove (Alberton Gorge)

From Alberton to Tarkio the quiet Clark Fork changes as it churns through Cyr Canyon for roughly 12 miles. This is a truly dangerous stretch for all but the most talented whitewater rafters. There are standing waves, powerful whirlpools, and five major rapids—Rest Stop, Shelf, Tumbleweed, Boat Eater, and Fang. Just looking at the river here is a bit frightening.

It is difficult to hike down into the canyon, and once there it is impossible to walk far up or down the river. The only way to effectively fish the gorge is by floating it. Why bother? The gorge has incredible habitat. Fish, Wildlife & Parks biologists say that this is the only section of the lower river with high numbers of trout per mile. Many of those trout, with prime holding spots, abundant food supply, and virtually no fishing pressure, are trophy specimens. The power of the river through here at high water is impressive. The thundering current vibrates through the ground. Caution is advised.

One of the best ways to catch a trophy fish here is to throw streamers with a sinking line. Woolly Buggers, Hornbergs, and Matukas are good, but the best fly, imitating a major food item, is a crayfish imitation. The largest trout jump a pattern such as the Bugskin Crawfish.

The water at the bottom of the gorge is a short transition zone between fast and slow sections. The walking angler can find some fine hatches here, including a great skwala flight (and, according to area resident and expert angler Dean Ludwig, there is no one down here in March).

Forest Grove to Paradise

The fish populations get spotty again once the river leaves Alberton Gorge, and this section is even wider and flatter, with more space for the trout to spread out in, than other parts. The bonus is that the fish—rainbow, brown, and cutthroat trout—run a bit larger here.

Salmon flies show in late May and last through June, but this is often a period of high water. Dark Woolly Buggers retrieved slowly or drifted near the shoreline imitate the behavior of migrating nymphs and often take trout in turbid conditions. By mid-summer, and clear water, the best flies for the flats are the exacting imitations, but on the riffles Wulffs or Trudes, approximating the shape, size, and color of the naturals, are good plays. They are easy to see for both the angler and the trout. Summer is also a great time to blast hoppers noisily to the banks.

PARADISE TO THOMPSON FALLS

From Paradise to the mouth of the Thompson River is warmer and still larger water due to the entrance of the Flathead River. There is some difficult, pounding water west of Plains known as the Plains Rapids, but most of the river is long, deep runs and large pools. Browns and rainbows grow well here, feeding on sculpins and other forage fish, but imitating these species by working streamers with sinking lines is hard, often unproductive work. Popular patterns include Matukas, Spruce Flies, Buggers, and Marabou Muddlers in sizes 1/0 to 4.

Northern pike over 20 pounds are found in this area. Red-and-white 2/0 streamers draw the northerns and also some of the best trout. Ten-foot sink-tip lines and 7-weight rods (at least) are required. Even largemouth bass are taken, usually unintentionally, by anglers swimming large patterns.

If intentionally targeting northern pike with a fly rod, consider using a wire-tippet section.

POPULAR FLIES

Adams	Kaufmann Stone
Black Mohawk	Light Cahill
Bugskin Crawfish	Mahogany Thorax
Casual Dress	Marabou Muddler
Clear Wing Spinner	Matuka
Comparadun	Outlaw Hopper
Diving Caddis	Red Quill
Double Spinner	Red Quill Parachute
Elk Hair Caddis	Spruce Fly
Hendrickson	Trude
Hornberg	Woolly Bugger
Humpy	Wulff

THOMPSON FALLS TO IDAHO

From Thompson Falls into Idaho, the river is a series of impoundments. In the running water between the lakes there are, aside from largemouth bass, smallmouth bass, crappie, northern pike, and yellow perch, some brown and rainbow trout. The browns provide some elusive but highly fascinating fishing as they move up into their spawning tributaries each autumn. Finding these big fish is, if anything, more hunting than fishing, and often the fall rains turn the streams muddy and unfishable.

Some of the state fishing access sites along the Clark Fork working downstream include Erskine, Petty Creek, Forest Grove, and Flat Iron Ridge. Forest Service camping areas are Quartz Flats, Trout Creek, Sloway, and Cascade.

FISHING WATERS IN THE LOWER CLARK FORK DRAINAGE

Arrowhead Lake: In the Thompson River drainage at the head of Big Spruce Creek, Arrowhead is only 12 acres, but it's fairly deep and has holdover cutthroats. The population is augmented by helicopter plantings every few years, and the number of trout can vary widely over the seasons. This is a lake where it's smart to call Fish, Wildlife & Parks to check the current status of the fishery before hiking to it.

Baldy Lake: Surprisingly, this 15-acre lake is not far from Mount Baldy, about 7 miles west of Hot Springs and 2 miles by trail from the McGinnis Creek Road. It also receives periodic plantings of cutthroats, which grow to maybe 12 inches, and it also has its up-years and its down-years.

Beaver Creek: Beaver Creek begins when Big Beaver Creek and Little Beaver Creek join and runs for 8 miles before dumping into Noxon Reservoir. It has small rainbows, cutthroats, and brookies, in roughly that order, as full-time residents, and some big browns move up into this creek in the autumn.

Big Beaver Creek: Followed by roads, this creek is popular with area anglers for cutthroats in the upper reaches, brookies in some beaver ponds, and rainbows in the bottom runs. Access, with a gravel road following the stream, is good from the flat land all the way up to the canyon headwaters.

Bonanza Lakes: Two lakes lie a stone's throw apart in the Bitterroot Range west of Superior. One lake is 10 acres; the other is just short of 20 acres. They are both filled with small brookies willing to jump on almost any fly.

Bull River: There are more than 20 miles of this locally popular stream. Anglers like it for the easy access off a good road and for consistent catches of 10- to 14-inch rainbow, cutthroat, and brook trout. There are also whitefish and, at certain times of the year, brown trout in the river.

The Bull River empties into the Clark Fork at Noxon Reservoir, and this makes the water interesting from late October into November. A couple hundred large browns run up out of the lake to spawn. These are big, wary fish, with all the fickleness of moving fish in an unfamiliar environment, and the problems are finding them and catching them.

Former FWP biologist Joe Huston first told me about the fall run of browns with fish to 30 inches. I fished the stream in October with sporadic results. Using a size 4 long-shank Woolly Bugger (prefer a Cree-hackled brown item that is heavily weighted with a dozen wraps of wire), I managed to connect with a half-dozen browns, all over 2 feet and one at 27 inches. This is hit-or-miss big-trout hunting that largely depends on the flush of autumn rains to move these big guys in the Bull. Overcast days are a must.

For the angler unwilling to hunt those elusive autumn trout, there is more consistent fishing in May, before the runoff. Some people even float the river during this period. There always seem to be nice browns—not the biggest ones, but fish up to 20 inches—that stay in the river after spawning. After a winter there they are acclimated to the environment and feed and act like residents. They don't leave for the lake until early summer.

Burdette Creek: With cutthroats to 10 inches, Burdette, up in the Fish Creek drainage, is a fine little stream for beaver pond lovers.

Cabin Lake: An easy hike, 1 mile from the West Fork Thompson River Road, makes this a popular spot. It's a beautiful little lake, about 20 acres at 7,000 feet, with good fishing for 8- to 12-inch cutthroats. The trout used to average a little larger, but the angling pressure has cropped the numbers of nicer fish.

Cabinet Gorge Reservoir: Twelve miles long and extending into Idaho, Cabinet Gorge is a wide, dammed spot on the Clark Fork that has brown and rainbow trout, plus large and smallmouth bass, kokanee salmon, yellow perch, crappie, northern pike, and trash fish. This place is a real zoo used by water-sports enthusiasts of all kinds during the summer months, but there are some big fish here. The head of the reservoir is the best bet for browns, except in late summer when these fish begin heading toward the creek mouths preparatory to spawn.

Cache Creek: The fun part of this stream in the Fish Creek drainage is that the angler can drive the South Fork Fish Creek Road to the mouth and then hike up it by good trail for 9 miles. Anyone with a bit of ambition is going to have a lot of water all to himself after a few miles. There are plenty of rainbows and cutthroats, 8 to 11 inches. My best fish was a 13-inch cutthroat.

Cataract Creek: Fast fishing for small cutthroats, 6 to 9 inches, for the angler tough enough to reach them. Cataract tumbles down from Seven Point Mountain, entering a gorge in its last 5 miles. There are, of course, plenty of deep pools within this crashing water.

Cedar Log Lakes: In hard-to-reach country, these lakes are snugged up against the Idaho border, up in the headwaters of Fish Creek (use a good topo map to follow the USFS trail). East Cedar is 44 acres, and West Cedar is 14 acres. Both are good fishing for cutthroats that run up to 14 inches. The trout in both lakes, when they aren't rising to surface food, relish olive scud imitations retrieved steadily along the drop-offs.

Cirque (Upper Wanless) Lakes: North of Noxon Reservoir in glaciated country, these four lakes are reached by a 6-mile trail. They all have good populations of cutthroats up to 14 inches. Cirque Lakes number one and number two are planted every now and then with supplementary stockings of small cutts.

Cliff Lake: Containing cutthroats, including some nice ones, just the sight of the aquatic vegetation at the outlet tells the angler that this is a fertile (and therefore not always easy) lake. It's in the Dry Creek drainage, which enters the Clark Fork a few miles northwest of Superior.

Duckhead Lake: In the backcountry of West Fork Thompson River country (3.5 miles by trail up Honeymoon Creek), Duckhead is good fishing for cutthroats that average 12 inches. There are larger trout, too, but they hang along the drop-offs of this deep, more than a quarter-mile-long lake.

East Fork Bull River: Not all that big, and tough to fish, there's so much brush crowding the banks that unless you have a good, tight roll cast, you're not going to be able to effectively present a fly. There are tiny cutthroats (10 inches is a monster) and a very few large brown trout up from Noxon Reservoir to spawn. A large streamer fished in the deeper holes and darker crannies always seems to produce a few surprising moments here.

East Fork Rock Creek: Perhaps 4 miles of fishable water from where it comes out of Rock Lake, this creek has a fine population of 6- to 10-inch cutthroats that are fools for a dry fly of almost any type and size. The special parts of this stream are the deep and beautiful pools in the lower 2.5 miles.

Elk (Sims) Lake: In this fertile lake the regularly planted cutthroats grow to a pound or more without much trouble. This 7-acre pond lies 2 miles north of the Vermilion River Road off the Sims Creek jeep trail. Because of the abundance of food, these fish are often selective (for cutthroats, that is). This is one of those waters that separate the real stillwater anglers from the floggers. It's probably best to use those imitations designed specifically for lakes, matching the items that dominate the food base.

The basic fact is that Elk Lake trout are never desperately hungry. They browse instead of hunt. During one of the major hatches, such as the Callibaetis mayfly of summer and early fall, these fish pick off flies that look and act like the nymph. My favorite lake pattern, the Biggs Special, works well here.

Fish Creek: Think of this stream as a slightly smaller version of Rock Creek. It is a rugged and beautiful watershed, one of the best places to glimpse wildlife. You might surprise a moose, mountain lion, or black bear.

Fish Creek flows into the Clark Fork near Tarkio, entering the Alberton Gorge section of the river. The lower 8 miles run mostly through a steep canyon, accessible only by foot trail. This is rough water, but large pools hold the trout. In late May, right after the season opens, there are still big rainbows here, to 5 pounds, that come up from the river to spawn in the canyon stretch. Large, weighted flies such as the Bitch Creek, or Montana Stone nymphs or Marabou Muddler or Dark Spruce streamers, take these fish.

The upper 7 miles are followed by a good logging road. This is popular water, but good fishing in spite of the pressure for mainly rainbows, cutthroats, and brookies. The insect hatches are so diverse, with different kinds of stoneflies, mayflies, and caddisflies on the water all the time, that the trout rarely get selective. They will generally take a Humpy or a Stimulator. Most of the fish measure under 16 inches, but they are willing feeders in this bouncing stream. It splits into North and South Forks above Clearwater crossing.

A small stream that runs really low in summer, Fish Creek at times has good fishing for several species of trout (and whitefish) on attractor patterns.

Fishtrap Creek: This pretty, pine forest stream, a tributary of the Thompson, is followed by a logging road for its entire length into the Cabinet Mountains. The cutts, brookies, and rainbows do not grow big here, although a few nice rainbows move up in the spring before the general season opens just to drive you nuts.

Fishtrap Lake: Mostly cutthroats, up to 14 inches. Skip the real deep water at the lower end. The bulk of the food (and the trout) are at the shallow, upper end of this 35-acre lake. Take the Thompson River Road past the Bend Ranger Station, then continue about 11 miles up the Lazier Creek Road.

French Lake: Fourteen acres in cirque country, French Lake nestles well back in the Fish Creek drainage. The cutthroats are small, with a few foot-and-a-half exceptions. This lake is good all-purpose Olive Nymph or Hare's Ear Nymph turf. Cast these flies far out on a floating line. Let them sink slowly and then begin a very slow, halting retrieve. The trout will find this hard to resist. If they do, lob large Olive Woolly Worms at them. If this fails, light a cigar and drink a beer.

Heart Lake: Heart Lake is in the headwaters of the South Fork of Trout Creek (Superior). You reach it via 3 miles of trail from the South Fork Road. There are 60 acres of water full of brook trout, mostly 8 to 10 inches, with the occasional big one.

Lawn Lake: In the Graves Creek drainage, and not famous for its fishing, Lawn nonetheless receives sporadic helicopter plants of cutthroat trout that offer fair sport.

Little McGregor Lake: Just north of US 2 with public access, Little McGregor is less than 100 acres with good numbers of brookies, some rainbows, yellow perch, and largemouth bass. The brook trout reach weights of a pound or two.

Little Thompson River: From timbered mountains in the east, this stream rolls through grazing country in its midsection and down a steep gorge in its bottom part, then flows into the Thompson River. It sees a good deal of action for small cutthroats, rainbows (the big ones are gone by opening day), brookies, and mountain whitefish.

Lowell Lake: Deep and fairly large for a cirque in the Cabinet Mountain country, Lowell is periodically planted with westslope cutthroats by helicopter. The fish do well. Lowell is reached from the end of the North Fork Bull River Trail in steep, rugged, and uncrowded country.

Lower Thompson Lake: Just to the south of US 2 between Kalispell and Libby, Lower Thompson covers 240 acres and is more than 140 feet deep. It is managed extensively for kokanee salmon and rainbows. Also, brown trout are planted here and, since there is plenty to eat, they grow quite large. The fly fisherman who tries big, perch-colored streamers along the shore and near the inlets in the fall might be surprised by the quality of the brown trout angling.

The attraction for the fanatic bass fisherman is the fine summer fly fishing. There really is no slump once the water warms enough—from late June until early fall this is a great topwater lake. The best area is at the inlet, with its long shallows and wide bays, or along the shorelines. The 12- to 15-inch largemouths hit the surface well in the clear water.

Favorite flies? A Sneaky Pete, a cork bug with rubber legs and a bullet front, fished with hard strips to make the fly dive in a shallow swim. The bass hit it on the pauses between the strips. Or a weighted Dahlberg Diver, a deeper-running fly with a deer-hair lip, worked with a sink-tip to make this pattern wobble over the bottom.

McGregor Lake: Over 2 square miles in surface area, McGregor lies right next to US 2 midway between Libby and Kalispell. There are summer homes and resorts, plus plenty of boat traffic on this lake. Some large mackinaw (lake trout) are caught with streamers in the spring and fall. There are also lots of rainbows and some cutthroat and brook trout. After ice-out this is not all that bad a place to cast a streamer, especially around the inlets. Also, in the early season, focus on Mackinaw Point. A bar runs across the lake here, concentrating the gamefish in reasonably shallow water.

Middle Thompson Lake: Almost a square mile in area and right by US 2, Middle Thompson has plenty of summer homes. This lake is planted regularly with rainbow and brown trout that do well. There are also kokanee salmon, cutthroats, and maybe a big lake trout or two, and populations of yellow perch, northern pike, and largemouth bass.

A number of small creeks run into the lake, and they are prime locations for rainbows early in the year and for browns (especially around Davis Creek and Tallulah Creek) in the fall. Streamers that look like small perch may pick off any of the predators, from a bass to a marauding northern.

Moore Lake: A 13-acre mountain lake, you get to Moore by logging road up the South Fork of Little Joe Creek west of St. Regis. This lake is fairly fertile, with deep water in the middle and aquatic weeds around the edges. An excellent population of brook trout, including a few in the 15-inch range, cruise the shoreline, hunting the vegetation.

These aren't dumb, hungry brookies. Good matching flies, especially a Green Damsel Nymph or a Flashback Scud, take the best fish when nothing is on the surface. The damsel hatch, lasting through June and July some years, is highlight time on this water.

Ninemile Creek: About 25 miles west of Missoula, this stream used to be excellent fishing for cutthroats, along with big rainbow and bull trout up from the main river. The lower 3 miles of Ninemile, which should be prime spawning habitat, is hammered by sedimentation from flood irrigation return flows. The Soil Conservation Service is working on a project to recover this stretch.

I used to live up this way in the early seventies, and the fishing was wonderful way back then using almost any dry fly. Instead of attending classes at the University of Montana in Missoula, I spent my time on this water. By the mid-seventies you could tell the fishing was going to hell—an inverse correlation between the number of homes and the number of trout. Most of the access is gone to private landowners. There were elk and black bear here, too, with big elk in the high timber and lots of ducks on the beaver ponds. Some wolves tried to establish a home, but they were shot. Get the picture? Sometimes if you look at things too hard, you get a damn hollow feeling in your gut. One of the streams that's all but gone, and I miss it so.

Noxon Reservoir: Lying behind Noxon Rapids Dam, the reservoir is about 38 miles long by 0.5 mile wide; MT 1 follows it on one side and county roads flank the other side. This lake needs to be fished from a boat unless you are of the "heavily-weighted-dough-ball" school of fishing made famous on the Rock River in Beloit, Wisconsin. Everything has been planted here, from burbot to brown trout to kokanee salmon to smallmouth bass to rainbow trout to largemouth bass. There are also northern pike and yellow perch. If you must fish this water, try the upper end or near the mouths of the many creeks pouring into the reservoir. Try fall for the browns and spring for the rainbows. The smallmouth fishing sounds as good as anything.

Petty Creek: This used to be a pleasant little mountain and meadow stream to fish for small brookies and cutthroats, but subdividers have ruined the country and access is marginal at best. The lower end goes underground for the last quarter mile during low-water years. A few large trout sneak up the creek a little ways in the spring and fall, but that's about all the action for the remainder of my lifetime.

Prospect Creek: Across the river from Thompson Falls, Prospect Creek flows over 20 miles, offering rainbow, bull, and brook trout in the lower reaches and cutthroats above. Once in a while a good brown cruises upstream. Fish streamers for the brown and attractor dry flies for everything else.

Rattlesnake Creek: A Clark Fork tributary entering the river right in Missoula, Rattlesnake provides much of the city's water supply. From the mouth of the stream up to the Mountain Water Company Dam, roughly 6 miles, the creek is very good for rainbows and cutthroats up to 14 inches. This is fun water to cover with a Royal Wulff or a Renegade. The 7 miles from the dam up to Beeskove Creek, along with all of the tributaries in this section, are permanently closed to angling. Above Beeskove fishing is catch-and-release only with artificial lures.

Rock Creek: Followed by logging road from its mouth north of the Noxon Dam, this Rock Creek is fished a lot by locals for 6- to 10-inch cutthroats and lesser numbers of other species.

Rock Creek Lake (or simply Rock Lake): Cutthroats—some of them very large (over 20 inches) and difficult to catch cutthroats. This mystery lake, just below Rock Peak and 3 miles off the East Fork Rock Creek Road, is on my "must see" list for some future summer.

St. Paul Lake: A high, above-timberline cirque lake reached by trail from the end of the East Fork Bull River Road, it is planted now and then with cutthroats, and they grow to better than 12 inches. As with most of these small, deep lakes, the trout concentrate around the lake edges and are easy to find.

St. Regis River: A nice little stream from a scenic perspective, the St. Regis runs along I-90 from the headwaters near the Idaho border at Lookout Pass down to the Clark Fork. The fishing isn't much, with the catch consisting of modest numbers of cutthroats and brookies. There are some bigger fish up from the main river in the lower stretch. This pretty flow is very slowly improving with time as it recovers from past logging and mining abuses.

Siamese Lakes: Both are about 30 acres and deep. They are reached by 13 miles of trail up the West Fork of Fish Creek. The fishing is good enough for 9- to 11-inch rainbows and cutthroats for the lakes to receive a lot of pressure from July until the snow flies. The way to avoid the crowds is to get there early. Sometimes that means hiking through lingering snowdrifts in June, but the closer to ice-out the better the fishing, especially on Lower Siamese.

Silver Lake: Reached by jeep road, Silver Lake lies near the Idaho border a few miles south of Saltese. It is deep enough to avoid winterkill, so there is a stable population of 8- to 10-inch brook trout. They are free-rising little buggers, working the shallows at the lower end, and they take dry flies well every evening.

Stony Lake: In the Fishtrap drainage, Stony is not very deep, but a few springs save the cutthroats during the winter. It is reached by poor road, so it gets hit by locals and visitors with nearly equal intensity. Fortunately, it is planted once in a while.

Swamp Creek: Not bad action early in the season for rainbows up from the Clark Fork. Browns move up in the fall, and cutthroats hang out all year. Timing is important for finding the good fish here. This stream is a few miles west of Plains, easily accessible all the way by road.

Terrace Lake: This lake, like many mountain lakes, has a naturally reproducing population. But even on these backcountry waters, rough winters and excessive angler pressure often decimate trout populations, so stocking is needed to maintain the alpine fishery. Terrace is planted every couple of years with cutthroats and they average about a foot, with a few bigger. You'll find it about a mile from the end of the road on the West Fork of Fishtrap Creek.

Thompson River: The Thompson flows from Lower Thompson Lake for over 50 miles to the Clark Fork above Thompson Falls, followed on both sides by the most confusing, braided network of logging roads found in the Northwest. Watch out for the constant flow of logging trucks on these narrow byways that are made all the more dangerous by the clouds of dust generated by the big rigs. The river is excellent, though according to Hugh Spencer of Spencer's Hackles in Plains, the increased levels of sediment from logging are having a deleterious effect on the numbers of large rainbows. From December to the general season opener in May, the water is catch-and-release only.

Years ago I was told by a FWP biologist that if this stream was managed as a quality fishery, the biomass of insects and attendant fish populations would rival Rock Creek. It's never reached this potential, but it's still a fine piece of water. Recently in the fall, Ginny and I camped along the upper river and caught browns averaging about 13 inches, along with some brookies. A Brown Hackle in size 14 was excellent. The peacock herl body was irresistible to the trout.

Up above, the stream is characterized by riffles and pools, but as you move downstream, there are deep runs, large pools, small cascades, and rapids cutting through igneous rock shelves. With some planning and caution, wading is not difficult, although chest waders are advised. The middle section, roughly 20 miles long, starts holding larger trout. Rainbows up to 3 pounds will rise freely during the best hatches. This rich little river has a fine emergence of green drakes and brown drakes, for example, and anglers ready with flies such as the Paradrake or the Mess take the best and fussiest trout.

In early May the grannom caddis appears in good numbers. A good population of salmon flies hatches from mid-May through June, bringing the hefty rainbows to life. During the summer months, caddis imitations, especially brown-wing and rusty-yellow-body variations in sizes 14 and 16 to match the spotted sedge, consistently produce. Some gray drakes show up in August and last into fall, along with tricos and Baetis.

The Thompson is an underappreciated dry-fly river, especially in the lower reaches. Courtesy of Jake How

Among terrestrial insects, there are usually grasshoppers around, but in some years the major news is the spruce moth. This chunky, size 10 or 12 bug lands on the water, gets trapped, and struggles feebly. Even a few of them attract attention, but when the population cycle is high and moths are landing on the stream by the thousands, the trout focus on nothing else. A good imitation, such as a Spruce Moth, is critical.

Stonefly nymphs are consistently effective searchers, but you'll need weight and a sink-tip line to reach the fish in the deepest, heaviest waters. Those fish will include a good number of eager mountain whitefish to maybe 2 pounds. They love to roll and twist up your tippet, but they mean well.

There are also brookies and cutthroats in smaller numbers and size. Beginning in August, big browns and bulls (to several pounds) up from the Clark Fork can provide excitement on streamers. Almost any pattern works if stripped and wriggled through the current seams and between the rocks, but I prefer a Woolly Bugger, size 6, weighted at the head, fished with a floating line and a 6-foot leader tapered to 4X. Buggers always work anywhere trout swim, and I've developed a strong (unhealthy?) attachment to the pattern.

Trio Lakes: You can reach the trailhead from the end of South Fork Trout Creek Road. Then there's several miles of tough hiking up to three lakes that offer brookies, rainbows, and ever-increasing numbers of cutthroats and rainbow-cutthroat hybrids that may reach 15 inches or so. Not many people come here, or could find the place even if they wanted to. This is topo-map country for sure.

Trout Creek: This is a very popular stream near Superior for spunky cutthroats and some rainbows. Logging is beginning to hurt the drainage. Mining already has damaged the stream in the lower reaches, although this is ever so slowly flushing itself out and on down to the river. Caddis patterns are popular here (the Elk Hair and Goddard rank one and two), mainly because there always seem to be fine evening hatches. In the lower water, near the Clark Fork, fair numbers of whitefish show up.

Trout Creek (Noxon Reservoir): This small, brushy stream bounces through a canyon. Local anglers work it over for rainbows, brookies, and cutthroats. A few fat browns sneak up here in the fall, but not in sufficient numbers to warrant a concerted angling effort.

Upper Thompson Lake: Another one of the numerous large lakes lying right next to US 2 between Libby and Kalispell, it is the shallowest in the Thompson chain. It doesn't get hit hard because boating access is poor, but this just makes it a great float-tubing spot. There are largemouth bass, yellow perch, and northern pike in this 230-acre lake, along with cutthroats and a few other trout.

Upper Thompson may not be one of the best lakes in the area for trout, but it's full of willing warmwater fish. There are extensive shallows between two deeper basins, and this middle band of the lake gives up bass all summer long (including eight large-mouths between 2 and 4 pounds on a Purple Leech one July evening).

Vermilion River: Followed by road for its 25 miles through a couple of deep gorges and timbered hills, mining and logging have sped up the rate of water delivery during runoff and rainstorms raise havoc with the streambed. Insects and habitat are regularly washed away. Cutthroat, rainbow, and brook trout provide marginal action. The scrubbing of the stream gravels has attracted the attention of the Noxon Reservoir browns. Maybe a hundred or so of the big browns migrate to reproduce each fall. Finding them, as always, is tough.

Wanless Lake: Deep and big water, Wanless Lake covers 120 acres at the end of a spectacular glacial cirque up Swamp Creek from Noxon Reservoir. It was originally planted with Yellowstone cutthroats, years ago, but it is being turned into westslope water now. Wanless produces a lot of trout up to 16 inches. It's on the same trail as the Cirque Lakes, sitting about 1 mile below them. Wanless is proof that anglers use and love (maybe too much) our high country.

West Fork Thompson River: Not a lot of water to work here, but it's still heavily fished for small brookies and cutthroats. A good road running alongside it makes it easy to hit anywhere.

West Fork Trout Creek (Noxon Reservoir): If you don't mind walking from the end of the Trout Creek Road, this is a pretty stream to try for cutthroats and brookies up to 14 inches. This is nice country that has been hammered by loggers. Hike the stream, use the campsites, and release the fish.

Scenic, big, deep water surrounded by the Swan Mountains and pine forests, Flathead Lake is best fished by trolling metal stuff with hooks. John Holt

Flathead

FLATHEAD LAKE

Dragging balsa wood logs for lures and doorknobs for sinkers through 200 feet of water in hopes of hooking a lake trout is not fly fishing. But trolling big stuff on downriggers is what Flathead Lake is famous for as a fishery.

Still, there are some intriguing prospects for fly fishers, such as the almost unfathomable amount of large Lake Superior whitefish, some approaching 10 pounds, which will take nymphs. And there is an abundance of 3- to 8-pound lake trout. With the collapse of the kokanee years ago, lake trout and lake whitefish make up 80 percent of the biomass in Flathead Lake. There are also fair numbers of cutthroat and bull trout (any bull trout that is accidentally caught must be released immediately).

To say that Flathead is huge is an understatement of considerable proportion. It is the largest natural body of freshwater west of the Mississippi, running 28 miles long by an average of around 6 miles wide. The lake covers more than 200 square miles and is the repository of the Flathead, Swan, Whitefish, and Stillwater River drainages, an area that includes Glacier National Park, much of both the Bob Marshall and Mission Mountains wildernesses, and the Whitefish Mountains. The Missions rise over a mile straight up along the eastern shore, and gentle hills of native grasses and pines roll off in the west. Good highways surround the lake and connect towns like Polson, Elmo, Somers, and Bigfork. Numerous state and tribal parks provide camping and access to the lake.

The lake is so big, it creates its own microclimate. Huge storms come up out of nowhere, killing unwary anglers with some regularity. Waterspouts have been sighted here.

Early fall is one of the best times to chase whitefish in the shallow-water areas of bays like Woods and Yellow. The species congregate in these areas, and if you are lucky, they will be holding in 20 feet of water or less.

Using a sinking line and a leader of about 6 feet tapered to 3X and a Hare's Ear Nymph, you probe the water from boats (which are easier and safer to fish from than float tubes or canoes on Flathead) until the whitefish are located. This is not all that difficult. Many people fish for them, and you'll often see several boats working a productive spot.

Catch-and-release is appropriate in almost all salmonid angling in the state, but according to Region 1 fisheries manager Jim Vashro, the whitefish population needs to be kept in check (along with the lake trout in the "smaller" 3- to 8-pound class) and may someday need to be reduced to protect the other native species. So if you want to

Flathead

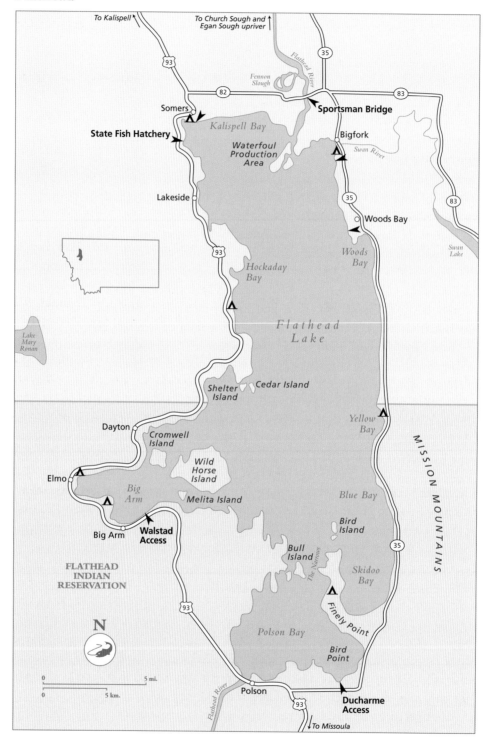

To Kalispell

To Church Sough and
Egan Sough upriver

95

35

82

83

Fennon
Slough

Flathead River

Somers

Sportsman Bridge

Kalispell Bay

State Fish Hatchery

Bigfork

Swan River

Waterfoul
Production
Area

Lakeside

35

93

Woods Bay

*Woods
Bay*

Swan
Lake

*Hockaday
Bay*

Lake
Mary
Ronan

*Flathead
Lake*

*Shelter
Island*

Cedar Island

Dayton

*Cromwell
Island*

*Yellow
Bay*

*Wild
Horse
Island*

Elmo

*Big
Arm*

Melita Island

Blue Bay

MISSION MOUNTAINS

Big Arm

**Walstad
Access**

*Bird
Island*

**FLATHEAD
INDIAN
RESERVATION**

*Bull
Island*

The Narrows

*Skidoo
Bay*

35

N

93

Finely Point

Polson Bay

*Bird
Point*

0   5 mi.

0   5 km.

Flathead River

Polson

**Ducharme
Access**

93

To Missoula

keep a few for a decent fish dinner, go ahead. You will actually be helping to restore the natural order of things in Flathead, at least to some minor extent. Whitefish will not provide the excitement or challenge of browns or rainbows, but for easy, steady action, they're a worthy quarry.

The cutts and bulls have provided good action in the past, but at the moment this intriguing, quality fishery is being threatened (as are many waters in the West) by the introduction of unwanted creatures. It is a serious situation.

Walleyes have their place in the world, but not in Flathead Lake. There has been a distorted suggestion by a northwest Montana angling group (obviously not Trout Unlimited) to introduce these overgrown perch into Flathead Lake. To its credit, the Montana Department of Fish, Wildlife & Parks has opposed the introduction of walleyes into coldwater fisheries.

Add to this the illegal "introduction" of northern pike, largemouth bass, yellow perch, and others, and the threat to Montana's native trout becomes obvious. These "exotics" thrive on salmonid eggs, fry, and, in the case of northerns, trout exceeding 12 inches. The number of trout a 20-pound pike eats in a year or the number of eggs and fry a 5-pound walleye ingests in a season is significant.

Anyone interested in cropping the pike population is invited to Flathead. The spring fishing with large streamers in the sloughs (especially Church, Egan, and Fennon Sloughs) can be productive. The pike are in the shallows to spawn.

Once the exotics are in lakes, they often quickly spread throughout the rivers, streams, and creeks, devastating a drainage with frightening speed. Those who want their favorite exotic introduced into prime trout water are extremely vocal about their desires. Walleyes Unlimited, for example, has been known to make life miserable for fish and game personnel throughout Montana.

The argument against stocking walleyes often is countered by saying that brown, brook, golden, and, in many cases, rainbow trout are not native to Montana. To a certain extent there is some validity to this viewpoint, but for the most part these salmonids have either so firmly established themselves in rivers like the Madison or Missouri or in barren mountain lakes and streams, that any initial damage that may have been done has long since been compensated for by the creation of quality fisheries.

Also, for the most part, species like walleye, perch, and northern pike are successful in outcompeting trout for both food sources and habitat. You really cannot have walleyes and trout hanging out in the same river.

Obviously this is not a minor problem. Trout populations can disappear rapidly with the introduction of a "few buckets full" of northerns or walleyes or perch or baitfish. "I don't think most anglers realize the effect they have on a fishery when they empty their bait buckets into a lake at the end of a day's fishing," Vashro said years ago. "We have to educate people as much and as quickly as possible."

"The potential for disaster from illegally introducing exotics is truly terrifying," concludes Vashro.

As mentioned earlier, cutthroats live in Flathead Lake, but many of them spend a large portion of their lives moving out of the lake and upstream beginning prior to spring runoff to reach spawning tributaries pouring into the Middle, North, and South Forks of the Flathead River. Following spawning, some of these fish drop back down the tributaries and rivers to rest up in the lake for the winter. There are times when the cutts rise to mayflies from late spring into early summer near shore, providing interesting fishing on drys with green drake overtones.

The most interesting action on Flathead Lake occurs in the fall when the big lake trout—to over 20 pounds—are spotted cruising near shore. This is streamer fishing for what amounts to very big brook trout. George Widener, former owner of Lakestream Outfitters, turned me on to this action in the late eighties. George is a very knowledgeable angler who was generous to a fault with his information.

You need a 14- to 16-foot (at least) flat-bottom boat both for stability in the often choppy water and for use as a casting platform. Depending on shoreline structure, fish will be swimming in 10 feet or maybe a bit more water. Using a 7-weight, 10-foot sink-tip and a large streamer—size 2 and larger—imitating another fish (trout, cisco, perch), the idea is to spot a lake trout, anticipate its movement, and then cast far enough ahead of its perceived course to allow the fly to sink to the bottom. When the trout closes in, a few tantalizing strips will do the trick most of the time. The fish are aggressive at this stage of their life cycle, and they attack a streamer with an obvious display of territorial imperative.

So, the best bets are to work the bays and other shallow-water areas from late summer into autumn for whitefish and lake trout. Spring and early summer in the same spots are good for cutthroats. Flathead Lake is very big water with a lot of good-size fish.

Lake whitefish make up much of the biomass of Flathead Lake and tributary streams.

FLATHEAD RIVER

The Flathead River is large by any measure. Water from an immense wilderness drainage pours in from three main forks—Middle, North, South—and the Swan River plus lesser waters including the Stillwater and Whitefish Rivers.

Big trout swim here, even in the section running between the head of Flathead Lake and the South Fork's confluence. Below the lake and Kerr Dam not only are there a few big trout, but there are also large northern pike and some largemouth bass. With so much wilderness and national forest water available, few anglers bother or even know about the opportunities in the main Flathead, but there is some quality action here.

You can reach the upper river both from the highway and by state fishing access sites. Fishing from shore or wading is not only difficult in most situations, but dangerous as well during high flows and below Kerr Dam when power generation is taking place.

Anglers with rafts or boats will find good summertime action for cutthroats and rainbows reaching a few pounds on the river between Columbia Falls and Kalispell. The population explosion in the Flathead Valley has led to a dramatic increase in the number of rafters on the main river and its three main tributaries. Starting early in the morning or late afternoon helps with this problem.

Toward evening larger caddis imitations cast next to the banks or run through the graveled riffles will produce. During the days, drys will work, but large nymphs—stonefly patterns, Prince Nymphs, Montana Nymphs, and the like—or big streamers turn the trout's heads.

Blankenship Bridge

Autumn and winter are catch-and-release seasons for trout, including a burgeoning population of lake trout moving into the river from Flathead Lake. Large—to 10 pounds—Lake Superior whitefish are present in astounding numbers in the upper river, especially from the Old Steel Bridge in Kalispell up through Presentine Bar north of town. Sink-tip lines with large nymphs take both species, and streamers stripped along the bottom trigger the lake trout.

Essentially the Flathead Lake system is out of balance with the introduction of mysis shrimp and the collapse of the kokanee salmon population. Lake trout and whitefish (mainly whitefish) make up over 80 percent of the lake's biomass. This is one place where you would be doing the trout a favor if you kept your limit of lake trout (averaging around 3 or 4 pounds) and whitefish (averaging around 4 pounds with a 100-fish limit). These species are threatening the native bull trout and cutthroat trout, and their numbers need to be substantially reduced to improve the odds.

You can reach the upper Flathead at Blankenship Bridge, near the mouth of the South Fork, at Teakettle, Kokanee Bend, and at the mouth of the Stillwater. The Blankenship float often produces good numbers of large rainbows and cutthroats

Main Flathead River

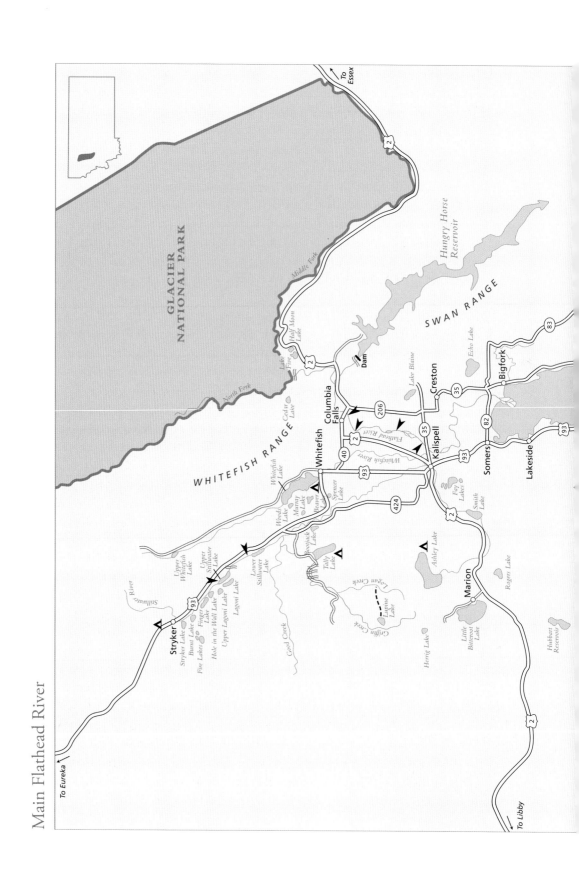

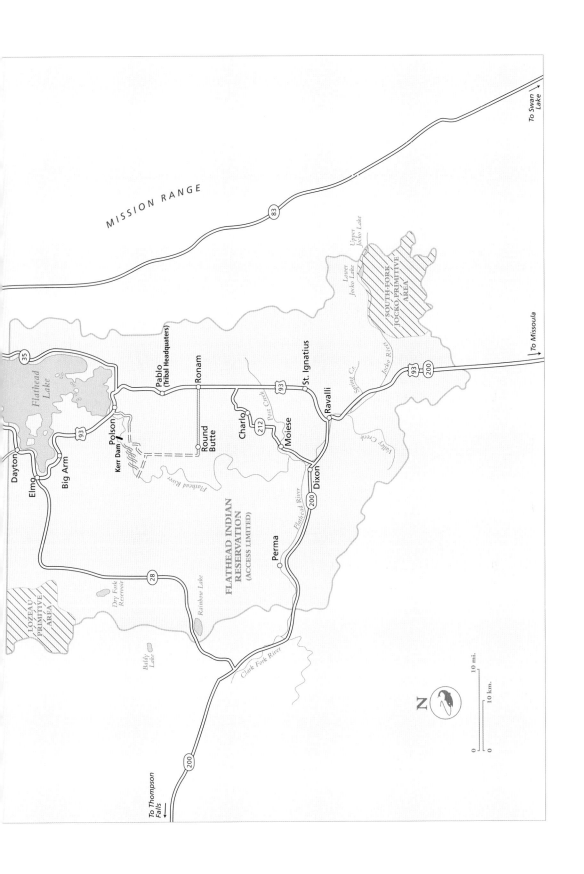

The Flathead is not difficult to float, but this is big water and there are strong eddies and currents that can suck a swimmer or anyone else under with ease. Wear your life vest.

The secret to fishing this river is cutting the water down to size. Look for smaller current seams, braided channels, cover along the banks, or midstream obstructions—any place offering shelter for the trout. While caddisflies are ever-present, any large—size 10 to 12—high-floating dry fly will take fish if presented properly in prime locations.

The River Below Kerr Dam

While the upper river is a straightforward angling proposition, the lower Flathead below Kerr Dam is a complicated management mess—a situation that is currently harming a potentially top-notch tailwater environment.

The river below the dam flows through a steep-walled narrow canyon for a brief distance before opening up to drift through a valley bordered by gentle (for Montana) hills of native grasses, scattered pines, and rattlesnakes. This is drier, more open country than the river's glacier-carved mountain headwaters to the north. Scattered among the few trout are some northern pike that the area's fisheries biologists say provide little if any serious competition for trout. Each lives in its own world, so to speak.

According to anglers who remember such things, prior to the 1930s the Flathead River below Kerr Dam was an excellent fishery for native species of salmonids. Large westslope cutthroat trout and bull trout were relatively common catches here. Since the late 1930s operation of Kerr Dam by Montana Power for generation of electricity has caused wildly fluctuating water releases that have unseasonally flooded or dried up shoreline and shallow-water habitat critical to many insects that are important food sources for trout.

It's still good for those who know how to fish it, though. It's not bad for cutthroats in the canyon stretch below the dam and for browns farther down. While water temperatures vary from around 70 degrees Fahrenheit in the summer to near freezing in the winter, a measurable population of insects including Baetis, Ephemerella, midges, and caddis thrive in the permanently wet areas of the stream course. Drys in the evening along with big stuff on sink-tips worked down deep are the tactics of choice in this water.

Large trout do swim in the few miles of cold water below the dam, and trophy northern pike fishing exists near Dixon. All of this water is on the Flathead Indian Reservation, requiring a tribal permit, and there is limited roadside access. MT 200 parallels the river from Ravalli to Paradise, and there is some access at Dixon. Once on the water, fish the extensive weed beds and sand and gravel bars along the edges of the strong current. The big pike—over 20 pounds—hide here waiting for smaller forage fish and even trout to swim past. Shock tippets and at least 7-weight rods are needed. Any large streamer of 1/0 and up, especially in red and white, will take the pike. Cast in and along the bars and weed beds, then strip the pattern swiftly and erratically.

Below Kerr Dam, the Flathead River can be a modest tailwater fishery for cutthroats, browns, and rainbows.
John Holt

Bass are fewer in number and normally taken in the sloughs and slower water on leeches and poppers in the evening. Just be dead sure you are not trespassing on tribal members' land. This is not worth the trouble (nor for that matter is it a good practice anywhere in the state—respecting private property is the basic axiom for preserving public access to prime waters).

So, for now the trout fishery below Kerr Dam is in doubt, but the fishing is still adequate for cutthroats, browns, and a few rainbows. Action for pike is very good and for bass, average. On the upper river the fishing is varied and good throughout the season after spring runoff.

The Flathead River offers fly fishers cutthroat, rainbow, brown, and lake trout and northerns to over 20 inches. Not bad for a no-name river.

The Whitefish River is best known for big northerns taken during the spring.

Fishing Waters in the Main Flathead River Drainage

Ashley Creek: This is a pretty little stream with some good water between the outlet of Smith Lake near Kila and the water treatment plant in Kalispell. Fish for rainbows up to 15 inches and a few brookies and cutthroats. Development has hit hard here. Access is not easy, but the stream is crossed and paralleled by county roads here and there, and you can see some of the best runs from US 2. Below the treatment plant, which has cleaned up its act in recent years, the fishing is still good but somewhat short on aesthetic values. Above Smith Lake the stream flows through, in descending order, Ashley Lake, Lone Lake, and Lake Monroe (Lower Ashley). This is good hopper water in July and August.

Ashley Lake: It's about 9 square miles and over 200 feet deep in spots, with summer homes all over the place and clear-cuts scarring the hillsides. The world record rainbow-cutthroat hybrid came out of here and meat-and-trophy hunters poach the spawning streams with gay abandon. Some good cutthroat and large—over 5 pounds—rainbows cruise the shallows, especially near inlets and outlets. But during spawning season give the trout a break.

Beaver Lake: Beaver, 5 miles west of Whitefish, is stocked yearly with rainbows that do well, along with a few large brookies, in the 106-acre, deep-blue water, but they get hammered by the local bait-flinging contingent. There are some white-mud sandbars, points, and beaches along the southern end that fish well with leech patterns around dusk.

Bootjack Lake: If you care about yourself or your car, you will pay a local fly fisher to take you here. The 65-acre lake is good fishing for some decent cutthroats and rainbows, especially from a float tube. It's on private land with some public access about 8 miles west of Whitefish. The fish are cruisers, and it takes two anglers to set each other up as the trout work back and forth.

Burnt Lake: An up-to-date Flathead National Forest travel-plan map will get you started on the diminishing lane into this water near Stryker. Managed for cutthroat and not too bad if you can find it.

Good Creek: This tributary to the Stillwater used to be decent fishing for brook trout, but access is limited in the best stretches and there are a lot of people living up here with guns and signs on their access roads indicating they know how to use them. Despite the logging, this is pretty country but full of strange people. Have you ever seen *Deliverance*?

Griffin Creek: This used to be a beautiful, fun little stream to fish for cutthroats with an Adams and a 6½-foot rod. Now the whole area is logged to hell. The Tally Lake

Ranger District is a disaster, a national sacrifice area that looks like it was bombed, scalped, and burned.

Hubbart Reservoir: Hubbart is drawn down a bit in the summer, but it's good float-tube fishing for rainbow trout (and there are some kokanee here also). Located west and south of Kalispell, it's over 400 acres with weed beds. Leeches, damsel nymphs, and the like produce.

Jocko River: The Jocko flows for about 20 miles from its junction with the Middle and South Forks of the Jocko past Arlee on the Flathead Indian Reservation. It joins the Flathead River at Dixon. The water is visible and crossed by US 93. Good dry-fly water for brown trout with some rainbows, brooks, cutthroats, and a lot of whitefish that love nymphs (catch-and-release for all except lake and brook trout). You can reach it by road most of the way, but keep an eye out for rattlesnakes dozing in the hot summer sun. This can be a wonderful stream at times.

Lagoni Lake: This one is managed for rainbow and cutthroat with a few holdover brook trout from earlier days. Hard to find, but there really are 20 acres of deep water just west of Upper Stillwater Lake in timber-and-rock-cliff country. There are plenty of northern pike here that gorge on small trout. Lug in a float tube. Big streamers in spring and early summer are effective for the slashing pike.

Lake Mary Ronan: Some 400,000 kokanees are dumped into this 1,506-acre lake 8 miles northwest of Dayton off US 93 every year along with 50,000 cutthroats. Rainbows and some nice largemouth also cruise the shorelines here. Opening day (unlike most still waters that are open all year, Lake Mary Ronan is closed from March 15 through the third Saturday in May) looks like Woodstock with boats. By early June things settle down a bit and float tubers have a fighting chance if they are interested.

Little Bitterroot Lake: There are summer homes, resorts, and lots of boats on this 3-by-1.5-mile lake 25 miles west of Kalispell. It's easy to find and it has a state park on the north end. A few large trout here.

Logan Creek: This is a scenic, little freestone stream that flows in the logged-over Star Meadows area, where there are brook trout in brushy-shored beaver ponds. The fast-water reaches hold 6- to 10-inch cutthroats that love attractor patterns popped into the pocket water before the creek enters Tally Lake. Stream cleats help when the water is high early in the season. There are some rainbows and whitefish in the lower reaches.

Lower Stillwater Lake: It's scenic, 248 acres with shallow drop-offs. The fishing for rainbows is mediocre, but in the spring, fishing is excellent in the shallows for northern pike up to maybe 10 pounds. Early in the day and toward evening, a streamer cast to shore and stripped in will take a lot of pike that really tear up the water and your leader—shock tippet helps.

Lupine Lake: Lupine is 13 acres, reached by marked trail from Griffin Creek Road. It's about 2 miles in, and there are still some trees left here despite the best efforts of the Forest Service on the Tally Lake District. It's managed for westslope cutts.

Murray Lake: There are lots of lure and bait fishermen at this 45-acre lake a few miles north of Whitefish off US 93. Murray offers westslope cutthroats and rainbows. A few nice ones work the shoreline near evening sipping caddis, mayflies, and flying ants.

Ninepipe and Pablo Reservoirs: Fishing is allowed on both reservoirs in accordance with applicable state and tribal regulations. Yellow perch and largemouth bass at Ninepipe, 1,200 acres at 3,000 feet elevation, and rainbow trout at Pablo often furnish excellent fishing. Ice fishing is permitted after the waterfowl hunting season has ended. Because anglers are confined to the shoreline, long rods casting DT7 or WF8 lines help. Streamers and poppers take fish. Can be a fun place, but the fishing is sporadic. I've also taken some pumpkinseeds to a pound on small nymphs—any pattern will do. Boats or floatation devices are not permitted on either reservoir, and a tribal recreation permit is required. Wildlife viewing is incredible here, with dozens and dozens of bird species.

Post Creek: This fine, little stream was a favorite of the late Harmon Henkin, who first schooled me in the ways of bamboo and mayflies. The outlet of McDonald Lake, it flows to the Flathead River a few miles above Dixon on the Flathead Reservation. It's posted in spots, but good for rainbows, cutthroats, hybrids, and sometimes a brown in the lower reaches.

Rainbow Lake: Out in semiarid farmland north of Plains on the Flathead Indian Reservation, Rainbow is primarily a northern pike and yellow perch fishery with an occasional stocking of brood stock rainbows. Off the beaten path but offers good action on the surface.

Rogers Lake: This was once an excellent grayling lake until some subnormal introduced "exotic" species that wiped out the sail-finned natives. It is still good at times, like in the spring.

Smith Lake: It looks interesting from the road, but this wetland, 300-acre lake is better known for its winter perch fishing than for the few rainbows taken each year. There is an access site 10 minutes west of Kalispell if you are interested in the perch.

Spencer Lake: Sporadic for warmwater species, Spencer is just out of Whitefish on the south side of US 93. Early and late in the season, it's an entertaining lake to float tube. Nymphs cast into the weed beds on the east shore work well at times. Sunfish sneak in from nearby Skyles Lake.

Spring Creek: This beautiful little creek meets the Jocko River just south of Ravalli on the Flathead Indian Reservation. Fished a lot, it is still good dry-fly water for brown, brook, and rainbow trout. It runs along US 93.

Stillwater River: The lower reaches from the town of Stryker down to the Whitefish River near Kalispell wander through farm and ranch land and some timber. The water is mostly slow, but there are some rainbows and lesser numbers of cutthroat and brook trout. The lower water is locally famous for the huge—over 30 pounds—northern pike that are infrequently taken each spring on large streamers. The water above Stryker flows out of the Whitefish Range and offers limited fast-water angling for small cutthroats and other salmonids. This is pretty country, but the fish are small. Ten inches is a trophy.

Strawberry Lake: Up near the Swan Crest west of Bigfork, this small lake used to have some trout but is no longer on the stocking program, so the action may be a bit slim. So what? This is a nice, steep hike for a couple of miles in pretty country. Take a chance.

Stryker Lake: This used to be an excellent brook-trout lake with fish to a few pounds and loons swimming here and there with their broods in the spring, but meat fishers hammered the water and there are not many fish left. It's about 40 minutes north of Whitefish below Stryker Ridge.

Tally Lake: Large (1,326 acres) and almost 500 feet deep (deepest in the state), but it is lousy fishing. Whatever was planted here never really took. There are still some remnant cutthroats, rainbows, kokanees, whitefish, and brook trout. About 30 minutes west of Whitefish with a large campground, it's more a party lake these days.

Upper Stillwater Lake: About 1 square mile and shallow, it's average fishing for several species of trout, trash fish, perch, and northern pike (especially early in the year). Twenty-five miles north of Whitefish, west of US 93.

Upper Whitefish Lake: You can reach this one by gravel road from Olney east off US 93. It's pretty but only mediocre for small cutthroats to maybe 10 inches or a touch larger. The campground is always crowded in good weather, and there have been weddings, beer busts, and human sacrifices here in the past. It's somewhat of a zoo for this far back in the woods.

The Stillwater is a classic mountain stream in its upper reaches, with fair numbers of cutthroat.

Swift Creek has spotty fishing for cutthroats up to 16 inches. The access, through thick new- and old-growth forest, is hard work, and there's always a threat of bumping into a wandering grizzly.

Valley Creek: Good for brookies and cutthroats, Valley empties into the Jocko near Ravalli on the Flathead Indian Reservation. Like most of these winding meadow streams, the biggest trout hold under the brush at the deep bends. Try slapping a hopper pattern as far back into the sticks as possible, and the average size of the fish in this creek might surprise you.

Whitefish Lake: A resort lake surrounded by summer homes, this is one of the best lakes in the country for lake trout up to 30 pounds. Trolling is the preferred method, but you can turn up fish by slowly working a Hi-D line down deep with big streamers in the swirling water at the inlet of Swift Creek, especially in the fall. You'll need to put a boat in at the south end and head up-lake 6 miles to this water. Cutthroats take mayflies in late spring and early summer near evening along the west shore in the bays. Some also cruise the points and shallow-water areas. Lots of kokanees (how exciting!) are also planted here each year.

Whitefish River: A slow-moving stream for most of its length from the lake down to the Stillwater River just east of Kalispell, the Whitefish River is best known for big northern pike taken in the spring. There are also some good rainbows in the weed beds

We used to be able to fish for bull trout, but no more. They're in slow recovery, but their numbers are still dangerously low. John Holt

growing below the sewage treatment plant outside of Whitefish and in the water near the Stillwater (but there is no easy access here).

MIDDLE FORK OF THE FLATHEAD RIVER

Flowing for 90 miles from its formation at the confluence of Strawberry and Bowl Creeks in the heart of the Bob Marshall Wilderness, the Middle Fork of the Flathead River is a remarkable stream.

Even running alongside US 2, it looks wild and free. Creeks wind northward into the jagged peaks of Glacier National Park. Standing waves and severe rapids pound through towering, narrow canyons. Acres and acres of charred trees stand as testimony to lightning-inspired wildfires. Dark green pine forest cloaks the mountains to timberline, where rock and ice then hold sway. The northern east–west line of Burlington Northern clings to the mountainsides. Piles of graying snags, some several feet in diameter, lie in huge piles on midstream gravel bars, reminders of the tremendous power of the Middle Fork during its swollen, ferocious spring runoff.

Elk, eagles, grizzlies, deer, mountain goats—all can be sighted along the river. The wind blasts through here in the winter, and US 2 is no place at all to be during a snowstorm. This is rough country masquerading as scenic splendor.

One of the wildest streams in the Lower 48, the Middle Fork of the Flathead nevertheless gets a little crowded during peak season.

This used to be a river where fly fishers were a rarity, but nowadays it's jammed with rafters running sports and anglers madly downstream. Aesthetically, from a fly-fishing perspective, it's hammered, though still worth the effort in the spring before runoff and in the fall when the chill weather drives away the tourist hordes. Yet, in the wilderness, fishing is good for westslope cutthroat trout that hit dry flies with little selectivity from the end of runoff through October if the weather holds. Fish to 16 inches are not uncommon.

The first dozen or so miles from the headwaters down to Schafer Meadows is an easy float through unspoiled country. Below Schafer for 32 miles to US 2, the river tips through a steep-walled canyon. In June and July this is an exciting float for experienced rafters. Others should hire a guide. Fishing here is best from July into early fall, but low water levels make floating difficult.

Ephemerellidae and Baetidae lead the mayfly parade, but in numbers rank far, far below that associated with waters like the Missouri. Bull trout of size use this stretch as a corridor to reach isolated spawning grounds far back in the forest. Finding these fish is difficult. Most of the cutthroats are small (a 12-incher is above average), but fairly numerous. They will hit small drys drifted near shore and around midstream boulders.

The fishing below West Glacier is similar, except that in some of the narrow canyon runs, some good-size rainbows will occasionally hit streamers or even hoppers, Sofa Pillows, and the like. When these fish are on, usually near evening in late July and August, the action is quite good. Unfortunately, no one has been able to predict this outbreak of rainbow enthusiasm with any consistency. If you've got several weeks and wish to float from West Glacier to Blankenship every afternoon and early evening, a number of local fly fishers, including myself, would probably buy you a drink or two in exchange for a glance at your angling log.

One technique that seems to produce results, though infrequently, is to use a super-fast-sinking 15-foot sink-tip and something like a Woolly Bugger. Dropping this down through the eddies and then pulsing it near bottom sometimes triggers a response, which often includes a rainbow arcing above the water, pulling 20 feet of slack fly line and leader. Such is life.

The main company you will have on the Middle Fork are large numbers of tour-operated rafts filled with giggling floaters soaking up cold water, hot sun, and cold beverages (quite original). The Middle Fork below town consists of boulder runs, riffles, deep holes, and some relatively tame whitewater. Not the stuff of thrilling rafting memories. There are plenty of small cutthroats, and the float is a dandy way to kill an afternoon.

Fishing Waters in the Middle Fork Drainage

Bear Creek: Bear Creek parallels US 2 for 13 miles before making a break for freedom, turning south into the wilderness. Large bull trout move up here to spawn, which is a marvel considering how small the stream is as it vanishes from roadside view. Some wild cutthroats also swim here.

Bull trout make their way up Bear Creek from as far away as Flathead Lake to spawn in their natal wilderness waters.

Flathead River Middle Fork

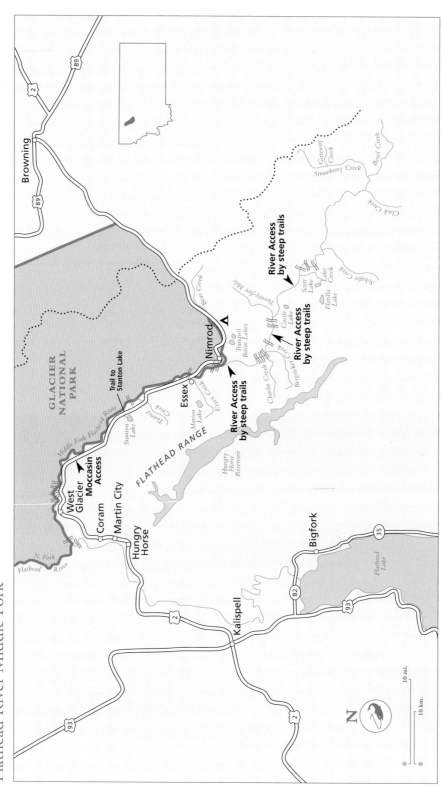

Way back in the mountains across the North Fork from Glacier National Park, Cyclone Lake holds westslope cutthroat.

Bergsicker Creek: Heading below Prospector Mountain, Bergsicker is not much to fish above, but down by the Middle Fork it offers some runs and holes for cutthroats. By trail, it's 8 miles below Nimrod.

Bowl Creek: Way back in the wilderness, this true mountain stream meets the Middle Fork 20 miles above Schafer Meadows. The fishing diminishes the farther upstream you travel, but there are fair numbers of 6- to 9-inch cutthroats. Lots of people on horseback or foot hit this water. Hike in from the Middle Fork of the Flathead or the West Fork of the Teton River.

Castle Lake: A steep hike of a mile or so above Twenty-five Mile Creek, there are nice cutthroats here in good country.

Essex Creek: Here, just off US 2, you'll find a few small cutthroats that receive more attention than they deserve.

Flotilla Lake: Lots of people stagger in here on a good trail north of Miner Creek, and it is big—146 acres—with plenty of cutthroats to 17 inches. They're spooky but the cruisers will hit a nymph twitched in front of their epicurean snouts. Even with all the people, you feel like you are in wild country.

Marion Lake: Another roadside attraction that gets some backcountry pressure mainly because it has lots of cutt-rainbow hybrids up to 15 inches. Pack snowshoes and time ice-out perfectly on the 80-acre, 145-foot-deep lake, and the action is sporting. It's 4 trail miles from the Walton Ranger Station on US 2.

Stanton Lake: Only 20 minutes from US 2, Stanton gets hammered constantly, but sometimes yields a rainbow or cutthroat of some size. This is a decent-quality wilderness day hike.

Tranquil Basin Lakes: These small lakes of 10 and 8 acres are about a half hour south of Nimrod. Some big fish, for cutthroat anyway, are here. This is glacial cirque country.

Tunnel Creek: Small and flowing through the forest, Tunnel Creek is fun to fish on your knees with a short rod for small cutthroats. You can get to it from US 2 about a mile or so west of Pinnacle.

NORTH FORK OF THE FLATHEAD RIVER

Wild, unspoiled, pure, and, at best, a modest trout fishery pretty much sums up the North Fork of the Flathead River, which has its feral beginnings in the McDonald Mountains of British Columbia, the Whitefish Range to the west, and the Livingston Range to the east in Glacier National Park.

Fires in recent years have burned most of the timber in the tributary drainages, but the forest is coming back and in ten years the setting will be pleasant. More and more people are moving here, but it's still wild, good country.

Grizzly bears, black bears, gray wolves, bald eagles, lynx, ptarmigan, porcupines, possible caribou, bull trout, and westslope cutthroat trout thrive in the drainage's heavily timbered acres. Many of these species are on threatened or endangered lists.

Three of Montana's native salmonids are found in the river—westslope cutthroat trout, bull trout, and mountain whitefish (which you will catch on occasion without trying). The cutthroats are found hiding behind rocks and boulders and beneath logjams all year long, while the bull trout migrate up from Flathead Lake 50 miles to the south.

From spring through early September, the river is filled with countless silvery cutthroats that run small—8 to 12 inches—with maybe a few up to 19 inches. They are easy pickings for dry flies such as the Royal Humpy, Elk Hair Caddis, and hoppers, and wet flies such as the Hare's Ear and Black Gnat. Whether you wade from shore (be careful, this river is much faster and deeper than it first appears) or fish from a raft, cast the fly near shore toward any submerged or partially submerged rocks and boulders. Pay particular attention to seams or channels through underwater rocks. You may take larger fish in these mini-runs. Sometimes a Woolly Bugger worked like a snake will move the larger fish.

Both the gravel and dirt North Fork Road and the dirt inside road (in Glacier Park) provide ready access to the river. Both roads are tough to negotiate in wet weather due to mudslides, gumbo, etc. Access is also abundant for the floater, and one of the easier floats is from the Big Creek Access down to Glacier Rim—an easy four hours of fishing runs, glides, flats, riffles, pools, and banks. Taking a few dozen cuts is possible. Ford Creek ranger work station down to Polebridge is a longer float, taking all day.

Unlike many rivers that are noted for having certain species in specific stretches of water, the North Fork is egalitarian in this respect. Any of the three species may be found more or less equally in any part of the river, though numbers decline somewhat as you move upstream.

The river near its confluence with the Middle Fork and at Moose City where it enters this country is turquoise clear, swiftly flowing, and has rock and boulder substrate. The Ford Creek float, beginning near the Canadian border, is best from mid-July into August, and the float below Polebridge works as the runoff ends. Never hit this river at peak flow. You will probably die. House-size boulders and 100-foot deadfalls are propelled downstream like toys at runoff. Near the end of high water, as the North Fork lowers and begins to clear, this compression can trigger some fairly good action and the cuts will run a bit larger. Even without the trout, the scenery is worth the float, though caution is advised. Even in low water, turbulence created by shelving and the large snags takes a few souls each year.

Because the North Fork is a low-productivity system, it cannot stand much fishing pressure (like that found on even the upper Clark Fork). Any significant deterioration in the water quality could be devastating. Timber harvest and the cumulative effects of canopy removal could cause a rapid melting of the snowpack, increasing sedimentation and bank erosion. Sedimentation chokes bull trout eggs and they die. Add to this possible threats from proposed coal mines in Canada, oil drilling near the river, and housing development, and it is easy to understand how tenuous the bull trout's hold on life is here.

But for now this is still one of the finest wild rivers in the world, as its Wild and Scenic River designation indicates. The cutthroat and bull trout are doing pretty well, and the fishing is active enough to hold an angler's attention for a few hours.

Fishing Waters in the North Fork Drainage

The following lakes and streams are found only on the western side of the drainage. North Fork country is filled with running water. Every trickle seems to have a name, even the ones that dry up by July 15. These are not mentioned and are so small you

Flathead River North Fork

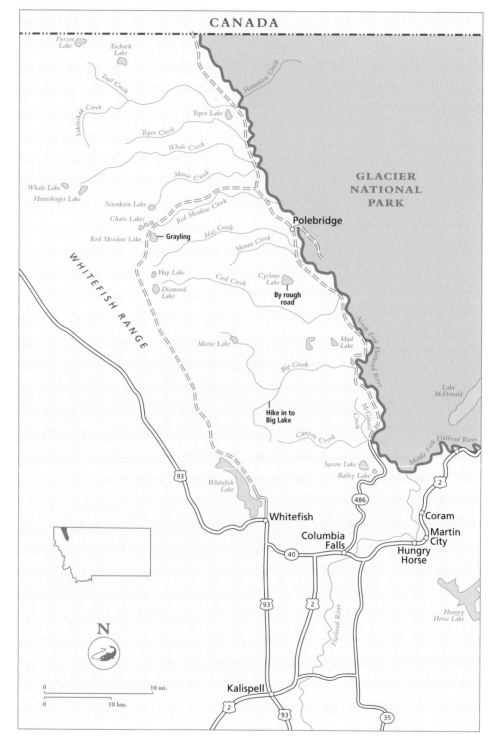

CANADA

Frozen Lake

Tuchuck Lake

Trail Creek

Yakinikak Creek

Tepee Lake

Tepee Creek

Whale Creek

Moose Creek

Whale Lake

Huntsberger Lake

Nasukoin Lake

Chain Lakes

Red Meadow Creek

Red Meadow Lake — Grayling

Hay Creek

Moran Creek

Polebridge

GLACIER NATIONAL PARK

Starvation Creek

WHITEFISH RANGE

Hay Lake

Diamond Lake

Coal Creek

Cyclone Lake

By rough road

Moose Lake

Mud Lake

Big Creek

North Fork Flathead River

Lake McDonald

Hike in to Big Lake

McGinnis Creek

Canyon Creek

Spoon Lake

Bailey Lake

Middle Fork Flathead River

93

Whitefish Lake

Whitefish

486

Coram

Martin City

Columbia Falls

Hungry Horse

2

40

93

2

Flathead River

Hungry Horse Lake

N

Kalispell

2

93

35

0   10 mi.

0   10 km.

would not be likely to notice them as you drove or walked over them. The waters on the eastern side are located in Glacier National Park and are discussed in that chapter.

Pattern selection is not sophisticated for cutthroats. The fish are wild and not selective. Drys such as an Adams, Royal or Green Humpy (this one is superb in fast water), Goddard Caddis, Hare's Ear Nymph, size 8 Brown Stone, Prince Nymph, and Olive Woolly Worm will cover the action. Simple but fun. The challenge on mountain lakes is anticipating the trout's feeding route and then making the appropriate cast. On streams, hitting pocket water is the game.

Canyon Creek: A pretty stream, Canyon Creek flows beneath the North Fork Road and has average fishing for small cutthroats for a few miles. Goddard and Elk Hair Caddis country.

Chain Lakes: You can get to these four pretty lakes in the Whitefish Mountains on a rough road just over the crest from Red Meadow Lake. Three of the lakes, averaging about 15 acres each, used to be excellent fishing for large, fat cutthroats. Wilderness advocates, in an attempt to publicize the location's attributes so that they would be included in a wilderness bill, turned northwest Montana on to the spot and now the place is overrun with hikers and anglers. You always hurt the ones you love. Still, on occasion, especially from late September on, when the weather turns cool and often ugly and the yupster masses have turned their attentions to the impending cross-country skiing, Lycra-fashion explosion, the fishing can be fun like it should be with small drys, including caddis, or a nymph slowly stripped near the surface.

Coal Creek: It's closed to protect spawning bull trout, but if I ever find out I only have weeks to live, I'll fish this one. One of the best-looking pieces of water in the region—deep runs and clear pools highlighted by weathered gray logjams.

Frozen Lake: This lake is located in some weird country along the US–Canada border. After turning off US 93 at Grave Creek and driving to and then along Weasel Creek Road through massive clear-cuts following the signs to Frozen Lake, you come to land that is so intensively logged over, it looks as though the two countries had a tag-team clear-cutting contest. The place looks like an asteroid having a bad day. A walk of about a half mile down an old skid trail takes you to a timbered shoreline where you can cast from a float tube streamers like Matukas, Buggers, and Zonkers to cutthroats up to 4 pounds.

Hay Lake: This lake lies in clear-cut, swampy country at the end of the Hay Creek drainage. The road is often closed to protect wildlife, but it's worth a mountain bike ride to get to. A float tube would be good, too. All the same, there are some pretty cutthroats of maybe 10 or 11 inches here that hit any dry fly thrown their way.

Fishing the North Fork of the Flathead, expect to see some westslope cutthroats and mountain whitefish, and maybe a bull trout. If you accidentally catch a bull trout, treat it gingerly and release it as soon as possible.

Huntsberger Lake: Huntsberger is a nice fishery for colorful, wild cutthroats that are fat and maybe 12 inches on a generous day. Take the Whale Creek Road. Very good bear country.

Moose Creek: This is not the outlet of Moose Lake, but flows to the North Fork a few miles south of the Ford Work Center. A pretty stream running next to a logging road with small native cutthroats, it's tough to fish because of the brush.

Moose Lake: Moose Lake is fished a good deal by locals for small, planted cutthroats that will take a slowly retrieved Hare's Ear Nymph (and drys when the wind is not blowing). Few fish are over 10 inches in this deep blue water. There is a campground. Pretty lake in wild country, but the fishing is nothing much.

Nasukoin Lake: Small (7 acres) but fairly deep, Nasukoin is filled with 12-inch cutthroats that are boring to catch on drys after the first half dozen or so. Walk in from where the Moose Creek Road is closed off.

Red Meadow Lake: Small grayling (to 7 inches) and a few big ones abound, and there are some nice cutthroats to maybe 16 inches. A few westslope cutthroats swim here, too. Try small drys for the grayling, and nymphs worked deep for the cutts. This place is nailed by weekend and out-of-state traffic all summer. I once saw an older lady with pink and blue hair playing "Cocktails for Two" on an organ that was set up outside a motor home at the campground here. Too strange for me. This one is located on Red Meadow Creek Road, 40 miles north of Columbia Falls.

Tuchuck Lake: In world-class bear country that is wild and moonlike in appearance, Tuchuck Lake is just a couple of miles south of Canada. It's only 8 acres, but there are some fair cutthroats in here.

Whale Creek: This stream is closed from the North Fork to Whale Creek Falls, about 10 miles upstream. Some decent cutthroats hold in upper reaches above the falls. It's a fine creek to visit in early September with a camera and polarizing filter. You can spot bull trout to 20 pounds (rarely) holding on the colorful gravels. Their redds are huge and over a foot deep at times. Magic stuff.

Whale Lake: Eight miles or so from the end of the road lies this shallow 20-acre lake. It has some springs that concentrate cutthroats of maybe 12 inches or a shade longer.

Yakinikak Creek: This Trail Creek tributary is small and brushy with some 8-inch or a bit larger cutthroats. I once saw a sow grizzly and her cubs romping away in the upper reaches. Chasing cutthroats on this water is an adrenaline trip.

SOUTH FORK OF THE FLATHEAD RIVER

Forty years back, the South Fork was too easy. Westslope cutthroat trout of 3 or 4 pounds fought to hit a fly on every cast. Then the word spread with vengeance and the river got hammered (and the fishing edged toward mediocre). This fine, world-class trout stream dancing and rushing through the Bob Marshall Wilderness for 52 miles was about to be trashed from a fly-fishing perspective.

People came in on foot to fish the South Fork. They flew in aboard flimsy Cessnas or lurched in on top of jaded pack horses to cast over the sapphire-clear waters. Hundreds of prime fish were derricked from the river, gutted, and grilled in oil over campfires. The population was decimated.

The first time I saw this stream was in the early seventies after hiking in from Holland Lake down the Little Salmon River drainage. My first cast took a 20-inch cutthroat. So did the next dozen. In two days on a mile stretch of the South Fork, I caught over twenty dozen trout of 15 inches and longer on sophisticated patterns ranging from Sofa Pillows to Renegades to Hornbergs.

People still come to the river each year by the thousands, but thanks in part to stricter possession limits, including no trout over 12 inches, the situation has improved. And many outfitters are educating clients about the obvious merits of catch-and-release. The river is once again wonderful angling but probably still receives too much pressure (by backcountry standards anyway) to be called world-class. All the same, the South Fork ranks with the best, and the Bob Marshall is beautiful, unspoiled country. Also,

It can be a long hike into the South Fork of the Flathead, but very good cutthroat fishing is your reward.

a healthy run of large spawning bull trout moves upriver each season, providing sport for fish that may reach 20 pounds. Mountain whitefish are abundant. They are native salmonids deserving of far more respect than they currently receive from anglers. True, they can be a nuisance, especially when nymphing, but they fight (at least a little) and have their place in the natural scheme.

Wilderness in the Upper River

You can reach the river via myriad trails coming in from the Swan and Flathead valleys on the west, from the Middle Fork just south of Glacier on the north, along the Rocky Mountain Front on the east, or through the Spotted Bear Wilderness lying to the south. If you walk, you will need at least one week, three being better, to feel the country and explore not only the South Fork, but streams such as the river's headwater, Danaher Creek, or Gordon Creek, or one of the lakes tucked back in the many glacial cirques. And you will want to walk along the 1,000-foot-high Chinese Wall or along Big Salmon Lake.

This is the South Fork before it empties into Hungry Horse Reservoir, formed by the construction of the Hungry Horse Dam in the fifties. The reservoir is 32 miles long, deep but filling with glacial silt, and the fishing is good at times but declining, as it inevitably does on man-made impoundments. Below the dam for a half-dozen or so miles to the Flathead River, the fishing is lousy due to the constant fluctuations in water level caused by power generation regimes. A re-reg dam may change this in coming years, forming a fairly good tailwater fishery, but for now the water is marginal.

If you like to hike, the river is easily accessible. Just avoid the obvious campsites that have been staked out by outfitters. You'll soon have plenty of company. One trick when hiking along the tributaries is to explore the smaller, marginal paths that break off into the trees. These often lead to hunters' camps that lie unused until fall elk hunting. They offer solitude, comfort, and streamside convenience.

Horse and raft trips, offered by several outfitters, are easy ways to see this country. Floating on your own is possible if you arrange to have your gear flown in, leave the river well above the impassable gorge near Bunker Creek, make a 3-mile portage, and then continue downstream. Life is good but rafts are heavy. Arrangements to tote this gear should be made in advance.

As for the fishing, a 5- or 6-weight rod of 9 feet is fine. Bring a sink-tip for the lakes. A 3-weight of 8 feet is ideal for the tributaries. Fly selection is truly catholic. Sofa Pillows, Royal Wulffs, Humpies, Adams, Bucktail Caddis, Hare's Ear Nymphs, Woolly Worms, Muddlers, and hoppers border on overkill. The water is cold, so bring chest waders and be careful. Runs that look 3 feet deep are often over 10. Fall into the main stream and you will be in trouble.

The South Fork, like its siblings, the Middle and North Forks, is included in the Wild and Scenic River system. The reasons are many and obvious.

South Fork Flathead River

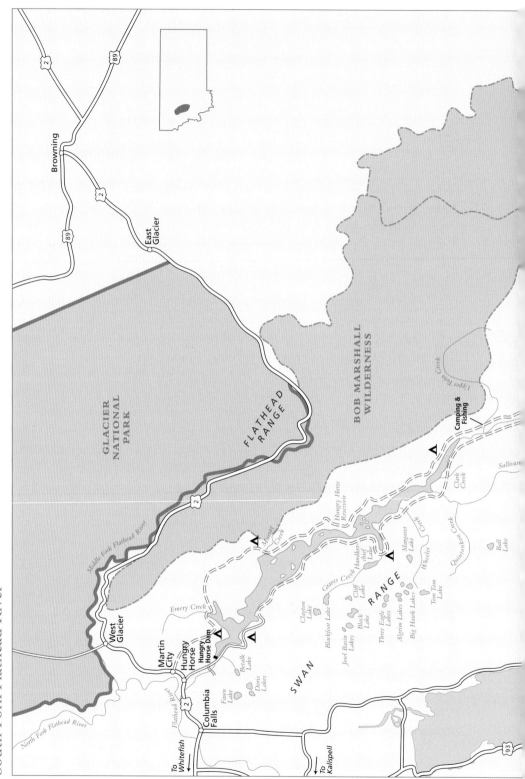

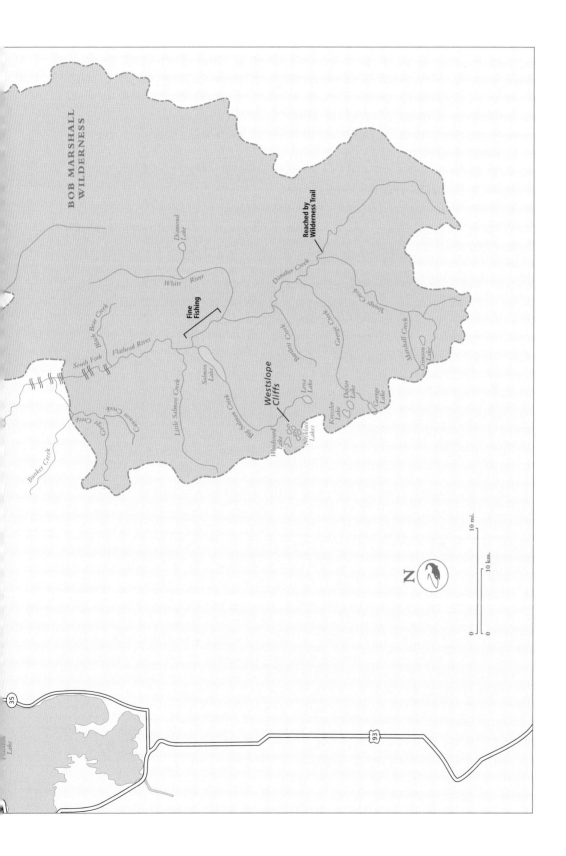

BOB MARSHALL
WILDERNESS

Diamond
Lake

White River

Reached by
Wilderness Trail

Danaher Creek

Fine
Fishing

Black Bear Creek

Youngs Creek

South Fork

Flathead River

George Creek

Bartlett Creek

Marshall Creek

Salmon
Lake

Westslope
Cliffs

Lena
Lake

Crimson
Lake

Little Salmon Creek

Big Salmon Creek

Koessler
Lake

Dodge
Lake

George
Lake

Camman Creek

Cooze Creek

Woodward
Lake

Necklace
Lakes

Bunker Creek

Lake

35

93

N

0   10 km.
0   10 mi.

Most of the lakes in the South Fork drainage were originally barren, but often have become excellent fisheries following stocking. Some do freeze out but are normally replanted. Trekking into unnamed, alpine lakes is a crapshoot, but fun all the same. On the other hand, fishing every named creek in the drainage would be a severe waste of time. Some of them are a foot wide, and some of them hold charming populations of 2-inch cutthroat.

Fishing Waters in the South Fork Drainage

Bartlett Creek: An easy and enjoyable piece of water to work, with some nice 10-inch cutthroats holding in small pools and behind boulders. It's 2 miles above Big Prairie Ranger Station.

Big Hawk Lakes: You can get to Big Hawk Lakes in the Jewel Basin Wilderness by trail from either the Flathead Valley to the west or the Wheeler Creek Road on the South Fork to the east. It's good fishing for 15-inch or larger cutthroats.

Big Salmon Creek: This beautiful stream above Big Salmon Lake is filled with cutthroats in all the right places—logjams, pools, runs, buckets between the current seams. And there are some big bull trout. All of this is below the barrier falls 3.5 miles above the lake. Above here the fishing is average for cutthroats. Below the lake the fishing is slightly above average for 12-inch cutthroats.

The section below the lake has a fabulous golden stone hatch in July. Maybe the lake serves as an enrichment basin, feeding enough nutrients into the short stretch of river between the lake and the main South Fork to create an ideal food base for the carnivorous golden stone nymphs. When those nymphs emerge, and the egg-laying females fly back to the river, the trout feed in a frenzy. Any big, straw-colored dry fly works. To impress the trout with your sophistication, show them imitations such as the Yellow Fluttering Stone or the Ginger Flex-Stone in size 6. Do the trout from the lake drop down into the river to feed on this hatch? I've often wondered because suddenly the trout run a larger average size, with fish 14 to 16 inches not uncommon.

Big Salmon Lake: Next to the South Fork, this is the best-known water in the Bob Marshall. Twenty miles above Spotted Bear Ranger Station, it receives a lot of horse and foot traffic. All the same, it's a beautiful lake that has plenty of cruising cutthroats of around 12 inches.

Black Bear Creek: An average fishing stream (for the wilderness), Black Bear Creek has 8-inch cutthroats and the usual gang of spawning bull trout. It's about 5 miles of water down to the river and an hour's walk below the Black Bear Guard Station.

Blackfoot Lake: This one is 16 acres in timber 4 miles above the end of the Graves Creek Road. It's home to rainbows, cutthroats, and hybrids to 15 inches.

Bunker Creek: This stream was logged all over the place, but some of the riparian zone was saved, resulting in adequate fishing for small cutthroats and decent spawners in May and June. Bull trout move up here also. Every season hunters get lost and sometimes die in this drainage. The country looks deceptively mild, but when a storm cruises in, getting lost does not require any special talent. Flowing from the southwest, Bunker Creek joins the South Fork near the Meadow Creek Trailhead.

Clayton Lake: Another pretty lake in the Jewel Basin that is large (over 60 acres) and deep (over 100 feet in the middle) with brushy shorelines, Clayton has a decent population of Yellowstone cutthroats averaging around 15 inches and running larger. At ice-out drys work well, but as the season progresses this action stops. Most people give up. Try a Gold-Ribbed Hare's Ear Nymph or even a Prince cast well ahead of the easily spotted cruising trout. The old "twitch-and-wait" method will take fish. You can get there via 3 miles of trail from the end of Clayton Creek Road, off the west-side road along Hungry Horse Reservoir.

Cliff Lake: In the Graves Creek drainage, like many higher-elevation lakes, Cliff at 5,500 feet is stocked periodically with cutthroats. The second year following stocking is normally the best, with the action declining into the next stocking cycle. Check with the local Fish, Wildlife & Parks office for the stocking schedule of the region's lakes if you like to plan ahead. Take the trail up Graves Creek for 3 miles, then go up the drainage to the west for a mile.

Danaher Creek: This beautiful headwater stream of the South Fork wanders across a wide mountain meadow after breaking out of a steep, timbered canyon. There are beaver dams here and there. There is also a lot of traffic because the valley provides wilderness for people entering from the Rocky Mountain Front. Still, this is a fine stream to fish if you don't mind company this far back in the woods, with lots of cutthroats to maybe 15 inches and a few bull trout and native mountain whitefish. By trail it is 5 miles above Big Prairie.

Doctor Lake: On the eastern side of the Swan Crest, Doctor Lake is usually reached from trails out of Upper Holland Lake. Lots of 12-inch cutthroat trout—overpopulated, actually. A good place to keep some fish for an evening meal.

Emery Creek: Small, brushy, and, like a dwindling number of streams of this type, it holds lots of 2- to 7-inch pure-strain westslope cutthroat trout. Years ago, while on an electroshocking survey with Fish, Wildlife & Parks biologist Joe Huston, I was amazed at the number of trout he and his crew turned up. But Huston said, "Those fish are as safe as a baby in Jesus's arms," referring to the extreme difficulty of catching more than a couple. Emery flows into Hungry Horse Reservoir near its northeast end.

George Lake: Heavily stocked by helicopter (an amazing sight in its own right) with westslope cutthroats, getting in requires an act of faith and good conditioning. Come in from Upper Holland Lake to Shaw Creek, then George Creek, then bushwhack straight up for 75 miles (really 2) and you are home. If you come before late July, bring ice skates.

Gordon Creek: Lots and lots of people hit this stream on their way to the South Fork from Upper Holland Lake. Still, it is classic, beautiful wilderness water with 8-inch cutthroats and some spawning bull trout that average a few pounds.

Gorge Creek: This stream drains three fairly good fishing lakes—Inspiration, Olor, and Sunburst—near the Swan Crest. A trail follows the creek as it cascades and sparkles its way down a deep, humbling rock gorge until it merges with Bunker Creek 11 miles later. The lower stretches have some cutthroats to 10 inches. Farther up, the fish are smaller.

Graves Creek: About a mile of fishable water flows in this stream below Handkerchief Lake that has some 10-inch cutthroats and rainbows and a few grayling. As with all Hungry Horse tributaries, there is usually some fishing for larger spawning cutthroats near the mouth in late spring and early summer. Above the lake the fishing is marginal.

Handkerchief Lake: This water is reached by road just up from the mouth of Aeneas Creek along Hungry Horse Reservoir. It's often crowded in the summer with small boats and a few float tubes as anglers search for another state-record grayling. There are some cutthroats also and a US Forest Service campground.

Hungry Horse Reservoir: When the dam was completed in the fifties, some of the finest wilderness river in the world was covered. Now there is a lake filling inexorably with silt, and the fishing for cutthroats and whitefish is often mediocre. The reservoir is reached by paved road south from the town of Hungry Horse (lots of neat curio shops and the like) and followed on both sides by roads that are much longer than Hungry Horse's 34-mile length. They twist and turn around the shoreline. This is still beautiful country and there are campgrounds dotting the shore at places such as Lid Creek, Doris Point, Murray Bay, and on Elk Island. Fishing the outlets early in the season is the only hope for cutthroats and in the fall for whitefish.

If the water is drawn down for power generation, in low-water years the place looks like a muddy, dusty, fly-infested bathtub and getting down to the water is a bitch. Also in late summer during huckleberry season, pickers get very territorial. Acrimony runs rife at this time, so be cautious.

The good camping opportunities around Hungry Horse Reservoir somewhat make up for the mediocre fishing.

Jewel Lakes, North and South: In the Jewel Basin Wilderness, both lakes are managed for cutthroats and are good fishing for hungry trout. Lots of hikers and a few grizzlies make use of this area. You get there from the well-marked foothills road west of Kalispell.

Koessler Lake: Just north of Doctor Lake with no trail, it's now managed for cutthroats which grow well in this deep 45-acre subalpine body of water.

Lena Lake: Reached by the Holbrook Trail just west of the divide, Lena Lake is heavily planted annually with cutthroats. A nice, off-the-beaten-trail alpine lake.

Little Salmon River: Followed by trail for 15 miles, the Little Salmon River meets the South Fork at the Black Bear Guard Station. It's beautiful water for cutthroats to 15 inches and, from late summer into fall, large bull trout—over 10 pounds. Some brush and timber make the fishing sporting.

Margaret Lake: Large cutthroats live in this deep, 46-acre lake, an hour's hike from the Forest Creek Road. Regular stocking keeps the numbers up.

Necklace Lakes: These are a half-dozen ponds on the Swan Crest about 5 tough miles from Upper Holland Lake. Cutthroat trout do well here, and there may be some rainbows left. Nice mosquito country. Bring a head net or you won't fish long.

Quintonkon Creek: Located just west of Hungry Horse Reservoir, this stream has some good early-season cutthroat action and late-season whitefish angling. Lots of brush and deadfalls and very few fly fishers in the course of a season. Bring the cheap waders for this one.

Shelf Lake: Reached above the Spotted Bear River, Shelf Lake always has a few good cutthroats and a bunch of smaller fish.

Spotted Bear Lake: This lake is muddy, swampy, buggy, and fairly good fishing for cutthroats, some nearing 20 inches. It's not far above the Spotted Bear Ranger Station.

Spotted Bear River: Followed by road and trail for 30 miles and then just trail for over 30 miles, there are a lot of people wandering through here both going in and coming out of the wilderness. Still, it is not difficult to disappear and have some fine fishing all to yourself. Above Dean Falls the fishing is typically for small cutts. Below is excellent fly fishing for cutthroats to 20 inches and lots of whitefish. Impressive limestone cliffs dominate the skyline.

White River: This stream hits the South Fork, coming in from the east, not far from the Holbrook Guard Station. It's a main thoroughfare, especially for those using the Sun River country, but it is good fishing for cutthroats over a foot long. Above Needle Falls the river often runs nearly dry in late summer, and the cutthroats pack into any cool pool or run remaining. Not my idea of a sporting proposition.

Wildcat Lake: Take the Noisy Creek Road to this lake alongside the Alpine Trail. Managed for cutthroats, the trout grow well here and take any small dry fly eagerly. There probably aren't any of the 10-pound-plus monsters left that were here before the road opened up the lake to heavier angling pressure.

Woodward Lake: This lake sees a bit of pressure and is good fishing for cutthroats that run around a foot long and sometimes larger and fat. The best way in is cross-country about 3 miles north from Necklace Lakes, through the mosquitoes. You can't miss this one: It's 65 acres. The scenery is worth the bug fight.

Youngs Creek: This is the headwaters of the South Fork at the south end of the wilderness, flowing for 15 miles with some big cutthroats in a few of the beaver ponds and in the larger pools. Some bull trout cruise up here also. Its trail starts 6 miles above Big Prairie.

Flathead Indian Reservation

Imagine owning 1.2 million acres of some of the most spectacular land in Montana—and that's saying a lot. Country filled with staggering mountains, dense forests, and rolling grass-covered hills stretching off into the distance. Throw into the mix hundreds of alpine lakes, a few choice rivers, miles of sparkling streams, some valley reservoirs, and a spring creek or two. This is the home of the Confederated Salish and Kootenai Tribes.

For many fly fishers this is a basic "died-and-gone-to-heaven" scenario. Spending the rest of your life chasing native cutthroats, browns, rainbows, brookies, and even lake trout, along with a collection of very large northern pike and good numbers of largemouth bass, has a certain appeal for some of us.

For the Salish and Kootenai Tribes of the Flathead Indian Reservation, such a fantasy is indeed a reality, and they are making the most of the opportunity. Located about 25 air miles south of Glacier National Park and just north of Missoula, the reservation takes in a large portion of the Mission Mountains, the southern end of Flathead Lake, the majority of the lower Flathead River, and the National Bison Range at Moiese.

Some of the better trout waters like the Jocko River and lower Flathead River, along with the valley lakes, ponds, and creeks, are discussed in the appropriate drainage sections. Both Kicking Horse Reservoir and Ninepipe Reservoir are locally renowned for providing quality largemouth bass action. The fish run to 5 pounds in the latter and occasionally over 2 pounds in the former (along with a rainbow or two of some size). Leech patterns work well in the shallows and along weed beds at any time, and deer-hair poppers produce in the evenings in the same locations.

You'll need a tribal fishing permit and should become familiar with the tribal regulations. They are available at the tribes' Division of Fish, Wildlife, Recreation and Conservation office at 406 Sixth Avenue East in Polson, as well as from various vendors throughout western Montana.

For those willing to backpack up steep (borderline death march in many cases) trails, the Mission Mountains Tribal Wilderness Area offers unspoiled fishing for cutthroat trout in wild, alpine country. Woolly Worms, Hare's Ear Nymphs, and Adams are representative of productive patterns in these high-altitude lakes. Some of the best reservation mountain lakes include:

Finley Lakes: These lakes are located below Murphy Peak in the Jocko Mountains and reached up the East Fork of Finley Creek by road. Rainbows and cutthroats are in the lower lake, and stunted cutthroats are in the upper.

First Lake: This is really a group of lakes hiding below McDonald Glacier in a beautiful valley. There is no trail, and the first time I tried to reach this region coming in from the Swan Valley on the east, I got lost and had to scramble over scree slopes and eventually slide down a tall pine to reach Ice Flow Lake at the head of the drainage. No fish here, but emerald-turquoise water shaded with glacial flour and waterfalls shooting out all over the place. Come in from the reservation side—it's longer but easier hiking. Topo maps help, as does a compass and plenty of luck. This is not for the faint of heart.

Disappointment Lake at a little over 6,000 feet holds Yellowstone cutthroats, but the area is closed to protect grizzlies (they have to live someplace) from July 15 through October 1. If the fall is warm, you have maybe a two-week window to get in and out of here, but you will be risking severe snowstorms coming out of nowhere and sending you for a ride on the oblivion express. Life is short, take a risk.

Kicking Horse Reservoir: The spectacular, rugged west face of the Mission Mountains provides the visuals for this 657-acre impoundment that on still days reflects the mountain grandeur. Good fishing for largemouth bass that will smash poppers and hoppers, but dearly love a large black leech pattern slowly wriggled through the weeds and grasses. All fish between 12 and 15 inches must be released. Some perch, pumpkin-seeds, and a rogue rainbow or two live here also.

Lost (Morigeau) Lakes: In Crow Creek country lying at about 6,000 feet, Upper is 15 acres and Lower is 8 acres. Both hold Yellowstone cutthroat of around 10 to 12 inches that are the result of old plantings from airplanes.

Lucifer Lake: Way up there, sitting below the most spectacular glacial cirque in the southern end of the Missions, a decent trail leads the way to healthy cutthroat fishing. Picture Lake, a quarter-mile farther upcountry, is currently barren—too high and too cold. All of this is fine, remote country that takes more than a few hours of rough hiking to reach.

Mud Lakes: Four lakes with trout lying between 5,500 and 6,500 feet, they are anywhere from 35 to 145 feet deep. The first has brookies and rainbows. The second holds rainbows. The third has cutthroats and maybe a few rainbows. The fourth has

A beautiful setting and fair bass fishing at Kicking Horse Reservoir on the Salish-Kootenai Reservation
John Holt

good fishing for cutthroats. The Mud Lakes Trailhead has been moved 1 mile north to Minesinger Road.

South Crow Creek (and Terrace) Lakes: About 5 miles east of Ronan, near the top of the Missions between 5,900 and 6,500 feet, 30 and 55 acres, up to 100-plus feet deep, and filled with cutthroats that will reach 12 inches—good fish for this far above the sea. This is spectacular glacial cirque country that is a killer to get into. The "trails" are rough and seem to go straight up. If you've never backpacked and wish to discover how "enjoyable" this masochistic pursuit really is, this is a good place to find out.

Other reservation mountain waters of marginal interest to anglers are Ashley Lake and Creek (day use only due to presence of grizzlies and closed from July 15 through October 1), Crazy Fish Lake (tribal members only), Crow Creek, Duncan Lake (barren), Eagle (tribal members only), Finley Creek, Lost Sheep Lake, Lower Jocko Lake (tribal members only), Meadow Lake (tribal members only), Minesinger Creek, North Fork Crow Creek, South Fork Crow Creek, and Upper Jocko Lake (tribal members only).

Here in the twenty-first century, while the rest of the state wrangles over stream-access laws, clear-cutting in sensitive drainages, irrigation allocations, and fisheries management directions, to mention just a few of the problems, the Confederated Salish and Kootenai Tribes have designed, adopted, and implemented a management plan for their abundant natural resources that is progressive by any management standards. The tribes have far fewer agencies, departments, directorates, and other bureaucracies to contend with, and this streamlined situation has made the implementation of a fisheries management plan on the reservation a relatively straightforward process.

Adopted in 1985, the plan first inventoried all waters and fish populations on the reservation. Following this, various population goals were drawn up for specific locations. Reaching these numbers entails habitat improvement, stocking, possession limits, guaranteeing stream flows, and, in some cases, closing streams to fishing.

What the Flathead Reservation fisheries management plan means to anglers is that for less than the cost of a tank of gas, you can purchase all required tribal permits and then spend a morning wading a small river taking numerous browns of 15 inches or so, enjoy lunch, and then drive up the road a piece to catch largemouth bass on deer-hair poppers on cast after cast. The next day you can float the lower Flathead River, working large streamers along weed beds and gravel bars for northern pike exceeding 20 pounds. Then you can hike into the mountains and fish high-country lakes for black-backed, crimson-slashed native cutthroat trout. All of this while surrounded by steep glacial cirques, remnant glaciers, and waterfalls shooting out of massive snowfields. If you are in good shape, you can visit lakes that are seldom fished. You will not see other people—only elk, eagles, and maybe grizzlies or goats.

Glacier National Park

When people think of Glacier National Park, mind-blowing vistas, the Going-to-the-Sun Road, and grizzly bears leap to mind. Mention fishing and you will draw blank stares and often less-than-tactful chuckles.

The trout fishing in Glacier will never compete with the top-of-the-line action found in Yellowstone, but there are some compelling arguments for the northern park. Chief among them are lack of crowds and relatively untouched angling.

Of the two million or so visitors to Glacier each year, less than one in twenty does anything more than cross the park from east to west. These hordes never fish, or if they do, the action consists of winging a Royal Wulff onto the virtually barren waters of McDonald Creek or maybe flinging a red-and-white spoon into St. Mary Lake. These normally futile endeavors lead to Glacier's reputation as a poor fishing location.

I discovered that there is a good deal of quality fishing in the park. Walk just a mile or so from the road and you will be alone, working untouched water in many cases. Walk even farther into the interior and you may be fishing a lake or stream that has not seen a fly cast with serious intent for several years. Big fish swim here—Yellowstone and westslope cutthroats, rainbows, bull trout, lake trout, and brook trout.

The fact that this is prime grizzly habitat is worth mentioning. First of all, I am all in favor of the great bears. The northern Rockies without them would be an empty, shallow place. If a human or two get eaten every now and then, those are the breaks as long as it isn't me. The bears are taking a beating, too. There may be as many as 200 grizzlies in the park, and they can be aggressive. In fact, many bear experts fear park bears more than their brothers found in national forest and wilderness areas and the larger specimens found in Alaska. Glacier's grizzlies have been exposed to humans for many years, along with an absence of gunfire in their direction, and this familiarity and resulting loss of fear of humans make their behavior unpredictable.

Whenever a bear sighting is reported, rangers close appropriate trail(s) for as long as necessary. Whenever you see bears at a distance, leave the area immediately. Make noise when you are hiking, especially when near rushing water. If confronted by a grizzly at close range, avoid direct eye contact and any other aggressive behavior. If a tree is nearby, get up it—fast. Don't worry about such things as "I've never climbed a tree before." When you see a grizzly, you will discover abilities you never thought you possessed.

Glacier National Park

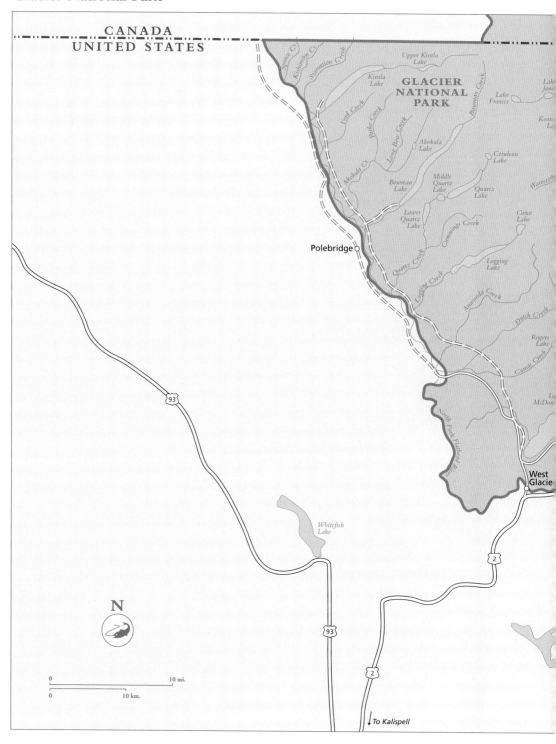

CANADA
UNITED STATES

GLACIER
NATIONAL
PARK

Upper Kintla
Lake

Kintla
Lake

Lake
Frances

Lake
Jane

Koote
La

Bowman Creek

Spruce Cr.
Kishinehn Cr.
Starvation Creek

Ford Creek

Jorde Creek

Long Bow Creek

Akokala Cr.

Akokala
Lake

Cerulean
Lake

Bowman
Lake

Middle
Quartz
Lake

Quartz
Lake

Waterton

Lower
Quartz
Lake

Cummings Creek

Grace
Lake

Polebridge

Quartz Creek

Logging Creek

Logging
Lake

Anaconda Creek

Dutch Creek

Rogers
Lake

Camas Creek

La
McDon

North Fork Flathead River

West
Glacie

93

Whitefish
Lake

2

93

2

↓ To Kalispell

N

0   10 mi.
0   10 km.

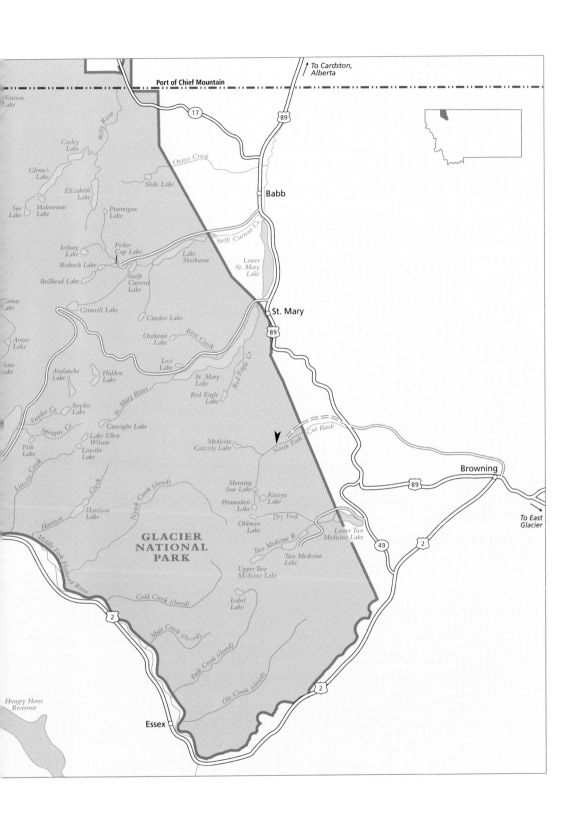

To Cardston,
Alberta

Port of Chief Mountain

17

89

Waterton
Lake

Cosley
Lake

Belly River

Glenn's
Lake

Elizabeth
Lake

Slide Lake

Otatso Creek

Babb

Sue
Lake

Makowanis
Lake

Ptarmigan
Lake

Swift Current Ck.

Iceburg
Lake

Fisher
Cap Lake

Lake
Sherburne

Lower
St. Mary
Lake

Redrock Lake

Bullhead Lake

Swift
Current
Lake

Camas
Lake

Grinnell Lake

Cracker Lake

St. Mary

89

Arrow
Lake

Otokomi
Lake

Rose Creek

Trout
Lake

Avalanche
Lake

Hidden
Lake

Lost
Lake

St. Mary River

St. Mary
Lake

Red Eagle Ck.

Red Eagle
Lake

Snyder Ck.

Snyder
Lake

Sprague Ck.

Gunsight Lake

Fish
Lake

Lake Ellen
Wilson

Lincoln
Lake

Medicine
Grizzly Lake

North Fork

Cut Bank

Lincoln Creek

Browning

89

Morning
Star Lake

Katoya
Lake

To East
Glacier

Nyack Creek (closed)

Pitamaken
Lake

Harrison
Lake

Harrison Creek

Oldman
Lake

Dry Fork

Lower Two
Medicine Lake

49

2

GLACIER
NATIONAL
PARK

Two Medicine R.

Two Medicine
Lake

Middle Fork Flathead River

2

Upper Two
Medicine Lake

Cold Creek (closed)

Isabel
Lake

Muir Creek (closed)

Park Creek (closed)

Ole Creek (closed)

2

Hungry Horse
Reservoir

Essex

If attacked, the common advice is to drop to the ground and "ball up," protecting your head and stomach. Most recent reports of bear attacks suggest that this may make things easier for the bears. People who have survived bear encounters with only a few hundred stitches and few broken bones usually have attempted to fend off the attack by punching the animal in the nose or anywhere else reachable. In fact, one elderly woman ran off a grizzly that was chewing on her husband by beating the bear with a stick. By the time you are in this situation, luck plays a far greater role in survival than advice and calm behavior.

While the threat of grizzly attack scares off many would-be anglers, the truth is that if you keep your eyes open, make noise in the backcountry, and use common sense, a bear encounter is extremely unlikely. Grizzles want even less to do with humans than we do with them.

On a more relaxed front, be sure to pick up park fishing regulations when entering Glacier and get current information at the ranger station near your destination. Lakes in the high country often freeze out or are closed because of bears. Five minutes of conversation with a ranger can save several hours of futile hiking. Also, most backcountry lakes and trails are not free of snow and ice until July, at the earliest. Campsites must be reserved in advance at the St. Mary or Apgar entrances or at major ranger stations no more than twenty-four hours in advance on a first-come, first-served basis—sort of a Motel 8 wilderness gig.

Finally, there are times when any pattern will take fish (as is true with all alpine fishing), but a varied selection of nymphs, drys, and streamers always helps. In other words, if you've got a box of weirdly colored streamers, bring them along. They may save the day. If I were limited to just three patterns, they would be Gold-Ribbed Hare's Ear Nymphs, sizes 12 to 18; Adams, sizes 12 to 20; and Olive Woolly Worms, sizes 6 to 10. High-country fishing is not sophisticated from a selection standpoint, but it is frequently exasperating.

The standard fishing season for all waters in the park is from the third Saturday in May through November 30, with the following key points:

- Lake fishing open all year.

- Waterton Lake season and catch and possession limits are the same as set by Canada. Check Canadian regulations before fishing these waters.

- Lower Two Medicine Lake season and catch and possession limits are set by the Blackfoot Nation. Check Blackfoot tribal regulations.

- To protect spawning cutthroat trout, and to reduce the potential for bear-human conflicts, Hidden Lake outlet creek and the area extending into Hidden Lake for a radius of 300 feet from the outlet is closed to fishing during the cutthroat spawning season.

- When fishing from park lands along the North Fork of the Flathead River, park catch and possession limits, as well as other park fishing regulations, are applicable.

- When fishing from park lands or bridges along the Middle Fork of the Flathead River, a Montana fishing license is required and state regulations are applicable.

- The following areas are closed to fishing: Kintla Creek between Kintla Lake and Upper Kintla Lake, Upper Kintla Lake, Bowman Creek above Bowman Lake, Logging Creek between Logging Lake and Grace Lake, Cracker Lake, Slide Lake, and the impounded pond below the lake. The following streams are closed for their entire length: Ole, Park, Muir, Coal, Nyack, Fish, Lee, Otatso, Boulder, and Kennedy Creeks; North Fork of the Belly River; and North Fork of the Flathead River within 200 yards of the mouth of Big Creek.

The Continental Divide splits the fishing in Glacier into eastern and western regions, with a third area in the north along the Canadian border.

Eastern Waters

The lakes and streams on the east side of the park are influenced by a drier and much windier climate. Forests are not as thick, tall, or dense as the west side. Rivers and creeks, as is true in most of the park, have either few trout or populations of very small fish, usually brookies.

Belly River: An early-season stream, the Belly has brook trout, rainbow trout, and grayling. A Goddard or Elk Hair Caddis, Adams, or Royal Wulff will handle the situation. The Blackfoot name for the river, *Mokowanisz*, refers to the digestive system of a buffalo.

POPULAR FLIES

Adams	Humpies
Biggs Special	Partridge and Orange Soft
Elk Hair Caddis	Hackle
Goddard Caddis	Royal Wulff
Gold-Ribbed Hare's Ear	Woolly Bugger

Cut Bank Creek: Brooks, cutthroats, rainbows. I had a glorious summer afternoon some years back taking cutthroats to 15 inches on cast after cast using Royal Wulffs. Mountains, warm summer breezes, puffy clouds in a soft blue sky, crystalline water, and the fish—it was heaven.

Elizabeth Lake: Nine miles from Chief Mountain Customs Station on the US–Canada border, Elizabeth offers nice angling for grayling. There are also rainbows and brooks in lesser numbers. One story suggests that legendary mountain man Joe Cosley named the lake for one of Theodore Roosevelt's daughters, who happened to be named Bertha. Spend a few days in the country and you begin to see how things are easily confused. Wild stuff here.

Francis Lake: Francis is good for rainbows. You can get there from the Upper Waterton boat dock in Canada.

Glenn's Lake: Brook, cutthroat, and lake trout and some whitefish live in this lake located 11 miles from Chief Mountain Customs.

Grinnell Lake: This lake sees a good deal of pressure by Glacier standards because it is only 1 mile from the Upper Josephine Lake boat dock, which is a mile from Many Glacier. You'll find some fishing for brook trout, and the same holds true for Josephine.

Gunsight Lake: Some good-size rainbows abide here. The lake is 6 miles from Going-to-the-Sun Road.

Hidden Lake: A couple of miles of up-and-down hiking from the Going-to-the-Sun Road near Sun Point, this water is small, but deep, and has trout.

Kennedy Creek: Small stream, cutthroats, whitefish. Grizzlies hide in the thick willow and alder. A high-octane place.

Kootenai Lakes: Superb brook trout fishing found in even better bear country means that these lakes are often closed. They are only 2.5 miles from the Upper Waterton boat dock. Lots of mosquitoes.

Medicine Grizzly Lake: Plenty of slightly stunted rainbows around a foot long live here. This is an 11-mile round-trip hike from the Cut Bank Campground.

Oldman Lake: This one provides good fishing for cutthroat trout and sees a bit of action despite being 6 miles from Two Medicine Lake. The last stretch of trail travels through a pleasant, open forest.

Accessible from the Logan Pass Visitor Center, Hidden Lake offers spectacular views and not-bad fly fishing. Habituated goats and sheep may join you, looking for a handout.

Two Medicine River is a beautiful little mountain stream with grizzlies and small cutthroats.

Lower Two Medicine Lake is windswept, spectacular, and often good fishing along windward shores, using streamers or nymphs.

Otokomi Lake: *Otokomi* means "yellow fish" in Blackfoot. The lake has large, cruising cutthroats that are quite spooky, but a nymph, cast well ahead of their perceived cruising pattern and then jerked a few inches when they are about 10 feet away, works wonders. This small lake is nestled in a glacial cirque with scree slopes plunging to the shoreline. The trail climbs steadily for 5.5 miles from Rising Sun Campground to an altitude of 6,482 feet.

Ptarmigan Lake: Five miles from Many Glacier, Ptarmigan has fine fishing for brook trout.

Red Eagle Lake: Some large rainbows and some cutthroats swim here. The water is 8 miles from St. Mary. The trail forks at about 5 miles. Take the right-hand path.

St. Mary River: Cutthroats, rainbows, and whitefish to some size. Best the month or so after runoff with attractors, then progressing through the summer with hopper patterns and streamers in early fall.

Swiftcurrent Lake: Brook trout, rainbows, kokanees, but not in good numbers and often buffeted by hurricane-force winds.

Two Medicine River: Brook and cutthroat trout in modest numbers that take a shine to nearly any small dry, especially a Hendrickson.

Upper Two Medicine Lake: Has some fat brook trout (and a few rainbows) that often hit small dry flies around dusk. Take the Two Medicine Lake (large water with brook and rainbow trout that may be spotted cruising near shore on occasion) tour boat to the head of the lake and then hike 5 miles from 5,164-feet elevation to a little over 5,550. There is a campsite at the head of the lake.

This area offers some of the finest, most remote fishing in Glacier, especially for brook trout and grayling. There is more precipitation here than along the Rocky Mountain Front of the eastern side of the park, resulting in denser forests. This is also some of the best grizzly habitat around, so many areas are frequently closed for lengthy periods.

WESTERN WATERS

The western section of Glacier is bordered by the Middle and North Forks of the Flathead River. Each of these rivers has its own section in this guide, but the tributaries located in the park are discussed here. This region is marked by thick pine forest, including some red cedar. The fishing in the streams is usually marginal, but migratory movements of westslope cutthroat trout can liven things up for a few weeks in July and

Lake McDonald is large, beautiful, and, at best, only average fishing along the shore.
David Restivo/National Park Service

August. These species are alive with spawning colors at this time and also under a good deal of stress. Play and release them quickly. A number of lakes are quite good.

Akokala (Indian) Creek and Lake: Both are good for small (to 10 inches) westslope cutthroat. The lake is 5.5 steep miles above Bowman Lake. Due to oil exploration many years ago, this used to be known as Oil Lake.

Arrow Lake: Located 7.5 miles up Camas Creek (a mile or so above Trout Lake) in prime bear country, Arrow Lake has good fishing for cutthroats.

Avalanche Lake: This is one of the more popular hiking destinations, lying in a beautiful waterfall-filled cirque a couple of miles east of Going-to-the-Sun Road. The far end of the lake is not bad for small cutthroats. Don't bother with the creek unless you own an 52-inch, 2-weight rod.

Bowman Lake: You can drive to Bowman up the North Fork. A canoe or float tube is best to work the shoreline for bulls, cutts, and whitefish. Not great fishing. The creek can be fun for small fish. Bear vibes are strong here.

Camas Lake and Creek: This tributary to the North Fork is in "bear valley," but the lake has fair fishing for Yellowstone cutts.

Cerulean Lake: Some large and small cutthroat trout. Site of the infamous "Grizzly Hilton." Extreme caution is advised.

Fish Lake: Just a few minutes through the woods from Going-to-the-Sun Road, this marshy lake offers fair cutthroat fishing. Bring waders unless you like leeches.

Grace Lake: Grace offers good fishing for big westslope cutthroat trout, but the hike is 12 miles from the inside North Fork Road at Logging Creek.

Harrison Lake and Creek: Harrison Lake is most easily reached by floating the Middle Fork and then hiking 4 miles to the lake. Or you can hike 11 miles east from West Glacier for cutthroats. Good brookies in beaver ponds along the creek.

Hidden Lake: About 3 miles from Logan Pass, Hidden Lake has some nice Yellowstone cutts that will take a twitched nymph provided it is cast far enough ahead to avoid spooking the fish. The hike out is steep. Offers nice fishing in early September, which is true of many Glacier lakes.

Isabel Lake: It may or may not be worth the 33-mile round-trip for anglers. Conflicting reports (no one fishes here much) suggest populations of cutthroat and brook trout. You get there by hiking up Park Creek, across the river from Essex. Mind-blowing beauty.

Kintla Lake and Creek: Some cutthroat trout live here, and you can drive right in and watch the tame deer and the not-so-tame campers. The lake is big water, requiring a canoe or float tube. Upper Kintla Lake is 8 miles from Kintla in spectacular cirque country.

Lake Ellen Wilson: This excellent brook trout lake is located 9 miles from Lake McDonald or 2.5 miles from Sperry Chalet.

Lincoln Lake: Lincoln lies at the foot of 1,300-foot Beaver Chief Falls, a couple miles south of Gunsight Mountain. The 8-mile trail dead-ends here. Scenic action for cutthroat.

Logging Lake and Creek: With average fishing for small cutts, the lake is 4 miles above the inner North Fork Road. The creek is closed to fishing between Logging Lake and Grace Lake.

McDonald Lake: Fished more than any other lake in the park, McDonald is lousy action for a little of everything. On occasion a few nice cutts can be seen working near shore along the Going-to-the-Sun Road and they can be fun.

McDonald Creek: Below Apgar, McDonald Creek offers very spotty fishing for cutthroat trout and a few rainbows (of some size on occasion) on drys. The upper creek is beautiful and almost devoid of fish, but this does not dampen the enthusiasm of thousands of eager anglers who try their luck on the fighting 4-inch cutthroats hanging out here, except the section from the lake to McDonald Falls is closed to fishing. The creek flowing below Apgar to the Middle Fork of the Flathead is fine dry-fly water, with some large rainbows, westslope cutthroats, and hybrids. The fishing is not what it once was because it's now hit hard by guided floaters.

Quartz Creek and Lower Quartz, Middle Quartz, and Quartz Lakes: These waters have cutthroats and a few bull trout. The lakes are 4 to 6 miles from Bowman Lake.

Trout Lake: This is another "bear valley" lake on Camas Creek that is fly fishing only for cutthroat trout. You get there via a 4-mile trek over the ridge from Lake McDonald.

Kootenai

The Kootenai flows through wild and beautiful country. When I lived in nearby Whitefish, I used to fish around here a lot. I always preferred the tributaries running through even wilder country. The river never grabbed my heart like, say, the Swan or the North Fork of the Flathead for some reason. Maybe it's the intrusion of Libby Dam. Maybe it's the wide-open size of the river.

Rumors and the Kootenai River seem to go together these days like fly fishing and trout. You often will hear stories about how strong the river's rainbows are or how big they can grow, but is any of this true? After all, anglers and truth are not always on speaking terms.

Tucked away in the northwest corner of the state and flowing past the logging community of Libby, the Kootenai is not as well-known as other waters in Montana. Much of the river was destroyed with the completion of the Libby Dam in 1972.

Kootenai rainbows are strong fighters that love nymphs and, at times, dry flies. John Holt

Kootenai

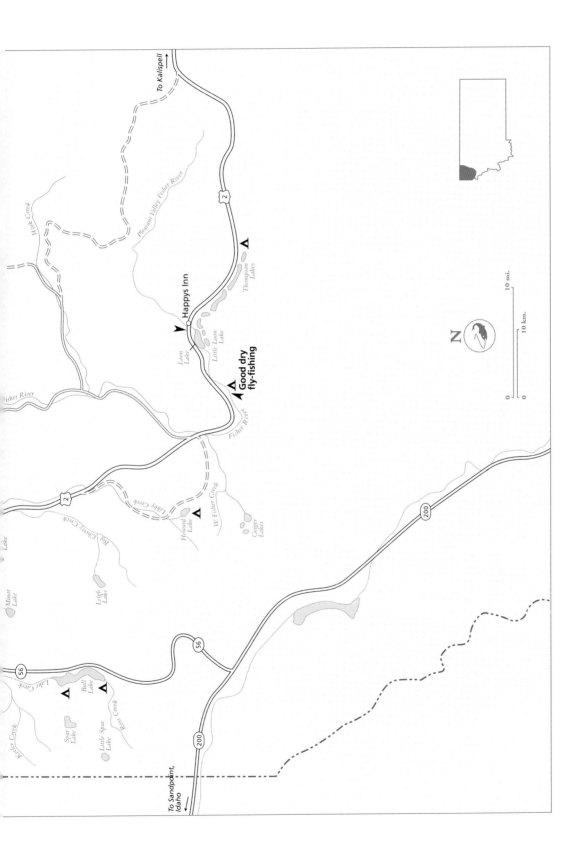

Ninety miles of the river (48 in the United States and 42 in Canada) are buried under many feet of water known as Lake Koocanusa. Much of the remaining 48 miles in Montana now provides a quality tailwater fishery.

The source of all this water—4,000 cfs is the normal flow, but this jumps up to 30,000 cfs during peak power-generation periods—are the rugged ice- and snow-capped peaks of the Canadian Rockies to the north. The Kootenai is one of the largest rivers in terms of water flow in the state.

The rainbows fight well for their size, which averages in the 1-pound-plus range for most of the floatable length of river, though they may run up to 5 or more pounds, especially in the spring near the mouths of tributaries such as the Yaak River and Callahan Creek. Some hefty bull trout live here, too, as do mountain whitefish and hordes of big suckers.

In recent years meat fishers (and an occasional fly fisher) have taken rainbows exceeding 20 pounds (with some approaching 30) out of the Kootenai just below the dam. The trout line up below the power-generating dam and feed on a chum line of chopped-up kokanee salmon and trout that have passed through the turbines.

This situation could be an interesting fishery for those willing to use Hi-D sinking lines and large streamers. But those using bait and lures are depleting a finite resource and, as Region 1 fisheries manager Jim Vashro said, "There are only so many of those tremendous fish, and even if they are the fast-growing Kamloops strain, once they are gone, it will take quite a few years to grow some more."

Most of the rainbows you will catch in the river run between 12 and 15 inches, but they are wide, thick, and silvery.

BELOW LIBBY DAM

The section of the river from the dam to Libby is paralleled by both MT 37 and a county road. Access for waders and floaters, while not abundant, is adequate. The same holds true for the stretch between Libby and China Rapids about 9 miles downstream. All told, there are about 30 miles of floatable water. This part of the river is open year-round, and on "warm" winter days you will see anglers working nymphs or even dry flies if a hatch is one. The river is never crowded with either waders or floaters. This is just too far off the beaten track. For the rest of the way to the Idaho border, US 2 is the major source of access.

The first stretch of the river (above Libby) is marked by large riffles, runs, and quiet glides with sections of large bankside boulders. Try working large streamers between the rock formations. Sink-tip lines will help you reach the calmer bottom areas where the big fish hang out. When the trout are rising, cast to the pods of fish in midstream. Weed beds and deep pools are also productive areas.

This is big water and it's easy to get intimidated by the sheer size of it. The best approach here is to cut the river down to fishable size. Experienced anglers work to fish

The Kootenai is big water with fluctuating flows caused by Libby Dam.

for trout within 30 or 40 feet with accurate, controlled, and calculated casts. Even with the large numbers of slurping trout, sloppy casting can put a damper on the festivities.

Below town the boulders along the banks and out in the current are the best bets (the mouths of creeks are the next best). When floating, look ahead for any "buckets," big patches where the water slows down and the insects concentrate, or even small pockets of calm water along the seams of two different currents. Good fish always hold and feed in these spots. They feel safe here because the surface is broken enough to provide at least a little cover, and they take with less discrimination than, say, out in the middle when a hatch is breaking. The trick when floating and fishing this seamy water is to plan the cast well in advance, leaving time to drift the fly right into these prime places.

BIG WATER COUNTRY

Even though it's not a wilderness river, timber-covered mountains drop down to the water and the Cabinet Mountains are visible to the southwest. Eagles, deer, and other wildlife are common. This is a peaceful float until a hatch of insects starts popping on the surface. Then the rainbows turn on and literally hundreds of fish will begin dimpling the smooth river.

The river is managed to hold over 1,300 trout per mile, with 5 percent exceeding 14 inches. There is sufficient aquatic life to support 2,500 catchable-size trout per mile. So when nature throws the switch and the heavy feeding begins, the angler with good skills will catch a lot of trout, often to several pounds. And on small drys.

Area guide Dave Blackburn describes the daily and yearly hatch cycles as follows: "Sporadic hatches of iron duns and blue-winged olives occur year-round, as do the midges. Salmon flies hatch from late May to early June. Although the population of these insects is on the rise, there is no intense, concentrated activity.

"Consistent, prolific hatches of mayflies and caddisflies don't start coming off the water until June when the river warms. Blue-winged olives, iron duns, and grannom caddis are the main attractions early in the summer, replaced later by spotted sedges, little sister sedges, and pale morning duns (which, in spite of the name, linger into the evenings). Late in the summer, heavy swarms of spotted sedges and little sister sedges smother the river with their mating flights. Tricos and spotted sedges provide the main staple through November.

"Most surface activity occurs in the evenings, when even the largest trout can't pass up food available in such dense concentrations."

While there is some cloudy runoff in April and early May, especially below the Fisher River, the upper 3 miles below the dam are always clear. Early-season angling from March through May produces the larger rainbows, as these fish move upstream on their spawning migrations. Nymphs and streamers, both bounced on the bottom, are the most productive flies at this time.

WARM WEATHER ACTION

Dry-fly action picks up in June and peaks in July and August. Days are long this far north, and rises that begin around 7 in the evening often last until almost 11. Streamers come into play again from September through October. Nymphs hold sway in the winter.

In the summer, when the water level kicks up from a 30,000 cfs release from the dam, the rainbows often move into the newly submerged, grassy banks to pick off terrestrials washed into the river. Ant, beetle, and grasshopper imitations, cast into the grass, can produce some very hot action—kind of like fishing your unmowed back lawn after an extended rain.

Despite the fact that it is large water, an 8½-foot, 5-weight rod for dry-fly fishing is ideal for the Kootenai. Bring along a 9-foot, 7-weight rod for large nymphs and streamers. A double-taper floating line and a sink-tip wet line cover the action in the main river. Anyone fishing for the monsters below the dam should bring appropriate equipment—a 10-weight rod, rigged with a Hi-D or lead-core, 30-foot shooting head for throwing 3/0 streamers, wouldn't be out of place.

Cliff Dare, the first guide on the river, has seen changes since the dam was completed: "In the early years, everyone used big dry flies on the Kootenai, size 10 and 12 Renegades and Adams, the same ones they'd use on other local rivers. Now the normal dry-fly sizes are 16s and 18s. The nymphs have also become exact imitations, and scud patterns are very popular. Even with streamers, the smart fishermen are using flies that look like kokanee salmon, especially near the dam, and crayfish."

The same types of flies that work on other tough tailwater rivers will catch trout on the Kootenai. During the aquatic insect hatches, emerger patterns are often more effective than dry flies. The smooth stretches of surface develop a thick meniscus, and insects struggle for a disproportionately long time in the film, creating a concentration zone. An imitation half in and half out of the water often works when a true dry fly, sitting completely on the surface, fails on critical fish.

Is the Kootenai a destination river? For some it is. Those who have experienced a summer evening filled with clouds of caddisflies and dozens of rainbows tend to keep coming back.

Fishing Waters in the Kootenai Drainage

Big Creek: Big Creek enters Lake Koocanusa on the west side, after flowing through rich, thick forest. A short rod and a tight roll cast help here. Some nice spawning cutthroats and rainbows show up in the spring and stay maybe as late as July. Try large attractor drys, like a Wulff or a Humpy, or flashy streamers. The resident cutts are somewhat smaller.

Blue Sky Creek: A small tributary of Grave Creek south of Eureka, this stream used to be paralleled by an old logging road that is now blocked off. Some nice cutthroats move up in early summer. This used to be a fun one to fish, but it's now closed year-round for all species to protect the bull trout.

Closed to fishing to protect the bulls, Blue Sky Creek is a wonderful little mountain stream that is fun to just watch and enjoy.

Bluebird Lake: Bluebird is a few miles up the trail from Little Therriault Lake at the end of the Grave Creek Road. It holds some cutthroats, and the 3-mile hike is easy and scenic. This is a good place to break in the kids on carrying your gear. It is in treeless mountain country below the crest of the Galton Range. Drys, nymphs, whatever—they all work. You'll pass Paradise Lake on the way. There are sometimes cutthroats swimming here, too. At other times it is barren.

Callahan Creek: A marginal fishing stream for rainbows and cutthroats, this tributary of the Kootenai (just west of Troy) is of interest because some big spawning rainbows can be taken on big streamers near the mouth in the spring. As with most of the good things in life, timing is everything, and this is usually a function of luck during late spring runoff.

Cedar Lakes: Reached by the Cedar Creek Trail west of Libby, the upper lake is 54 acres and the lower one is 21. A lot of backpacking traffic strolls into this country due, in part, to the mountain and cirque scenery, and a little bit because of the fishing for 10- to 12-inch trout.

Crystal Lake: Crystal Lake lies right next to US 2 halfway between Kalispell and Libby. Lots of rainbows and kokanee salmon are dumped in here each year. It is large—175 acres—and deep. There are also perch and northern pike and plenty of small boats trolling for salmon. Most people probably know this as the water behind Happys Inn.

Dickey Lake: Right next to US 93 south of Eureka, this is very large water for this country (nearly 600 acres) and has all kinds of species in it, including cutthroats, rainbows, brookies, largemouth bass, and northern pike, along with motorboats and the like. Summer homes dot the shoreline in this rolling, timbered country. The shallow-water areas at the inlet on the east end have that aqua-blue Caribbean look, and local rumor consistently vibrates to the tune of "there are some huge brook trout in that lake." Sinking lines and big streamers in the evenings during the fall may tell the story.

Dickey is so deep that you are pretty much limited to pecking at the edges. Most people make the mistake of positioning a boat 30 or so feet out and casting toward the shore. In areas with sharp drop-offs, which includes the entire north and south shorelines, they are retrieving flies far over the heads of the fish. They'd do a lot better standing on the bank, or putting the boat next to the bank, and either casting out into the lake so that the fly follows the contours of the bottom upwards, or casting parallel to the shoreline.

East Fisher River: This pretty stream, located 40 miles south of Libby on US 2, is followed by a good road all the way. There's not much water in the summer, and the

The fishing at Dickey Lake is usually slow and peaceful, and sometimes you can come across some rather large brook trout. The scenery is always prime.

headwaters have been logged to death. In spite of this rainbows, cutthroats, and those ubiquitous brookies hang around waiting for a well-placed dry fly.

East Fork Yaak River: This used to be a beautiful stream, but most of the drainage has been logged to oblivion. The little pools and quiet runs are silted up. There is still some good water in the lower stretches where the riparian areas are left alone. Once in the stream, you can pretend you're in a real forest and take some nice rainbows and brookies and a stray cutthroat on general searching flies, such as Elk Hair Caddis, and attractors. It's hard to believe that 20-inch-long trout once swam here. Take the Yaak River Road 4 miles above Upper Ford Ranger Station.

Fish Lakes: Three of these five lakes—North, Middle, and South—are managed for westslope cutthroat trout. The lakes nestle high up in the Cabinet Wilderness, which is not huge as far as Montana wilderness areas go, but contains some beautiful high country and a few hold-out grizzlies. The trail in is steep, but the place receives some pressure in July and August when snow levels drop enough so that people can hike in. These lakes are about 4 miles up Vinal Creek from the Vinal Creek Road.

Fisher River: In spots, this is still a classic Northwest forested stream, but heavy logging in the region has hurt the drainage to the extent that the fishing is now average, at best. During spring runoff the Fisher is the major contributor of silt to the Kootenai. As a matter of fact, anytime it rains, it runs mud into the river. Some cutthroats, rainbows, brookies, and whitefish are still taken in the stream. US 2 crosses Fisher about 14 miles south of Libby.

Five Mile Creek: MT 37 crosses this stream as it runs along the east shore of Lake Koocanusa above the dam. It is small water, but in early summer some good-size cutthroats move upstream. You'll also find brook trout here.

Fortine Creek: Access is not always easy but is available from a country road running east from US 93. Resident trout are small, but some of the spawning cutthroats are a good size in early summer.

Frank Lake: Frank is 10 miles south of Eureka off US 93 on poor, rutted road. The closeness to the town, and the fact that it is very good fishing, makes this a popular spot. It's hit hard all year, especially by ice fishers. Its size, over 100 acres, gives the trout some protection.

Almost three-quarters of Frank Lake is very shallow, never getting much deeper than 10 feet. There are two islands at this shallow end, and both of them are fish magnets. During June the lake has a fine damselfly hatch and trout cruise over the weed beds, intercepting the swimming nymphs. A size 6 or 8 Olive Marabou Damsel, retrieved with a "jerk, jerk, and pause" movement, will take these fish.

Frozen Lake: This lake straddles the US–Canada border and, if you pretend real hard, the logged-over country you drive through to reach the trailhead won't remind you of Gary, Indiana. There is a boat launch on the Canadian side, and a good number of put-puts smoke up the water in the summer. Just the same, if you are willing to lug a float tube down an old logging road to the lake, you can catch big cutthroats (I've taken a couple over 20 inches) with flashy streamers worked into and along the downed shoreline timber. To get there, go 30 miles up Grave Creek Road, then east to the end of Frozen Lake Road, and hike about a mile into the lake. This lake actually lies in the North Fork of the Flathead drainage, but you get there from the Kootenai side.

Glen Lake: Six miles southeast of Eureka, Glen is large (340 acres) and managed for rainbows. It's not much for aesthetics, especially during the midsummer drawdown, but there are some nice fish and lots of anglers and boats and trucks. The structure of the lake is equally uninspiring. It's a dammed-up bowl, the shore all the way around sloping down steadily to a maximum depth of 38 feet in the center. The way to find trout is to cast parallel to the shore, moving systematically outward into deeper and deeper water until you start getting strikes.

Grave Creek: Grave Creek flows into the Tobacco River (which empties into Lake Koocanusa) from the northeast. A good run of spawning cutthroats moves upstream from late spring until July. Late summer finds the bull trout and mountain whitefish doing the same. This is a wide, swiftly flowing mountain stream with riffles, whitewater, pools, and downed timber. Pretty stuff. Fish attractors like Royal Humpies and Air Heads with short, accurate casts, hitting the pockets.

All of the tributaries play host to at least a couple of nice, spawning trout. When the fish are in the small streams that are open to fishing, leave them alone. Working these during spawning is kind of like having your car tipped over while hugging your sweetie at the drive-in. Go about 8 miles south of Eureka on US 93 to get on Grave Creek.

Accessible by a paved then gravel road, Grave Creek holds good numbers of small- to medium-size westslope cutthroats.

Hawkins Lakes: These lakes are not far from the upper reaches of Pete Creek in the Yaak drainage. Upper (2 acres) and Lower (4 acres) are managed for cutthroats and are fairly good for fish running 12 to 14 inches. Both ponds are really weedy. Bring scud imitations. All of this country is going fast (it will grow back but not in our lifetimes), so you'd better fish it now if you like shade. Logging road north from the headwaters of Pete Creek will get you within a half mile of these lakes.

Hoskin Lake: Hit the Forest Service trail 2.5 miles north of Yaak. Hoskin is planted with westslope cutthroats every other season and is good fishing for trout in the 1-foot range. The Dirty Shame Saloon is nearby and worth a stop if you're dry or in need of a T-shirt. Some time back a couple of the boys got a little buzzed up and blew some fingers off playing with dynamite outside the tavern. My kind of place.

Howard Lake: Thirty miles south of Libby on Libby Creek and Howard Creek Roads, Howard is planted with Arlee rainbows every year. The paved road and the public campground make this a popular spot. It's good fishing from float tubes (watch out for trollers). Gold-Ribbed Hare's Ears and Marabou Damsels are effective nymphs. Zonkers, Krystal Buggers, and Rabbit Leeches also work well.

Kilbrennan Lake: This one is popular with people around Troy. Kilbrennan is northwest of the city, roughly 10 miles of gravel road away. It's a good lake for float tubing for brookies and cutthroats. Much of the bottom is mud, and midge larvae are abundant on this type of substrate. There are weed beds on the west end, with large populations of crayfish and bullheads. Brookies like bright flies, too, especially in the fall, and a Mickey Finn is an effective streamer here.

Lake Creek: The big flood in the winter of '74–75 wiped out pools and logjams, and even straightened out sections. This stream is still good, but not as good as it was before the flood. It's best when the spawners are in it. Fish can only come up a quarter mile from the Kootenai before running into generators. Most of the spawners come downstream from Bull Lake. Those rainbows stay in the stream from mid-June to mid-July. They take dry flies well, especially a size 14 and 16 Parachute Adams and Elk Hair Caddis. Lake Creek has excellent caddisfly populations, and for an all-around searching nymph pattern, nothing beats a Free-Living Caddis Larva. Take the Lake Creek Road turnoff about 2 miles south of Troy off US 2.

Leigh Creek: The outlet of Leigh Lake and a tributary of Big Cherry Creek, this is a fine little hike-in fishing stream for rainbows and brookies. There's a pretty falls on it, and no angler worth his graphite (or bamboo for traditionalists) would pass the big spill basin without trying a few casts.

Leigh Lake: Leigh can be good fishing for brook and rainbow trout (with some trophy specimens over 5 pounds). The lake lies blow Snowshoe Peak in the Cabinet Mountains. It's a good 3-mile trek in nice country that is popular with backpackers. Woolly Worms sometimes take trout when they turn difficult here (or in any other high-country lake).

Lake Koocanusa: The result of the completion of Libby Dam in the 1970s, Koocanusa can be good fishing for cutthroats and Kamloop rainbows along the shore, especially by creek mouths, from late spring into summer. There are also lingcod, kokanee, and whitefish, and some bull trout on occasion.

The reservoir's main problem is that the Army Corps of Engineers often draws the water level down over 150 feet during the late summer and early fall for power generation, which is the main purpose of the dam. The Corps stated years ago that recreation values are 1 percent of the overall operating scheme. When Koocanusa is drawn down this low, huge muddy beaches are exposed, making boat launching next to impossible. Hordes of flies swarm in the air. The place resembles a very large sewer. The Corps doesn't care. Why should you? There are plenty of other places to fish in the region in the summer.

Leon Lake: This is another large lake lying near US 2 between Kalispell and Libby. It's planted with cutthroats and rainbows, which do well in the 87-foot depths, and it is often decent fishing.

Libby Creek: Eight miles east of Libby, this creek goes under US 2 and dumps into the Kootenai. It's good-looking water, but is heavily polluted with mining waste. It does get some rainbow, cutthroat, and bull trout that run up from the river. Fishing is best in the spring, when nymphs, like an Olive Hare's Ear or a small Montana Stone, work well.

Little McGregor Lake: This muddy-bottomed lake near US 2 covers 38 acres and is 30 feet deep. It's average fishing for rainbows and sometimes good fishing for large brook trout. The marshy shoreline dictates the use of float tubes.

Loon Lake: Over 200 acres in area, Loon is full of panfish, trash fish ("Who you callin' trash, boy?"), small- and largemouth bass, and some fat rainbows. You should try for the rainbows early in the season, before the water warms up. Work the narrow neck between the two basins thoroughly with poppers for largemouths in late May and June. It's located about 3 miles southwest of Fortine.

Marl Lake: Not far from Fortine, Marl is over 100 acres and planted with generic rainbows. It can be good from a float tube with leech patterns. Take Meadow Creek Road about 3 miles west of Fortine, then go south 1.5 miles on rough road.

Moran Lake: About 8 miles northwest of Eureka and 0.5 mile east of Sophie Lake, this water has brookies and rainbows and can be good. Not much over 30 feet anywhere, and it's always possible to find the trout. There's a long point near the center of the lake, and off the point is a flat no more than 10 feet deep. The rainbows cruise that area in the evening.

Mount Henry Lake: There are a number of ways into this lake in the Yaak drainage, all indicated by signs that point to a trailhead. This is still pretty country, and you will get wonderful views of the clear-cuts once you reach the 8-acre lake. It's managed for cutthroats and is good fishing most of the time from July until the snow flies in the fall.

Murphy Lake: Just east of US 93, south of Eureka, this lake is overrun with summer campers. You can catch largemouth bass, yellow perch, northern pike, and rainbow trout. You need a boat or a float tube. The southeast shoreline is the most productive.

Pipe Creek: Pipe Creek enters the Kootenai 3 miles west of Libby and is readily accessible, heavily hit, and contains cutthroat, rainbow, and brook trout. As with most creeks in this country, beaver ponds lie about in the swampy, meadowy sections. Brookies of some size often inhabit them. A leech pattern underwater or a Mosquito dry fly on the surface turns trout's heads.

Pleasant Valley Fisher River: Much of this stream is on private land, but a number of miles parallel US 2. Most of the rainbow and brook trout in this fishy-looking stretch average around 7 inches, but away from the road near evening, a few larger ones can be taken on drys like a Hairwing Adams or a White Wulff.

Seventeenmile Creek: The road follows this stream in the Yaak drainage. It offers fair angling for resident cutthroats and rainbows, plus some spawning fish up from the Yaak. During midsummer, when the Yaak gets too warm, brookies come up for the cool water. It's overgrown along the banks.

Sophie Lake: Sophie is over 200 acres of lake about 8 miles northwest of Eureka. It has a population of cutthroats and rainbows. Leeches and damsel nymphs work as imitations, but a gaudy streamer does even better. During the heat of the day, a hopper dropped next to the shore and occasionally twitched will also pull trout a long way.

Spar Lake: Twenty-five miles south of Troy via Iron Creek or Lake Creek Road, nearly 440 acres big and 200 feet deep, Spar is intensively managed for kokanee salmon. There are also brook trout and some lake trout. The Forest Service manages the campground, picnic area, and boat ramp. It's popular with Troy anglers.

Big Therriault Lake is fair fishing for cutthroat, though the campgrounds tend to get crowded.

Ten Lakes: Most of these lakes are barren, but Rainbow has cutthroats that get hit hard once the snow leaves this high country just south of the Canadian border. Near the end of Grave Creek Road, take Wigwam Creek Road for 3 miles, then hike 2 miles cross-country to get there.

Therriault Lakes (Big and Little): Both have campgrounds, and both are always crowded. Lying below a rugged ridge at the end of the Grave Creek Road, each lake has good numbers of small cutthroats. Small nymphs and dry flies fool these fish. The yahoos have found these lakes, and the campgrounds are now filled with crazies driving like lunatics and playing loud music or something.

Timber Lake: Rainbows do well in this water. Timber Lake is 5 miles of rough road south of Eureka. It has plenty of food, and the trout average a little over a pound. Scud, leech, and damsel imitations work well from a float tube or canoe.

Tobacco River: Access is limited on this Lake Koocanusa tributary, but you can get on it at the county road bridges. The fishing is good with drys for spawning cutthroats early in the season. The cutts like bushy flies like Wulffs, Trudes, and Humpies. There are lots of runs and pools in this underfished (by fly fishers anyway) stream. A 2-pound cutthroat in this river is an intriguing problem, especially on a 3-weight.

Tom Poole Lake: Reached by a couple hundred yards of trail off the Yaak River Road, this lake is planted with westslope cutthroats and is good fishing for fat trout. This is rich water, full of scuds, leeches, and aquatic insects.

Topless Lake: The name is probably politically incorrect these days, but there are some nice rainbows in this small pond lying near Horseshoe Lake. There are trout in the 17- to 20-inch range. Emergers worked in the surface film are productive.

Vinal Lake: Go north on Pipe Creek Road out of Libby, then about 5 miles south of Yaak, take the Vinal Lake Road northeast. Finally take a short hike on level ground to the lake. Good cutthroat fishing in this 18-acre lake for 12-inchers.

Weasel Lake: This is an easy-to-reach lake in relatively unspoiled country in the Whitefish Range. It used to be a great place to go and catch a dinner of cutthroats. But then some government agency in its infinite wisdom built fishing decks around the western shore and a cute little wooden bridge across the creek. The place is now full of tiny (4 inches) cutthroats and some larger ones to over a pound. Radios blast, children frolic, dogs bark. It's good water turned into a Brady Bunch nightmare. Go 30 miles up Grave Creek Road, then follow the signs.

West Fork Yaak River: The West Fork is an average, at best, fishery for small cutthroats that average maybe 6 inches, except in early spring. This time of year bigger fish move up from the main Yaak and you can find 12-inchers.

Wigwam River: The Wigwam flows into Canada not far from the Grave Creek Road. The stream looks like superb fly-fishing water, but holds only a few cutthroats until you sneak across the border and work your way downstream several miles. Pools, runs, and logjams hold trout to 15 inches, and you won't have any company except for the grizzlies, wolves, and perhaps a caribou or two. This is tough country best saved for those who know their way around the woods (and the wildlife).

Wolf Creek: This tributary of the Fisher River looks like fine water early in the year before it shrinks way down. It's followed by paved road most of the way. There is less-than-average angling for small cutthroats, brookies, and some rainbow trout, plus whitefish in the lower reaches.

The Wigwam runs into British Columbia and is a wild, wonderful flow with small cutthroats.

Wolverine Lakes (Upper and Lower): These lakes are reached by a 2-mile hike up Grave Creek Road in the Ten Lakes area. Cutthroats swim here, and the ones that aren't hammered in the early season (July and August after the snow melts some) are good sport in late September. They average a pound or better by that time of year.

Yaak River: Formerly one of the best unknown rivers in the state, logging, second-home yupster style, and increased recreational pressure have hurt this stream a lot. The lower stretch below the impassable (unless you're insane) falls holds some good rainbow, brook, bull, and cutthroat trout up from the Kootenai, plus chunky whitefish. This is bouncing, canyon water, and short casts on the deeper creases and pools work

The Yaak can be good at times for nice-size cutthroats and brook trout. John Holt

best. There are still old-time wet-fly fishermen on the Yaak, and they catch their share of trout on western favorites like the Picket Pin and the Western Bee.

The upper river, much slower water, has nice brook and cutthroat trout, and also ferocious whitefish. Use more delicate dry flies and nymphs here. The upper river is floatable, but *do not* go over the falls. The trip would be painful. Campgrounds and plenty of national forest allow ample opportunity to spend some time in the woods.

Young Creek: Flowing from the west into Lake Koocanusa about 10 miles north of Big Koocanusa Bridge, Young Creek, like most of the reservoir's tributaries, now has good runs of spawning cutthroats (but when any spawning fish is on its redd, leave it alone) that can offer exciting action for fish of several pounds in cramped circumstances. The only problem with all of these streams is that when the snowpack is low and the Corps draws down Koocanusa, the fish have a bit of trouble crossing the mudflats to reach the forest segments of the creeks. No one said life was easy, did they?

Swan

If rivers were conscious entities capable of speech, the Swan River would say something like, "You've clear-cut my drainages and you've scalped my mountainsides, but I still have trout and I always will."

The Swan has endured an incredible amount of logging, both on Forest Service and private land (much of the latter owned by Plum Creek). There has even been some illegal cutting in the Mission Mountains Wilderness Area. Still, there are cutthroat, rainbow, brook, and bull trout in the river.

The size and numbers of the rainbows are rebounding slowly, mostly due to the healing of some old clear-cuts. The Swan is a stronghold of the endangered bull trout.

Although Elk, Goat, Squeezer, and Lion Creeks comprise the annual index, assistance from the US Forest Service and Plum Creek has allowed Montana Fish, Wildlife & Parks to complete total basin-wide counts annually since 1995. The basin-wide redd count averaged 555 during the nineteen-year period from 1995 to 2013. The 2013 basin-wide count of 335 was similar to the previous three years, and was approximately 40 percent below the nineteen-year average.

The exact reasons causing the recent decline in bull trout redd numbers is unknown, but it is likely that twenty years of increasing lake trout numbers is a factor. Lake trout have led to declines in bull trout populations in waters similar to Swan Lake across the region. Biologists began an experimental lake trout removal in 2009 using gill nets as the primary method. The bull trout bycatch associated with this ongoing lake trout removal likely is also reducing bull trout numbers. FWP made a regulation change in 2012 to allow only catch-and-release fishing for bull trout in Swan Lake to offset bycatch mortality.

The populations are also threatened by overfishing, siltation in the spawning tributaries from excessive clear-cutting, and hybridization with another char, the eastern brook trout, but the state is implementing corrective measures to spur a bull trout recovery.

Headwater Tributaries to Lindbergh Lake

The river originates in the snowfields of the Mission Mountains. It has its beginnings in wild waters such as Gray Wolf Lake and Crystal Lake. The streams in this country cascade in a shower of perpetual whitewater, falling toward the valley floor at over 400 feet per mile before leveling out at Lindbergh Lake. The water is not particularly fertile, but some cutthroat and brook trout, a few over 15 inches, are found here.

Swan

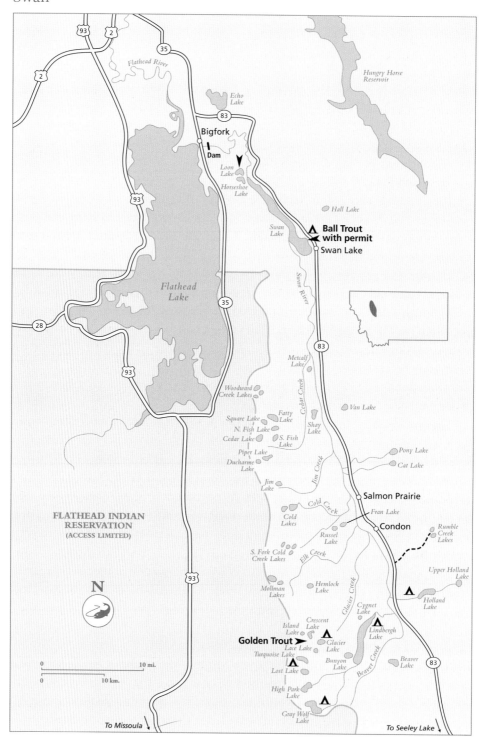

- 93
- 2
- 35
- 2

Flathead River

Echo Lake

- 83

Bigfork
Dam

Loon Lake

Horseshoe Lake

Hall Lake

Swan Lake

Ball Trout with permit
Swan Lake

- 93

Flathead Lake

- 35
- 28
- 93

Swan River

- 83

Metcalf Lake

Woodward Creek Lakes

Van Lake

Square Lake

Fatty Lake

N. Fish Lake

Cedar Creek

Shay Lake

S. Fish Lake

Cedar Lake

Piper Lake

Pony Lake

Ducharme Lake

Cat Lake

Jim Lake

Jim Creek

FLATHEAD INDIAN RESERVATION
(ACCESS LIMITED)

Cold Creek

Salmon Prairie

Fran Lake

Cold Lakes

Condon

Russel Lake

Rumble Creek Lakes

S. Fork Cold Creek Lakes

Elk Creek

N

Mollman Lakes

Hemlock Lake

Upper Holland Lake

Glacier Creek

Cygnet Lake

Holland Lake

- 93

Crescent Lake

Island Lake

Lindbergh Lake

Golden Trout

Glacier Lake

Lace Lake

Turquoise Lake

Bunyon Lake

Beaver Lake

Beaver Creek

- 83

| 0 | 10 mi. |
| 0 | 10 km. |

Lost Lake

High Park Lake

Gray Wolf Lake

Hungry Horse Reservoir

To Missoula ↓

To Seeley Lake ↓

Mouth of Lindbergh Lake to Swan Lake

The Swan doesn't have great numbers of trout. The population of small fish is fair, at best. There are enough rainbows, cutthroats, brookies, and whitefish to provide steady action on a generous day, but even if it had hordes of trout, the Swan would be a tough river to work with a fly in many places.

Most of the private land is posted. You can get in the stream at numerous logging roads, at bridges (at Piper Creek), or at state sites (at Cold Creek and Fatty Creek). But once you reach the water, you still have to fight the brush. Piles of snags and fallen trees break up the stream, forming deep pools that give way to long runs of turquoise water. The swift current cuts under rocky banks. It is hard to wade very far between the high-water marks until well into the summer.

Spring runoff makes the Swan tough and dangerous to fish until late June at the earliest. The current is deceptive and you have to be careful when wading, especially above the snag piles. Being swept underneath one of these—even if you survived—would not be enjoyable. Those same snag piles and the fallen trees make floating for anyone who doesn't know the river intimately extremely dangerous all year.

As the water level starts dropping in late June, decent rainbows and cutthroats can be taken during the day on nymphs worked through, along, and around cover and undercut banks. Good patterns include Marv's Stone (sizes 8 to 4), Hare's Ear (sizes 14 to 10), and Tear Drop (sizes 18 to 12). The key is to get the drifting fly deep, down to the eye level of the fish.

The river doesn't have huge numbers of any one mayfly, just a smattering of various species, but the heavy caddis hatches spark good dry-fly fishing. The Swan supports high populations of net-spinning spotted sedge, little sister sedge, and case-making grannom. Evenings are the best time of day on the Swan to fish; through midsummer the insects draw the fish out from the cover into feeding lanes.

As summer progresses the terrestrials become important on this overgrown water. Hopper patterns, especially a Joe's Hopper fished wet, are consistent. The spruce moth can trigger spectacular surface activity when it is abundant. The evergreen forests of the Swan River corridor provide excellent habitat for the spruce moth, rivaling Rock Creek and the Thompson River as the place to be for the fanatics who chase this bug around the western half of the state. Ants and beetles are other important terrestrials.

One hatch worth chasing in early September on the Swan is the giant orange sedge. This size 8 caddisfly is abundant enough to bring the best fish to the surface, the occasional 15- to 20-inch trout appearing from slots that only seemed to hold 10-inchers before the evening hatch. An Orange Bucktail Caddis standard matches the insect.

The favorite attractors on the Swan are not the most garish ones. More subtle patterns, such as the Irresistible, the Humpy, and the Stimulator, do better for the rainbows. Even the fly sizes should be on the small side, the size 16 to 12 range working better than the 10 to 6 range.

In its upper reaches the river offers a mix of brook, rainbow, and cutthroat trout. As the Swan grows in size, the brook trout give way to the other two species and the overall size of the fish increases somewhat, averaging perhaps a foot, although there are trout considerably larger. Currently the water from Piper Creek down to Swan Lake is under catch-and-release management.

In late May and early June, there are longhorn sedges flitting around and the trout slash and jump for them all day. The fish are chumps for any skittering imitation, such as a size 14 Dark Ginger Dancing Caddis. The best retrieve is a steady, two-handed "run," the rod tucked under the arm and the fly pulled in hand over hand.

FISHING WATERS IN THE SWAN DRAINAGE

Cat Lake: Situated just below Union Peak and 1 mile above Pony Lake, Cat is only 14 acres, but it's over 50 feet deep. There isn't much use fishing anything but the edges. There are cutthroats up to 14 inches once you get here, but this is not easy country to move around in.

Cedar Creek: The upper 8 miles are followed by trail (all the way to Cedar Lake); the lower 3 miles are followed by logging road. Cedar is good cutthroat and brook trout water.

Cold Lakes: Pretty country to hike into, access is by a mile of good trail starting at the end of the Cold Creek Road. The two lakes are each about 80 acres and very deep. Like most of the higher-elevation lakes in the Missions, they are not fishable until well into the summer. Snow and ice make hiking tough, and the waters are sometimes still frozen over until July. Both lakes hold good numbers of cutthroats up to 16 inches.

Crescent Lake: Crescent was planted with goldens years ago, but there are few (if any) of these left. The trail is a steep mile or so of switchbacks from the end of Kraft Creek Road. Crescent is now stocked periodically with cutthroats, and fishing is nice in September following the plant. Dry flies, especially generic types such as the Adams or the Black Gnat, produce as the fish cruise back and forth in groups along the shore and across the inlet.

Fatty Lake: Go to the top of the Fatty Creek Road and then hoof up a poor trail that follows the creek for 1.5 miles to this 21-acre lake. The shoreline is swampy and brushy, and there is mud in the shallows. This makes Fatty a spot for the float tube or a canoe. The fishing is fast and furious on a good day for regularly planted cutthroats that average 12 inches and a few rainbows that are 18 to 20 inches.

Fran Lake: Located in timbered and logged country on the Swan Range side of the river, Fran is reached via logging roads near Condon. The lake is small but good for rainbows and cutthroats up to 15 inches. There are also a few Kamloop rainbows cruising here, and these fish (a wonderful strain of stillwater trout originally from British Columbia) grow bigger and fatter than the other residents.

Glacier Creek: This ice-cold, sapphire-blue stream, the outlet of Glacier Lake, looks wonderful for trout, but except for some swampy, meadow stretches in the middle, it's not too hot. That middle section (also known as Glacier Slough) is worth fishing from July to September with ant, beetle, caterpillar, and grasshopper imitations. The fish there are more plentiful and a bit larger (up to 12 inches instead of 10 inches). In the creek section just below Glacier Lake, there are some good trout, too—cutthroats, rainbows, and brooks. This is beautiful forest where it hasn't been logged, but the pristine areas shrink yearly in this country.

Glacier Lake: Reached by a 30-minute walk on the trail at the end of the Kraft Creek Road, this 103-acre lake sits in scenic country (overrun with hikers in the summer) and is good fishing by wading or float tubing (if you drag one in) for cutthroats averaging 10 inches. The exciting aspect of Glacier Lake is that there are a few fish that grow out of the "cookie-cutter" mold of the planters and get much larger.

Gray Wolf Lake: Reached by a steep, 9-mile climb from the end of Beaver Creek Road, this lake sits below a glacier (telling the wise man something about the climate up there). The ground around 300-acre Gray Wolf is mostly rock slope and boulders. With nothing to slow down the wind, the lake surface is typically churned to a froth. Gray Wolf is extremely temperamental for 10- to 20-inch cutthroats, but the fish cruise the shorelines on occasion. Try a Hare's Ear Nymph worked parallel to the bank.

Hall Lake: The hike in is only 5 miles from scenic downtown Swan Lake, but it is a 3,000-foot climb up to this 12-acre, deep water. Hall Lake is planted heavily with cutthroats. The average fish is 12 inches, but a good trout runs 15 inches.

Heart (or Hart) Lake: The middle lake in the Island-Heart-Crescent chain, it's the best of the three. Unfortunately they have all been hurt by overfishing. Goldens were planted in the 1960s, but except for some bright cutthroats that apparently had licentious relationships with their California cousins, there are none of those goldens left here. The fishing ranges from poor to fair for 12- to 16-inch cutthroats.

Hemlock Lake: Not far up the Kraft Creek Road (there are signs), it is about a 4-mile hike into this 30-acre lake. Hemlock is not as wild or scenic as the higher-up stuff in the Missions, but there is a nice population of 10- to 13-inch cutthroats here.

High Park Lake: This is another high-elevation, way-back, big-water, quite-windy-most-of-the-time lake in the Missions. To get there, go to Lindbergh Lake, hike 2.5 miles to Crystal Lake, and then hike another 2 miles to High Park. It is not easy to get to, but the fishing is often solid during the calm morning hours for 10- to 15-inch cutthroats. They hit all manner of flies well (out of loneliness, if for no other reason). This is good country in the fall if winter doesn't sneak up out of nowhere. Then you are in trouble.

Holland Lake: A summer-home lake replete with a nice log lodge, it is pretty water, with too many boats in the summer. But there are some very nice trout here. The best fly-fishing months are early and late in the year. Rainbow and cutthroat trout, along with kokanee salmon and lots of whitefish, are found here. The cutthroats especially seem to like dry flies, and they'll cruise the shoreline all day looking for something to eat (except in the summer when watercraft make this life-threatening). There are public and private campgrounds here also. This is one of the "gateways" to the Bob Marshall Wilderness.

Horseshoe Lake: Smallmouth bass (and very fat sunfish) live here. If this lake was in the Ozarks, it would attract hordes of eager bass anglers. It is 9 miles east of Bigfork. Lots of people fish for the 1- to 4-pound smallmouths found here, but few anglers really seem to understand the habits of this species. You can use a float tube or boat

Horseshoe Lake offers some very good smallmouth bass fishing.

to cover the main basin (which never gets deeper than 15 feet). The smallmouths in Horseshoe feed as much on insects as they do on minnows and crayfish. They gorge on damselfly nymphs, and they rise to Callibaetis mayflies. The south shoreline, with dense beds of lily pads, is a consistent area for active fish. The water is clear, and a leader tapered to 4X, and sometimes 5X, is often the secret to fooling the smallmouths.

Island Lake: Even with a map, this is a difficult lake to find. The trail fades away to nothing a mile or so above Heart Lake. Most of the time you end up bushwhacking through steep, brushy, wet country. It's a tough go in alpine country. Island has a few small goldens (to 10 inches?), remnants of a 1960s plant. The fish are finicky, and the best bet is to cast a small Olive Woolly Worm, let the thing sink, and then give it a few twitches.

Jim Creek: This creek drains out of the Jim Lake complex. The private holdings were ravaged by logging into the nineties, destroying not only the aesthetics of the area, but also the trout population of the west fork of the stream. Decades more are needed for recovery.

Jim Lake: This used to be fantastic timbered country full of grouse, elk, bear, deer, woodpeckers, and fish until Plum Creek ravaged the timber on its holdings (and left an eyesore for years to come). There is an ongoing management program in the basin for cutthroats, but the clear-cuts spoil the fun.

You can drive right into the first lake, which used to be wonderful for cutts (as did several of the upper waters). North of Condon, take the Cold Lake Road west and follow the signs. Above the first lake there are maybe a dozen more, along with ponds and bogs, in the Mission Mountains Wilderness. All of them have cutthroats up to 12 inches, a few larger.

Lace Lake: Lace lies just below Turquoise Lake in the Missions (and is connected to it by a small stream). There are lots of fat, dark-sided cutthroats up to 15 inches in this 18.5-acre lake. It is much easier pickings than Turquoise.

There are lots of shallow-water depressions in this country that pretend to be lakes, but instead are just barren potholes. Two of those, Jewell and Lagoon, are especially easy to confuse with Lace. An angler's instinct plays an important part in avoiding "lakes" like these, but when in doubt, an hour of observation will usually save a lot of casting.

Loon Lake: Drive the 1.5-mile gravel road off the Swan Lake highway to reach the public fishing access. Loon has planter trout, mostly rainbows, in the cooler sections, but it is an especially fine place for warmwater fly fishing, featuring both smallmouths (to 3 pounds) and largemouths (to 5 pounds). The 44-acre lake is mostly deep water (50 feet maximum), except on one end.

The entire shoreline is good wherever there's structure. There are fallen trees and a few docks spaced around the lake. The north end is shallower, with bays and weeds. The pre-spawn period usually runs from the third week of May until mid-June. The key water temperature for the best topwater action is 58 degrees Fahrenheit. Once the shallows get into the 60s, the bass are looking up. Leeches and Woolly Buggers in black, olive, brown, and burnt orange complete a good basic selection for bass. All of these patterns can be carried in sizes 4 to 2/0.

Metcalf Lake: One of the premier trophy trout waters in the state, Metcalf is currently under special regulations—one trout daily in possession with a 22-inch minimum length; artificial flies and lures only. It is a 13-acre, lowland lake 14 miles south of Swan Lake. There are no real inlets, but there are underwater springs at the north end. This is the best area during June and July to find rising rainbows, the fish sometimes leaping to take adult damsels in the mornings. Either adult damsel imitations on the surface or damsel nymph imitations on the bottom (especially the Floating Damsel Nymph worked with a fast-sinking line so that it swims just over the weed tops) are effective around the springs for trout up to 26 inches. Metcalf warms up too much in August, pushing the fishing into a brief slump. The trout start feeding heavily again in the fall.

Mollman Lakes: These two lakes and a pothole lie way back in the Missions. A trail comes up the North Fork of Elk Creek, but it wanders around some. All of these waters are managed for cutthroats, which average 12 inches but occasionally top 16 inches. The difference in elevation between the two lakes may be the height of a bar stool. Don't overlook that little pond below the lower lake—it can be good at times.

North Fish Lake: One of those spots for anglers who dislike crowds. It is not easy to find, but take a good map and a compass and work up the North Fork of Cedar Creek. The cutthroats planted in North Fish do very well.

Notlimah Lake: Sometimes confused with the Glacier Sloughs, this 1.25-mile "wide-spot" is several hundred swampy yards farther upstream. There are cutthroat and brook trout here up to roughly 12 inches. Tough maneuvering in the bog, with mosquitoes and bears.

Rumble Creek Lakes: These two lakes (27 acres and 11 acres) hold out high up on the flanks of Holland Peak in the Swans. They are good for cutthroats ranging up to 14 inches, especially just after ice-out (surprise!). They are a bit tough to reach because there is, at best, a faint trail. The Rumble Creek drainage is not the easiest route in. Go to the Cooney Lookout, hike the main ridge until the lakes are in sight, and then head cross-country.

Russ Lake: One of three lakes, Russ lies in the Swan River bottomlands. They are easy to reach by a logging road (across from the Condon Ranger District building). Russ, at 10 acres, is the uppermost and largest of the three. It's fine fishing for cutthroats and rainbows, with good numbers of trout up to 15 inches.

Shay Lake: Rainbows and grayling inhabit this deep, 20-acre lake not far off the very rough Fatty Creek logging road. The grayling are an oddity in this area, and that alone makes it worth a visit. The rainbow fishing is good for 8- to 14-inchers.

South Fork Cold Creek Lakes: This long string of thirteen lakes, as small as 3 acres and as large as 20 acres, chains through rough, buggy, and swampy country. Not all of these lakes have fish, but all of the larger ones do. The better ones harbor good populations of 10- to 15-inch rainbows. The hike to the first lake, starting from the South Fork Road, is only a mile, but this country is still not overrun with people carrying fly rods.

Square Lake: Good for 10- to 16-inch cutthroats, Square Lake is up in the Fatty Creek drainage in country so rough, with no real trail, that reaching it is a much greater challenge than fishing it.

Swan Lake: Thousands of acres, 10 miles long by one mile wide with an average depth of 52 feet. This is a tough piece of water for the fly fisher unless you happen to be out when things are calm and some cutthroats or rainbows are rising (a rare occurrence) along with nonnative lake trout.

The fifth year of targeted gillnetting by FWP to remove nonnative lake trout in Swan Lake wrapped up in late October 2013. A total of 6,988 lake trout ranging in size from 5 to 36 inches were removed by gill nets during the juvenile netting portion of the project, which was conducted from August 12 to August 30, 2013. This time period was chosen because most adult bull trout are on their spawning run in the Swan River system and are absent from the lake. Bull trout bycatch was 200 fish. Similar to previous years, 64 percent of these bull trout were able to be released alive (72 actual mortalities). Netting conducted along the lake trout spawning area later in the fall (October 7–25) resulted in catching an additional 210 adult lake trout. Spawning lake trout ranged in size from 20 to 36 inches. Bull trout bycatch was consistent with previous years, with an additional 135 bull trout captured during fall netting (67 percent of these bull trout were released alive, with 44 actual mortalities). All lake trout less than 22 inches in length were cleaned, packed on ice, and sent to local area food banks for distribution.

The best places to fish Swan Lake blind are off the river mouth or along the flats on the south end (and this is also the prime area for bass and pike). There is a large wildlife refuge at the southern end of the lake; a campground, a restaurant, and summer homes are scattered along the rest of the east and north shoreline. MT 83 runs the length of the east side of the lake.

Turquoise Lake: More big water high up in the southern end of the Missions. The few trout I've seen here have been either 12 inches or several pounds, and neither cared much for my offerings. A lot of people come in here (although anglers generally concentrate on Lace Lake right below it). The entire drainage is pretty, but crowded in the summer.

Upper Holland Lake: Go to Holland Lake to hit the trailhead for the 2.5-mile hike to Upper Holland. This lake sits way up near the Swan Crest. It has spooky cutthroat trout that grow long and snaky. These can be caught by the stealthy angler, but even in choppy water a 16-foot leader tapered to at least 6X is a necessity. And don't go big on the flies—size 16 is about the maximum in my experience. There is a campground on the east shore.

Van Lake: Accessible by 2 miles of logging road off the Swan River Road, signs lead the way. Van is managed for rainbows and is fair to good for 12-inchers. It is especially good in the spring. A boat or a float tube is essential equipment; trees and bushes crowding the water all the way around the lake make walking brutal.

Woodward Creek Lakes: Reached by decrepit logging road, these lakes are managed for cutthroats. There's not a lot of pressure here.

DRAINAGES EAST OF THE CONTINENTAL DIVIDE

The Beaverhead is one of the top big-brown trout waters in Montana, but it can be quite tough to fish. Access is difficult, unless by raft. This is water for the experienced fly fisher. John Holt

Beaverhead River

The Beaverhead is one of the premier rivers anywhere to connect with large browns, and to a lesser extent, rainbows—fish well over 5 pounds—but it is rarely easy. It is the type of river that humbles even the most skilled anglers all too frequently, but then there are other times when the rainbows and browns pounce on any fly drifting by their noses. The amount of light, as much as anything, seems to control the fishing. A bright sun is tough; to find rising trout after late June, fish early or late in the day or on overcast days.

Tuck casts, mending the line in the air, pinpoint accuracy to tiny pockets that fly by in an instant, maintaining steady contact with a couple of down-deep nymphs—all of these skills are needed to fool the big trout holding in the river. And once hooked, bringing the fish to net is another matter.

The river features a difficult array of undercut banks, thick weed beds, runs, riffles, and deep pools. This water can be as challenging as fly fishing gets in Montana, or anywhere else for that matter. As a friend of mine once said after a tough October outing, "If you can catch fish on the Beaverhead, you can catch them anywhere."

Because of its popularity and heavy use by anglers, new regulations are constantly evolving. The following are now in play. (It cannot be stressed enough how important it is to consult current FWP regulations for this and all rivers in Montana. The situation is extremely fluid—no pun intended.)

- Clark Canyon Dam to Pipe Organ Bridge: open third Saturday in May through November 30.

- High Bridge FAS to Henneberry FAS: closed to float fishing by nonresidents and float outfitting on each Saturday from the third Saturday in May through Labor Day.

- Henneberry FAS to Pipe Organ Bridge: closed to float fishing by nonresidents and float outfitting on each Sunday from the third Sunday in May through Labor Day.

- Downstream from Pipe Organ Bridge: open entire year.

- Highway 91 South Bridge (Tash Bridge) to Selway Bridge: closed to float outfitting from the third Saturday in May through Labor Day.

Beaverhead River

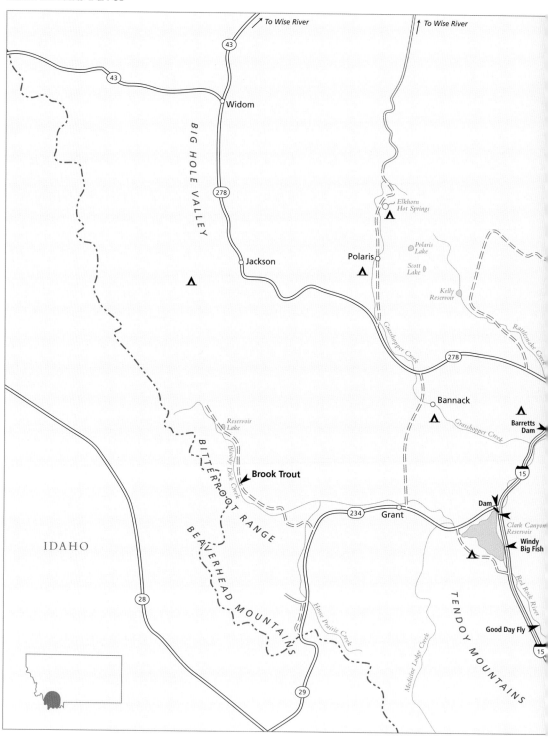

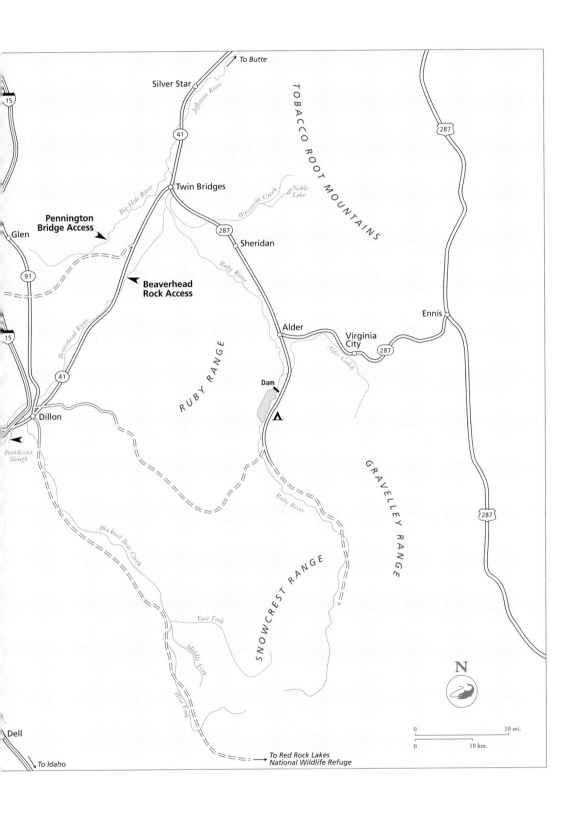

To Butte

Silver Star

15

Jefferson River

41

TOBACCO ROOT MOUNTAINS

Twin Bridges

Wisconsin Creek

Noble Lake

Big Hole River

Pennington Bridge Access

Glen

287

Sheridan

91

Ruby River

Beaverhead Rock Access

15

Beaverhead River

Alder

Virginia City

Ennis

287

287

RUBY RANGE

Dam

Dillon

41

Poindexter Slough

Alder Gulch

GRAVELLEY RANGE

287

Ruby River

Blacktail Bear Creek

SNOWCREST RANGE

East Fork

Middle Fork

West Fork

N

Dell

To Idaho

To Red Rock Lakes National Wildlife Refuge

0   10 mi.

0   10 km.

There is an "old" way and a "contemporary" way to fish the river. The Beaverhead's reputation for large trout was built with the old-style, chuck-and-duck methods. Anglers hammered large weighted streamers, or two big Girdle Bus, tight to the bank. The leaders were short, minimum 15-pound test, and when the fisherman either hooked the overhanging willow branches or a very big trout, he just leaned back and hoped that something would come out of the tangles.

"It's not really a Woolly Bugger, Yuk Bug, and Girdle Bug river anymore," says Tim Tollett, a Dillon Outfitter and guide. "You can still catch big fish that way, but the trout see those flies so much that they become extremely wary.

"Even when somebody's home in a good hole and you make a perfect cast and retrieve, the trout won't always take."

State fisheries biologist Dick Oswald agrees, saying that pattern selection has become more varied and the size of the flies has gone way down. "The overall trend in the last nine years has been from crude fishing with Girdle Bugs and 15- to 20-pound tippets to smaller nymphs and finer leaders. The big, ugly stuff used to hold sway, but it is not very often that you do well with that approach now."

So is the old way ever worth trying? On overcast, windy days, the fish still seem to get silly and will chase the big flies. The most popular patterns for this method are the simplest ones to tie and the reason is plain—this is not for the timid. You have to slam the flies back into the cover cast after cast, expecting to lose a dozen or so flies in a day.

The contemporary way uses nymphs that at least generally imitate the predominant insect forms of the river. Some of the best patterns are the Partridge and Peacock, Red Squirrel Nymph, Hare's Ear, Dark Olive Brown Flashback, Callibaetis Nymph, Little Beaverhead Stone, George's Brown Stone, Bead-Head Pheasant Tail, and Deep Sparkle Pupa (especially as the tail fly on a two-fly dropper rig) in sizes 10 through 16. It's also possible to do well with larger patterns, such as T's Crane Nymph, that imitate the abundant cranefly larvae of the river.

POPULAR NYMPHS

Bead-Head Pheasant Tail	Little Beaverhead Stone
Brown Flashback	Prince
Copper John	Partridge and Peacock
Dark Olive Brown	Red Squirrel
Flashback	Scuds—pink, gray, tan
George's Brown Stone	T's-Crane Nymph
Hare's Ear	Tungsten Tailwater
Lightning Bug	

The upper Beaverhead can be slower, placid, and, as always, tough to fish. It's shown here not far from the interstate south of Dillon.

The modern style of blind fishing the Beaverhead still focuses on those overgrown banks and the deeper pools. The key is a dead drift instead of an active retrieve. The problem is the dead part of the drift. It ain't easy and it ain't pretty. Whether wading or floating downstream in a boat, you are always casting across the swift water in the middle of the river. You have to mend a big, upstream belly of line to get any kind of drift.

With a river current greater than 5 miles per hour, running against tight corners and through swirling holes more than 10 feet deep, fishing from a boat can be really frantic. There isn't much time to plan the cast and drift. You get a quick glance ahead to find the next pocket, and then you have to throw the fly almost instinctively dead tight to the bank.

Your casts have to angle downstream. You can't wait until the line is on the water to mend—you have to loop the big, upstream belly while the line is still in the air. There are probably at least one or two lead twist-ons on the leader to make the nymphs get down quickly. There's probably a big strike indicator, which hinges the leader and catches air. And remember, the casts have to be dead accurate. All this adds to the casting excitement for angler and guide alike.

Leave the 3-weight rods at home; 6- and 7-weight rods are more practical. Weight-forward and shooting-taper lines predominate around here. The leaders run from 7 to 12 feet. A 3X tippet is nice for feel, but a good fish will smoke this like it's a spider web. But if you go larger than 3X, you lose contact with the flies and have trouble detecting the strikes.

Sound like fun?

The Beaverhead can be a great dry-fly river, but three factors control the fishing. The light conditions, the intensity of the hatches, and the rate of water flow all determine how many fish come to the surface. For most of the summer, during a normal year, the only chance the angler has to find feeders is either early, from daybreak to 6:30 a.m., or late, from 8 p.m. until dark. And even then, it takes a heavy hatch to get the trout interested in the surface.

The flow of the river is controlled entirely by Clark Canyon Dam. The water is delivered from Clark Canyon to Barrett's Diversion for irrigation. During a hot, dry summer, like 2012, the Beaverhead roars bank full down to the diversion because the fields need a lot of moisture. Below the diversion, it can be reduced to a trickle. But during a cool, wet summer, the river above Barrett's runs low and very fishable because the fields get enough water from nature.

POPULAR DRY FLIES

CDC Caddis	Little Olive Trude
Elk Hair Caddis	Little Yellow Trude
Flame Thrower	Olive Serendipity
Fluttering Damsel	Sparkle Spider
Get-R-Dun	Tim's Cicada
Goddard Caddis	

The upper Beaverhead offers the occasional opportunity to take big browns on tiny flies.

During almost any year the river offers excellent dry-fly fishing before the irrigation season begins in the spring and after the irrigation season ends in the fall. There's always a lull in irrigating during August, too—the ranchers stop watering so that they can get their first cutting of hay.

Even during the heaviest flows, there's the chance to catch large trout on dry flies in the huge backwaters on the Beaverhead. These are scum-covered, swirling eddies that collect bits of vegetation, occasional logs, lots of foam, and uncountable dead or dying insects. The trout sit in these reverse currents and sip insects for hours. These spots can't be fished effectively from a boat; you have to know where the eddies are on the river. You can creep up to one and work fussy trout for hours.

Biologist Dick Oswald says, "The weather makes or breaks you. One day I hid in the willows during a real goose drowner—thunder, lightning, wind, rain. In the two hours after this storm, I had some of the best fishing ever. I suppose if somebody really studied this, they would figure it out, but I haven't."

Like most tailwaters, the Beaverhead has a "small community" of insects. This means that there aren't many different species of mayflies, caddisflies, stoneflies, and two-winged flies, but the ones that are there occur in incredible numbers. The outbreaks of huge hatches must be experienced to be believed. A fly on the surface is often lost in the thundering herd of emerging, breeding, egg-laying, and just plain dying bugs.

The important hatches include mayflies such as the blue-winged olive (especially since they appear in the spring and fall during low water), pale morning dun, trico, Callibaetis, and little blue-winged olive; caddisflies such as the grannom, longhorn sedge, spotted sedge, and little sister sedge; the smaller stoneflies such as the little olive stone and the little yellow stone; and one great two-winged fly, those monstrous parodies of mosquitoes, the cranefly.

The hatches of craneflies, those semiaquatic larvae that live in the soft, muddy edges, can be phenomenal. The Beaverhead, with its overgrown banks, provides the perfect habitat for this insect. On summer mornings, at the first glow of dawn, the adults fly and lay eggs, skimming the surface. The trout roll and jump for these big, size 6 to 10, flies. A matching orange fly, maybe a variant-style pattern, such as the Flame Thrower, or even a Hewitt Skating Spider, draws the same kind of splashy, heart-bumping strikes.

The popular emergers and dry flies on the Beaverhead contain a mix of proven standards and new inventions. The Elk Hair Caddis, Goddard Caddis, and Emergent Sparkle Pupa are standard for the caddis hatches—the CDC Caddis is finding a place among that famous trio. The Sparkle Dun and the Parachute are the main styles for adult mayflies—no single emerger has caught on for the river, maybe because it is so hard to float and see a flush fly on this turbulent water. Little Yellow and Little Olive Trude patterns match the stoneflies. The Olive Serendipity is a popular midge imitation.

CLARK CANYON DAM TO BARRETT'S DIVERSION

Clark Canyon Reservoir was completed in 1964, and the tailrace of this concrete dam is the beginning of the Beaverhead. The releases, although they fluctuate widely, now insure adequate flows of cold water. Moisture patterns in this part of Montana have been capricious in the past few decades, to say the least, but enough precipitation normally falls to fill the reservoir partially if not brim full.

Under so-called ideal conditions, starting in May the rate of flow rises to around 500 to 700 cfs, compared to the winter rates in the 200 to 250 cfs range (some dry winters see flows dropping down into the 35 to 50 cfs range). During the peak of the irrigation season in June and July, the releases rise to 900 to 1,100 cfs, but drop for the haying season in August to 600 to 700 cfs.

The Beaverhead doesn't lie in a valley surrounded by towering mountain ranges like many of the quality streams in the state. It flows through irrigated pastureland. Rolling hills studded with rugged rock outcroppings flank the river.

Water flow is still the most important factor for fish populations. After a series of good winters, there are literally tons of trout present in every mile of water. A general figure would be 2,500 pounds of browns and 1,500 pounds of rainbows per mile. Dick Oswald, not totally at ease with using these numbers, prefers to cite 550 trout of 18 inches and up per mile.

"The river has an incredible capacity to bounce back from bad periods," says Oswald. "During electroshocking surveys in the spring and fall, I handle a hell of a lot of fish between 5 and 10 pounds and a few of the bizarre monsters up to 15 pounds in the upper river."

BARRETT'S DIVERSION TO DILLON

Because of the rather gentle topography surrounding the Beaverhead drainage, the river is almost totally dependent on releases from the dam to maintain adequate flow and temperature for the fish. The effects of runoff and summer snowmelt are not as dramatic here as on other rivers in the Rocky Mountain West.

Twelve miles below Clark Canyon Dam, Barrett's Diversion siphons off as much as two-thirds of the water in the river. The effect of less flow, leaving the fish to freeze in the winter and bake in the summer, depresses both the number and size of the trout. And there are fewer rainbow trout down here, making up only 5 percent of the population by the time the river reaches Dillon; the rainbows virtually disappear below town.

This is not as depressing as it sounds. The stretch from the diversion to Dillon is the favorite water on the Beaverhead for many fly fishers. This section is easily wadeable, whereas the upper river is mostly float fishing. There are good hatches of pretty much the same insects as the upper area, and the trout rise well when the bugs are out. There's the occasional big fish here, but most of the browns are 10 to 16 inches. The trout are so much more accessible on this portion that the numbers caught during a typical day can be much higher—twenty to thirty fish on the water below the diversion versus six to ten fish on the water above it.

The fish are primarily brown trout, and that means casting close to or into cover. The banks are much more open down here. Some sections were riprapped for the highway; even natural sections have as much grass as trees on the banks. Bulky, attractor dry flies, such as a Humpy or Madam X, pounded into the notches of the boulders, or buggy nymphs, such as a Zug Bug or Fray Nymph, washed against the rocks, can pull fish out all day long. If the riprap sections don't produce, small streamers, such as a Muddler or a Brown and Yellow Matuka, work consistently in areas with standing clumps of willows, with deep shade and dark water, against the bank. And if the trout won't cooperate during the heat of the day, there are plenty of whitefish in the riffles and pools that will take any small nymph.

But the real fun here comes with the dependable rises every evening during the summer. This is great caddisfly water. The spotted sedge (size 12 or 14, with brown wings and a yellowish body) and the little sister sedge (size 16 or 18, with tan wings and light ginger body) start flying as soon as the heat of the day fades and build in numbers until dark. The trout feed on all stages—an Emergent Sparkle Pupa works for the emerging insect, the Elk Hair Caddis works for the clumsy, mating adults that fall on the currents, and the Diving Caddis matches the egg-layers that go underwater.

DILLON TO THE MOUTH OF THE RUBY RIVER

The river below town is capricious. It's really sucked low and it gets too warm most of the summer for good fishing. There is some irrigation return as you move downstream, but that water is not only warm, but overfertilized and murky.

In the fall, when the river runs clearer, fish streamers for the browns. There are few anglers and a good fish now and then. The biggest ones are in the 4- to 5-pound range. The way to cover this section is with a canoe or similar watercraft, getting out and concentrating on the mouths of some of the spring creeks. The access isn't good, so not many waders here.

MOUTH OF THE RUBY RIVER TO THE BIG HOLE RIVER

If there is a "sleeper" section, this is it. The Ruby River (source of so much litigation and bad vibes) enters the Beaverhead 3 miles above Twin Bridges. The cold, clear, and constant flow of the Ruby sparks a jump in trout populations. Some of these fish—the browns still predominating—are very good size.

The trick is to avoid high flows of the irrigation season and rainy periods. Either one of these situations mucks up the water, turning the river to brown soup. It wasn't always this way on the lower Beaverhead. The river used to run cleaner, if not crystal clear, through Twin Bridges. The banks are so eroded now by cattle that any flush of water washes dirt into the flow. The state biologists in this region are studying this problem and might be able to work with the ranches to stabilize the stream margins.

This is dry-fly heaven when the water is fairly clear. The best months are September through November. Until the first frosts, grasshopper imitations, anything from a Joe's Hopper to a Dave's Hopper, pull up fish. With the overcast days of fall, and the start of the blue-winged olive hatches, the browns take positions in every good feeding lane and rise with that nose, back, and tail sequence from 1 p.m. to about 3:30 p.m.

The Beaverhead offers something for most fly fishers. The upper water demands long, hard days, usually from a boat, for the chance to catch trophy trout. The section below the diversion, easily waded, is more consistent fishing for smaller trout. Anyone who wants to be alone on a stream can explore the lower river. A visitor, to do justice to the river, should spend a minimum of five days in the area. Anyone who tries to figure out this stream by himself the first time is going to have some long, frustrating hours. On the Beaverhead, more than on most rivers in the state, a guide is a good investment. But even for the devoted do-it-your-selfer, the truly masochistic, the trout are here and waiting.

ALDER GULCH AND THE VIRGINIA CITY DREDGE PONDS

Alder Gulch runs right beside MT 287 east of Virginia City. The creek has some rainbows and brookies, but is small and brushy. The many dredge ponds dotted along the stream course provide much more interesting action for larger fish up to several pounds. Low profiles, long leaders, and small nymphs are most often successful, but there are hatches (including a consistent Callibaetis) on the ponds, and dry flies come into play on occasion. Always watch the head of any pond, too, where the creek enters—hatching stream insects drift down into the still water and trout line up to sip on these lost souls. The ponds are not the most aesthetically pleasing fly fishing in the world, unless you really like mine tailings and dredge holes, but they are challenging spots.

BLACKTAIL DEER CREEK

Near its mouth this stream suffers all the typical degradations of a ranchland stream—the cattle-pounded banks, the herbicide and waste runoffs, and the water extractions—but a few miles above Dillon it becomes a great-looking, quality stream. The Blacktail muddies quickly with even a modest rain (and should be avoided at these times) even in the upper stretches, but there are lots of deep holes connected by gentle runs. The stream is filled with brookies, fat and beautifully colored fish up to 14 inches, with some rainbows and the occasional fat brown running up from the river.

CR 202, just south of Dillon, follows the stream most of the way, right up to the headwaters in the Snowcrest Range. There's good access outside of town. What works in the Beaverhead works here, but with less effort. Bright streamers, such as the classic Mickey Finn, do wonders with the brookies if the water is at all cloudy. With clear water conditions, simple upstream presentations with dry flies or nymphs take fish from runs and pools. The most notable hatches are the early June caddis flights.

FISHING WATERS IN THE BEAVERHEAD DRAINAGE

Bloody Dick Creek: Bloody Dick has superb brook trout fishing for fish up to a foot or so in world-class mosquito country (.28 gauges recommended). Access is spotty; your best bet is west of Clark Canyon Reservoir from Horse Prairie Creek. It is extremely overgrown and difficult to fish in some stretches; other parts of the stream are more open, meadow terrain. Guess which sections have the biggest trout? Some rainbows and mountain whitefish also swim here.

Clark Canyon Reservoir: This is a quality, big-fish water planted with several hundred thousand rainbows each year. These rainbows, some browns, and plenty of battling carp regularly reach weights of over 5 pounds. This is one of the best places in the state to wear your arm out playing big trout at certain times of the year. When it's hot, it's hot.

Some of the prime areas of the lake include the inlet areas of both the Red Rock River and Horse Prairie Creek, especially in the spring and fall, and the east side of the lake (the highway side) at Willows Beach. The rainbows, looking for spawning areas, cruise the long gravel flat in the spring. In front of Lone Tree Campground, there's another long flat that extends to the west, attracting rainbows in the spring until the water level of the lake drops and exposes the bottom. The south side of the big island is a good midsummer spot, but the trout hold deep during midday and it takes a sinking line to reach the 8- to 15-feet-deep holding water. At the west side of the dam the trout congregate during the summer at the 15-foot level. And a quarter mile off Lookout Point is always a good area for blind prospecting.

The fish that are growing well, reaching 14 to 15 inches as two-years-old, are the Eagle Lake strain of rainbows. These trout are stocked in such huge numbers, and they're such aggressive feeders, that they actually make it harder for anglers to take the bigger rainbows and browns. The trick when the schools of young fish are grabbing everything is to use larger flies on the bottom. The 4- to 8-inch tiddlers will keep tapping big streamers, such as a size 2 Clouser Minnow, Olive Zonker, or Silver Crystal Flash Woolly Bugger.

There is an old road that heads out from the south and offers easy access for float tubers and boaters to bays and submerged brush along the southeastern shore near the inlet of the Red Rock River. This is the prime area for insect hatches—at ice-out it's midges; by June the damselflies are emerging; the Callibaetis mayflies show up for most of the summer; there's a spotty hatch of tricos, but the spinner fall attracts gulpers from August through early October.

There are other good locations, many of them, on Clark Canyon Reservoir, but on this 5,000-acre (in rare years when it reaches full pool) lake, cutting the water down to size is a necessity. There are tons of trash fish here also. Keep an eye on the winds, usually from the north to northwest. They can make life in a float tube a difficult and dangerous proposition.

Grasshopper Creek: This stream is like a little Beaverhead. It has most of the same hatches—the mayflies (blue-winged olives, pale morning duns, and tricos) and the caddisflies (grannom, spotted sedge, and little sister sedge)—and when the water is clear and the trout are rising, a decent match takes more fish than a general fly. Drys like small Humpies, especially an Adams tie, for the mayflies and Elk Hair Caddis for the caddisflies are standards. Of course, grasshopper imitations work well here all summer, but the smaller, size 8 to 12 patterns are better for the 10- to 16-inch fish than the monstrous imitations. The only problem with this creek is that it muddies immediately and badly with the slightest rain, and runs so turbid that it even discolors the entire Beaverhead once it joins with the main river.

Grasshopper takes its time flowing down through open, hay-and-sage flat country, on past the ghost town of Bannack, alongside some mining areas, through a dozen miles of canyon, and then into the Beaverhead. The upper reaches are about 20 feet wide with undercut, grassy banks. Some brown trout of size move up from the river into this stretch, providing good fall action on streamers. The resident trout do well all year, including rainbows and brookies. Don't worry about the rattlesnakes. They're too busy fighting off the mosquitoes.

Kelly Reservoir: This one lies above 7,000 feet west of Dillon and is reached by a real bad road up Rattlesnake Creek. To the native Montanan a road like this is the reason companies make four-wheel-drive trucks. Nonetheless, it's popular and good fishing for 7- to 11-inch brookies and rainbows.

Poindexter Slough: Extremely well known, particularly by spring creek fanatics, it's a classic; and, thanks to the efforts of the Nature Conservancy working with the Montana Department of Fish, Wildlife & Parks, it's available to everyone. It's easy to find—I-90 passes directly over it right outside Dillon. There are deep holes and narrow channels surrounded by thick beds of aquatic plants that wave gently in the clear currents. During the summer the hummocks of watercress get so thick that they force the water out of the streambed. The fish can graze in this salad for scuds anytime, but they quickly focus on the surface during the hatches.

 The fishing is year-round. There are no crowds. A recent October trip found the water deserted and the fishing good with a size 16 Pheasant Tail. When midges are on the water, a Griffith's Gnat for the adult usually works. Caddisflies abound here. The early grannom caddis, also known as the Mother's Day hatch, doesn't wait for May. In a warm year it is going well by mid-April. A dark Elk Hair Caddis is an effective

Sometimes slow-moving Poindexter Slough can be easy to fish with small drys. At other times, trying to predict the behavior of these capricious, difficult trout is like playing chess with a madman.

match for the egg-layers. Some of the species of small, spring creek caddisflies are very important here—the speckled peter has a concentrated emergence during late June; the weedy water sedge shows during June and July; the little sister sedge peaks in July but stays around all summer; the midsummer grannom becomes very important in August; and the varicolored microcaddis may be only a size 22 insect, but in the fall it is so abundant that the trout feed on emergers readily. It seems that with all of these small caddisflies, the trout lock onto the emerging, pupal stage.

Terrestrials are important all summer—a tribute to the lush meadows of this protected area—and not only grasshopper patterns but beetle and ant patterns make good searching flies.

Blue-winged olives hatch well in both the spring (April 10 through May 10) and the fall (September 10 through October). The pale morning duns and the tricos—the latter with a wonderful, 9 a.m. spinner fall during August and September (best matched with a Black Clear Wing Spinner)—are important mayfly species. But the highlight of the season for the matching-the-hatch fanatic can be the tiny blue-winged olive, a size 24 insect that appears in such great numbers that it overwhelms other emergences, and during this "masking hatch" the fish are selectively taking the small flies and ignoring the more obvious, larger ones.

When in doubt on Poindexter (and other spring creeks), strap on a Pheasant Tail, Brassie, or Brown Tear Drop—streamlined and weighted nymphs that will sink quickly even in sizes 16 through 22—and work the seams between the weed beds. A scud pattern, a size 14 or 16 Olive on this stream, is the main choice in a bigger fly.

Numbers of big fish are down from the glory years of decades past, but there are still plenty of 10- to 18-inch fish, adequate numbers of 18- to 22-inch fish, and even a smattering of true brutes. The angling pressure has increased on the stream, however, and these trout see a tremendous number of flies. There are no second chances at this ballpark—use 14-foot-plus leaders tapered to 7X or 8X, delicate presentations, and the right fly for consistent results.

Polaris Lake: Polaris is a deep, 11-acre hike-in lake at over 8,000 feet (and at this elevation there are no easy walks). It's over 4 miles of steep trudging up the Lake Creek drainage. Go to the town of Polaris up Grasshopper Creek to hit the trailhead. The reward for the rough climb is the chance at rainbows and Yellowstone cutthroats up to 24 inches, but these are selective and spooky fish. They might take a small Olive Woolly Worm if it's not cast too rambunctiously. A more consistent producer is a tiny midge pupa imitation, something like a size 20 Black Serendipity, retrieved slowly, on a fine tippet.

Reservoir Lake: Reservoir Lake is up the Bloody Dick Road (FR 181), an easy 19-mile drive on improved gravel. There's also a nice Forest Service campground on this 40-acre lake at over 7,000 feet. It's worth bringing in a float tube or a cartop boat. There are steep drop-offs around most of the shore, and during the day deep techniques, with sinking lines and weighted nymphs, are productive for brookies to a foot or so. But there's also a shallow, weedy shelf at the upper end, and in the morning and evening, trout cruise and rise well in this water.

Ruby Reservoir: When it's at full pool, it's 1,000 acres of water behind an earthen dam 6 miles south of Alder on MT 287. This one doesn't get for me—not the most attractive, and the fishing is so-so most of the time. The reservoir is stocked with rainbows, and there are big browns and some cutthroats that work their way down from the upper river. Also, there are lots of suckers in the reservoir, which the browns gorge on. A larger streamer (like a 3/0-or-so Hair Sucker), imitating these beautiful trash fish, worked deeply and slowly, is very boring, unless a huge brown nails the thing. There are roads around most of the water, which even during a good year is drawn way down for irrigation in the summer, exposing big mud flats that create wonderful breeding habitat for all sorts of flies.

Ruby River: Access fights, legal and otherwise, are the current hallmark of this beautiful stream that "feels unwelcoming" according to my wife. I agree. It was called the Passamari by the native tribes, and the Stinking Water by the early white pioneers. The Ruby heads in the Snowcrest and Gravelly Ranges. The upper stretches (followed by the Upper Ruby Road) offer good fishing for rainbow and cutthroat trout to a foot, along with some browns. The fish run a few inches larger below the confluence of Warm Springs Creek (which adds the smelly, sulphuric flow that taints a small section of the river). Between the end of the Forest Service land, north to the Ruby Reservoir, the river travels through private land. Stream access according to state law seems, at times, to go out the window as contentious billionaire landowners go out of their way to make things difficult. Hopefully there's a proper place in hell for these soulless bastards.

Below the reservoir the Ruby (followed by Ruby River Drive) is a perfect stream for big brown trout as it winds, bends, and twists through a wide-open valley. There are miles of undercut willow and grass banks, logjams, gravel runs, and sandy-bottomed pools. The "rip and strip" tactics of the Beaverhead, with a big streamer or a pair of Girdle Bugs on a short, 20-pound-test leader, work on the overgrown sections of the Ruby, but with excellent populations of aquatic and terrestrial insects in or around the river, this is also a fine wet-fly and dry-fly stream.

The early grannom, a size 14 or 16 caddis with gray wings and a dark green body, starts emerging and egg-laying in early to mid-April. The spring blue-winged olive pops at the same time. The runoff, moderated by the dam, is brief, if there's any at all, and hatches stay important through the late May to early June period. The caddis flights are heavy, with the spotted sedge and little sister sedge appearing in late afternoon and

The subject of a well-publicized Montana stream-access fight, the Ruby is a wonderful brown trout water with unwelcoming vibes. Fish it hard anyway.

early evening through the summer and into the fall. The fall blue-winged olive, lingering into November if the weather holds, is another highlight on the river.

The Ruby is known for its exceptional grasshopper action. The valley has everything necessary for great hopper conditions. It's dry, even drier than Montana's prevalent semiarid climate. The fields, expanses of generally flat grassland, give the hoppers plenty of room and food. The warm summer winds off the hills blow the insects into the stream. During good-weather years, the fish begin keying on natural grasshoppers by late June, and keep watching for them until the hard, killing frosts of October.

The Ruby has been hurt in recent years. There is the continual problem of over-grazing in the upper river, and in 1995 state biologists found whirling disease in the trout population. Even with these assaults, it's still a wonderful fishery. Unfortunately, the area is being bought up and then subdivided into "vacation" or "retirement" lots, and access is all but gone on the Ruby. If you know someone who lives here or are willing to pay a stiff fee, you'll find fine action for browns of a couple of pounds or larger. If you are like most of us, you'll have to gain access from county roads and you can plan on getting plenty of grief working the river, even if you obey the state's stream-access law. This river is becoming a playground for the wealthy "elite," although there are still a dwindling few gracious landowners along the stream course.

Sawtooth Lake: A 500-foot wall towers over the lake, the bare rock along the ridge jagged like saw teeth. This 16-acre lake is up Clark Creek in the Pioneer Range west of Dillon at 8,500 feet. It's beautiful and lonely, the perfect wilderness hideaway for nice golden trout that, as always, are tough to catch.

Larger goldens are primarily benthic (bottom) zone feeders that take advantage of available populations of caddis larva, midge larva, and mayfly nymphs at times, and that is when they can be caught consistently, although it means digging out the Hi-D lines and twist-ons. At other times they ingest daphnia, smaller than any hook, and then they are all but impossible to catch.

Scott Lake: Take FR 192.2 to the Upper Rattlesnake Trail northwest of Dillon, hike the 1.5 miles over to Estler Lake (poor fishing), and then struggle the 2 miles up the inlet stream to Scott Lake. You'll find beauty, solitude, and some healthy Yellowstone cutthroats, and possibly some rainbow/cutthroat hybrids up to 24 inches if the lake hasn't frozen out. It receives periodic plants, and there are usually nice fish here. Ask questions before hiking into this lake, unless the beauty and solitude are enough for you.

The Big Hole can be good fishing, especially during the salmon fly hatch, but it's just about always full of floaters.
John Holt

Big Hole River

The Big Hole starts in the Beaverhead Mountains south of Jackson at an elevation of over 7,300 feet. The river is 160 miles in length. Running through the canyon stretch in Divide and into the farmlands below Melrose, this freestone river has a varied character as it winds its way to Twin Bridges. With over 3,000 trout per mile, it's easy to see why the river receives so much attention from fly fishers.

For much of the year the Big Hole is not all that crowded, relatively speaking. The exception is during the salmon fly hatch in June. Commercial outfitters from outside the area converge on the river. Why? There are three reasons: The hatch on the Big Hole occurs from early to late June, when there are no fishable salmon fly hatches on other rivers. The Big Hole runs high, and even gets tea-colored with heavy runoff, but it seldom turns into a mud bath, and it's a fine dry-fly river most years. And finally, there's always the chance to catch a big brown or rainbow.

But first off, some recent regulation changes need to be listed. Starting on the third Saturday in May through Labor Day, recreational use of the Big Hole River from its headwaters to Notch Bottom fishing access site is allowed and restricted by defining eight river zones, with one zone closed to float outfitting each day and with the zone that is restricted on Saturday and the zone that is restricted on Sunday also closed to nonresident float fishing.

The eight river zones are defined by river reach and restricted each day of the week as follows: a) all seven days of the week, the river reach from the headwaters to Mudd Creek Bridge BLM recreation site is closed to any float outfitting; b) each Sunday the river reach from Divide Bridge BLM recreation site to Salmon Fly fishing access site is closed to any float fishing by nonresidents and to any float outfitting; c) each Monday the river reach from Salmon Fly fishing access site to Glen fishing access site is closed to any float outfitting; d) each Tuesday the river reach from Mudd Creek Bridge BLM recreation site to Fishtrap fishing access site is closed to any float outfitting; e) each Wednesday the river reach from East Bank BLM recreation site to Jerry Creek Bridge BLM recreation site is closed to any float outfitting; f) each Thursday the river reach from Fishtrap fishing access site to East Bank BLM recreation site is closed to any float outfitting; g) each Friday the river reach from Glen fishing access site to Notch Bottom fishing access site is closed to any float outfitting; and h) each Saturday the river reach from Jerry Creek Bridge BLM recreation site to Divide Bridge BLM recreation site is closed to any float fishing by nonresidents and to any float outfitting.

Big Hole River

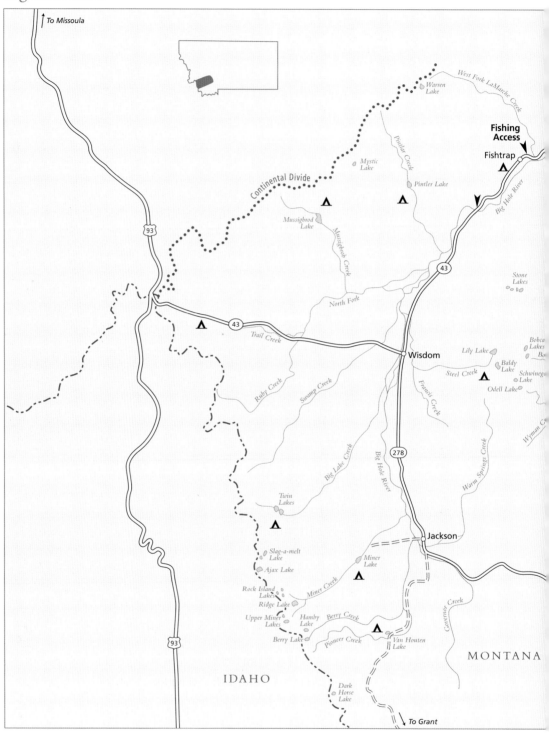

To Missoula

West Fork LaMarche Creek

Warren Lake

Fishing Access

Fishtrap

Continental Divide

Mystic Lake

Pintlar Creek

Pintler Lake

Big Hole River

Mussigbrod Lake

Mussigbrod Creek

93

43

Stone Lakes

North Fork

Trail Creek

43

Wisdom

Lily Lake

Steel Creek

Bobca Lakes

Baldy Lake

Schwinegar Lake

Odell Lake

Ruby Creek

Swamp Creek

Franzi Creek

Odell Lake

Wyman C

278

Big Lake Creek

Big Hole River

Warm Springs Creek

Twin Lakes

Jackson

Slag-a-melt Lake

Ajax Lake

Miner Lake

Governor Creek

Rock Island Lakes

Ridge Lake

Miner Creek

Upper Miner Lakes

Hamby Lake

Berry Creek

Berry Lake

Pioneer Creek

Van Houten Lake

MONTANA

93

IDAHO

Dark Horse Lake

To Grant

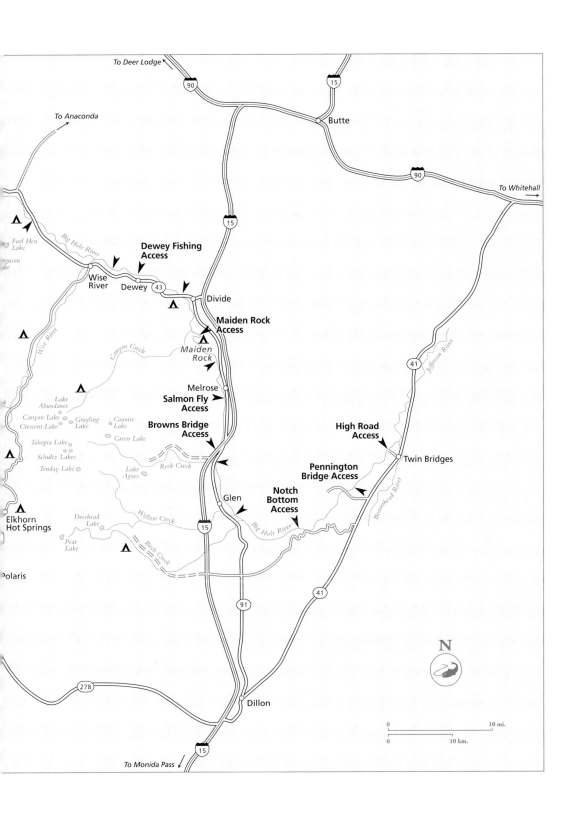

To Deer Lodge

To Anaconda

To Whitehall

90

15

Butte

90

15

Fool Hen
Lake

Big Hole River

Dewey Fishing
Access

Ferguson
ke

Wise
River

Dewey

43

Divide

Wise River

Maiden Rock
Access

Maiden
Rock

41

Jefferson River

Canyon Creek

Melrose

Salmon Fly
Access

Lake
Abundance

Canyon Lake

Grayling
Lake

Granite
Lake

High Road
Access

Crescent Lake

Green Lake

Browns Bridge
Access

Twin Bridges

Tahepia Lake

Schultz Lakes

Lake
Agnes

Rock Creek

Pennington
Bridge Access

Tenday Lake

Beaverhead River

Elkhorn
Hot Springs

Deerhead
Lake

Willow Creek

Glen

Notch
Bottom
Access

15

Big Hole River

Pear
Lake

Polaris

Birch Creek

41

91

N

278

Dillon

0   10 mi.

0   10 km.

15

To Monida Pass

All float users, including each float outfitter, are limited to a total of two launches at or near each official access site per day on the Big Hole River. If a boat is launched at an unofficial site, the launch will be counted as occurring at the nearest official site in determining the two-boat limit at or near each official access site.

With more and more anglers, an increase in regulations is likely to continue. Consulting the current regs is a must to avoid unpleasantness, disappointment, and fines.

Now back to the fun stuff. The salmon fly hatch usually begins around June 10 in the Twin Bridges area and is pretty much over four weeks later. Cold or hot weather can shorten or eliminate the hatch some years, but usually it progresses upriver 4 to 6 miles a day on the Big Hole.

There's a common strategy for salmon flies—fish the head of the hatch, where the insects are just starting to emerge and lay eggs. On some rivers it is almost a waste of time to fish in the middle of the hatch, where the large salmon flies are so abundant that the trout get satiated and stop feeding. The Madison River is like that; so is the Henry's Fork in Idaho. But the Big Hole isn't. The angler can work nymphs in areas where the hatch hasn't started, and work active dry flies at the head of the hatch. Even in the middle of the hatch, there always seems to be some cooperative trout, but the trick is to fish the dry fly in a dead drift over the best holding spots against the banks.

In most areas there will be plenty of other boats and rafts, crowds walking the shore, and the usual madness associated with the salmon fly hatch. A few days of this intense activity turns the trout wary and seems to make them less willing to come to the surface.

A trick of the locals is to let all of the out-of-area guides start floating early. The locals put their own boats in later in the day and cover rested water. Often, they'll still be floating during the early evening hours and the female salmon flies won't be flying in the chillier air, but for the last few miles of the trip, they'll match the big, size 8 great gray spotted sedges instead with a gray-and-green Emergent Sparkle Pupa and catch a lot of trout.

Most people concentrate their efforts during the salmon fly hatch on the 30-mile stretch between Wise River and Glen. The river is the perfect size for floating, and there are large trout in this water. Dry flies such as the Bird's Stone, Sofa Pillow, and Fluttering Stone (this last pattern developed by Big Hole guide Nevin Stephenson), or nymphs such as a Montana Stone, Kaufmann's Stone, or Natural Drift Stone bounced on the bottom, take trout consistently.

There are populations of salmon flies above Wise River, and they'll still be hatching into July some years. The key is knowing the river—one section will have insects and another one won't. The best populations of salmon flies are in rougher, steeper areas.

After mid-July the water level stabilizes and a good portion of the crowd has moved on to other western rivers. There are still plenty of anglers fishing the Big Hole, but it's possible to find some solitude.

POPULAR FLIES

Bird's Stone	Matuka Sculpin
Black Creeper	Montana Stone
Brooks' Stone	Natural Drift Stone
Crowe Beetle	Pheasant Tail
Crystal Bugger	Prince Nymph
Dark Spruce Streamer	Rusty CDC Spinner
Double Wing	Sofa Pillow
Egg-Sucking Leech	Spider
Elk Hair Caddis	Stimulator
Fluttering Stone	Ted's Stone
Goddard Caddis	Woolly Bugger
Humpy—larger sizes	Wulff
Kaufmann's Stone	Yellow Marabou Muddler

The Big Hole's reputation is deserved, but on some days the river shuts down and no one can take decent fish with any consistency. Return a few days later, and the surface will be alive with feeding trout of all sizes. Then, a few more days down the calendar, the trout will seem to have vanished from the face of the earth. This fickleness may be due to stresses from irrigation, especially on the lower river. The return flows off the fields are warmer and saturated with nutrients. With any stretch of warm, still days, the river seems to get tough during the summer months. If there's some rain, or just a few cold nights, it can suddenly get generous.

HEADWATERS TO WISE RIVER

The river begins in the Beaverhead Range of the Bitterroot Mountains south of Jackson, running by Wisdom at 6,058 feet, and then on to Wise River about 30 miles downstream. From the headwaters to Wisdom, there are brook, cutthroat, and rainbow trout, along with a remnant population of the nearly extinct fluvial (stream-dwelling) grayling. Around Jackson there are about 300 brookies per mile, with a few reaching 18 inches. Montana Department of Fish, Wildlife & Parks (FWP) biologists have supported an aggressive harvest of the brook trout in the upper reaches to make room for the grayling, but as a result, the remaining brook trout, on average, are getting larger. Rainbow numbers increase steadily as the river winds toward Wise River, both brook and cutthroat numbers decrease, and the grayling get really scarce.

Really just a creek, this is the home of the last significant population of fluvial grayling in the Lower 48. Water depletion and warming from irrigation, overgrazing, and destruction of the spawning tributaries; competition from nonnative fish; and proposed logging in the drainage threaten to eliminate even these few wild fish. To protect the species, FWP has instituted grayling catch-and-release regulations along the entire river.

The trout are smaller in the upper water (as is surprisingly true with most rivers), but this is a great area to wade. In many sections it is a meadow stream. The river stays cool enough through the summer months for good terrestrial fishing. A good grasshopper imitation usually takes trout. The fish aren't extremely critical during the hatches, and general dry flies and nymphs work consistently.

WISE RIVER TO MAIDEN ROCK

During the winter it's easy to see where the river changes character. Just above Wise River, where MT 43 crosses the river, springs enter the Big Hole. The upper river will be frozen until it reaches those springs, and then suddenly it will be ice-free. The springs signal not only more constant temperatures, but also richer water for both insects and trout.

From Wise River to Maiden Rock, the Big Hole holds 2,000 rainbows and 300 browns per mile, some approaching 5 pounds (or, rarely, larger). The hatches are heavier in this section, and the trout can get fairly selective at times. The early grannom appears in May and triggers heavy feeding. The salmon fly dominates most of June, but there are good hatches of the great gray spotted sedge and the golden stone, too. In early July two large mayflies, the brown drake and the green drake, emerge in good numbers. The pale morning dun and the trico are the main midsummer mayflies. The little sister sedge (with massive flights every evening) and the spotted sedge are important summer caddisflies. In the fall the blue-winged olive and the tiny blue-winged olive are dependable hatches. There are enough of the giant orange sedge in the fall to attract trout, too.

The trout are becoming more selective as the years pass. There's still a great "Royal Wulff hatch," when the fish are looking up and a general attractor works, but when the hatches are happening, the size and outline of the fly becomes critical.

On the Big Hole, with the glare bouncing off the riffles, a flat, drab dry fly can be impossible to see. The Parachute caddis is tied with matching wing and body colors, but there's a white post of hair sticking up. The Parachute mayfly has the post, but the favorite variation also has a trailing shuck.

The Big Hole is a great terrestrial river. The spruce moth goes through its cycles. This is one river where you don't want to be caught without a flying ant imitation. During August and September, flights of black ants spatter the water and the trout go berserk. It's a grasshopper, size 8 or 10, stream all summer, with the combination of grassy meadows and regular warm winds that push insects out onto the water.

MAIDEN ROCK TO THE MELROSE BRIDGE

From Maiden Rock to the Melrose Bridge, the river has 3,500 trout per mile, equally divided between browns and rainbows. There are also lots of mountain whitefish (just try drifting a nymph through certain runs). This is bigger water, and for many anglers it is more challenging. The simple act of wading on slick, round boulders in a fast current can be tough for less agile fishermen.

Early or late in the season, this section fishes fine all day, but by midsummer it can slump. In the bright hours in the middle of the day, the fish, especially the browns, go into hiding. If the day isn't too hot, there may be a good evening rise. There are fine caddis flights, and standard patterns, such as the Elk Hair Caddis, are effective. On really hot days, or after a stretch of warm ones, the only good surface fishing may be in the morning. There always seem to be straggling mayfly spinners, left over from the nighttime egg-laying, and a size 14 Rusty CDC Spinner is an especially consistent searching pattern.

When trout aren't looking to the surface, you can work nymphs effectively through the runs and riffles, but the catch will be predominantly rainbows. A standard selection of nymphs—Hare's Ear, Prince, Pheasant Tail—will work in the moderately broken water, but the big stonefly patterns take larger fish in the heavy runs. Good patterns include weighted versions of the Brooks' Stone, Kaufmann's Stone, and Ted's Stone, but the traditionalist might consider George Grant's woven-bodied stonefly nymphs, such as the Black Creeper, developed for this river. No flies sink faster than these patterns, the hard bodies cutting through the currents, and no other flies have caught as many 5-pound-plus trout on the Big Hole.

MELROSE BRIDGE TO GLEN

In this stretch the number of trout drops to 2,000 trout per mile, with about 1,700 of these being browns. Perhaps 150 per mile are in the 18- to 22-inch class. All of the standard techniques and flies will work at times in this water, but the preponderance of browns means that you will have to focus on cover. The fish hold especially tight to banks, sunken logs, and large rock shelves when they're not actively feeding.

Streamer tactics work throughout the drainage, but they are especially important in this section. The main fly is the Woolly Bugger, in all of its variations, from a Crystal Bugger to an Egg-Sucking Leech.

GLEN TO THE CONFLUENCE WITH THE BEAVERHEAD

This final section is primarily big brown trout water. Don't bother with this stretch until autumn unless you really know the water, or are a fan of futility. The trout are hiding in cool water away from the warm flows of the main river. But come autumn, work this water hard with a Matuka Sculpin, Yellow Marabou Muddler, Dark Spruce Streamer, or Woolly Bugger. Fishing this stuff is not glamorous, but it is productive. Size 4 up to 2/0 is not out of line.

While the Big Hole (and the Bighorn and the Madison and the Missouri) has taken some heat from fly fishers and writers about the number of angler-use days it receives each season, this is still a river that every fly-fishing addict should spend some time discovering.

FISHING WATERS IN THE BIG HOLE DRAINAGE

Ajax Lake: You reach Ajax by rough road (when open) west of Bannack. It is 20 acres and 100 feet deep in places. Ajax is fun fishing for the cutthroats, rainbows, and hybrids that swim around the downed timber and along the drop-offs. The biggest fish top out at 15 inches or so, but the numbers are good. It's a good place for spotting and casting to individual trout.

Baldy Lake: You have to hike several miles from the end of the Lacy Creek Road, starting at the point where it's closed, up and into this one at over 8,000 feet. Baldy is deep and over 30 acres, with Yellowstone cutthroats, rainbows, and hybrids over a foot.

Berry Lake: Berry is up in the Pioneer Creek country and way back away from the crowds. This lake is 11 acres, deep, and full of fat cutthroats to several pounds. A serious effort is required to reach this place, and the fishing can be tough. It's the kind of lake where you go in and camp for three or four days, hoping to be there when the fish go on a feeding spree. Take small (size 16 or smaller) terrestrials, such as a Foam Ant or Crowe Beetle, for the evening rise.

Start at the Pioneer Creek Trail and trek from Pioneer Lake (may be barren) to Highup Lake (certainly barren) to Skytop Lake (also barren). From there it is 1.5 miles along the Divide to Berry. Watch out for weather up here. Lightning in the exposed rocks is nasty, and sudden storms with cold rain or snow sweep over the crest in the fall.

Bobcat Lakes (North, South, West): Up the Wise River drainage at over 8,000 feet, the chief attraction in these small lakes are the grayling that on rare occasions may top a foot.

Canyon Creek: A typical pretty mountain stream with brushy, downed-timber banks and lots of pocket water and rapid riffles before running into the Big Hole not far from Maiden Rock. There is a campground on the upper reaches, which have a few small trout. The lower stretch has cutts, rainbows, and brookies to maybe 12 inches.

Most of the tributaries of the lower Big Hole also have good runs of brown trout in the fall, usually beginning in mid-September and running through the end of the season, November 30. These trout will strike streamers and larger nymphs drifted in front of them. At this time of year, walk the stream banks quietly until you find the fish under the banks or other cover. Many fly fishers do not like to fish for trout when they are on their redds. A number of fisheries biologists now believe that trout are stressed less here (if played fairly and quickly, and properly released) than when taken well below their spawning gravels downstream, when they still have several miles to travel. My experience shows otherwise, but it's hard to argue with science. The choice is yours, but always put the welfare of the trout first.

Canyon Lake: Canyon is reached by 4 miles of good trail above the campground, at the base of 9,810-foot Maurice Mountain. Marshy, shallow, and around 20 acres, it has good numbers of cutthroats in the 10-inch class and a few up to several pounds.

Dark Horse Lake: Dark Horse is reached by too many trucks, cars, mountain bikes, nomadic camel caravans, etc., for obvious reasons—it is a beautiful cirque lake with decent fishing for healthy cutthroats that are fools for dry flies and flashy streamers. Fish the lower end, with its shallow bench, morning and evening. The road from Skinner Meadows is poor but usable all summer.

Deerhead Lake: Deerhead is on the trail from the Dinner Station Campground northwest of Dillon. Used as irrigation storage, it is still good action for some sizable cutthroats. It's small (15 acres), shallow (15 feet), and weedy. It doesn't take a genius to figure out that damsels are important here.

Ferguson Lake: In the Alder Creek drainage, less than 20 acres, it has cutthroats, rainbows, and hybrids. Ferguson has extensive shallows surrounding a middle basin that's nearly 50 feet deep. The fish, up to 15 inches, are real cruisers and will rush a long way for a fly.

Francis Creek: Southeast of Wisdom, running through national forest, then sage flats to Steel Creek, this is still a pretty much unspoiled stream that has brookies, whitefish, and a few small (but eager) grayling. Easy and enjoyable dry-fly water with light rods at ten paces.

Hamby Lake: Hamby is about a half-dozen miles southwest of Jackson, with fair numbers of grayling that reach 15 inches or a bit larger along with some cutts and brookies and even rainbows. It's over 35 acres in timber-and-rock high country about 8,000 feet.

Lake Agnes: Agnes is full of grayling of around 10 inches. It's almost 100 acres, located above the Brownes Lake Campground up the Rock Creek Road. It's a short hike from the campground—less than a mile—and that makes it a popular spot. Fishing pressure doesn't seem to educate the grayling, however.

Lily Lake: Lily is about 10 miles east of Wisdom and has some cutthroats, rainbows, and hybrids. There seems to be a real split in the trout population—most of the fish are in the 8- to 12-inch range, but there are some real trophies here.

Miner Lake: You can reach Miner by road west of Jackson, so it's quite popular with area residents and visitors alike. It's good for brook trout and grayling, especially along the channel near evening. There are some cutthroats, too. Canoes or float tubes help reach the fish.

Mystic Lake: Mystic has lots of rainbows that are hit by the horseback crowd. A float tube would play well here, especially along the edges of aquatic growth. Try slowly working a small nymph, like a Pheasant Tail or a Pearl Serendipity, parallel to the weeds. Mystic is in the Anaconda-Pintler Wilderness north and west of Wisdom.

North Fork Big Hole River: The North Fork wanders through grass and willow country to the Big Hole north of Wisdom. It's mainly brook trout water, with some of the fish growing fat and over 15 inches. There are also whitefish, and maybe a stray grayling. Z-Wings and Elk Hairs for the caddis and Sparkle Duns and Parachutes for mayflies will usually fool the brookies, though some nymphs are not a bad idea either.

O'Dell Creek: A small stream followed by road and trail, O'Dell Creek receives quite a bit of pressure for its size, but still manages to produce good numbers of small brookies, grayling, and some rainbows.

O'Dell Lake: Lots of people reach this one by trail from the end of the Lacy Creek Road. They come here mainly for the 10- to 14-inch grayling, and they stay at the campsite at the south end. It's a pretty busy spot in the summer, but after Labor Day the hordes diminish and it's fun to use a float tube to fish the shallows on the north end, where the fish seem to concentrate. Pattern type isn't critical, but grayling have small mouths and any fly larger than size 14 is not as effective as tinier offerings.

Pintler Lake: Less than 40 acres and only 20 feet deep, Pintler has mainly cutthroats along with some rainbow and brook trout. About 30 minutes north of Wisdom, you reach it by road and it has a campground. There is some draw-down. Float tubes or canoes make the fishing a little easier. Strip a dragonfly or damselfly nymph slowly along the bottom.

Ridge Lake: Ridge Lake is west of Jackson, off the Rock Island Lakes Road, in high country. It's a short hike up to the lake. Ridge is good action for cutthroats of 10 to 15 inches. Try skating a caddis or spider pattern when the water goes flat in the evening.

Rock Island Lakes: These four lakes are up 4 miles of trail heading off from the Miner Creek Road west of Jackson. There is some decent fishing for cutthroats and a few rainbows.

South Fork Big Hole River: This stream forms the Big Hole when it joins forces with Governor Creek above Jackson. It's good fishing for brook and rainbow trout, but most of the water is on private land, making access sporting. Irrigation takes its toll on this stream.

Steel Creek: Steel hits the Big Hole north of Jackson. It's good autumn fishing for brook trout to 15 inches and a few grayling. Something like a Royal Trude or an Orange Double Wing make good attractor drys, as do Humpies in the fall.

Stone Lakes: In the mountains on the west side of the Wise River, these two small lakes provide decent fishing for cutthroats running from 8 to 15 inches.

Tahepia Lake: Tahepia is a rainbow trout lake at almost 9,000 feet in glacial cirque country in the Wise River drainage above the Mono Creek Campground. It's a little over 15 acres and only 20 feet deep, but something keeps it from freezing out and it grows healthy fish to 15 inches.

Tendoy Lake: This one is high in the Pioneers. It is ice-free only a few months of the year, but offers average fishing for average cutthroats after ice-out. It's only 30 acres, but it's 100 feet deep (which is what saves it from freezing out).

Ten Mile Lakes: These are a half-dozen small lakes above 8,800 feet in the Anaconda-Pintler Wilderness. They were originally managed for rainbows but have been taken over by cutthroats that do well in the clear water. You can reach them by a lengthy hike from the end of the Grassy Mountain Road.

Twin Lakes: You'll find these lakes 25 miles south of Wisdom. They're fished by just about everyone owning fishing gear in the area. The two lakes are joined by a small channel and combine for 75 acres of water. They hold large lake trout to 20 pounds, plus brook trout, grayling, and rainbows. You can catch those lake trout in the fall on streamer flies when they cruise the gravel shallows. The nastiest weather is the best fishing time.

Warm Springs Creek: A headwaters stream of the Big Hole, Warm Springs passes just south of Jackson and provides nice dry-fly action with Wulffs, Humpies, and other delicate patterns for 10-inch brook trout and some whitefish. This one is open from June 13 through September 30.

Warren Lake: Warren Lake is in the Anaconda-Pintler Wilderness far back up the West Fork of LaMarche Creek. It's a 9-mile hike (enough to discourage the backpacking wannabes), but this 18-acre lake is good fishing for cutthroats to a couple of pounds.

Willow Creek: This 20-mile-long stream flows north behind Twin Adams and Sugarloaf mountains in the Pioneers. There are lots of cutthroats and rainbows to a foot or a little more, plus some nice browns in autumn in the lower reaches (as is true of most of the Big Hole tributaries between Twin Bridges and Wise River). Streamers will take these fish when they are on the run as winter approaches. You can get away with floating lines in the smaller streams, making casting much easier and safer. A 20-inch trout in a 20-foot-wide stream is an engaging proposition.

Wise River: The Wise River flows for about 30 miles through the Pioneer Mountains and joins the Big Hole at the town of Wise River. It's beautiful water that offers some good fishing in spots, but pollution from mining, scouring from floods decades ago, and heavy dewatering from irrigation do a number on the populations of catchable brookies and rainbows. The low, clear water of midsummer also makes the fish very spooky; as a result, most anglers do poorly here. This is a beautiful stream to fish on a nice early-autumn afternoon whether you catch fish or not.

It's amazing how good this stream becomes once you start creeping and crawling among the boulders. The trout concentrate in the pools, and when they're not frightened out of their holding areas, they'll take any reasonable dry fly. Goddard Caddis, Stimulators, Wulffs, Humpies, and Renegades all work well, but for special excitement try Spiders skittered across the river's surface on hot, windy summer afternoons. This pattern drives trout crazy throughout the state when the caddis and the wind play together.

Blackfeet Reservation

"Wind-blasted, wide-open country dotted with glacier-scoured depressions that are now spring-filled with nutrient water that grows very large trout" conveys a superficial sense of the fishing opportunities lying out on the wild grass prairie of the Blackfeet Indian Reservation.

Rainbow, brook, and cutthroat trout regularly grow past the 5-pound mark by feeding on the abundant populations of damsel- and dragonflies, midges, leeches, caddis, mayflies, terrestrials, scuds, and smaller fish. In mild years, growth rates of an inch per month have been documented.

With all of these big fish cruising around like out-of-control Trident submarines in search of a vanished communist threat, why isn't the reservation overrun with fly fishers?

The reasons are simple. The wind often blows for weeks straight at over 30 miles per hour, making fishing, especially from a float tube, difficult, if not impossible. There are also times when the trout head for deep water and sulk, especially during the heat of summer. And, finally, quality food, lodging, and equipment outlets are in short supply. Browning, the largest town on the reservation, does offer a couple of motels, restaurants, and cafes, and there's some fishing gear available. But that's about it, if you plan on staying on the Blackfeet Reservation. Except for private campsites, there is no camping allowed on the reservation. Most people who fish here are from west of the mountains—towns like Whitefish and Kalispell—or from Great Falls and Helena to the south.

I used to have a love-hate relationship with this place when I lived in Whitefish— love the chance for big fish and the scenery, hate the wind. Living in Livingston makes fishing the Rez a long drive, so I don't get up here as much anymore.

One other frustrating fact is that non-tribal members cannot fish after sunset, a time when some huge fish begin to suck down insects with loud slurps, making large rise forms out there in the gloom of dusk. Nor can you cast a line before sunrise.

So why bother coming to the reservation at all?

Well, there is the sight of the Rocky Mountain Front rising snowcapped into the sky across the entire western horizon. There are elk, sharp-tailed grouse, grizzlies, Hungarian partridge, deer, eagles, and other animals roaming the million-plus acres. The prairie grasses light up in emerald green in the spring, with bunches of wildflowers glowing all over the place.

Blackfeet Reservation

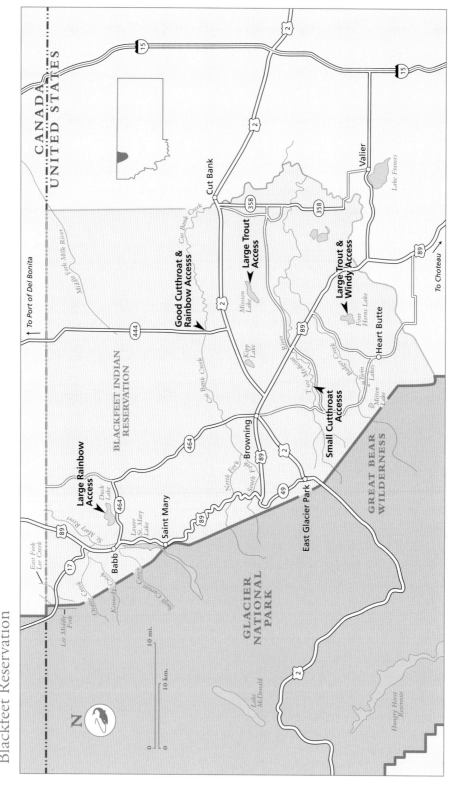

A cutbow hybrid like this is what makes anglers drive long miles to the Rez. John Holt

And there are the trout. Sure, there's a good chance that the wind will blow you off the water or that the fish may do a vanishing act, but if you are willing to fish hard all day for a week, you will catch a large trout. Perhaps one over 10 pounds if you are fortunate.

Lakes like Mission, Mitten, Duck, Kipp, and Four Horns hold plenty of sizable trout (and those are just a few of the waters). A set of current regulations are a must. They contain a map that will help you navigate out here. Roads not marked with brilliant neon signs often degenerate into two-lane ruts that really do lead to fine lakes. Other waters have frozen out or are temporarily closed. The situation is in a constant state of flux. A little inquiry is often needed to find out what is what. This is all part of the adventure, so relax, keep your eyes open, and go with the flow.

There is big water here, and a float tube or kick boat is helpful. So are neoprene waders, even in summer, because springs keep most of the lakes cool all season. You'll need 7-weight rods, or larger, to punch casts into the winds and to shoot long casts out to cruising fish. Shooting heads are also gaining in popularity. Other than sunscreen, sunglasses, rain gear, warm clothing, a cooler full of chilled beverages, tribal permits (never forget these), a stout vehicle for the rough "roads" that quickly turn impassable with rain or melting snow, and a CD or two of Béla Fleck to fill the drive time between lakes, you really don't need anything special.

Pattern selection is not elaborate. Hare's Ear Nymphs in tan, gray, and olive, sizes 12 to 18, cover a lot of insects. Some damsel patterns, especially Biggs Specials in 8

Duck Lake is big-fish water, often cold and windy, but it can be excellent, especially at ice-out.   John Holt

and 10, are necessities, as are brown, black, and purple Marabou Leech patterns in sizes 2 through 6. A good choice for a scud imitation should include an Olive-Gray Bead-Head Scud and an Olive Rollover Scud in sizes 8 through 14—the size 8 is there for shocking the spoiled, overfed trout into striking sometimes. Prince Nymphs also take fish, especially when worked in the wind over exposed points (cast perpendicular to the direction the waves are running, and strip the fly quickly back to shore). An Olive Halo Emerger for the escaping nymph, a Speckled-Wing Paradun for the resting dun, and a Gray Clear Wing Spinner for the spent egg-layer, all in sizes 14 to 18, handle the Callibaetis mayflies, which seem to hang around most of the warmer months but peak in August and early September. An Adams will approximate the clumps of midges that sometimes appear. Hoppers, ants, and beetles are good in July, August, and the first part of September.

In March and April big rainbows move up to the gravel shorelines of the wave-swept southeastern shores of the larger lakes and go through a daisy-chain, false-spawning ritual. Large, gaudy streamers cast over and in front of the fish provoke severe responses. Many of the best rainbows of the year are taken at this time. This is also a time of wind, sleet, snow, and rain, so you've got to want this type of action to enjoy it. Finding the fish is a matter of walking the banks and looking for the dark, swirling shapes. The trout move back and forth between deep water and the shallows. Often they will circle madly for only a few minutes before vanishing for an hour or a day. And there are times, when the ice is pulling back from the shoreline, that a small nymph cast onto the frozen floes and then jerked into the water will trigger a strike from trout hiding just below the shelf. They can hear the fly scratching across the ice. This is big-fish, capricious angling at its elaborate best. The rainbows are firm and full of fight at this time of year, running and jumping at the first tug of the fly when it interrupts their wild, futile procreational ritual.

Navigating this wild country can be tough. Using a quality guide like Joe Kipp of Morning Star Outfitters is money well spent. Ice-out from approximately April 15 through May 15, depending on weather, elevation, and the severity of the previous winter, is the best time to take large trout. Reservation permits are available by the day ($20) or season ($50). You will also need an additional permit for a boat ($10) or float tube ($5). These permits are available from any area sporting goods store, as well as a host of grocery and convenience stores, etc., or anywhere that sells Montana licenses within a 100-mile radius of the reservation.

FISHING WATERS OF THE BLACKFEET RESERVATION

Duck Lake: Duck is justly famous for large rainbows during the spring season, but the setting is trailer-court decor wall-to-wall. The drill is to stand half-frozen as deep as you can wade and make long casts with Woolly Buggers out into the lake. The earthly reward for this is a ripping strike just often enough to keep you out there.

East Fork Lee Creek: This creek heads below Chief Mountain and flows for 6 miles before crossing over into Alberta. Not bad fishing with drys for brook trout and cutthroats to 12 inches.

Four Horns Lake: Four Horns sits in a valley that just funnels the wind. It is often too covered in whitecaps for safe fishing, but when it is calm, it can be especially good at the top end where an inlet stream enters. This little stream winds across a high plateau and picks up drowned terrestrials. There are few fish in the stream to intercept this food line, and all of the insects are dumped into the lake. The trout (and some walleyes) stack up in this area. Early morning is calmest.

Kipp Lake: Kipp is ugly and great fishing. It is a featureless bowl that sits out on the prairie. The bottom is thick with both weeds and food forms for the rainbows. The secret on Kipp is to move the fly very slowly, because these trout don't have to rush to feed.

Mission Lake: Mission is richly carpeted in weeds, and so full of bottom-food forms that it's hard to get the fish to strike at times. It sits in a beautiful, high valley and is sheltered a bit by the winds. The most reliable summer action comes with the damsel emergence every morning. If you get there at sunrise, you will find rainbow trout snatching some of the millions of hatching insects that are swimming into the shore. Get there later in the morning, and you might find the water covered with Callibaetis duns, the wings so thick that they create a silver shimmer, but often there's not a single fish rising anywhere on the lake because they've glutted themselves on those early damsels.

Mitten Lake: This is another scenic, high-valley lake. It's the place to go for sinking-line, slow-retrieve tactics during the middle of the day. Here's where the scud patterns work well. Some areas of the lake are better than others, and the regulars seem to know where the good weed beds are located—it seems to be a matter of depth. The trout on Mitten might be concentrating at certain levels at different times of the day. A friend and I were run off by the approach of a mountain lion some years back, and I've seen grizzlies and moose in the area.

St. Mary River: Running very swiftly and sapphire clear out on the high plains east of the Rocky Mountain Front, the St. Mary River is a wild, little-fished stream with decent numbers of cutthroats, rainbows, and a few brook trout. The river flows onto the Blackfeet Indian Reservation before disappearing into Canada with its load of snow and ice melt from the distant peaks of Glacier National Park. Access is not the greatest, and the fishing can be average at best. All the same, I've caught nice fish on large attractor patterns and colorful streamers on this beautiful river.

A bit on the sterile side, there are nevertheless some sizable trout in the St. Mary River.

Almost no one fishes here, but large cutthroats can be taken at brief and rare windows of opportunity that open just a crack. The formula includes periods of consistent and diminished release from Swiftcurrent Dam; periods of warm, high overcast when hoppers are leaping blithely to their deaths on the river; or when large, dark stoneflies are crawling out from the water to dry on warm rocks and then take

POPULAR FLIES

Adams	Joe's Hopper
Biggs Special	Kaufmann's Stone
Black-Nosed Dace	Marabou Leech
Brooks' Stone	Prince Nymph
Dave's Hopper	Scuds—olive, pink
Double Wing	Speckled-Wing Parachute
Gray Ghost	Woolly Bugger
Hare's Ear Nymph	Wulff
Humpy	Zonker

flight in the pure sky above. Then the trout can be fooled. The big cutthroats in the river are spooky and hard to catch, and discharges from Swiftcurrent Dam screw up the fishing more than occasionally, but there are those moments when everything is right on the St. Mary.

The best patterns are likely to be things like Joe's Hoppers and Dave's Hoppers in sizes 6 to 10 from early July into the summer, but some anglers do well with large attractors like Goofus Bugs, Wulffs, Double Wings, and Humpies. Big stonefly nymphs, such as the Kaufmann's Stone or Brooks' Stone, sometimes fished in tandem with a smaller fly, such as a Prince Nymph, Hare's Ear, or Bead-Head Twist Nymph, drifted along the bottom (with a few twist-ons to offset the current), will often take the trout and always entice the greedy whitefish.

The St. Mary does not open until the first of June, and the runoff from the Rockies is often in full swing at this time. By July the levels have stabilized and fishing can be quite good for the smaller trout, especially toward evening (no fishing after sunset is allowed).

Streamers like the Zonker, Gray Ghost, Black-Nosed Dace, and similar flashy patterns, cast across stream and allowed to swing with the current, will pull up reluctant fish. So will large wet flies fished the same manner. Using two or even three wets can simulate a hatch of artificial food that fools the cutthroats into feeding.

This river is not exceptionally fertile despite its verdant surroundings (from late spring into midsummer). Any fly that reflects the light and acts lifelike will probably attract a strike. Catching fish in the St. Mary is not all that important—just being alive in this wind-blasted, wild country is what matters.

Twin Lakes: These are not the "big fish" lakes. They are separated by the road between Heart Butte and Browning, about 4 miles northwest of Heart Butte. Anglers who tire of the slower trophy hunting should know about these waters. They can come here and fish for trout that rise all morning to the Callibaetis hatch. The rainbows are mostly under 14 inches, but there is the occasional bigger one in these lakes.

By midsummer the waters have warmed to the extent that most of the lakes are in the doldrums, though fish will be taken working down deep, along weed beds, around springs, and on the surface during cooler, overcast days. From September into winter (lakes are open all year), the trout key at first on various autumn caddisflies, the late stragglers of the Callibaetis hatch, and then on small fish as the thick growth of aquatic plants dies back. The withering of the vegetation allows fly fishers to work the bulky patterns more effectively. Trout will often be seen prowling near shore. A cautious approach and well-timed cast ahead of a cruiser consistently takes such a fish.

Many of the creeks, which have specific regulations, are a joy to fish for cutthroat, brook, and rainbow trout. And every now and then, a large one to 20 inches shows up.

All in all, the Blackfeet Indian Reservation is a land where serious fly fishers (read: those willing to put up with austere conditions and willing to work at their fishing) can reasonably expect to take one or more trout over 5 pounds in a week's fishing. This time frame includes at least one-third of the daylight hours rendered unfishable because of high winds.

If you can handle arm-numbing casting, rough weather, hot sun, and perhaps a large trout, this is not a bad spot to spend some time. The Blackfeet Reservation and its permit fees should be considered a bargain and a privilege for non-tribal members. The place is a hell of a lot cheaper (and often better fishing) and just as scenic in its own way as New Zealand.

Born in the mountains, in its lower reaches the Clarks Fork of the Yellowstone is less attractive from a fishing perspective.

Clarks Fork of the Yellowstone

The Clarks Fork of the Yellowstone does not look like much of a trout stream after leaving the mountains along the northern border of Yellowstone Park, but looks can be deceiving. Wide, smooth-flowing, sometimes turbid water holds plenty of trout, some of them large.

At its beginning, the Clarks Fork is a true mountain stream. Formed by snow and glacier melt in the barren reaches of the Beartooth Plateau just a few miles east of Cooke City on the northern border of Yellowstone National Park, the Clarks Fork is a fast-flowing, riffle-and-pocket-water stream. It runs south into Wyoming for a crooked piece before crossing back into Montana about 10 miles south of Belfry.

Near the headwaters a dry-fly attractor, as subtle as a Deer Hair Woolly or as garish as a Royal Humpy, from size 12 to 18, will turn Yellowstone cutthroats and an occasional brook trout up to 10 inches on a good day. You can easily reach much of this alpine water by short hikes from the Beartooth Highway. In the spring and summer, wildflowers brighten the landscape and hoary marmots whistle back and forth among themselves in the jumbled, shattered rock. The country is spectacular, with ragged peaks over 12,000 feet, remnant glaciers, snowfields, and sapphire blue lakes clouded with glacial flour of ground and pulverized rock. Storms roll by swiftly overhead, filled with thunder and lightning. The air is often charged with static electricity and the scent of ozone drifts by. These disturbances disappear as quickly as they come, rumbling out onto the flatlands.

The river is born in Montana but after a quick 3 miles passes into Wyoming (where it is also good fishing). When it reenters Montana, MT 72 parallels the Clarks Fork. The river from the Wyoming line downstream to Bridger is also rapid, pocket-and-riffle water with mainly mountain whitefish and some large browns. There are also a few brookies, cutthroats, and rainbows. This water would be truly classy stuff if it were not so heavily dewatered for irrigation, a problem that rivals logging in many state drainages. Low flows, the flush of returning water, and overgrazing by cattle cause severe sedimentation that chokes both insect life and spawning gravels. Clean up this problem and you immediately create another excellent trout stream.

Past Bridger the same problems exist, exacerbated by natural sedimentation and alkalinity from surrounding unstable soils. There are a few impressive browns up from the Yellowstone, plus some rainbows, ling (ugly, ugly fish), sauger (a lethargic version

Clarks Fork of the Yellowstone

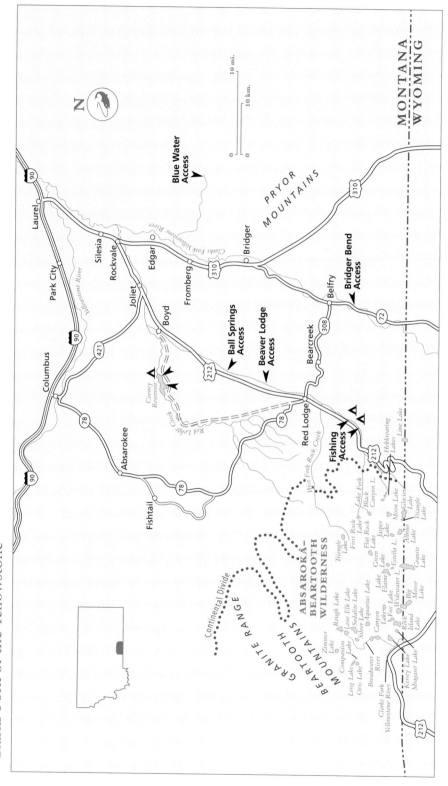

of the walleye), and some muscle-bound catfish. Big streamers imitating forage fish will take the browns in the fall in this often turbid situation.

In the Beartooths the river drains less than 120 square miles, but there are hundreds of named and unnamed lakes in this small area. Many freeze out on a regular basis and are subsequently barren. Most of the water is between 9,000 and 10,000 feet, and one lake is at 11,200 feet, the highest in the state. Crazy Lake, Daisy Lake, Goose Lake, and Lulu Pass jeep trails lead into the backcountry, but these conduits are often narrow, rocky, and hazardous to travel, especially during and after the frequent snow and rain

Yellowstone cutthroats can be found all along the headwaters of the Clarks Fork.

storms. Grizzlies also make this country home, but are little trouble if you keep a clean campsite. The lakes around Cooke City are usually free of ice by late May or early June, but the higher-elevation waters often do not clear until August.

From a great beginning in pristine country, the Clarks Fork dies a quick death from a fly-fishing perspective almost as soon as the river wanders back into Montana. Perhaps someday the river will have an opportunity to show us what kind of trout stream it was in the past.

POPULAR FLIES

Dave's Hopper	Muskrat
Deer Hair Woolly	Olive Woolly Worm
Flashback Callibaetis	Pink Trude
Gold-Ribbed Hare's Ear	Red Serendipity
Griffith's Gnat	Royal Humpy
Henry's Fork Hopper	Timberline Emerger
Humpy	Twist Nymph
Krystal Egg	Woolly Bugger

FISHING WATERS IN THE CLARKS FORK DRAINAGE

Albino Lake: Albino is way up in the clouds—over 10,000 feet—on the Beartooth Plateau (no trees here), and 40 acres with well-defined drop-offs. The 5-mile hike into Albino starts at Island Lake on the Beartooth Highway. This lake has good numbers of Yellowstone cutthroats (the species of choice in this area) that grow to 15 inches. They occasionally feed on the surface, especially at dusk, as with all mountain-lake trout, but nymphs work better, especially if they have just a hint of flash. A Flashback Callibaetis, Twist Nymph, or Gold-Ribbed Hare's Ear are all good patterns. These flies reflect the available light, drawing the curious but finicky fish. Greasing the nymph so it rides in the meniscus is also a productive ploy. For deeper presentations, don't forget the Olive Woolly Worm with a tuft of red at the tail.

Big Moose Lake: This one's an 84-acre lake on the Montana-Wyoming line. Take the Crazy Lakes Trail out of the Cooke City area. Big Moose has a few large brook trout, some rainbows, and plenty of gregarious grayling that love tiny drys—size 20 and smaller. It's fun to use a Griffith's Gnat or a Black Halo Midge Pupa and wait to see what will hit it.

Black Canyon Lake: Every six years or so, over 8,000 Yellowstone cutthroats of 2 inches are air-dropped into this 60-acre lake lying at the foot of Grasshopper Glacier. The fish average less than a foot but sometimes reach a couple of pounds in this 185-foot-deep, cream-and-jade-colored lake. You'll climb high enough to look the mountain goats in the eye at 9,400 feet. Start at US 12 and hike 2.5 miles up the Broadwater Creek Trail to Curl Lake. Circle past Broadwater Lake (connected to Curl) and climb 3 miles up the Lake Fork Rock Creek Trail to Black Canyon.

Bluewater Creek: This is a little gem for spring creek lovers. There's 13 miles of it, flowing from Bluewater Springs to the Clarks Fork of the Yellowstone. The lower reaches are hammered by irrigation and only poor fishing. Drive up a good county road (across the river from Fromberg) 5 miles and start there. It is rattlesnake infested all along (crowd control). The stream has good numbers of fat, 1- to 2-pound browns that rise well to terrestrial imitations. The best fish hold increases under the brush, and a daring caster who hammers a fly deep into the thickets takes trout all day.

Canyon (Crazy) Lake: Canyon Lake is long, narrow, and deep (like most lakes formed in a steep canyon). Hit the trail at the north end of Fox Lake, which isn't far from Cooke City, and hump the 1.5 miles up to Canyon. There are very big cutthroats and rainbows here, along with the regular foot-long variety, but they hold so deep that unless they're feeding, they are hard to take with a floating line. A few people fish it with fast-sinking lines and weighted nymphs.

Elaine Lake: Hit the trail off the Beartooth Highway 20 miles east of Cooke City. It's 8 miles up to Granite Lake and then another 2.5 miles up to Elaine. Is there any doubt why this is known as a good place for horsepackers? The lake is packed with small brook trout that thrive in the 100-plus acres.

Estelle Lake: This is another good spot for small brookies. It's on the same trail as Elaine, sitting about a mile east of that lake. It's only 18 acres, but it seems like every foot of it has a willing trout. If you put two or three wet flies on a leader, you will hook more than one trout often enough.

Flat Rock Lake: At almost 10,000 feet, the site of the annual Flat Earth Society Convention, this is a windswept, 35-acre lake on the desolate Beartooth Plateau. Hop from Long Lake to Star Lake to Green Lake to Summerville to Lake Flat Rock Lake. It's a wicked, high-elevation jeep ride and 2-mile climb. All this work is for cutthroats up to a foot or so. Don't worry about the crowds.

Fox Lake: Fox is about 10 miles east of Cooke City off US 212. It has good populations of 10- to 12-inch grayling, brookies, and rainbows. Long, narrow, and fairly deep, covering 120 acres in all, it's only the length of a football field from the highway.

Glacier Lake: You can get to within a mile of Glacier by the Rock Creek Road. It sits near the Wyoming line and is about 180 feet deep and nearly 180 acres. Glacier is planted with cutthroats, which grow to 2 or 3 pounds if they live long enough. It is a popular place, heavily fished for both the cutthroats and resident brookies.

Granite Lake: Twenty miles east of Cooke City, Granite lies in both Montana and Wyoming. It's reached by an 8-mile hike up Muddy Creek to 8,625 feet, where you will find 8- to 14-inch brookies and rainbows in this deep, 250-acre lake.

Green Lake: Green is about a mile southeast of Elaine Lake and filled with 10-inch brook trout, whose ancestors must have been glad to leave the blighted streams of the East to the hardier brown trout and come West where they could overrun so many waters perfectly suited to them. Anyway, they thrive in this 36-acre, 130-foot deep lake.

Hellroaring Lakes: These are a dozen miles south of Red Lodge off US 212. There are twelve lakes in all, and about half of them are barren (the secret is knowing which ones). Anyone lacking local and current information can play safe and fish Hellroaring Lake #2. It's planted with cutthroats regularly, and in peak years it's good fishing for trout up to 3 pounds. This is serious thunderstorm country.

Jasper Lake: Go to Albino Lake and then hike a half mile north to 55-acre Jasper. It sits at over 10,000 feet and is planted periodically with cutthroats that will reach 4 or 5 pounds before the cycle begins to decline and populations dwindle toward its next eight-year stocking.

The most consistent fishing in these lakes (and most others) is in the third, fourth, and fifth years after stocking. Information on plantings is available from regional headquarters of the Montana Department of Fish, Wildlife & Parks. It's worth checking on specific waters before wandering into this hard-to-reach country. Often a lake that was hot last year is dead this year, while a water just next door is prime this season. A quick visit or phone call can eliminate a lot of frustration (and useless hiking if trout are the major goal of the expedition).

Kersey Lake: Kersey is easy to reach by four-wheel drive up Sedge Creek just 3 miles out of Cooke City. It is nearly 120 acres by 70 feet deep with good-size brookies, some cutthroats, and maybe a stray lake trout or two.

Lake Creek: Lake Creek begins as ice-melt from Castle Rock Glacier. It flows through lakes such as Long View and Green before emptying into Granite. The water between the various lakes is worth fishing. This is good pocket water for brook and cutthroat trout. Nothing fancy is required here in the way of patterns, but pick something buoyant and visible, such as a Humpy, in sizes 14 through 18.

Lake of the Winds: This one is planted every so often with cutthroats and is good fishing for fat trout. It was once planted with goldens, but they're long gone. It's 40 acres at almost 10,000 feet in barren, windy country. Hike about 3 miles from Fox Lake to Russell Lake to Marianne Lake and north to Lake of the Winds.

Line Lake: Line is very good for cutthroats that average a pound or more, but it's tough fishing because of the steady and hard winds. It's small, only 5 acres, and there's no place on it to escape the gales. You can reach it by going up Line Creek from the Beartooth Highway.

Lone Elk Lake: Climb above Broadwater Lake, up beyond 10,000 feet. The lake is green from glacial flour, and dark, high-contrast flies are consistently better than lighter ones in Lone Elk. A Timberline Emerger is one of the best patterns. Brookies to 16 inches and grayling over a pound do very well here.

Long Lake: This one is easy to drive to with a four-wheel-drive vehicle off US 212. Wind 5 miles up the Goose Creek jeep trail to reach Long (and go another half mile to reach Ovis). It's filled with smallish brook trout and a few cutthroats that have washed down from Ovis Lake. Long is well named, stretching over a third of a mile, but covering only 12 surface acres.

Moon Lake: Moon is well above 10,000 feet in barren rock and wind country in that Glacier Lake cluster. Ever try breathing at 10,000 feet? This is not the place for aerobics. Altitude sickness (with a throbbing headache being one of the first symptoms) is a possibility. Moon, at roughly 80 acres, is planted periodically with cutthroats that might reach 20 inches on rare occasions.

Ovis Lake: Ovis is below Sheep Mountain, not far by jeep trail from Long Lake. It's the better of the two lakes, with bigger fish that average maybe 12 inches. It's a popular drive-to spot throughout the summer, but crowds disappear after Labor Day.

Red Lodge Creek: Followed by road all the way from Joliet to the confluence of the East and West Forks, Red Lodge has two distinct sections. The 15-mile stretch above Cooney Reservoir has undercut, brushy banks that hold plenty of brown trout. The fish run mostly between 10 and 15 inches, but there are bigger ones to 24 inches. The broad valley is good grasshopper country, and by late July patterns such as the Dave's Hopper and Henry's Fork Hopper are the most consistent midday producers. The lower stretch, below Cooney Reservoir, is marginal fishing. It runs through open grass and cottonwood country, too, but there are mainly trash fish, whitefish, and a few large brown trout here.

Rock Creek: This Rock Creek originates on the Beartooth Plateau in Wyoming and flows for 27 miles to the Clarks Fork near Joliet. There are five public access sites and it's fished quite a bit for browns, brookies, rainbows, and whitefish. Willows and cottonwoods line the banks, providing excellent cover that protects the fish and also eats a fly every now and then.

Rock Island Lake: Rock Island is planted from the air every three years with lots of cutthroats that grow to a couple of pounds. There are also some naturally sustaining (it's almost impossible to eradicate them) brook trout. Reached from Cooke Pass, 7.5 miles up the Crazy Lake Trail, the lake is 137 acres by 110 feet deep. It's known locally for big trout that are sometimes easy to catch and sometimes impossible to even find when they disappear into the deep.

Rough Lake: Rough Lake is over 100 acres, deep, high (over 10,000 feet), and not far from Lone Elk Lake. It is filled with nice brookies to 3 pounds and pitifully small grayling that spawn in the clear gravels at the base of a waterfall.

Silver Lake: Accessible from the Sky Top Creek Trail, in the Rough Lake area, it's only 7 acres and shallow, but Silver Lake holds some big brook trout that wander down from Hunger Lake just upstream.

Sodalite Lake: Start at the Broadwater Creek Trail off US 212, hike up past Curl Lake and Broadwater Lake, and after about 5 miles you'll reach Sodalite. This lake is in the Broadwater drainage at 9,840 feet, measures 26 acres by 90 feet deep, and is loaded with skinny brook trout that grow to a big-headed 14 inches.

Triangle Lake: Triangle is managed for cutthroat trout, which do well in this 6-acre pond (small but surprisingly deep at 35 feet). This is another of those "can't get there from here" waters—start at the West Fork Rock Creek Trail, and with the aid of a compass and good topo maps, head west to find Triangle.

Widewater Lake: Reached from the popular Crazy Lakes Trail off US 212, it sits a half mile below Fox Lake. Widewater is about a 6.5-mile hike. It holds good numbers of grayling, brookies, and cutthroats to a couple of pounds.

Zimmer Lake: Go to Broadwater Lake and hike 5 miles up the Broadwater River–Zimmer Creek Trail. It is 26 acres by 55 feet deep and sits not far from Grasshopper Glacier. Zimmer has good-size cutthroat dependent on the planting cycle. Beautiful, out-of-this world country.

Gallatin River

This was the second river I ever fished in Montana (the first was the Taylor Fork) way back in the early sixties when I was staying at the Nine Quarter Circle Guest Ranch. The Gallatin River is a nice place to spend a summer afternoon casting Wulffs of one color or another along the bankside runs, around midstream boulders, or along bouncing riffles. The trout will be mostly rainbows and they will not often exceed 12 inches, but you'll catch plenty of them, and wading along the river as it dances over a colorful streambed on a warm July day is a simple pleasure.

This doesn't mean that there aren't good-size rainbows and browns in the 115 miles of river between Yellowstone National Park and the headwaters of the Missouri. Browns of over 5 pounds are taken each year, especially in autumn. Rainbows of similar size are also taken, usually by anglers working large nymphs along the bottoms of deep, fast runs.

Big fish are always a top attraction on Montana's rivers, but a day making short casts with an easy-to-see dry and taking fish without constant mending and reaching is a pleasing change of pace from the intense techniques often required to connect with the big boys. To escape the increasingly annoying levels of entomological Latin dogma that pervade some of the corners of fly fishing is a relief, too. The upper stretches of the Gallatin are the spots to view mountain vistas and striking cliff formations. And, since most of this river is within yards of US 191, you just pull over to one side of the road, rig up, and start casting.

BOUNDARY OF YELLOWSTONE PARK TO THE TAYLOR FORK

Upstream from the Taylor Fork, the river is narrow, shallow, and often braided as it flows over a gravel streambed along willow-lined banks. The Madison and Gallatin ranges dominate the skyline. There are mainly rainbows with some browns in this water. The populations aren't high—just 350 trout per mile over 8 inches—but there are bigger fish in the scattered deep holes. Find those holes and their concentrations of trout, and this part of the river suddenly becomes a fine little fishery.

The wild part of the upper river that breaks away from the highway, and runs north and east, has a good trail running up into the alpine headwaters and the mountains of Yellowstone. You will see moose, elk, deer, and perhaps a grizzly along the way through beautiful country.

Gallatin River

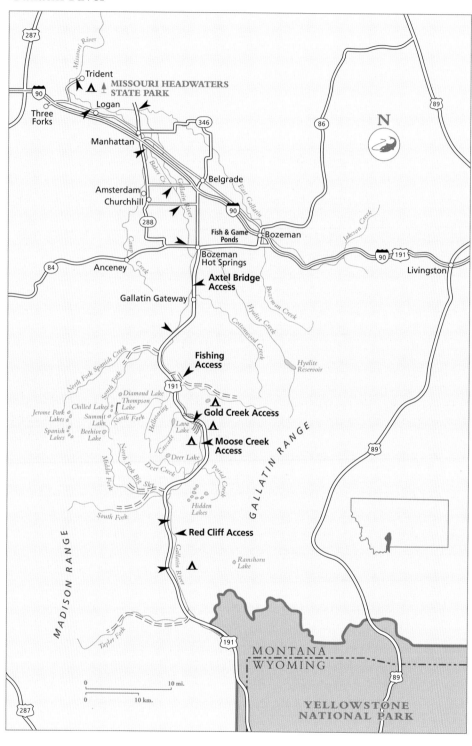

Trident

MISSOURI HEADWATERS STATE PARK

Logan

Three Forks

Manhattan

Belgrade

Amsterdam
Churchhill

Fish & Game Ponds

Bozeman

Anceney

Bozeman Hot Springs

Axtel Bridge Access

Gallatin Gateway

Fishing Access

Gold Creek Access

Moose Creek Access

Red Cliff Access

MADISON RANGE

GALLATIN RANGE

Livingston

Hyalite Reservoir

Diamond Lake
Thompson Lake

Chilled Lakes
Jerome Park Lakes
Summit Lake
Spanish Lakes
Beehive Lake

North Fork

Lava Lake

Deer Lake

Hidden Lakes

Ramshorn Lake

MONTANA
WYOMING

YELLOWSTONE NATIONAL PARK

N

0   10 mi.

0   10 km.

For some reason, I seem to take the most trout in this small water on soft-hackled patterns cast quartering upstream and then pulsed lightly just below the surface, especially in the bankside runs and through the sapphire pools. Large fish are present but uncommon, but the casting is rewarding if only for the fact that you are alive in pristine mountain terrain.

TAYLOR FORK TO GALLATIN GATEWAY

Mark well the location of the Taylor Fork (actually called Taylor Creek on the topographical maps). It is a major tributary and it, more than anything else on the river, controls the fishing downstream from its mouth.

The problem is the exposed banks and cliffs on the Taylor Fork. These natural formations dump gray soup into the water with any high runoff or even a good rain. The silt stays suspended and washes far down into the main Gallatin. Fly fishing suddenly turns nearly impossible for days at a time. During the high-water months of May through early July, the river is entirely "mudded out."

A big and obscene change over the years has been the rampant, obnoxious development around Big Sky, with gridlock traffic and LA rush-hour exhaust fume levels in midsummer. This place is trashed by developers. It's hell on Earth. Avoid it like you would a psychotic door-to-door salesman.

From the Taylor Fork down to Gallatin Gateway, there are populations of rainbows up to 5,000 fish per mile in some sections. Fish average about 12 inches, with some of several pounds holding in the deeper water or under banks. The salmon fly hatch comes off in June. After this, terrestrials play well in the summer, and there are also caddisflies from June into fall. Hoppers, beetles, and ants cover the warm-weather action, but these "occasional" terrestrials are overshadowed (as is every other food item) by one of the best spruce moth populations in the state.

The spruce moths flop down on the water by the millions in this forested, canyon stretch of the river during a good year from July through August. This is mass suicide—not the occasional, accidental blow-in. The insects don't belong on the water, and once their powdery, scaled wings get wet, they are trapped on the surface. These chunky, size 10 bugs are too much to ignore for even the best trout. Suddenly the river is producing 14- to 20-inch rainbows and browns on dry flies instead of the 10-inchers.

The trout feed on the spruce moths for weeks at a stretch and then suddenly do become selective. It's time to put away the Wulffs and the Humpies and tie on a matching size 10 or 12 Spruce Moth. And it's time to stop the blind casting and start stalking the trout making the biggest, slurping rise forms.

Throughout the summer, if the fish aren't up on dry flies, try a weighted stonefly nymph. Just about any pattern will do, as long as it's black and has rubber legs.

GALLATIN GATEWAY TO GALLATIN FORKS

There are good and bad stretches on this part of the Gallatin. Sections of it are sucked dry every year for irrigation. Anyone crossing over the river on I-90 in August must wonder about the bed of rocks. The dewatered areas never recover insect and fish populations from season to season.

The valley portion of the river in general is much slower and warmer than the upper river, which stays in the 60-degree range even in July and August, and the lower river offers much richer habitat wherever there's continual flow. Over 1,000 rainbows in the 12- to 14-inch range and an equal number of browns running to 18 inches were discovered in one survey. There are also very large browns that will come to large streamers in the fall. Try twitching sculpin patterns of 1/0 and 2/0 along the bottom and over the rocks to goad the browns into taking.

If you are in an aggressive mood and feel up to some challenging work, put on a short, stout leader at the end of a quick-sinking line and a large nymph, like Charles Brooks' Assam Dragon, and probe the depths of some racy, deep run. To fish water like this properly, you must cross well above the run so that you cast from just short of midstream. You will be in fast water well over your knees right next to even faster water over your shoulders. Fall here and you'll likely wind up rolling all the way to the dried out, lower river.

With a 6- or 7-weight sinking line, a 4- or 5-foot leader tapering to a delicate tippet in 1X or 0X, a size 4 Assam Dragon or a size 2 Girdle Bug, a lead twist-on or two (far-and-fine fishing at its delicate best), and a 9-foot rod, you begin your exploration of this deep, rough-water environment. Actually, this is not as awkward or as difficult as it may seem, and the technique works very well on similar waters throughout Montana.

Starting at the head of the run, cast the contraption about 20 feet upstream, allowing it to sink to the bottom, and work right through the run. Keep the slightest bit of slack in the line, but not so much that you can't feel, see, and sense (this comes on rapidly with experience) the nymph bouncing along the gravel and rounded rocks of the streambed. When a good trout hits here, it will be a vicious strike as the fish zips up after the food and then powers straight back to cover. You'll know when this happens.

At the end of the drift, allow the fly to swing in the current for a few seconds, enough time to take out the belly that accumulated in the line as it fought the many conflicting currents in the water column. On occasion a big boy will hammer the fly at the last moment. A half-dozen casts or more are needed to work a stretch thoroughly before lengthening the cast a few feet and repeating the procedure.

GALLATIN FORKS DOWNSTREAM TO THE MISSOURI RIVER

From the Gallatin Forks, where the East Gallatin empties in, down to Three Forks, the river runs through mostly private land. Floating is allowed in this section, and it is the best way to cast to a nice balance of rainbows and browns. For wading anglers the

From Yellowstone Park to the headwaters of the Missouri, the Gallatin provides 115 miles of wadeable, small-stream fishing.

bridges are the main public access in this section. There are soft, limestone walls where the water digs out deep, swirling holes. Trout hang in these pools and feed on good hatches of pale morning duns, tricos, and blue-winged olives—in this spring-creek-like environment, the Gallatin suddenly becomes a more technical river.

The best times of the year to fish the Gallatin are before the runoff in late spring and just after the runoff subsides and the water begins to compress. During the earlier period, in March and April, the river is in superb condition. It might muddy up on warm days, but it stays clear and fishes well on nymphs on cool days. Patterns such as the Prince Nymph and George's Brown Stone produce well anywhere on the river. Autumn isn't bad either.

During the later period, after runoff, a dark-colored streamer, like a Woolly Bugger, snaked through the rocks and along the bottom near shore or through the heart of strong runs, can turn some very big fish in the middle to lower sections of the Gallatin.

Autumn means big browns on the spawning move. This translates into streamer and nymphs, like Zonkers, Muddler Minnows, Matuka Spruces, Bitch Creeks, Girdle and Yuk Bugs, and, of course, Buggers. If you're floating below the confluence with the East Gallatin, cast one of these bank-tight and let it drift with a little action, or cast it to shore and quickly strip it back to the raft. When wading, cast upstream or work your way out into the river and cast to shore. Felt-soled boots help on the slippery rocks, as does a wading staff at times.

Blue-winged olives also provide some action, especially during the hatches on overcast or rainy autumn afternoons. A greased Olive Hare's Ear covers some emerging

POPULAR FLIES

Baetis Wulff	Olive Gold-Ribbed Hare's
Bitch Creek	Ear
Disco Midge	Parachute Adams
George's Brown Stone	Pheasant Tail
Girdle Bug	Prince Nymph
Goddard Caddis	Serendipity
Griffith's Gnat	Shroud
Humpies—especially red	Spent Partridge Caddis
and yellow	Timberline Emerger
Matuka Spruce	Woolly Bugger
Muddler Minnow	Yuk Bug
	Zonker

activity. Baetis Wulffs are nice, easy-to-see selections, as are light and dark Olive Comparaduns, for the adult insects.

Wherever and whenever you decide to fish on the upper river, the choices you make will not be disappointing. Because this water is closed to fishing from boats, it's perfect wading water. If you have the means to float, the lower river gives an added bonus of some truly large trout. The Gallatin is a fine trout stream in all aspects—scenery, water quality, and numbers of catchable fish—but it's under threat big-time from developers, ruthless modifiers all.

FISHING WATERS IN THE GALLATIN DRAINAGE

Baker Creek: This is an agrarian, small stream out in the open not far from Manhattan that has a decent run of brown trout in the fall, plus fair numbers of resident rainbows and browns. It is touched at various spots by a county road.

Benhart Creek: This fine, spring-fed water has brookies, browns, and rainbows in good numbers with some size, but the surrounding land around Belgrade is being cut up, subdivided, posted, and made more or less off-limits for most fly fishers.

Benhart is well known for its difficult trout. This is spring creek fishing at its most technical; it will make you start babbling Latin or discoursing on the qualities of 8X versus 7X, or wondering what you would ever do with a fly larger than size 20. The pale morning duns, the tricos, and the blue-winged olives are all important on this stream, but for really fussy fishing, try matching the tiny blue-winged olives, the size 24 Pseudocloeon mayflies that start blanketing the water in September.

Deer Lake: Deer Lake is in a glacial cirque above 9,000 feet. The Deer Creek Trail starts right off US 191 on the west side of the road about 20 miles south of Gallatin Gateway. It's a 5-mile hike to 7-acre Deer Lake, which has good numbers of grayling that reach a foot or so. They have moments when they display suicidal tendencies toward small dry flies—size 20 and down. Effective patterns include tiny versions of the Griffith's Gnat, Shroud, Parachute Adams, and Spent Partridge Caddis.

Diamond Lake: Everyone has to walk the last leg into this lake—the trail is too rough for horses. Go up the South Fork Spanish Creek Trail for 5 miles, then cross-country for about 2 miles, to a small, deep lake that has some very big rainbows that are tough to catch but have been known to hit a slowly sinking fly.

East Gallatin River: The East Gallatin drains both the Gallatin and Bridger mountains and flows for almost 40 miles to the main river near Manhattan. Most of the stream runs through private hay fields but there is public access here and there, so once you're on the water, if you stay below the high-water marks, you can fish to your heart's content. The river has good populations of aquatic insects because of the nutrients that enter the spring-fed water from the fields. Hoppers and other terrestrials are also present in significant quantities.

The upper dozen miles are mainly rainbow water. The lower stretches are brushy with undercut banks, providing excellent habitat for both resident and spawning brown trout that average 13 inches and run into several pounds. Streamers take the fish in autumn, and hoppers are productive from midsummer until the first succession of killing frosts. The hoppers will still work for a week or so after this period. The fish don't know any better. Baetis sometimes draw the trout to the surface in the afternoons in the spring and fall.

Hidden Lakes: Reached from the Portal Creek Road, there are eight lakes in all, lying at close to 9,000 feet. Several of the lakes have goldens ranging from a few inches to several pounds. The big ones are hard to catch unless they have moved into the connecting streams. When they're in the streams, a large, weighted Woolly Bugger or other streamer pattern worked across their noses will provoke strikes. The little goldens will take nymphs and drys worked near shore or along outlets. A Goddard Caddis works well in the outlets.

Hyalite Creek: Hyalite Creek flows from Hyalite Reservoir for 23 miles across an alluvial fan to the main river near Belgrade. The upper reaches, also known as Middle Creek, are good pocket water with Wulffs and Humpies and such for rainbows, cutthroats, brookies, and even grayling and a very few browns. The lower reaches are not all that great, except for an occasional fat brown in the fall. Sculpin patterns lobbed to the banks and bounced along the rubble and muck will do the trick. Maybe you'll catch a tiger trout. Who knows?

Hyalite Reservoir: South of Bozeman in a timbered canyon, it's about 200 acres when not drawn down 30 feet or more. You can reach it by road, and there is a boat ramp. Yellowstone cutthroats grow big here, and there are grayling that approach a couple of pounds. Thirty thousand cutthroats are planted each year to keep the numbers of fish up in the face of extreme angling pressure of all disciplines. Summer often sees a good hatch of Panther Martins.

Jackson (Rocky) Creek: Jackson forms the East Gallatin River when it joins Kelley Creek. Good fishing for small brookies, cutthroats, and rainbows, plus a few decent browns in the lower reaches in the fall.

Rat Lake: Made famous (or infamous) in *A View from Rat Lake* by John Gierach, it's up Squaw Creek. Rat Lake is 18 acres and shallow, and it's really popular because of rainbows that exceed 5 pounds. If you can lug a float tube in here, try working damsel-

or dragonfly nymphs tight to the aquatic plants. Let the nymphs sink and then crawl them back along the bottom. Slow, tedious work, but this will take the big trout. Other favorite nymph patterns for near-surface work include the Biggs Special, Pheasant Tail, and Twist Nymph. The unnamed tributary to the lake, inlet and outlet, is closed all year.

South Fork Spanish Creek: This is a good mountain stream with plenty of pocket water holding brook trout to perhaps 12 inches but averaging smaller. Beaver ponds hold the best fish.

Spanish Lakes: These two lakes in Spanish Peaks country are less than 10 acres, but have some Yellowstone cutthroats to 15 inches or a bit larger.

Squaw Creek: Squaw Creek is followed by road and trail into timbered mountain country. It's good fast-water dry-fly and nymph fishing for cutthroats, rainbows, and brookies. A wet fly worked through the pools near the main current seams will also take fish. Some browns head up the lower reaches in autumn.

Summit Lake: This one has some fat cutthroat trout in its 1.5 acres. To reach Summit, take a long walk up the North Fork Hellroaring Creek Trail.

Taylor Fork Gallatin River: The Taylor Fork is followed by a lousy gravel and dirt road that winds and lurches past the Nine Quarter Circle Guest Ranch, then on to Taylor Falls (the last couple of miles by trail). The stretches by the ranch and down to US 191 are heavily fished by dudes, but some nice rainbows, cutthroats, and a stray brookie or two can be taken with stealth. Use wet flies or nymphs around the large rocks and boulders or along the brushy banks. The same holds true for very few browns in the fall. A pretty, easy-to-wade, open, sagebrush-country trout stream with some nice mosquitoes in June and July. Hoppers play well here in the heat. The upper reaches can be good for fat cutthroats to 10 inches.

Thompson Lake: Thompson is in the Spanish Peaks area and gets hit hard by pack strings and hikers. Can you say "Woodstock"? All in all, there is still some fair fishing for cutthroats that average less than a foot.

West Fork of the Gallatin River: This used to be one of the prettiest little trout streams in the West, but the Big Sky development killed that off. Gone now are the wide-open sage benches and brushy runs that were filled with cutthroats, rainbows, and brookies that loved any type of dry fly they could clamp their jaws on. Now there are condos and paved roads and hotels and ski runs and poor fishing. You have a better chance of finding a golf ball than catching a trout. Can you say "trashed"? Thanks, Chet.

Floating the Jefferson River anywhere along its way to the Missouri can turn large trout.

Jefferson River

A recent late-October trip to this river produced several browns to 18 inches on first a size 10 Yellow Humpy and then on size 6 Woolly Buggers as I waded from a bridge access about 20 miles above Twin Bridges, working riffles and the inside corners of current seams. The browns and the day were gorgeous, highlighted by cottonwoods turned bright yellow-orange. I was reminded once again why I love the Jefferson.

Any fly fisher familiar with the Jefferson River immediately thinks of brown trout lying tight to brushy banks that line a meandering river of large holes connected by deep, dark runs that are fed by shallow riffles running swiftly over gravel bars and drop-offs. Logjams, cottonwoods, undercut grassy shorelines, narrow canyon stretches, and wide-open country studded with the isolated Tobacco Root Mountains on the east and the Highland Range off in the west complete the picture.

Formed at the confluence of the Beaverhead and Big Hole Rivers with a nice assist from the Ruby just upstream, the Jefferson runs 80 miles until it joins the Madison and Gallatin to form the Missouri. Over 200 feet wide for much of its length, the Jefferson can be divided into three general sections: the upper river between Twin Bridges and Cardwell, the canyon stretch, and the final lower river stretch downstream from Sappington Bridge to Trident.

Most of those who float or wade the river concentrate their efforts on the upper river, which has a faster flow, relatively speaking, than the rest of the river. This portion has the most catchable trout per mile and is considered the best water. Browns outnumber rainbows by about seven to one, with an average size of just under 15 inches. This brown-to-rainbow ratio holds up pretty well for most of the water. There are also large numbers of mountain whitefish that are always on the lookout for a nymph bounced along the bottom. Current regulations allow anglers to keep five browns, but the action is strictly catch-and-release for rainbows, which are making slow inroads on the population dynamics of the Jefferson. The river braids a good deal up here, and the current scours gravel sufficiently to attract fair numbers of spawning browns in the fall.

Probably the best times to work the Jefferson are from April through mid-July, using large nymphs like the Prince or Montana. Allow time off to let the spring runoff have its way. As soon as the water begins to lower and clear, pound the current seams and buckets (convergences of varying speeds of water) with Woolly Buggers, Girdle Bugs, Matukas, and similar large patterns. Some of the best action of the season takes

Jefferson River

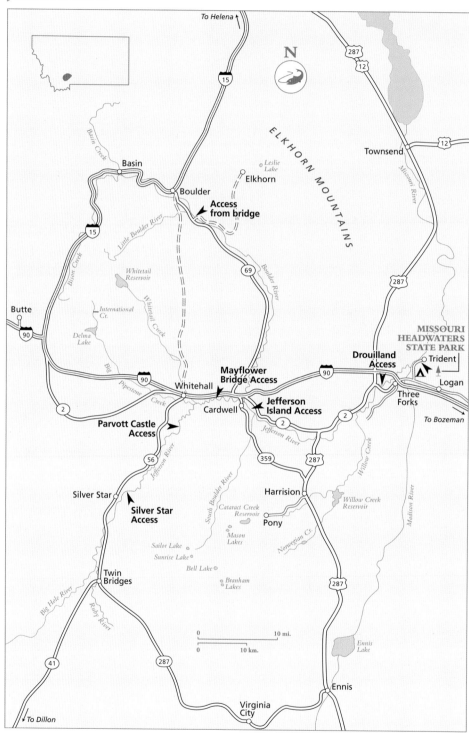

To Helena

N

ELKHORN MOUNTAINS

287
12

Townsend

12

Basin Creek

Basin

Leslie Lake

Elkhorn

Boulder

Access from bridge

15

Little Boulder River

69

Boulder River

Missouri River

287

Bison Creek

Whitetail Reservoir

International Cr.

Butte

90

Delma Lake

Big Pipestone Creek

90

Whitehall

Whitetail Creek

Mayflower Bridge Access

90

Drouilland Access

MISSOURI HEADWATERS STATE PARK

Trident

Logan

Three Forks

2

Parvott Castle Access

2

Cardwell

Jefferson Island Access

Jefferson River

To Bozeman

56

Jefferson River

359

287

Silver Star

Silver Star Access

South Boulder River

Cataract Creek Reservoir

Harrision

Pony

Norwegian Cr.

Willow Creek

Willow Creek Reservoir

Madison River

Mason Lakes

Sailor Lake

Sunrise Lake

Bell Lake

Branham Lakes

287

Twin Bridges

Big Hole River

Ruby River

0   10 mi.
0   10 km.

287

Ennis Lake

41

287

Ennis

To Dillon

Virginia City

place on the Jefferson, and most other rivers in the western third of the state, during this week-long-or-so period of compression.

From September through the cold of November, diehard anglers work the river for large spawning browns that will top 5 pounds. If you're willing to heave large (1/0 or 2/0) Matuka Sculpins, you'll turn some impressive trout with sink-tip lines cast quartering upstream along the banks, and then working the sculpin along the bottom rocks and gravel. Lobbing the heavy stuff slightly sidearm avoids potential midflight collisions between weighted streamer and skull. The casting can be tedious, but if you work the stretches of the river that are flushed clear of irrigation silt, you will normally take several hefty browns. Dead sculpins, with mouth-shaped chunks missing from their sides, are not an uncommon sight in the still water near shore. Fishing Matukas is not the thrill-a-second angling in the caddis falls of evening, but the browns you connect with are worth the effort.

While weighted streamers and sink-tip lines are usually the most effective approach for browns, there are periods when the trout hold near the surface—under banks, just below foam eddies, or beneath logjams. A pattern retrieved along the bottom may miss these trout entirely. A floating line with an unweighted Bugger or similar fly cast line-tight across stream, then dead-drifted or twitched slightly, often spells the difference between few, if any, browns and steady action. Allow the streamer to swing out with the current and flutter at the end of the line for a few seconds. Big trout often snap at the fly as it hangs suspended in the river's current. When the usual, down-deep, quickly-stripped approach proves unproductive, thirty minutes playing around with this variation is often useful.

State fishing access sites and bridges on county roads provide access to the upper river. For the floater, several large irrigation diversions present potential hazards that require caution and often a brief portage. From a mile above Ironrod Bridge to below Silver Star, irrigation diversions can lead to extremely low water levels in the summer. In the drought of 1988, the river was sucked almost bone dry, with miles of streambed exposed to the sun. How sufficient numbers of trout survived to repopulate the river is something of a mystery and a minor natural miracle. Irrigation damages much of the river, and in dry years, some potentially top-notch tributaries. When the water is returned to the riverbed, it is often choked with silt and chemicals and warmed to near lethal levels. Another diversion to watch for is at Guy George Bridge near Waterloo.

The canyon stretch of the river below (east of) Cardwell is quite deep and slow. Along here you can get to the river both from the road and from railroad tracks. The fishing is often good because cliffs shelter the river from the sun during the dog days of summer.

The trout run about an inch or so smaller in the lower section of the Jefferson. US 10 and a couple of campgrounds provide access. An abandoned limestone quarry and the last, crumbling vestiges of an old wooden flume used to transport water to nearby

POPULAR FLIES

Adams	Pink Cahill
Bitch Creek	Prince Nymph
Clouser Deep Minnow	Renegade
Elk Hair Caddis	Trude
Girdle Bug	Woolly Bugger
Humpy	Wulff
Matuka Sculpin	Yuk Bug
Montana Nymph	

mining operations in the early 1900s are visible on the limestone walls. Full-sinking lines with big nymphs and streamers dredging the bottom are the best play.

The lower Jefferson runs over a gravel and small-rock bottom through fields of hay. Towering cottonwoods line the banks. The first part of this section is mostly one channel, but the river braids wildly between Three Forks and Missouri Headwaters State Park, creating some navigational problems for floaters. During low water you can drag your boat as much as you row it along here. Aluminum canoes can be heard for miles as they bang along the rocky streambed. Trout tend to shy from this cacophony. Hopper and beetle patterns are prime selections during the summer days, especially along the hay fields.

Work the undercuts and clear gravel areas of this part of the river. Yuk Bugs, Girdle Bugs, and Bitch Creeks are local favorites, though many anglers prefer drys from size 10 to 16. This approach makes sense in low, clear water conditions because the drys are less likely to be spotted for fakes than are the submarine-size streamers. Some obvious picks include Elk Hair Caddis in sizes 14 and 16, especially on overcast days and in the evenings in spring and fall, and, because of the slow current, some Callibaetis in the warm months. Adams, PMDs, Blue-Winged Olives, and perhaps a Cahill for the sake of impulse work well in the early morning and around dusk.

In the riffles, attractors like Wulffs, Trudes, Renegades, and the durable Humpy bring the trout up with some regularity. Most anglers use these patterns in size 12 and smaller. During bright light conditions on hot afternoons, try size 8 or 10. The big, bushy, imitation has a bit more appeal for the fish. On overcast days, try a Gray Wulff. Actually, large nymphs bounced along these riffles is the most productive technique, if you don't mind catching a crazed whitefish every now and then.

While floating the Jefferson is usually an all-day affair, wading presents problems that are borderline insurmountable on many sections. The river has steep banks and is too deep in many areas to wade comfortably or even safely. Choose your entrances and beats with care, or you'll wind up totally soaked. With a little scouting and caution, there are runs that can be fished adequately on foot, even from the banks.

Fishing Waters in the Jefferson Drainage

Big Pipestone Creek: Big Pipestone begins as the outlet of Delmo Lake and is followed by county road for 20 miles to the Jefferson near Whitehall. Good brown trout fishing in the lower reaches in autumn, and there are some cutthroats in the upper section.

Bison Creek: Heading northeast of Butte not far from Elk Park Pass, Bison runs mainly north for over 15 miles to the Boulder River near Basin. The upper section flows through open fields with small rainbows and brook trout. The canyon stretch is tough to fish but has some trout. The final section is silted up and hard-hit by local anglers for mainly put-and-take rainbows.

Boulder River: This was once a quality trout stream, and in spots it still is, but heavy-metal pollution from mining has choked the streambed and killed off much streamside vegetation that used to offer shelter for the browns. Stream alteration and cattle stomping along the riparian areas add to the woes of this little river. The upper 17 miles above Bison Creek are the best water, with over 1,500 brook trout per mile averaging about 9 inches with a few to 15. Dry flies worked tight to bankside cover take the trout, as do wets fished through the same locations. Try dead drifts, then some action, and finally allow the pattern to hold in the current, undulating from side to side at the end of a drift.

Remember that the river from the mouth upstream to the bridge on Boulder Cut-Off Road (mile 14.4) is open the third Saturday in May through September 30.

The stretch below Bison Creek runs through a canyon that is poor habitat due to the steep gradient and pollution. The upper part of this water is fair for rainbows and brookies. Nymphs down deep work best. Below severely polluted High Ore Creek, trout all but disappear.

The final 50 miles down to the Jefferson at Cardwell is mainly brown trout water with perhaps as many as 3,000 catchable fish per mile. Once again, metal contamination and high water temperatures combine to slow growth rates and depress trout numbers. The last few miles of the river are flushed to some extent by springs and small creeks. Browns are found at well over 1,000 per mile. Unfortunately, most of the best water flows through private land and is posted. You need to wade a good piece to reach the best fishing. A run of large browns heads upstream in the fall, but the fish are blocked by an irrigation diversion, which has led to the closure of four "airline" miles of the river up from Cardwell after September 30.

The upper run is paralleled by I-15, and the lower part is followed by MT 69. An interesting sidelight of dubious distinction lies just to the west as you look back from

Sometimes around dusk, big browns in the Boulder River rise to mayflies and caddis. So, too, do hordes of whitefish.

the river's mouth along I-90. A mining company has blasted and hauled away the entire eastern face of Dry Mountain. And we all thought ants were industrious.

Branham Lakes: These two lakes are less than 20 acres each in the Tobacco Roots at over 9,000 feet. They're managed now for Lake DeSmet rainbows that grow to a couple of pounds on occasion.

International Creek: Some good rainbows are taken in the lower reaches above Delmo Lake on drys in this small stream.

Leslie Lake: Leslie is about 9 acres and fairly deep in a glacial cirque below Crow Peak. A rough 6-mile jeep road from the ghost town of Elkhorn goes within three-quarters of a mile of the lake. It's fished a good deal but is still quite decent for cutthroats up to 3 pounds and averaging a bit less than a foot.

Little Boulder River: This one heads below Haystack Mountain and joins the main river southeast of Boulder. The lower willow-lined stretches have nice browns and brook trout. The upper section provides fishing for rainbows and cutthroats holding in the headwaters. Smaller—size 8 or 10—weighted Woolly Buggers with even a No. 1 egg shot crimped at the head work wonders, though you'll lose more than a few in the brush.

Mason Lakes: Not too far from Pony in the Tobacco Roots, both are less than 5 acres, dammed, and reached by trail for fair catches of rainbows. You'll do well if you're up to lugging a lightweight float tube into the ponds.

Norwegian Creek: Norwegian flows to Willow Creek Reservoir 8 miles through open, hilly country, including some beaver ponds, for nice rainbows, some brookies, and a few good browns. You can get to it by county road. Make sure you check your regulations on this one.

South Boulder River: You'll find classic pocket water in the upper reaches of this 20-mile stream that heads above Mammoth. Brookies and rainbows nail Wulffs, Renegades, and Humpies in the fast water, and there are some nice browns in the lower, slower private reaches.

Sunrise Lake: In the Tobacco Root Mountains at 9,300 feet in a glacial cirque, this small lake has good numbers of eager cutthroats in the 12-inch range.

Whitetail Creek: Whitetail heads a dozen miles east of Butte and flows first through canyon country, then rangeland to the Jefferson several miles west of Whitehall. There is good fall fishing with streamers for brown trout in the lower portion of the creek. Up above in the holes and in some beaver ponds, there are brookies, rainbows, and browns.

Willow Creek: Willow originates at the confluence of the North and South Forks of the creek not far from Pony, west of US 287. Good fishing in the open country below for rainbows and browns and perhaps a few brook trout, but landowner permission is needed (good luck!). The canyon stretches are filled with venom-spitting rattlesnakes that leap through the air from nearby rocks aiming for your throat. The venom can blind you and will eat through your blue jeans. If you are willing to risk potentially lethal attacks from these aggressive reptiles, there is good nymph and wet-fly fishing for larger fish that hold around submerged rocks. Bring a shotgun—these rattlers are dirty business.

Willow Creek (Harrison) Reservoir: This reservoir is nearly 4 square miles of water in the Tobacco Root Mountains east of Harrison, with naturally reproducing rainbow trout and browns to over 4 pounds. It's best in the spring and fall, fished from a float tube.

Particularly in its upper reaches, the Madison can be fast, braided water holding big trout. Mike Cline

Madison River

The Madison is often overrun with anglers, driftboats, and non-anglers rafting the river during peak times of the summer, but in spite of all the traffic, it's still one of the best trout fisheries in North America. The secret to fishing it successfully and enjoyably is to avoid the crowds. How? Avoiding the boats is simple. There are main put-in sites and main take-out sites. Fish near the take-out sites in the morning, long before any boats reach the area, and fish near the put-in sites in the evening, long after any boats leave the area. Avoiding the foot traffic is simple, too. A 15- to 20-minute hike from any access site leaves many of the anglers behind.

Once you get away from the hordes, you can usually use your favorite method, no matter what it is, and catch trout. Nymphs worked through the riffles, runs, and pockets are almost always successful. Classic wet flies, as well as soft-hackle patterns, still fool fish on this river. Streamers, wigged and danced through the current seams, drive the browns and rainbows crazy. Dry flies, from subtle hatch-matchers to garish attractors, will bring trout to the surface most days. The Madison, because it is so consistent, is just plain, flat-out a world-class trout stream in every sense of the term.

All great rivers display a variety of personalities as they tumble, wind, and drift their way downhill. Habitat, stream flow, water quality, species distribution, and fish numbers all combine to present a changing fly-fishing experience for the angler. Solutions gleaned on a headwaters stretch may have only limited application just a few miles downstream. The Madison is no exception, and it offers myriad challenges that even the most observant and skillful among us will never fully solve.

The Madison has specific regulations for each stretch, so consulting the regulations is important. It begins where the Gibbon and Firehole Rivers join in Yellowstone National Park. From this point until its juncture with the Jefferson and Gallatin Rivers to form the Missouri River, it flows mainly north for 140 miles through virtually every type of habitat and climate found in Montana—volcanic and mountainous, glacial and high plains, sedimentary and agrarian.

JUNCTION TO HEBGEN LAKE

The Madison in the park (much of it technically in Wyoming) wanders through lodgepole pine forest and mountain meadows. Wildlife, including elk, buffalo, moose, and grizzles (and now, even a few wolves), is abundant. Despite lying well above 6,000

Madison River

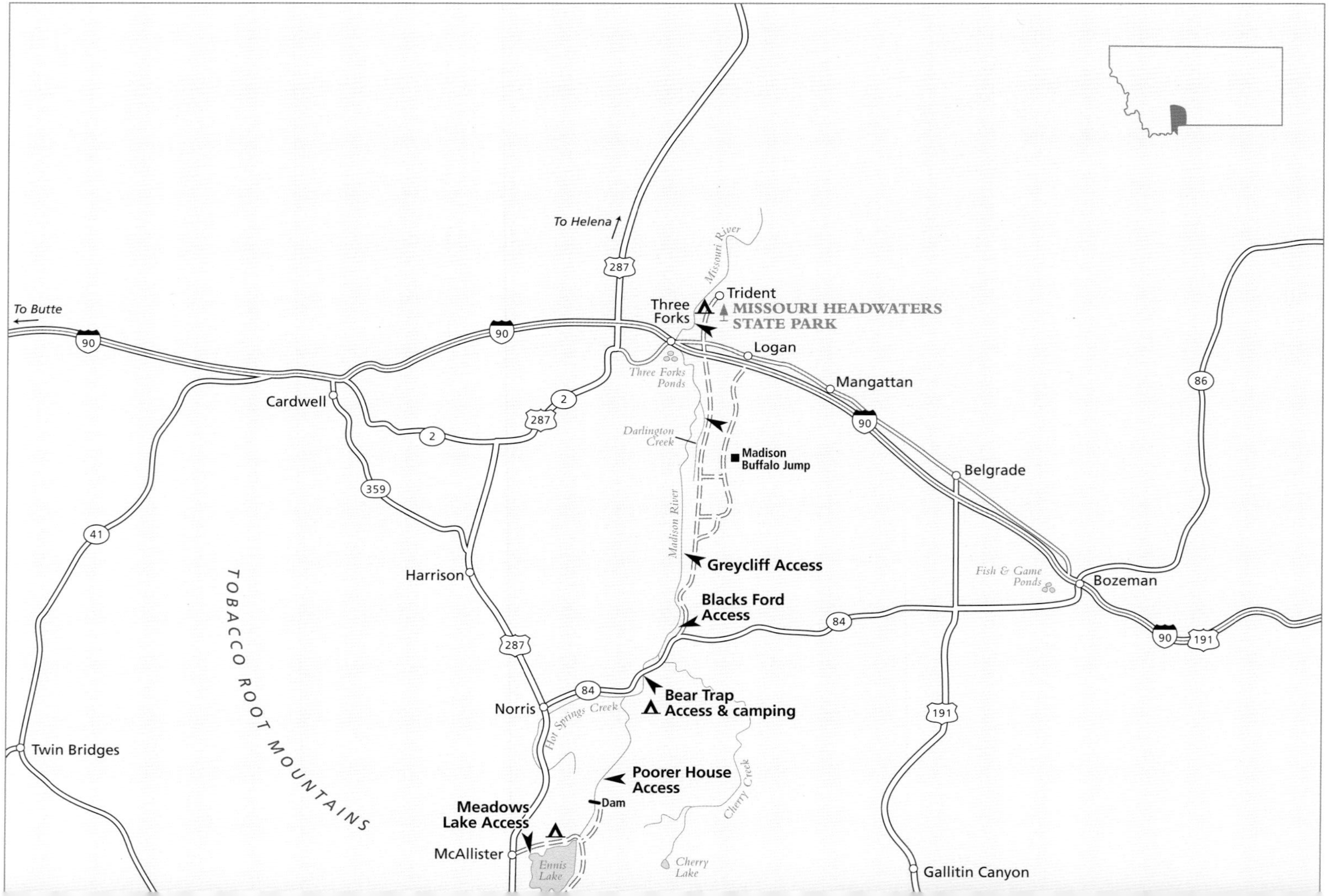

MISSOURI HEADWATERS
STATE PARK

Trident

Three
Forks

Logan

Mangattan

Belgrade

Bozeman

Madison
Buffalo Jump

Greycliff Access

Blacks Ford
Access

Bear Trap
Access & camping

Poorer House
Access

Dam

Meadows
Lake Access

McAllister

Ennis
Lake

Cherry
Lake

Cherry Creek

Hot Springs Creek

Norris

Harrison

Cardwell

Twin Bridges

TOBACCO ROOT MOUNTAINS

Gallitin Canyon

Darlington
Creek

Three Forks
Ponds

Madison River

Missouri River

Fish & Game
Ponds

To Helena

To Butte

86

191

90

90

90

90

90

191

84

84

287

287

287

2

2

359

41

Three Forks
Ponds

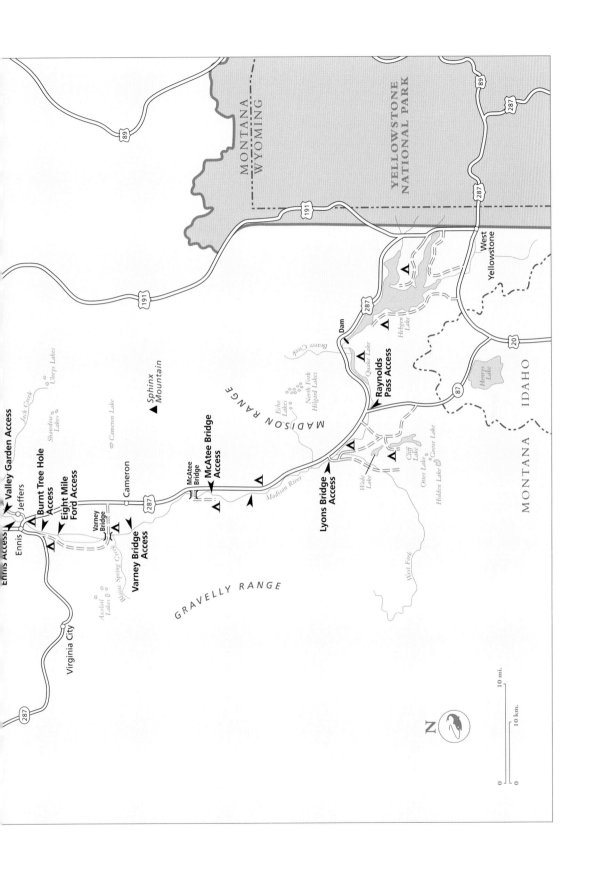

The Madison in its lower stretches above its confluence with the Missouri is wider, slower water and good for nymphing and fishing small drys and hoppers.

feet, the Madison is quite warm here, often reaching temperatures of 80 degrees Fahrenheit or more. This is due to the influx of hot water from geysers and hot springs that pour into the Firehole. This region is essentially a giant volcanic caldera, holding the largest concentration of thermal features in the world. Their influence is not lost on the Madison. Riffles, deep holes, and dark, mossy, glassy-surfaced runs mark the water in Yellowstone. The water is nutrient-rich—the late Charles Brooks called it the "largest chalkstream in the world." Browns, rainbows, cutthroats, and whitefish predominate.

In the spring, rainbows move up from Hebgen Lake into the river. In their spawning run, with the lake serving as their ocean, these fish act just like steelhead. During a low-water year, it's possible to bring a trout slashing up to the surface with a Bomber or a Slider, but usually this spring fishing is a bottom-bouncing game. The most popular flies are either insect imitations, such as a Golden Stone Nymph, RAM Caddis, or Brown Drake Nymph, or gaudy attractors, such as a Glo Bug, Marabou Single Egg, or Babine Special. A two-fly rig, with the bright fly up the leader and the imitation at the bottom, fished with a large indicator and weight, and drifted dead near the bottom, covers both pattern options.

The brown trout, running up from Hebgen in the fall, are another story. The water is typically low and clear, and these fish can be taken on lighter tackle and unweighted flies. Early morning and evening are the prime time for swinging a soft-hackle wet, maybe a Partridge and Herl or a Grouse and Orange, just under the surface. The key is finding the right "speed" for the smoothly swinging fly. You have to mend up- or downstream, making the fly move either slower or faster, until you find the right pace.

Reliable hatches occur throughout the season on this stretch. During the heat of the summer, however, the insects may not trigger a rise. The water, from all those thermal influences, gets too warm some seasons and the trout just don't feed for extended periods. The best fishing is in the spring and the fall. The early insects include the blue-winged olive mayfly (early April through late June), grannom caddisfly (early April through late June, but peaking in May), and pale morning dun mayfly (early May into July). The most consistent fall hatch is the blue-winged olive again, which lasts into October, but the tail end of both the trico and the Callibaetis mayflies can bring fish up once the summer water cools down. Midges are also active in September and October.

The trout in this rich section of the river can be picky. Flyfishing expert, fly shop owner and author Craig Mathews, for example, prefers Trico spinners tied with a green body and black thorax as opposed to an all-black fly. (Is that fussy enough for a size 18 or 20 imitation?)

HEBGEN LAKE TO QUAKE LAKE

The water below Hebgen Dam used to be an 8-mile run of bouldery pocket water known as Madison Canyon. In 1959 a massive earthquake registering approximately 7.8 on the Richter scale dropped the side of a mountain on top of a campground, burying people sleeping in their trailers and damming the river, forming Quake Lake.

The river between Hebgen and Quake is 1.5 miles of boulders, runs, and pools. It holds a resident population of trout and whitefish, but it isn't a great year-around fishery. There are public campgrounds along the river, and this stretch gets pounded throughout the prime tourist months. It can be excellent water early and late in the season. In the spring, when other parts of the river are muddy and high from the runoff, the half mile below the dam runs clear (up to where Cabin Creek enters). Some nice rainbows come up into this section. In the fall, from September through November, some of the heaviest browns taken all year anywhere on the river are hooked on large streamers like Woolly Buggers, Spruce Flies, Marabou Muddlers, Hair Suckers, and Muddler Minnows.

Quake Lake to Slide Inn

The Slide Inn section, racing below the natural rock jumble of the Quake Lake outlet, is the next major reach of the river. The water tears along at an impressive whitewater clip. This stretch can be intimidating to those unfamiliar with it. With a little experience, you can take trout after trout in this reach.

You have to choose either an inside approach or an outside approach. "Inside" means within inches of the banks, and it means surprisingly small flies. It is a visual spotting game. Make short, upstream casts with a small nymph or emerger pattern matching the predominant insect. For most of the summer, the fly will be a size 16 or 18 Quigley Cripple or CDC Emerger in the colors of the pale morning dun or a size 18 or 20 Clear Wing Spinner in the colors of the trico egg-layer.

With the outside approach, you will work the blue-green ribbons of comparative calm slipping between broken water. The key to this technique is to look for any run, pocket, or eddy that appears to be quieter than the rest of the river. The fast current delivers a steady supply of food, and the well-oxygenated water is ideal habitat for nymphs and larvae of stoneflies, caddisflies, and mayflies. In this water, it's almost impossible to spook the trout. You get second, third, and fourth chances to drift your fly through big-trout locations.

To take these fish, use a long rod, at least 9 feet, and make a short, upstream cast into the whitewater chute. The leader is roughly 7 to 8 feet, tapered to 3X. The fly, matching the green sedge, is a size 14 brown and bright green Emergent Sparkle Pupa. You won't see the fly, but you can keep almost direct contact by lifting the rod and pulling in slack with the line hand as the Emergent drifts downstream. You'll feel the strike, not see it, because the trout rise and dart back down to the bottom so swiftly that they quickly snub tight. It is a deadly method for large fish, and it covers water that no one else bothers to touch.

Slide Inn to Varney Bridge

Below Slide Inn, the Madison breaks free of the mountains and begins what is often referred to as the "50-mile riffle" as it bubbles and splashes over rock and gravel all the way down to Varney Bridge. This is the most famous stretch of the Madison. The river rarely reaches 70 degrees Fahrenheit, even at the peak of summer, and is usually below 65 degrees, ideal temperature for trout. The valley is spacious, sagebrush bench land with the Madison Range on the east and the Gravellys on the west. US 287 parallels the river as it cuts through prime cattle country. Rainbows (at least before the advent of whirling disease) and browns are the quarry, but the native mountain whitefish is the dominant species in terms of overall numbers.

On the reach between Lyon Bridge and Varney Bridge, before whirling disease decimated the rainbows, there were, on average, over 3,000 rainbow trout of over 7 inches per mile. By 1995 this population had dwindled to a little over 300 trout per mile. Fortunately, the brown trout have maintained, apparently less susceptible to whirling disease.

This part of the river is famous for the salmon fly hatch, which kicks into high gear normally around the end of June and bursts into full-tilt craziness through the first two weeks of July. Estimates suggest that 80 percent of the 90,000 angler days on the Madison are burned up in this brief period of fly-fishing madness.

The 2-inch nymphs and the huge, clumsy, winged adults drive the trout into a feeding orgy that translates into remarkable fishing. Sofa Pillows, Jugheads, Orange Fluttering Stones, and old license plates catch trout, but the smart anglers carry a mix of flush, low-floating dry flies and heavily dressed, high-floating dry flies. The low-floating flies, like the Jughead, are for chilly days when the insects ride the surface without a lot of fussing. The high-floating flies, like the Fluttering Stone, are for warm days when the insects kick and bounce all over the water.

The hatch typically moves upriver, the rate of progress depending on the weather. About 5 miles a day is a good average. Many anglers frantically try to find the "head" of the activity, where the salmon flies are hitting the air in a stream-wide front. This may seem like an exciting and profitable strategy, but in reality much of the best fishing is well ahead of this. The trout in front of the hatch are not yet satiated and the nymph action can be tremendous. Matching patterns, such as the Bitch Creek, Brooks' Stone Nymph, and Natural Drift Stonefly Nymph, can be deadly when fished close to the banks where fish stage to intercept the crawling, migrating emergers.

Many anglers prefer to work behind the main commotion. There are fewer anglers, and several days after the Pteronarcys front has blown past, the fish are hungry again and receptive to imitations. This "memory" of the big insects may last as long as two weeks. Fishing action slowly dwindles on the large imitations, but even at the last dying moments, the huge dry flies still take some of the biggest trout in the river.

In truth, only one in four years on average provides ideal conditions for the salmon fly hatch (also true on the Yellowstone and some other rivers). Bad conditions can bother the insects, the fish, or the fishermen. Extreme wind can make casting difficult for even the best anglers. High water may discourage the trout from feeding on the surface even when the insects are abundant. Cold snaps may delay or sharply reduce the hatch. But when it is right, the salmon fly hatch is a phenomenon that everyone should see at least once. It's worth coming back for year after year.

If the salmon flies fail to cooperate, there are always the early-season caddisflies. When in doubt on this part of the Madison, you can always depend on Trichoptera. Grannoms begin appearing in late April, followed by spotted sedges in mid-May. Great gray spotted, little sister, little tan short-horn, and green sedges show up throughout June, then the little plain brown sedge shows up in July with a steady run into the fall. Any of these species can divert the trout from the bigger, showier salmon flies.

There's another caddisfly species in the river if you want a serious challenge. The ring-horn microcaddis is tiny, size 20 or 22, but trout feast on them during the late June and early July hatching and egg-laying stages. With over 5,000 larvae per square foot on the riverbed in this section, they are one of the most abundant insects in the river. The egg-layers crawl down the downstream side of boulders and oviposit under-water. The fish sit in the slack pockets behind these rocks and sip in the drowned, drift-ing females. A small Black Diving Caddis wet fly, dangled off the back of a larger, more visible, indicator dry fly, is effective for even the large trout that focus on this activity.

In *Fishing Yellowstone Hatches*, John Juracek and Craig Mathews cover the major hatches of the entire region. They include the blue-winged olive (May 1 through June 7 and again September 1 through October 10), red quill (July 1 through the end of August), pale morning dun (June 25 through August 13), small western green drake (July 15 through August 10), and trico (July 13 through September 15) as major may-flies. The Sparkle Dun is the main choice for matching the adults.

The giant salmon fly isn't the only significant stonefly on the Madison. The golden stone pops in early July, right on the heels of the Pteronarcys, and even overlaps slightly. It provides more consistent fishing than the salmon fly and is nicely matched with a Stimulator. Later in the summer the little olive stone and the little yellow stone are both abundant and important. Match them with the dry flies of the same name, or with the Air Head in size 16 or 18 (body color the same as the naturals and the foam colored pale yellow or pale olive).

Fly selection for the Madison is always changing. Maybe there's a law on the city books in West Yellowstone: The hot fly on the local rivers has to be something new and different *every* season. It's a matter of local economics. The visiting angler might tie everything he thinks he needs the winter before, but when he starts hearing fish stories about the great new pattern, he still has to buy some flies at the area shops. This region, and the Madison in particular, receives so many out-of-state anglers that it launches many new flies to fame. Not all of the favorites are invented here, but many of them become popular across the country after a successful summer on the river.

The list of patterns that blossomed like this is impressive—a pair of good ones are the Serendipity and the Griffith's Gnat. Some general-purpose nymphs, for both float-ing and wading, are the Hare's Ear in sizes 12 to 18, Prince Nymph in sizes 10 to 14, Feather Duster in sizes 10 to 16, Pheasant Tail in sizes 12 to 18, Girdle Bug in sizes 2 to 6, and Fur Nymph in sizes 14 and 16. General dry flies include the Parachute Adams, Elk Hair Caddis, Bivisible, and Irresistible, all in sizes 10 through 18. Good terrestrial patterns, of course, have to feature grasshopper imitations, such as Joe's Hopper or the Madison River Stopper, but should also include flies such as the Foam Beetle and the Foam Ant. Soft-hackle wet flies, in a variety of colors, are standards on the river.

Float fishing presents a slightly different set of demands for dry-fly buoyancy and visibility. If you can't see the pattern on the water, you can't detect most takes, and if the bug is drowned most of the time, you can't get good drifts. With this in mind, some of the better attractor patterns for float fishing include the Wulff (various colors), Trude (various colors), Double Wing (color series specifically matched to the color of the prevailing light), Humpy, Madam X, and H & L Variant.

Fall is the time to take big browns, and a few rainbows, on streamers. The fish often hold in water along the banks that doesn't seem deep enough to cover their backs. Float fishing is the best approach for covering a lot of water without spooking these trout. For the wading angler, an upstream approach from out in the river, as far from the bank as possible, is best. Use a 7-weight rod, with stout 2X or 3X leaders, that can handle the large streamers in sometimes windy, snowy, wet conditions. The best of this fishing is after mid-October. Woolly Buggers, Whitefish Streamers, Woolhead Sculpins, Stub Wing Bucktails, and Marabou Muddlers will take fish. Cast next to or onto the bank and quickly strip the pattern back. The browns will hit as soon as they see the fly, often in water only inches deep.

Varney Bridge to Ennis Lake

Below Varney Bridge the river slows its pace and begins to braid and wander about. Small islands surrounded by deep channels hold some of the largest trout in the river. Undercut banks are more common and provide an abundance of brown trout cover. Ennis Lake, formed by a dam built by the Montana Power Company in the early 1900s, is usually too shallow and silted-in to offer significant habitat for trout.

Not as many out-of-state fly fishers bother with this section of the river for several reasons. The current is slower than the upper river, the channel is heavily braided, float fishing is not allowed from Ennis Bridge to Ennis Lake, and the fishing can be more demanding. Also, this section just is not as famous as the upstream reaches.

Nonetheless, this stretch holds some hefty browns. When they're feeding on a heavy hatch, they can be highly selective. When they're not feeding, they can be quite secretive. Large streamers or heavily weighted nymphs are the patterns of choice when the trout are tucked into the undercut, brushy bank habitat. You'll need 7-foot leaders of 1X or 0X to check the browns from breaking off in the mazes of exposed roots, tangled limbs, and other detritus. Large Marabou Muddlers, Woolly Buggers, Spruce Flies, Zonkers, anything hefty, in sizes 4 to 1/0, will sometimes move the fish if you hammer the cast right to the bank and then let the fly drift and pulse at least a few inches under the bank in the dark water.

Ennis Lake to the Bottom of Bear Trap Canyon

From Ennis Lake the river flows for 7 miles through the Beartrap Canyon Wilderness. The Beartrap section is remote and wild, and the fishing can be good in this whitewater. Hiking into it means a steep climb and a day of rattlesnake dodging; rafting it means battling dangerous Class IV rapids. It might be worth all that if the river here was as great as it was thirty or forty years ago. Since then Ennis Lake has silted in, becoming progressively shallower and warmer. While a good number of rainbows and browns are present, their growth is stunted by the high summer temperatures. Fishing in the summer is poor, at best, and fish kills are all too common.

The best season for the Beartrap is probably during early spring. The easiest access is at the mouth of the canyon, where MT 84 hits the river. The Madison flows clear in this section when many other rivers are muddy. There are great hatches of blue-winged olive mayflies and grannom caddisflies from mid-April through mid-May. The fish may not be large, a mix of mostly brown trout and whitefish up to 18 inches, but they turn the water to a froth in a splendid rise. As the water cools in the fall, you get a rerun of this action. A Parachute Adams, sizes 14 to 18, fished with a bead-head (almost any bead-head seems to work—try the ever-popular bead-head and bare hook) in the sane sizes, is a deadly combination.

Mouth of Beartrap Canyon to Three Forks

The remaining 28 miles of the river are slow, and water warms to near-lethal levels for trout in the summer. The best times are April through mid-June and mid-September through November for browns and rainbows that average from 10 to 15 inches. Mountain whitefish make up the majority of the fish in this stretch. Public access is poor after the first 15 miles, so the easiest way to fish the last 13 miles of the river is to float. Because of the slow current, these floats are all-day affairs. The Madison joins the Gallatin and the Jefferson at Three Forks to form the Missouri River.

This is wide water with nice riffle-run sections in beautiful open country. Looking upstream from the Blacks Ford access, the river wanders through a bluff-lined canyon. One fall day I used a size 12 Coch-y-Bondhu, a Welsh tie from a century ago that imitates a beetle. I tied some for the fun of it, and I've always been a fan of patterns using peacock herl. Working the riffles and runs near shore, I took rainbow after rainbow along with a few browns and whitefish—all of them in the 15-inch hefty range. Why this fly worked, I don't know. I didn't see any beetles. I can't argue with success, though.

Weather tends to be sudden and often violent in the Madison Valley. At Three Forks at about 4,000 feet, summertime temperatures can exceed 100 degrees, while air temperatures in Yellowstone National Park, lying at nearly 7,000 feet, can be in the mid-60s. Cold air will often build up and rush down the Madison Valley, creating violent winds as it pours off the plateau (summer breezes have been clocked at over 90 mph along the Madison). In winter, temperatures can drop to more than 60 degrees below zero.

Fishing Waters in the Madison Drainage

Axolotl (Twin or Crater) Lakes: These five alpine lakes lie in the northern end of the Gravelly Range below Baldy Mountain. They were once great fishing for large rainbows, but some of the lakes have been managed for the last decade or so for cutthroats, which are the predominant species now. Though they do not grow quite as large as the rainbows, they are easier to coax into taking a dry fly or a nymph or a Woolly Worm.

Cameron Lake: Cameron is about 11 miles south of Ennis at over 9,000 feet and requires a demanding, steep hike into its 4 acres. It's filled with 12-inch cutthroats that do not see many anglers. The lake is only 20 feet deep, so there is nowhere for the trout to disappear to.

Cherry Creek: This has been returned to a native Yellowstone cutthroat trout fishery in recent years with the help of a lot of money from Ted Turner. Fish numbers are good, size is increasing, and water quality is excellent. It's accessed by Trail #122 up Sweet Grass Creek.

Cherry Lake: Cherry Lake is on a rough trail from the Ennis Lake dam. This 4-acre lake has cutthroats to perhaps 18 inches. There are extensive shallows where the fish cruise, and a sharp-eyed angler can pick his targets for some fun sight fishing.

Cliff Lake: Cliff is close enough to West Yellowstone—only 30 miles by good road—to get heavily used. There's also a public campground on this 4-mile-long, narrow lake. It's popular because it has good numbers of rainbows, cutthroats, and brookies up to 3 or 4 pounds. There are some whitefish (good forage) in Cliff, too.

It gets decent hatches of pale morning dun and Callibaetis mayflies, but the main forage for the bigger trout is minnows. When the ice goes off, which can be fairly late around here, the rainbows and the cutthroats go on a hunting spree. They gather around the mouths of Horn Creek and Antelope Creek (where skilled angler Gene Turner caught a 20-inch cutthroat stuffed with small fish in early June).

Cougar Creek: Cougar runs into Duck Creek a mile from Hebgen. It's brushy and tough to fish for brookies, cutthroats, grayling, rainbows, browns, and whitefish. In the spring some decent rainbows sneak up here, but the stream is not yet open. A teaser. In the fall some big browns cruise their bellicose way upstream, providing interesting fishing (try controlling a 5-pound trout in this water). Large streamers work well, but are a bitch to cast in this narrow corridor.

Darlington Creek: Eight miles south of Three Forks, Darlington has the same insect profile as Blaine Spring Creek, plus a scud or two. The one big difference is the improvement to the stream made by the Madison-Gallatin TU chapter. There is a FWP fishing access called Cobblestone. It's nice, but difficult, fishing for big browns.

Duck Creek: Duck Creek flows through brushy, swampy land from Yellowstone National Park to the Grayling Arm of Hebgen Lake. There are plenty of smallish brookies, cutthroats, grayling, rainbows, and some fat browns in the fall. It's similar to Cougar Creek, but a bit wider and naturally richer. Maybe only one out of three casts will find the brush. The fact that the high grasses of the bottoms obscure the regular traffic of grizzly bears makes some anglers nervous on Duck Creek, but that just controls the fishing pressure on the stream.

Ennis Lake: This is really just a submerged meadow formed when the Madison Dam was built many years ago. The lake is full of sediment, often choked with weeds, and warms to lethal levels. All the same, some big browns and rainbows survive down deep along old channels where the water is cooler. Grayling to almost 2 pounds have also been caught. The best fishing is in the spring and later in the fall. You really need an area resident to show you the holes on this water.

Goose Lake: Goose is above Cliff Lake at "only" 6,600 feet. It's about 10 acres, with rainbows, cutthroats, and cutthroat/rainbow hybrids to several pounds. The fact that it is shallow and rich makes it a fine piece of fly-fishing water. The best flies are small nymphs that match the Callibaetis mayflies, and the best technique is that slow, crawling retrieve that skims the fly just off the bottom.

Grayling Creek: Grayling flows out of Yellowstone National Park, and the lower mile is on public land, allowing you access. This is another in the Hebgen Lake series of swampy, brushy creeks with good numbers of small resident salmonids and some large spawners, including cutthroats in late spring and early summer and the obligatory run of rowdy browns in the fall. A nice stream that is also wonderful grizzly habitat.

Hebgen Lake: Hebgen Lake is 16 miles long, 4 miles maximum width, and impounds almost 400,000 acre-feet of water. The dam was completed in 1915, and the rising waters covered numerous creek beds, the main river channel, and the small town of Grayling (sounds like grist for a Jimmy Buffett ballad). Hebgen is given credit for being the cradle of "gulper" fishing. This is where trout feed on the surface, literally gulping clumps of midges or individual caddis and mayflies.

During the main action of summer and early fall, created by trico and Callibaetis mayflies, the fish get selective about fly choice—try a Clear Wing Spinner for the trico egg-layer and a Gulper Special for both the Callibaetis emerger and egg-layer. This is float tube action, and the Madison Arm of the lake attracts a dedicated crowd. At least 9-foot 5-weights are needed, though you will rarely cast more than 40 feet. Wind and a low position in the tube make some demands on equipment. Trout will approach to within a few feet of anglers in tubes. They do not seem to find the profile of a fisherman dangling in the water threatening.

During early May there is a spectacular midge hatch in the shallow bays along the east shore. By mid-June those same coves will be choked with weed, but they are open and jammed with brown trout feeding on those giant, size 14 black midges early in the season. A single bay often has hundreds of fish in it rising in head-and-tail rolls. The browns aren't easy to fool, however—this may be tougher than the regular gulper fishing. One consistent method is to cast a midge adult pattern, a parachute for visibility, and behind that a midge pupa pattern, and just let the tandem of flies sit out there among the craziness until one of the trout takes one of your imitations.

During certain months you can work one bay and take nothing but browns, then paddle to another and find nothing but rainbows. The species seem to be quite territorial at times in Hebgen. Many inexperienced anglers also spend long hours casting to rising chub under the mistaken impression that these are actually feeding trout. A chub rise is a splashy affair often punctuated by a tail flip. Trout normally display the classic head-and-tail rise.

You can locate trout in several ways. The most obvious is to fish where others are casting (keeping a courteous distance). Also, creek inlets like Duck or Grayling are prime locations, as are the narrows near Red Canyon Creek. Another spot to try in early summer with more modestly sized midge pupa imitations (small finicky labor, but someone has to do it) is along the South Madison River arm. This area receives little pressure but offers excellent action. Rainbow Point and Rumbaugh Bay are good in mid-June. Rumbaugh is broad and shallow, and it fishes well with a Canadian Mohair Leech along the edge of the drop-off. By midsummer you have to avoid areas of heavy algae growth, but one of the best stretches (and one of the least fished) during July is the southwest shore from the dam up to Trapper Creek. It is consistent morning and evening for cruising and sipping trout. Concentrations of mercury are moderately high in Hebgen Lake trout, and you'd have to be as mad as a hatter to eat them.

Hidden Lake: Hidden is a popular lake in the Goose Lake and Cliff Lake cluster. It's only a half mile above Goose at 6,600 feet in elevation, and almost 150 acres and quite deep. The fishing is good for mainly rainbows up to 18 inches. There's just the perfect balance here for simple and fast fishing—good numbers of healthy trout, but not so much food that they are spoiled.

North Fork Hilgard Lakes: A bunch of small lakes and potholes up the Beaver Creek drainage above Quake Lake, they are quite popular with pack trips both on foot and via horse for cutthroats, rainbows, and cutthroat/rainbow hybrids. Expedition, Crag, Hand, and Blue Paradise are the best of the lot, producing fish up to 15 or 16 inches.

Quake Lake: Fishing below Hebgen Dam used to be an 8-mile run of bouldery pocket water known as the Madison Canyon. In 1959 a massive earthquake registering about 7.8 on the Richter scale dropped the side of a mountain across the river, forming Quake Lake. The quake lowered the ground as much as 30 feet in some spots. US 287 running alongside Hebgen Lake was fractured, and a large portion of the road slid into the water. Nearby ridges rippled like gelatin during the seismic event. Hebgen tilted sharply northward, with bedrock under the dam dropping nearly 10 feet. The upper end of the lake rose 12 feet. Homes built near the shoreline are now situated well back from the water.

The shift in the lake bed caused large waves to wash over the dam four times, sending walls of water crashing down the canyon with devastating results. Many of those staying at Rock Creek Campground below Hebgen were buried alive beneath 80 million tons of rubble that shook loose from the mountain. The rock traveled at almost 200 miles per hour, and the frontal wind created by this literally blew vehicles, tents, and people out of the path of the slide and to safety. If the earth slide had not destroyed the campground, the waves sloshing over the dam would have. As it was, sixteen people were killed.

Hebgen Dam was damaged but it was quickly repaired, while the river below the dam all but dried up, killing thousands of trout, whitefish, and forage fish, along with countless numbers of aquatic insects. As soon as the new lake refilled and the stream flow was restored, the river quickly healed itself. Quake Lake is now 180 feet deep by 4 miles long and 1,800 feet wide.

The skeletons of trees killed by the rising water are visible from the highway today, and they provide cover for some fair-size trout. They also serve as an eerie reminder of those people buried in the slide. Working along the old river channel is productive, but float tubers should be aware of the current that will suck the unwary down the outlet. Caddis hatches are frequent and often prolific on Quake Lake. Trout will work calm seams created by the wind on the surface, feeding on the spinners that accumulate in windows.

During ice-out, a Gold-Ribbed Hare's Ear Nymph cast onto the ice and stripped into the water will sometimes take large rainbows cruising for food just beneath the ice. The lake fishes well in the spring until it dirties from the muddy flow of Cabin Creek up the Madison. Sometimes it doesn't clear until June or even July, but when it does, there is good dry-fly fishing among the dead trees along the shorelines and good nymph fishing out in the center over the old riverbed.

South Fork of the Madison River: The South Fork parallels a road from its mouth at Hebgen Lake. It's fair for catches of rainbows, brookies, cutthroats, whitefish, and some large spawning browns in the fall, but anyone who has ever sampled the insect populations in this stream, and pulled up screens weighed down with all kinds of nymphs and larvae, has to wonder why it isn't a big trout fishery—too much pressure or undiscovered contamination?

Wade Lake: Wade is west of Quake Lake. It's 1.5 miles by 0.5 mile wide and planted with 30,000 Eagle Lake rainbows each year. There is a public campground and a tourist resort here—and big brown trout. One of 29 pounds was taken in 1967. The rainbows will grow past 5 pounds on the abundant feed that includes scuds, leeches, mayfly nymphs, caddis larvae, and damsel nymphs.

Marias River

Captains William Clark and Meriwether Lewis wandered across the country blithely replacing the Native American names for all sorts of physical landmarks. Traveling up the Missouri River in June 1805, their expedition reached the junction of two major rivers. After some indecision about which flow was the Missouri (and a couple days of reconnoitering), Lewis rechristened this one. He did not name the stream for the only

Access on the Marias can be difficult, but polite anglers often find that all it takes to access the river is a knock on a rancher's door and a gracious request.

Marias River

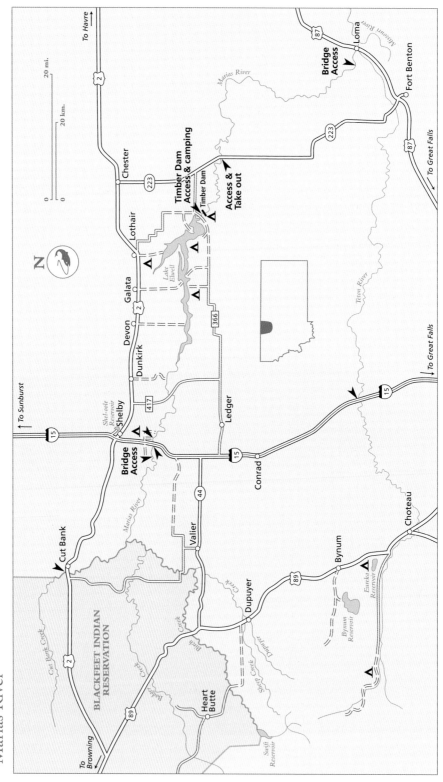

N

20 mi.

20 km.

0

0

To Havre

2

Chester

223

223

To Great Falls

87

Loma

Fort Benton

Bridge Access

Missouri River

Marias River

Timber Dam
Timber Dam Access & camping

Access & Take out

Timber Dam

Lothair

Galata

Devon

Dunkirk

Lake Elwell

Shel-oole Reservoir

Shelby

To Sunburst

15

417

Ledger

366

Teton River

To Great Falls

15

Conrad

15

Bridge Access

Cut Bank

2

Marias River

Valier

44

Dupuyer

89

Choteau

Bynum

Eureka Reservoir

Bynum Reservoir

BLACKFEET INDIAN RESERVATION

Cut Bank Creek

Badger Creek

Birch Creek

Dupuyer Creek

Sheep Creek

Heart Butte

Swift Reservoir

2

89

To Browning

man who died on the expedition (burst appendix), or for the young Shoshone woman who accompanied the group across the plains, or for any of the brave but common lads who toiled and fought for the party. He named it Maria's River in honor of his cousin, Miss Maria.

Not many people make the Marias River a destination for fly fishing. Most of the water holds species like sauger, walleye, northern pike (to over 20 pounds), burbot, goldeye, and perch. Places to stay or camp, along with other amenities, are few and far between, as are the rainbow and the brown trout along most of the stream.

From the confluence of Two Medicine River and Cut Bank Creek south of Cut Bank, the Marias wanders east and south for more than 125 miles to the Missouri River east of Vimy Ridge at Loma, way out on the prairie. Access is mainly across private land (permission is often granted with a polite request), or at several bridges above and below Tiber Dam.

The river fishes well for trout throughout the summer near Tiber Dam. There is a nice run of rainbows to perhaps 5 pounds each spring below the dam for about a dozen miles. The same spawning concentration occurs in the fall, with browns to perhaps 8 pounds. The river here offers clear, cool water that runs over clean sand-and-gravel streambed. Streamers on sink-tips, especially a Cree-hackled brown Woolly Bugger, worked along the bars, gravel shelves, deep down through the slow pools, and close to banks account for most of the good trout fishing early in the season. Nymphs, including the Prince, Hare's Ear, Cased Caddis Larva, and Serendipity (all in smaller sizes to match the food forms in a tailwater), and dry flies, including the Sparkle Dun (olive-bodied and size 16 to match the Baetis) and Dancing Caddis (olive-bodied and size 14 to match the grannom caddis), also take the trout and more than their share of whitefish. The Marias is not a river that sees the latest in patterns and tactics, but at times this upper water demands a refined approach.

In the summer there is fine fishing for mountain whitefish to 4 pounds using any small dry fly, say a size 16 or 18. In the warmth of a breezy summer day, this is a lot of fun. Some of the best action is in the shallow runs alongside the campground. A few rainbows up to a couple of pounds may be taken also.

The rest of the river gets warm and turbid, but it is ideal habitat for the warmwater species. The float fishing is good just as the high water subsides. A variety of fish come up from the Missouri, and it's not unusual to catch a mixed bag of bass, sauger, and catfish (along with the surprise brown or rainbow slumming in this lower section) on a drifted and twitched size 8 or 10 weighted Burnt Orange Woolly Bugger (which more than likely represents a crayfish).

The fishing on the Marias is out on the wide-open, windswept high plains. On clear days the Rocky Mountain Front is a shimmering illusion flickering across the western horizon. The countryside is often bright green and studded with clumps of wildflowers from spring rains. You will be alone here, possibly experiencing some quality fishing for the rainbows and browns. Even if the trout are uncooperative, the experience of this wild, empty land is worth the investment in time.

FISHING WATERS IN THE MARIAS DRAINAGE

Badger Creek: Badger begins below Half Dome Crag in the Rocky Mountains with the joining of the North and South Forks just east of the Continental Divide. The upper reaches on Forest Service land have silvery cutthroats to 12 inches that are not choosy about which dry fly they take. The lower reaches are on the Blackfeet Indian Reservation and mainly off-limits to non-tribal members. With a tribal permit, however, you can reach some of the water from state and reservation roads for limited fishing, once again mainly for cutthroats along with some brook and rainbow trout. You can also catch whitefish and assorted trash.

Cut Bank Creek: Cut Bank begins high in the mountains of Glacier National Park before wandering across Blackfeet Indian Reservation land that is mostly off-limits to non-tribal members. There are some nice cutthroats and rainbows that move upstream into open water on spawning runs, but those runs are difficult to time properly. Fishing with chunky drys—Wulffs or Double Wings or Stimulators—can be good if you can reach the water and find the fish.

Hidden Lake: This lake is located above the end of the South Fork Teton "road" and reached by trail from there. Hidden is only 5 acres, but there is good fishing for cutthroats that grow to a plump 14 inches quickly and sometimes get larger.

Lake Frances (Frances Lake): Five miles long and 5,500 acres, Lake Frances sits right off MT 44 next to the town of Valier. There are some nice rainbows swimming here with the northern pike and the walleyes, but not many people fish for them. They are an incidental catch. Large Buggers worked slowly along the bottom in the spring are best.

South Fork Birch Creek: There's not much water from the headwaters on the Continental Divide to Swift Reservoir, but this short piece is fair fishing for small cutthroats. A Forest Service trail provides access to the trout.

Teton River: The Teton is formed from the North and South Forks east of the Continental Divide about 25 miles west of Choteau. It flows for close to 200 miles to the Marias River at Loma. This stream was once good fishing, but a series of serious floods have badly scoured the stream course, eliminating most of the habitat for both trout and aquatic insects. The river from Choteau to the headwaters looks like someone used a D9 to pile up large mounds and ridges of gravel along the banks. Nearly fifty

Badger Creek is in grizzly country, in beautiful surroundings with westslope cutthroat finning away in eastslope water. John Holt

years later, the stream has still not fully recovered. Small drys and nymphs take mainly cutthroats. Below Choteau there are some enormous browns that take size 2, 4X long Woolly Buggers, but you'll have to work through muck that is like wet cement and smells like sewage from decaying vegetable matter. This is tough work that can produce a brown of a lifetime amid the hordes of mosquitoes. As it nears the Missouri, the Teton is drawn dry for irrigation.

For anglers who enjoy solitude and a sense of adventure more than blue-ribbon fly fishing, the Milk has plenty to offer.

Milk River

From a fly-fishing perspective, the Milk River is pretty slim pickings. Formed by the confluence of the North and South Forks (which head in the mountains of Glacier National Park), the stream flows for nearly 300 miles before joining the Missouri below Fort Peck Dam.

The 35-mile stretch on the Blackfeet Indian Reservation has some fair fishing for brook trout, rainbows, and a few cutthroats, but a tribal permit is required and access is limited. The banks are brushy and undercut, and the stream grows some nice trout, but this is also grizzly country.

The Milk spends some time in Canada before crossing back into Montana. It's captured in long and narrow Fresno Reservoir before it reaches Havre. Below the dam it drifts nearly 250 miles through wide-open, arid country that is pockmarked with glacial depressions, reservoirs, and streams that frequently go dry in the summer. Most of the fishing in this stretch is for warmwater species such as walleye, sauger, channel catfish, and some big northern pike. The bass provide some fine sport on streamers, and they will even feed on the mayflies that hatch sporadically throughout the season. The trout and a population of whitefish, well, they swim in this water, too, sometimes managing to get themselves stuck on a hook.

The Milk River drainage is not prime trout country, but it is some of the wildest, least-developed land in the state, with large populations of upland birds, waterfowl, and big game. This is good country, worthy of anyone's time. Camping along on the bluffs here will slam a sense of place and humility into a person in a hurry.

FISHING WATERS IN THE MILK DRAINAGE

Bearpaw Lake: Rainbows, Yellowstone cutthroats, and smallmouth bass are planted in the 55-acre, fairly deep reservoir lying in the open hills beneath the Bears Paw Mountains south of Havre. There's a good campground and spring fishing is fast for hordes of stocked rainbows, most cookie-cutter 12-inchers. The excitement comes from the occasional holdovers to several pounds. The planted fish grow quickly here, and by July they are silver and plump from gorging on plentiful food. Float tubes help; boats with motors are not allowed. This is popular water, and a nice place to camp on the weekdays.

Milk River

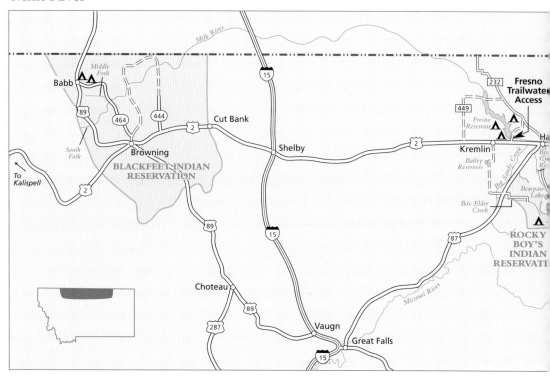

Beaver Creek (Bears Paw Mountains): This Beaver Creek runs for over 30 miles to the Milk just west of Havre along the Hi-Line (US 2). The fishing is relatively good though sporadic, even when there's enough water, all the way and accessible by road in most places. Brookies and rainbows hang out in the upper reaches, rainbows run the show in the middle section, and browns (some up to a few pounds) and rainbows cruise the slower lower reaches. There are good populations of hoppers and other terrestrials along this stream, especially in the open, grassy portions. This holds true for many streams in the region, though a lot of them either dry up or hold only warmwater fish. Channel catfish sucking down hoppers is a strange sight. So, when in doubt, use terrestrials out here in the big, open middle of wonderful nowhere.

Beaver Creek Reservoir: Known as "first lake" locally, this is one of the better impoundments in what must be a population of 10,000 reservoirs, ponds, and lakes splattered across the Hi-Line countryside beneath the Canadian border. If you fished a pond every day for the rest of your life, you might get to half of them, but it's doubtful. The best among them, like this 180-acre piece of work on Beaver Creek north of Bearpaw Lake, have good numbers of fast-growing rainbows that take leeches, scuds, nymphs,

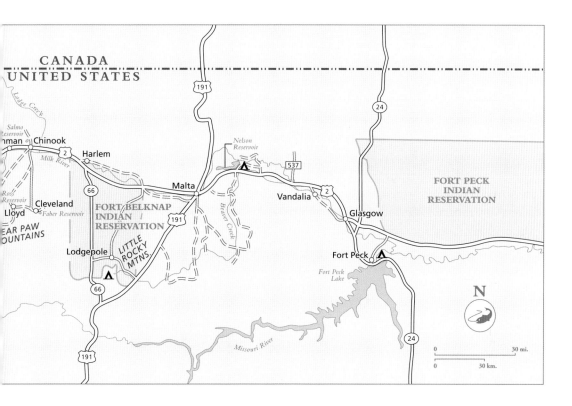

streamers, terrestrials, Callibaetis mayflies late in the summer, and even a stray band of marauding caddis once in a while. If the first thing you tie on fails to provoke the trout, keep experimenting. Once you discover what works, you are often in for some steady (if not spectacular) action for big trout that have nowhere to run or hide. And most of the time, the still waters out here are all yours, particularly on the weekdays or in the fall.

Take the Beaver Creek Road south of Havre to reach this reservoir. It fishes well early in the year. The most popular fly in the spring is the Bloodsucker Nymph in size 8 or 10—of course, it imitates a small leech and should be fished in a slow, slow swim over the bottom. Prince Nymphs are good all summer. By early June the lake becomes fine dry-fly water. Locally favorite patterns such as the Adams and the Mosquito have worked for years on Beaver Creek Reservoir. When the weeds get thick around the shoreline, usually by mid-July, the smart angler sits in a float tube or a canoe and casts back to the rim of vegetation.

Big Sandy Creek: Big Sandy Creek flows north-northwest through rolling hills and fields with a delightful sense of synchronicity toward the small town of Big Sandy, where Pearl Jam bassist Jeff Arment grew up. It's a fooler and tricky to fish. A handful of large brook trout swim here, but they're kind of shy and the walking is tough through alders, marshy grassy, and stream muck. A short durable rod, 7-foot 3X leader, and size 6X weighted Cree-hackled brown Woolly Bugger can make all of the effort a little bit worthwhile. Way-out-there country—give aliens the right-of-way. I like this one.

Bowdoin Lake: Bowdoin is 8 miles east of Malta along the Hi-Line (US 2) and better known for the staggering numbers of birds and other wildlife. The area consists of a number of lakes, including Bowdoin, Dry, Drumbo, Lakeside Marsh, and Lakeside Marsh Extension. There are over 15,000 acres set aside just south of US 2. Huge flocks of waterfowl move through here in the spring and fall. The bird list, resident and migratory, runs to 160 species. This is an impressive place, but there is little to attract the fly fisher. Look for a ranch pond.

Clear Creek: Clear Creek joins the Milk River at Lohman after flowing for 35 miles from the flanks of the Bears Paw Mountains. It's followed by gravel roads most of its course. Clear Creek is good fishing in the upper pocket water for brookies, the middle section for rainbows, and the lower grassy, undercut bank stretch for browns of a pound or so. Irrigation hurts the water, but some good browns move up after the fall rains.

Fresno Reservoir: Almost 6,000 acres of windswept water north of Havre in good mosquito country. Irrigation drawdown hurts the fishing for crappie, walleye, northern pike, and perch. A good dose of mercury contamination makes even these fish risky for human consumption. If you like trout, this is not the place to fish. Can be good for northerns, though.

Grasshopper Reservoir: This 20-acre reservoir south of Chinook is in rangeland north of the Bears Paw Mountains. Various strains of rainbows in varying size ranges are planted here every year—the mosquitoes, on the other hand, are a naturally reproducing, native population and they need no artificial enhancement. Get here in March, when the ice usually goes off, and the fishing is good off the gravel points. The lake goes through a period in late June when the fishing is very fast for 12- to 14-inch rainbows, with a few to 20 inches, but those mosquitoes are voracious by then. This "fast" time is good dry-fly fishing—try a Mosquito for sentimental reasons, but the Black Ant and the Renegade are the local choices. Grasshopper is good fishing through the summer, but the trout drop deeper in the warm weather. Cast olive-green damselfly nymphs along the edges of the thick weed beds, allow them to sink to the bottom, and strip them up and down in the water. Weeds make this one hard to fish after early July.

Middle Fork Milk River: This one is good for brookies and cutthroats on the Blackfeet Indian Reservation. A tribal permit is required, access is poor, the bugs are rough, and the grizzlies aggressive. So what? Live a little. Think of the stories they'll tell about you back home. "Yeah, that's right. Died on an Indian reservation. Killed by a crazed 3,000-pound grizzly that ate him whole." They'll buy anything in New York.

Nelson Reservoir: This is a special piece of pike water. There are warm, shallow bays up at the northern end, around Pelican Island. The fish move into 1 to 3 feet of water in these bays to spawn. They get very aggressive, nailing surface bugs and divers. Spotting the lurking fish is fun, and the strike is all visual in the clear water. This shallow-water fishing is good through May. After that the fish drop back to deeper water in the main lake around drop-offs, points, and weed beds. The pike run from 5 to 12 pounds and contain some mercury contamination.

South Fork Milk River: This is a beautiful stream that begins in Glacier Park and runs out onto the Blackfeet Indian Reservation. Open in spots. Brushy in spots. Beaver dammed in spots. Buggy everywhere. Access is somewhat limited, and a tribal permit is required for the brookies, cutthroats, and rainbows that sometimes reach a couple of pounds and love drys, hoppers, and Buggers stripped along beneath the banks. You are not going to outrun a grizzly in this stuff, but again, you only live once, and this is a pretty little stream in wild, electric country north of Browning.

Because of the periodic dams along its length and the resulting variety of water types, the Missouri River in Montana can provide good fishing year-round. Sherry Yates Young/Shutterstock.com

Missouri River

The fish of the Missouri are tremendous fighters. Couple this with spring-creek-like clarity in stretches, fantastic scenery, and rowdy rattlesnakes, the river is a true western classic, though during times of high-water runoff in the spring on other waters, it becomes crowded, to say the least, along certain stretches.

The Missouri River starts at Three Forks, not far from the speeding traffic of I-90. Three famous trout streams—the Jefferson, the Madison, and the Gallatin—combine at Missouri River Headwaters State Park. At their mouths, none of these famous waters is great fly fishing, however. The Jefferson, after receiving the muddy summer flow of the Beaverhead, is silty and warm; the Madison, coming out of Beartrap Canyon, suffers from fish kills during hot years; and the Gallatin is so dewatered in its lower reaches that if it wasn't for the inflow of its tributary, the East Gallatin, it wouldn't contribute any water in some summers. Not a very auspicious start for the mighty Missouri, but the situation improves downriver.

The Missouri takes its time as it winds though the Montana countryside, drifting through wide-open valleys defined by geologic structures with names like Giant Hill, Lava Mountain, Horseshoe Hills, and Hogback Mountains. On the bottomlands there are antelope, and up off the river, you can encounter grouse, deer, elk, coyotes, and, on rare occasions, mountain lions.

A series of dams slow the river even more, forming large bodies of water—Canyon Ferry Lake, Hauser Lake, and Holter Lake. Big trout hold in these lakes until the breeding drive moves them to upstream spawning gravels.

Along its course the Missouri becomes a geologic textbook. The river forces itself through twisted striations of sedimentary rock formations that were part of a vast inland sea 100 million years ago. It becomes canyon country. I-15 and many lesser roads bend and swerve as they conform to walls of ochre, pink, red, and oxidized green.

Neither the brown trout nor the rainbow trout populations are natural. Both species reproduce in the system, but the survival rates of young fish in the dewatered tributaries and in the main river are fair at best. The reservoirs are heavily stocked, however, and many of these trout wash over the dams in high water or through the turbines and accidentally populate the river. The most prevalent species in the Missouri is a native—the whitefish populations reach an astonishing 15,000 per mile in some sections, and they reproduce quite well.

THREE FORKS TO TOSTON DAM

There isn't much gradient to the river in this 23-mile section. It doesn't get squeezed by canyon walls until just above the town of Toston. It isn't classic trout water—it gets too warm in the summer, and there is usually a brown shade to the river. This doesn't mean that an angler willing to slam Woolly Buggers against the bank can't catch respectable trout, but neither the water nor the fishing methods are particularly pretty. The best times for dry-fly action are in the spring, from March until the end of April, before runoff, when there's a good hatch of blue-winged olive mayflies, and again in the fall, after the river cools down, and the lingering trico mayflies or the late-season blue-winged olives become important to the trout.

This is a good section to float with a guide who knows the moods of this upper water. There is public access at Fairweather, about halfway between Three Forks and Toston, and a boat takeout just above the Toston Dam. There are fly shops in this area that tout this water, but the key to fishing this section is knowing the "when" and "where" of it.

TOSTON DAM TO CANYON FERRY RESERVOIR

Toston isn't a "real" dam. It's a low irrigation facility that backs up a pool of water and, in the last few years, generates a bit of electricity for the state. There's no cold bottom flow, and when the water in the pool warms up and spills over the top of the dam, it can reach the high 70s. During midsummer these temperatures drive the trout down to Canyon Ferry Reservoir. The populations of full-time resident fish are pretty pathetic, less than a few hundred brown trout per mile in some parts of this 23-mile stretch.

One problem may be poor spawning rates in the few good tributaries in this area. The Montana Department of Fish, Wildlife & Parks has instituted special regulations to help the trout. Parts of the Toston to Canyon Ferry stretch are closed in the spring (check current regulations each season) to protect spawning rainbows, and three important tributaries—Warm Springs Creek, Dry Creek, and Deep Creek—have shortened general seasons. Parts of these streams have been opened to spawners and with the cooperation of local irrigators, rehabilitated; and rainbows are already using these waters extensively.

This Toston stretch does change from scrubwoman to princess in the autumn. Suddenly, this is a great place to catch large brown trout. Roughly 80 percent of the spawning female brown trout that run upstream from Canyon Ferry Reservoir are between 18 and 24 inches. So if 24 inches means a 3- to 4-pound fish, and many of the remaining 20 percent trout are larger than that, it's easy to understand the attraction the river has for the trophy hunter.

The deep methods, either streamers or nymphs, can work well in this stretch. For streamer fishing, use a Wool Head Sculpin, Hair Sucker, Egg-Sucking Leech, Double-Egg Sperm Fly, or a Crystal Bugger. For nymphing, use a Marabou Single Egg, Big

Horn Scud, Rubber Legs Bead-Head Squirrel Nymph, Brown/Orange Deep Sparkle Pupa, or Olive Hare's Ear.

You can fish shallow, too, but you have to concentrate on the lips of the pools at the heads of the riffles. The spawning females dig their redds in water so thin that it barely covers their backs. These fish will hit a small, unweighted wet fly better than they will a large streamer. A size 12 Partridge and Orange Soft Hackle is a proven pattern, used either separately or in a two-fly rig. Sneak into position, staying well back, and cast down and across. Try to "wake" the flies across the river just above the lip of the pool.

The brown trout don't start running heavy until mid- or late October. They stay in the river through November. Overcast, or even raining and sleeting, days are often the best. On sunny days the deep techniques prove most effective, but on the miserable days the active, shallow-water techniques take a fair share of the big fish. I caught my first browns of 5 pounds or more on Buggers along this stretch way back when.

CANYON FERRY DAM TO HAUSER LAKE

Below Canyon Ferry the river dumps pretty directly into Hauser Lake: There isn't much of a tailwater fishery here, but the old river channel is shallow enough to trap the outflow from the dam for almost a mile. You have to move out from the shoreline flats until you find the current and the channel. Then work a fly, either a nymph or a streamer, deep to reach the fish. There's a good population of fat, 12- to 22-inch resident fish here all the time, more rainbows than browns, and in the spring and the fall there's an influx of spawners.

POPULAR FLIES

Dry Flies/Emergers	
Buzz Ball	Henry's Fork Hopper
CDC Emerger	Humpy
Clear Wing Spinner	Mohawk
Comparadun	Parachute PMD
Double Wing	Serendipity
Elk Hair Caddis	Schroeder's Parachute Hopper
Emergent Sparkle Pupa	Stimulator
Fitzsimmons Adult Midge	Trude
Griffith's Gnat	Wulff

HAUSER DAM TO HOLTER LAKE

There are roughly 1,500 trout per mile, 90 percent of them rainbows, in this 3-mile stretch. The old state record brown trout, a 28-pound fish, came from the heavy turbulence just below the dam. It's big water and so varied in its 3-mile run that you can use just about any technique. And, if you're willing to do a little walking, you aren't likely to be bothered by crowds.

The huge fish of the early 1970s just below the dam are either gone or very rare now, but there are still plenty of browns and rainbows up to 5 pounds here. They sit below the generators and gobble the chopped-up or injured fish that come through the turbines. This was where the Hair Sucker made its reputation as a big-fish fly—on October 4, 1974, Bill Seeples caught five brown trout weighting between 6 and 11 pounds in four hours of fishing. He used a lead-core shooting head, short leader, and 3/0 weighted fly, casting as far as possible up into the turbulence of the outflow and mending repeatedly to let the line and fly sink as deep as possible.

Downstream from the dam the river is still big, but there are long riffles and flats that can be worked with a dry fly or nymph. A good bet is walking downstream from the dam. There's no road along the west side of the river, and floaters are rare on this stretch, so after a half mile you're pretty much alone. The fish, mostly rainbows averaging 14 to 17 inches, rise well all summer during the evenings.

POPULAR SUB-SURFACE PATTERNS

Nymphs
Big Horn Scud
Brown/Orange Deep
  Sparkle Pupa
Diving Caddis
Floating Damsel Nymph
Hare's Ear
Marabou Midge Larva
Marabou Single Egg
Partridge and Orange Soft
  Hackle
Pheasant Tail
Prince Nymph

Rubber Legs Bead-Head
  Squirrel Nymph
San Juan Worm

Streamers
Crystal Bugger
Egg-Sucking Leech
Hair Sucker
Marabou Muddler
Stub Wing Bucktail
Wool Head Sculpin
Woolly Bugger

HOLTER DAM TO CASCADE

This is the water most fly fishers hear about when the Missouri River is discussed. From Holter Dam to Cascade, roughly 35 miles of water, this is like a giant spring creek. The bottom is covered with weeds that harbor great populations of scuds and aquatic insects. Consistent hatches of midges, mayflies, and caddisflies bring trout to the top all year. Both rainbows and browns feed in pods, holding just under the surface and sipping mayfly duns and spinners.

The trout populations fluctuate a lot from year to year. The population of both rainbows and browns combined can run anywhere from 2,000 catchable (10 inches or larger) fish per mile to over 4,000 fish depending on conditions. After a few seasons of low water, the numbers of rainbows in the river drop off as spawning recruitment from dried-up tributaries declines—let there be one high-water summer, and the numbers increase sharply. One explanation for this strong correlation between high water and high fish populations suggests that, in part, it comes from rainbows stocked in Holter getting washed into the river.

The first dry-fly fishing of the year starts with the winter midges on any warm day. These aren't necessarily small insects—there are big black buzzers matched with a size 14 fly. Other species of midges are smaller and come in a full range of colors. Effective patterns include the Serendipity and Halo Midge Pupa for the emerger and the Fitzsimmons Adult Midge and the Griffith's Gnat for the adult. Another good pattern, the Buzz Ball, matches the clumped up, mating insects.

From mid-April through June, and again from September through mid-October, the blue-winged olives will emerge from late morning until around four in the afternoon. The dun is probably the most important stage for the angler, but the nymph just prior to emergence, caught in the surface film, can also take trout. Weighted Hare's Ears and CDC Emergers work well prior to and during the initial stages of the emergence. A generic pattern is a grizzly or olive Parachute. The size range varies from 16 through 24, with the smaller patterns being more prevalent in the fall.

The blue-winged olive hatch can sometimes be mystifying—fish rising everywhere to everything but your fly, no matter what it is. On these occasions it can be effective to strip a small bead-head or Pheasant Tail nymph back through the working fish in short (6- to 8-inch) strips. Blue-winged olive nymphs are swimmers, and this action will often trigger a strike when nothing else will.

The pale morning duns start in early summer and they are so steady that, in truth, they could be called "pale morning, noon, and evening duns." The fish get very selective after weeks of a steady diet of these insects. They'll ignore any presentation, no matter what the fly, if it has the least bit of drag. A good imitation, a Halo Mayfly Emerger or a Parachute PMD, for example, has to hit a feeding trout right in the mouth. Some days it doesn't matter how precise you are or how good your pattern is—the fish don't care. On those days your time might be as well spent in the cool recesses a local tavern, commiserating on the foul and fickle ways of trout.

Tricos hatch from July to September, providing plenty of action for the 1- to 3-pounders during the morning hours. These tricos tend to run a little larger in the Missouri than elsewhere. By "larger," this means sizes 18 and 20, instead of 22 to 26. The ambitious angler who gets out on the water before 7 a.m. will hit the emergence of trico duns, and this stage can actually provide better fishing than the spinner fall that occurs later in the day. The spinners typically start swarming between 8 a.m. and 9 a.m. and on a windless day they hover in heavy clouds. That's the problem—once they hit the water there are so many of them that it's hard to get a fly to a fish with so many naturals on the surface. Good patterns include the Clear Wing Spinner and the Goddard Caddis that imitates a cluster of bugs. Recognizing trico spinners is relatively easy. They are small, of course. They have three tails, with the male's about three times the length of its body and the female's the same length as her body. The wings are clear and there are no hind wings, unlike most mayflies.

Caddisflies are also important on the river. Every summer evening you'll see heavy hatches, with the mating flights cruising up the river. At times they're so thick, you don't dare breathe through your mouth. Right at dark the egg-laying and the general emergence begins, and the river boils with the slashes and splashes of rising fish. The trout could be feeding on the spotted sedge, which peaks in late June and early July, or the little sister sedge, which spreads out over the summer. Or in June or July, the fish might be taking the summer grannom (also called the black caddis). The following assorted color combinations should stand you in good stead: 1) brown wing and yellow body; 2) tan wing and ginger body; and 3) dark, almost black wing and very dark green body. All in sizes 10 through 16. Likewise, the Diving Caddis will imitate the egg-laying females of the spotted sedge and the little sister sedge (both of which go underwater to oviposit). A dark Elk Hair Caddis usually works when the grannoms fall and lay their eggs on the surface.

The one perplexing phenomenon on the river are the random "explosion" rises. All around trout are sipping the prevalent insect, and all of a sudden a big fish erupts through the surface. These rises are caused by one of three food forms: damsel nymphs, large emerging caddis, or minnows and fry. If the explosions are really random, and against the bank, the trout are probably busting fry. A Marabou Muddler, a Stub Wing Bucktail or a Woolly Bugger, cast into the shore and swung out into the current, looks like a minnow escaping into deeper water.

If the rises are swirls more than leaps, and happen with any consistency around the mats of shoreline weeds, the fish may be gorging on damsel nymphs—on a windy day they may even be taking the pewter gray, freshly emerged adult damsels that are getting blown back onto the surface. A Floating Damsel Nymph, cast from the shore out into the river and retrieved with spurts, fools these trout.

If the rises happen out in the main current, fish rocketing into the air, the trout are feeding on large, emerging caddisflies. This happens more in the fall, when the large, case-making types hatch on the river. A sunken fly dead-drifted over the tops of the mid-river weeds works better than a surface pattern for these feeders. Most of the time, these explosive main-current rises are so random that your time is better spent working the more regular hatching activity.

Even when nothing is hatching, the Missouri is a fine dry-fly fishery. In low-water years especially, this is a shallow river and trout always seem aware of the surface. As a result, terrestrial imitations produce consistently all summer. Good grasshopper patterns, such as Joe's and Dave's Hoppers and the Henry's Fork Hopper, can bring trout a long way. A good trick is to put on two or even three Henry's Fork Hoppers, cast them into the bank, and retrieve them with hard strips that make them swim and dive. An ant or beetle pattern, fished as a trailer behind a big dry fly, can be productive at times.

Even attractor dry flies have a place on the Missouri River. On this smooth, tricky tailwater the secret is often using very small attractors, 18s and 20s, or at the opposite extreme, very large attractors, 6s and 8s. The Wulffs, Humpies, Trudes, Stimulators, and Double Wings all have a place on this fishery. All too often first-time visitors to the Missouri resist using attractors.

Of course, you can always go subsurface when the trout aren't rising. Favorite nymphs on the river include not only the standards, such as the Pheasant Tail, Hare's Ear, and Prince Nymph, but also the types of flies that seem to work on tailwater fishers all over the West, such as the San Juan Worm, Hot Pink Shrimp, Brassie, Marabou Midge Larva, and Bead-Head Serendipity (in fact, a bead-head anything—possibly even on a bare hook—has become one of the most consistent producers year-round). Hanging the nymph off the back of a buoyant, visible dry fly, such as a Mohawk or a Stimulator, is a standard technique.

Visiting anglers need to master the "Missouri River lift." When a fish is hooked, either a rainbow or a brown, it might jump once or twice, but sooner or later it's going to dig into the heavy weeds. If too much line and leader gets wrapped in salad, the trout breaks off or pulls loose. To prevent this you have to lift your whole arm, mimicking the Statue of Liberty, as soon as you set the hook, and you have to keep that arm and the rod high throughout the fight.

The quality of the fishing, especially the dry-fly fishing, depends on the amount of water released from the dam. Holter is not a peaking power facility, so the flow through the dam pretty much mirrors the flow into the lake. The reservoir can smooth the highs and lows a little, but during a low-water year the river is going to run at roughly 2,500 cfs, and during a high-water year it is going to run as heavy as 10,000 or more cfs. Above 6,000 cfs the Missouri is a vastly different river than it is at even 4,000 cfs.

At first glance, even in low-water years, the Missouri can be intimidating. It is hundreds of feet wide, but this can be rapidly reduced to pockets along the banks, long riffles, and channels around the islands. Look at the detail of the river right in front of you, not the entire river.

CASCADE TO FORT PECK RESERVOIR

Below the city of Cascade, and the mouth of the Smith River, the river begins changing from a coldwater to a warmwater fishery. There are good fly-fishing opportunities for goldeyes—free-rising, insect feeders that reach 16 inches—and for smallmouth bass. There is also a scattering of trout down past Great Falls, until the river gets too warm, too sluggish, and too muddy. While this stretch may not be premier fly-fishing water, it is nonetheless worth the trip. Below Fort Benton, the Missouri River Breaks is some of the wildest country left in the Lower 48. An occasional fish on a fly is just a small bonus to a truly spectacular trip.

THE MISSOURI BELOW FORT PECK RESERVOIR

Several hundred lonely miles to the east, below mammoth Fort Peck Dam, steelhead-like rainbows thrive in a fresh, clear tailwater fishery, mostly unknown and only rarely fished over with a fly. This stretch of the Missouri has rainbow trout that have been reported to exceed 15 pounds. Less than two hours from the North Dakota border lies some tough, deep-water fishing for the diehard fly fishers.

Fort Peck Dam is earthen and 6 miles long with a highway running across the top. When you pull over on top of the dam, you can look back west across much of the 189-mile length of Fort Peck Lake. Most of the time when you do this, the wind will try to blow you down the hill and into the Missouri flowing out onto the plains hundreds of feet below.

The river is big here—too big to successfully fish the main channel. Again, as with the upper river, only more so, you must cut the water down to some semblance of fishable size. Do this by working a side channel, which is best done in the spring.

The Missouri River below Fort Peck Dam offers some of the most surprising tailwater fishing in Montana.
Robert Etzel/US Army Corps of Engineers

Rainbows are on the move at this time, and there is sufficient flow to float you over some gravel bars. The water is anywhere from 100 to 200 yards wide. The trout hold out in deep (8 feet or more) runs and chutes. This is where you will fish your streamer. A 1-mile section of prime spawning habitat is off-limits to anglers. Big signs make sure you are aware of this fact.

The only aquatic insect life of any note is chironomid and dipteran, which more or less eliminates matching the hatch. The water is deep and the fish concentrate on forage species. Use size 2 to 2/0 Zonkers, Matuka Sculpins, Stub Wing Bucktails, and similar-size streamers fished with a fast-sinking line and a short (6 feet), stout (2X) leader. Even in the best of conditions, this is tough work. Factor in gusting winds that come with sufficient strength to force you to shift your feet to maintain balance, and you're talking austere angling conditions, especially from a boat. You can handle some of the water from shore, but a stable flat-bottom craft will give you a decent casting platform away from bankside obstructions, and you can fish the water thoroughly.

Eight-weight rods are not too much in this section of the river. So, to fish here, you really must be excited by the idea of fly fishing unknown turf for big, frequently uncooperative trout. If you measure enjoyment in terms of numbers of trout caught and released, don't come to this reach of the Missouri. But, if you like wild surroundings and the chance to connect with a big, powerful rainbow and can accept fishless days, the river below Fort Peck Dam might be worth at least a day or two of your life.

THE UPPER MISSOURI

Fishing Waters of the Upper Missouri—Headwaters to Great Falls

Beaver Creek (below Hauser): This tributary is good fishing for rainbows and big brown trout up from the Missouri below Hauser Dam. It flows through canyon country, with good public access off the Beaver Creek Road on the lower and best-fishing sections. The upper reaches hold little brookies. This is a good fall stream for fat browns that will hit large streamers.

Canyon Creek: This tributary of Little Prickly Pear Creek is on the Lincoln Highway (MT 200). It offers good dry-fly fishing for brookies and rainbows plus some nice fall-run browns. There are some good stretches right along the road—tough casting but nice water. Hopper patterns work all summer, with the smaller sizes, 12 and 14, doing much better than bigger imitations.

Canyon Ferry Reservoir: Waters like this one aren't my cup of tea, but to each his own. This lake receives more fishing pressure than any other water in the state. It is a huge reservoir, about 15 minutes east and south of Helena, and it's followed by state and county roads. This water is 25 miles long by 4 miles wide and has some good fishing

Upper Missouri River

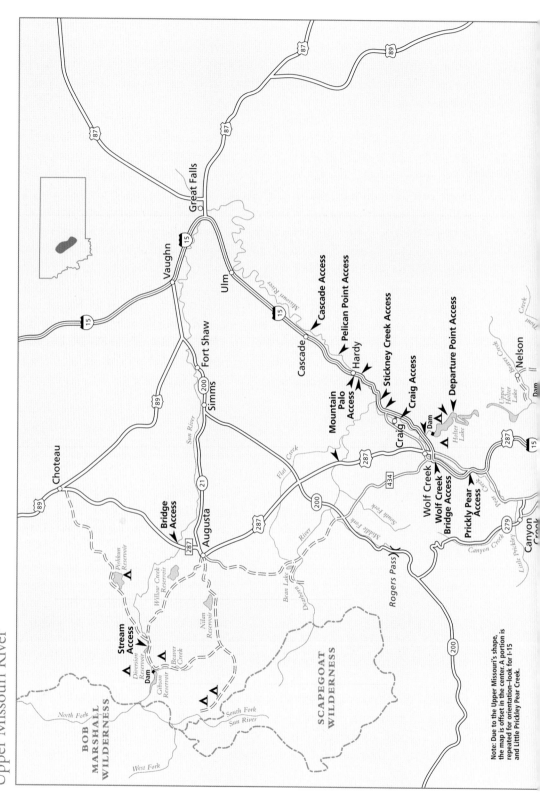

Note: Due to the Upper Missouri's shape, the map is offset in the center. A portion is repeated for orientation—look for I-15 and Little Prickley Pear Creek.

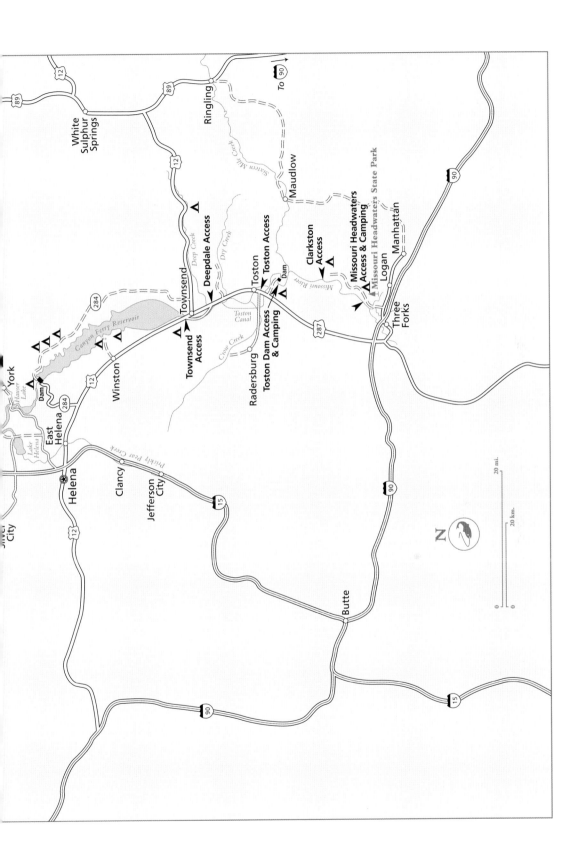

all season around small islands at the southern end, mainly for rainbows but also for a few big browns in the fall. There are also perch, pike, walleyes (the gift of some slack-jawed bucket biologist), suckers (many from out-of-state), kokanees, and brook trout. The best times to fish are in the spring for the rainbows and maybe in the fall for the browns that move quickly up into the shallows to spawn.

The easiest fishing is in the spring—at times it can be too easy and a fly fisher can get jaded with catching 2- to 6-pound Eagle Lake rainbows. It can get so easy when the spawning rainbows congregate along certain stretches of shoreline that FWP has to close sections of the lake to protect the population. After the ice goes off Canyon Ferry, the better areas include the bays on the north end of the lake, around the dam, along Magpie Point, and near Kim's Marina. The peak of the shoreline concentrations vary from year to year, but it generally happens sometime in May. You can walk the shoreline and spot cruising fish. Nonetheless, these fish put on quite a show. They nest and protect their territory with all the ardor of a Babine steelhead. At times they'll be rolling right at your feet, oblivious to you. The standard drill is to cast to them with a Woolly Bugger, a small nymph, or a small egg imitation below a strike indicator. Cast ahead of the cruisers and let it dangle, or maybe impart a small twitch. This is not a finesse game, and, at times, it can run dangerously close to bobber fishing.

After the spring flurry the rainbows drop into deeper water, but early-morning float tubing at the mouths of Goose Bay and Confederate Bay is still productive. Use sinking lines, but don't go too deep—search from the 6- to 12-foot levels until you find the trout (which hang just under the thermocline). The best flies are perch-colored and silver-colored streamers.

Crow Creek: This is a good fishery for rainbow, brook, and some brown trout. It enters the river near Toston. The stream suffers greatly, though, at the hands of irrigators and from mining pollution. Drive to Radersburg and start fishing upstream from there. There are more than 20 miles of good water in the Helena National Forest, but with easy access and public campgrounds, this becomes a popular area during the summer. It's a rich stream in the upper reaches, with lots of great deep-pool structure. When the mayfly and caddisfly hatches are happening, the trout rise freely to generally matching flies. At other times, they'll take a Parachute Adams or an Elk Hair eagerly enough.

Dearborn River: The Dearborn heads along the Continental Divide in the Scapegoat Wilderness, flowing for over 60 miles to the Missouri south of Great Falls. The mountains section is good riffle, pool, and pocket water for cutthroat and rainbow trout averaging perhaps 10 inches. The middle section is often hit hard by irrigation demands, but there are some brook and rainbow trout. In the canyon stretch north of Wolf Creek, some nice browns to several pounds and rainbows of similar size are taken by those floating the river.

The most popular put-in access is where MT 287 crosses the river, and the shuttle required for the trip is time-consuming. Large nymphs and streamers work well until midsummer, when water levels make floating difficult. Autumn precipitation raises the level of the Dearborn, and this is the best time for the browns. One notable hatch on the river is the skwala stonefly in March and April. This pre-runoff insect creates some of the best dry-fly fishing of the season. Access can be extremely difficult and contentious here.

Deep Creek: Much of this water is followed by US 12. It is a pretty little stream east of Townsend that flows through open sage flats with willow-choked banks and then through rocky, narrow canyon land above. There are nice browns to maybe a couple of pounds below, but access is tough. Small brookies and rainbows take a little bit of everything—drys, wets, and nymphs—in the small pools and runs up above. This valley gets heavy infestations of grasshoppers, making a good hopper imitation a must in the summer.

Flat Creek: Flat Creek is a meandering, small stream that begins south of Augusta and winds through open, grassy land with lots of undercut banks that hold some brookies, fat rainbows, and big browns. Much of it is posted, making access possible only when crossed by county road or through permission from area ranchers. All the same, intriguing water.

Gibson Reservoir: Gibson is over 5 miles long by 0.25 mile wide. You'll need a boat or float tube to reach rainbows and brown trout that will exceed 15 inches and smaller numbers of little brookies and cutthroats. The problem with this irrigation reservoir is the drastic summer drawdown (hurting both aesthetics and basic productivity). Working the creek inlets with streamers or nymphs is the best bet, especially early and late in the season. The estuary of the forks of the Sun River, at the upper end, is the only consistent area for rising trout.

Hauser Lake: This large impoundment on the Upper Missouri holds some big rainbows and browns. Hauser is about a dozen miles northeast of Helena and about 6 miles below Canyon Ferry and measures nearly 3,800 acres of surface area. There are public campgrounds, boating activity, and sapphires and garnets lying in narrow seams in the cliffs surrounding the lake. The fishing is best through the ice (which is tough with a Blue-Winged Olive), but there is also some action in the spring for the rainbows and in the fall for the browns. The lake also supports walleyes (which are fine sport in Wisconsin and Ontario, but have all the fighting qualities of a wet towel in Montana waters). Hauser has kokanees, which make the walleyes look like spectacular battlers, that average 1.5 to 2 pounds and run up to 4 pounds. Suckers and perch provide forage

Gibson Reservoir has some sizable trout despite drawdown problems.

for some large browns that rarely come up from the deep. There are also some truly huge carp if you're looking for a little different challenge.

Holter Lake: Holter covers nearly 8 square miles of water impounded along the Missouri above and below Gates of the Mountains 30 miles north of Helena. There are good numbers of rainbows and browns, some reaching 5 or more pounds, but these are usually taken by trollers working way down deep. Lots of boat traffic.

Lake Helena: This one is over 2,000 acres with tons of carp (for which there is a thriving commercial operation) and some nice rainbows that thrive on the small bugs lurking in the algae. It is best fished in the spring with large streamers.

Little Prickly Pear Creek: There's an inverse relationship—when the Missouri is fishing poorly, anglers come up here, but when the Missouri is prime, the stream is almost empty. One of the secrets then, for small-creek lovers, is to come here when the main river is sizzling hot.

There are three distinct sections. The upper reaches, from the mouth of Canyon Creek down to Sieben Ranch, meander through deep, slow pools and undercut runs. The resident fish, rainbows up to 16 inches and browns up to 18 inches, feed on good hatches of mayflies and caddisflies. A Stimulator is a good searching fly when there aren't a lot of bugs on the water; either a small Joe's Hopper or a Mohawk makes a good terrestrial fly; and an Olive Flashback Hare's Ear or a Red Fox Squirrel Nymph are effective subsurface patterns. This is also prime rattlesnake country, so watch your step.

The middle reaches, from the Sieben exit down to Wolf Creek, and the lower reaches, from Wolf Creek down to the mouth at the Missouri River, both get a lot of migratory fish. These trout, both rainbows and browns, stay in the stream long after spawning time. It's not rare to catch fish over 20 inches even during the summer on Little Prickly Pear. The water that runs parallel to I-15 has been rehabilitated and improved over the past decade to overcome the damage done by highway construction. There are some good pools and shelf water within walking distance of the road. The stream is closed in the fall to protect spawning browns from the Missouri.

Middle Fork Dearborn River: Heading near Rogers Pass and followed by MT 200 most of its length, it is fair fishing for cutthroat, brook, rainbow, and perhaps a stray brown trout up from the Dearborn. This is a fun stream to putter around with small fish on dry flies or nymphs.

Nilan Reservoir: Over 100 acres, up to 50 feet deep, and located about 15 minutes west of Augusta, Nilan is heavily planted with rainbows that quickly reach 15 inches and will top 5 pounds on occasion. It is a good streamer or Woolly Worm lake. There is occasionally some midge action where small gray or brown drys take the cruising trout. If you're in the area in August, don't pass up the Augusta Rodeo. Be prepared for a party that goes on "forever." And the rodeo isn't too bad either. One of these affairs in the early seventies changed my outlook on life.

North Fork Sun River: The North Fork heads below Sun River Pass at nearly 8,000 feet and drops swiftly down through wilderness to 4,750 feet at Gibson Reservoir. There are pockets and pools filled with cutthroats and brookies and some chunky rainbows. It is hike-in water all the way, with a good trail following the river. After runoff an angler can stop anywhere and pop a good dry-fly attractor on the river and consistently catch trout.

Pishkun Reservoir: Southwest of Choteau, Pishkun Reservoir is 1,550 acres with some drawdown in the summer due to irrigation. FWP plants it with rainbows that grow well. There are also northerns to 10 pounds (the fishing peaking in late June), some yellow perch, and maybe a holdover grayling or two. The rainbows have been recorded over 10 pounds. Try working a perch imitation, fishing the thing in the lanes between the weed beds in deep water (but use a wire leader to keep from getting chopped off by the pike).

Prickly Pear Creek: This small stream flows into Helena from the south, running down from some low mountains past Alhambra and Montana City and followed by I-15. It still suffers from mining and smelting pollution. The trout are here, maybe up from Lake Helena, and browns over 16 inches are not uncommon. The rainbows are smaller, mainly 6 to 10 inches. Bigger flies like a Woolly Bugger take the best fish.

Above the ASARCO plant, it is a different stream. The bottom is rocky and there's more gradient as it comes out of the Elkhorns. There are brookies, browns, and rainbows. The best area is at and just below the mouth of McClelland Creek. It's good up to Clancy. Above Clancy there are some beaver ponds with small brook trout.

Sixteen Mile Creek: Sixteen Mile heads just west of the Crazies below Punk Mountain and flows for 50 miles through open, grassy country up by Ringling, dumping down through a canyon that really is full of rattlesnakes before entering the Missouri several miles above Toston at Lombard. The upper reaches are too small to bother with. The snakes make fishing for the rainbows and browns (plus a few brookies and whitefish) a risky proposition once the weather warms. The stream is high and muddy in the spring, so fall is the best option, after the hard frosts have calmed the rattlers to a certain degree. Access is difficult throughout most of the best reaches, with much of the land tied up for outfitters/guides to use for their sports.

South Fork Dearborn River: Like the Middle Fork, this stream also begins near Rogers Pass and flows through pine forest and through cottonwoods and aspen. The fishing is similar to the Middle Fork, but it's not quite as good.

South Fork Sun River: It heads below Scapegoat Mountain and flows through wonderful, hike-in country to Gibson Reservoir. The upper reaches are barren, but below Pretty Prairie there is fine fishing for rainbows, brookies, and cutthroats. The water is very clear, running over the lightly colored gravel, and the trout blend with the bottom. They rush up, appearing like magic, to grab dry flies floating over their heads.

Sun River: The Sun has its beginnings on the eastern edge of the Bob Marshall Wilderness and flows into the Missouri near Great Falls. Gibson Dam discharges dictate the amount of water in this river, as do diversions at Diversion Dam. Those erratic releases from the dam also hurt the productivity of the river. The Sun is about 25 miles west of Augusta, and the Rocky Mountain Front dominates the western horizon. The upper section of the river, above Diversion Dam, has 10-inch or so, and a few larger, cutthroats, brookies, and rainbows. The quality of the angling here has decreased in the past few years for some reason. Maybe the trout are as afraid of the leaking, decrepit dam as I am. The river below has some good-size browns, along with rainbows, brook trout, whitefish, and more and more northern pike. In late summer well into fall, this

Erratic releases hurt the productivity of the Sun, but the dramatic scenery almost makes up for it.

can be good fishing for nice browns using streamers, large nymphs, and even hopper patterns. The browns I've taken along here have been lighter in color—"blonde," if you will.

Ten Mile Creek: This is the water supply for Helena. The stream follows US 12 out of town for a while and then curls up into the hills. The city takes its water out just above

Rimini. Above this juncture it is better fishing, mainly for brookies and cutthroats up to 10 inches. From Rimini down to US 12, there are brookies and a few rainbows, but the population is hammered by dewatering each summer. Below the Blue Cloud Ranch there are browns, brookies, and rainbows. Also in this stretch, with the limited spawning areas that crowd the brookies and browns together, there are a few of the rare and beautiful tiger trout, naturally produced hybrids between brook and brown parents.

West Fork of the South Fork of the Sun River: This creek joins the South Fork above Pretty Prairie Guard Station and is followed by trail to the headwaters. The lower stretches are good fishing for brookies and rainbows as the stream runs between timbered hills, with plenty of pools and gravel drops holding the trout.

Willow Creek Reservoir: Over 1,500 acres with good fishing for the many planted rainbows that grow quickly in the rich environment. There is a lot of boating activity that can make float tubing adventuresome, but working streamers, leeches, and nymphs into and then away from shore is productive. The summer highlight is the Callibaetis hatch, but it starts earlier than usual on this lake. The peak emergence happens between 5 a.m. and 10 a.m. As the trout cruise over the weed beds, try to plot the course of these rising, gulping feeders.

THE LOWER MISSOURI

Fishing Waters of the Lower Missouri—Great Falls to Border

Ackley Lake: About 250 surface acres fed by a canal from the Judith River, this lake is located southwest of Hobson and is popular locally with anglers, boaters, picnickers, and other outdoor enthusiasts. The state plants rainbows in here each year that reach 15 inches with ease. Some big brown trout also find their way in from the Judith—poor misguided souls. There are pike also, to 8 pounds. Action slows down in the summer for all types of tackle, but in spring and fall even fly fishermen can have good fishing from the shore.

Belt Creek: This stream is formed in the thickly timbered Little Belt Mountains and flows for more than 50 miles to the Missouri below Great Falls. Followed by US 89 and county roads, the best-known water on this pleasant stream is called the "Sluice Boxes." These are large pools that derive this nickname from past mining operations that have also caused some pollution problems that linger even today. The Sluice Boxes and much of the rest of the upper 40 miles are good fishing with dry and wet flies for rainbows to 15 inches and averaging about 10. The lower reaches are best for brown trout—some moving up the river during fall spawning are quite large and suscep-

Wide and slow, the lower Missouri River holds warmwater fish in abundance.

tible to streamers. There are also whitefish in good numbers. Use from non-anglers has increased greatly in recent years.

Big Horn (Brockton) Reservoir: Located in the northeast corner of the state, Big Horn is planted regularly with rainbows that grow quickly to several pounds. The trout will hit leeches, nymphs (especially dragon- and damselfly patterns), streamers, and olive scuds. This is just one of the countless ranch ponds, lakes, and reservoirs that are lying out on the plains east of the Continental Divide. The fishing is generally good for fat rainbows. Many of these waters are private and off-limits to all but family and friends. Others are planted with fish from state hatcheries and so open to the public.

Because some of these waters winter-kill or become too alkaline to support trout, their status is always changing. When traveling through the eastern portion of the state, the best way to locate these reservoirs or ponds is to call the appropriate Department of Fish, Wildlife & Parks office (numbers are at the front of each regional section in the current regulations) and inquire concerning names of waters, location, accessibility, and current fishing status. The information FWP has on waters is astounding and extremely accurate. Calling FWP is by far the easiest way to get onto some superb fishing for very big rainbows (or perhaps browns or brookies). A float tube is always a good idea, as is sunscreen and bug repellent.

Lower Missouri River

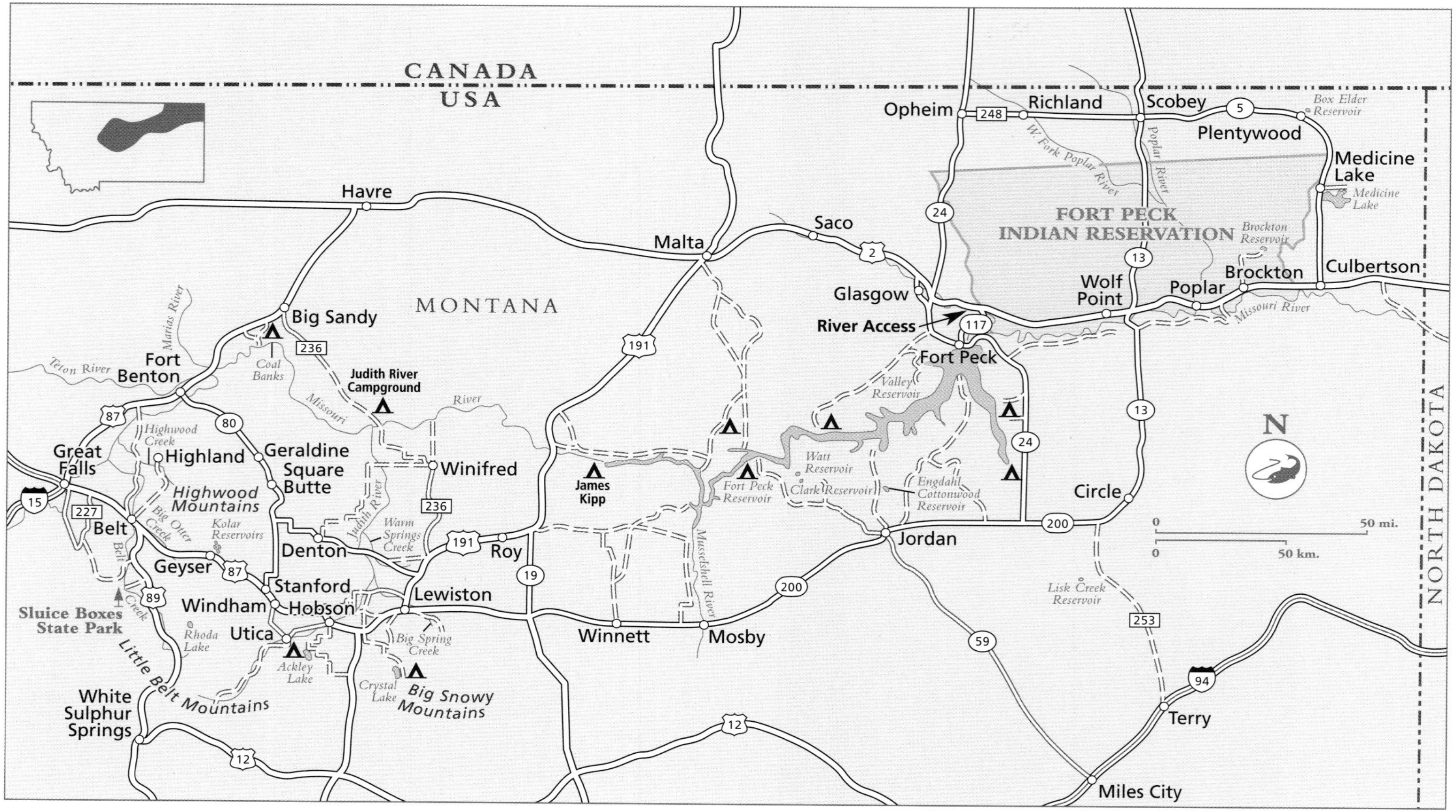

Big Otter Creek: Another in the famed collection of Montana trout streams overrun with rattlesnakes. In the summer, placing your hands or feet without looking can result in a very painful bite. Always keep an eye open for the reptiles, especially around rocks and cliffs where the snakes love to sun themselves. Snakebites are never any fun—painful, often necrotic, and even deadly. But don't be a wimp—this stream is worth the risk.

Otter has some fine fishing in its slow-moving miles of small water for browns that average 12 to 14 inches but with many that will go over 2 pounds. Going west from Raynesford, on US 87, the stream meanders back and forth from one side of the road to the other. Some of it is overgrown with brush and shrubs, but most of it is open meadows. The creek itself is plenty rich, with watercress and elodea covering the bottom, and tall grass on the banks contributes plenty of terrestrials to the food base. The best method is to crouch or kneel (eye to eye with those rattlesnakes) and move upstream, casting a dry fly or a nymph to the undercuts and deeper slots.

Big Spring Creek: Big Spring heads in the hills southeast of Lewistown and flows right through the town. It runs 31 miles from its origin to its mouth at the Judith River. The soul of the creek is the spring that pumps out 64,000 gallons of water a minute. E. Donnall Thomas Jr., writing about the stream in *The Big Sky Journal*, sums it up nicely: "For as spring creeks go, this is definitely a blue-collar version; beer rather than Chardonnay, bleachers rather than box seats, substance rather than style."

Big Spring Creek is famous for big rainbows that gather just below the hatchery west of town. The occasional one gets caught—8 pounds and up—but these fish are stuffed with the spillage from the hatchery and difficult to catch on flies. The real fishing starts a few hundred yards below the hatchery. Even there, however, it is not a "classic spring creek." It runs bank full and very fast; there are deep holes, but relatively few spots where trout can hold and leisurely sip insects from the surface. The key for the dry-fly fisherman is not only knowing the timing of the hatches, but also the backwaters and broad pools where the fish will hold and rise steadily.

The section above town is a series of deep pools connected by riffles and runs guarded by brushy banks. This upper stretch has fewer trout (mainly rainbows) than below town, but is prettier, more accessible water, with fish averaging 15 inches and running to several pounds. These trout are spooky in the very clear water, so you need light tippets, low profiles, and delicate casting. This applies to the nymph fishing during the non-hatch hours as well as to the dry-fly fishing. Pheasant Tails, Rubber Legged Hare's Ears, Bead-Head Twist Nymphs, Gray/Olive Scuds, and Prince Nymphs do well. Even with a sink-tip line, you'll sometimes need weight to get down to the fish, who run for their lives at the merest suggestion of drag. The steadiest dry-fly activity for hatch-matchers comes from the midge hatches during the winter on the Griffith's Gnat, the blue-winged olive hatches in the spring and fall on the matching Sparkle Dun, and the pale morning dun hatches all summer on the matching Sparkle Dun. A small rule of thumb at times: Nymph the deeper water and use drys in the riffles.

The demarcation zone between the upper and lower sections is the long concrete ditch that channels the stream through the middle of town. The lower stretch, with the Judith Mountains rising to the north, flows through rangeland and is marked by brushy and grassy banks. It's great water—better fishing even than the upper area. A large Woolly Bugger (olive) hammered along the banks will turn browns consistently, even along runs that look like poor habitat. Watch for shelves in the streambed that can wrench your knees or wet your shirt. These are also prime places to dead-drift the Bugger or a big cranefly imitation. Two nymphs on the leader usually do better than one—the best combination is a big pattern, size 10 or larger, and a small pattern, size 16 or 18. This lower water gets the same hatches as the upper stretch; the secret is knowing areas where the stream slows down enough for fish to rise efficiently to small food forms. Grasshoppers, so abundant in the meadows along the creek, are not tidbits, and even in the heavy water, both browns and rainbows rush the surface for them.

Access below town is at bridges off the city streets or off CR 238. There are three public access points, but these aren't well marked on the main highway. Camping is available southwest of town, if you do not mind a spot with no amenities (like water and toilets) and can handle barking farm dogs and bright barn lights glowing all night. Access is being bought up and posted, but there are still adequate places to get on and off the water. The access at Hruska off of MT 426 has been completely revamped and is now quite nice and functional.

The fish in Big Spring Creek are tainted with PCBs. A study by the Montana Department of Health and Environmental Sciences and the Department of Fish, Wildlife & Parks recommended, "Children up to age 15, nursing mothers, and women of childbearing age should be particularly careful about consuming these fish."

Carter's Ponds: The lower one is usually the best of the two, but the dam has been leaking and the fishing is deteriorating on this pond. They are planted yearly with rainbows that grow rapidly as they gorge on the tremendous numbers of olive scuds (sizes 14 to 16), damsel nymphs, and Callibaetis mayfly nymphs. A proven pattern here is the Rollover Scud, a fly with a distinctive motion that separates it from the hordes of naturals. The most consistent dry-fly fishing is at dawn during spells of warm (not hot) stable summer and autumn weather—the fish cruise and indiscriminately sip drowned and crippled naturals from the previous night. They even work the shallow, mossy bays, feeding in the open lanes; stalking these trout in the heavy vegetation feels like bass fishing. They stop feeding as soon as the sun hits the water. The shoreline is too weedy with cattails, reeds, and moss for easy wading. Either a float tube or a boat will help you get to the deeper water. There is a boat launch and a picnic area. The ponds are 7 miles north of Lewistown on US 91.

Crystal Lake: Crystal is about 40 acres in the Big Snowies (south of Lewistown), with a picnic area and campground. This pond provides average fishing for rainbows to 15 inches. Most of these die off over winter in the shallow water, and the road in is a bit on the unsafe side of life. The stream running out of here often goes dry and is barren.

Fort Peck Reservoir: Well over 100 miles long with 1,600 miles of shoreline, Fort Peck is surrounded by the 800,000-acre Charles M. Russell National Wildlife Refuge. It's planted with lake trout, northern pike, and walleyes. This is the location of the exciting Governor's Cup Walleye (and competition license plate drowning) Tournament each summer, where teams of eager anglers race all over the place in metal-flaked, high-powered speedboats chasing the elusive species and the financial awards attendant with derricking the fish into a live well. Great fun. There are also chinook salmon here. Other species include some browns, rainbows, perch, burbot, smallmouth bass, carp, suckers, paddlefish, sturgeon, and goldeyes.

Most of the fish taken in Fort Peck are caught either with bait or lures. One notable fly-fishing opportunity is in the bays on the southern shoreline (especially near any creek inlet) with large streamers for schools of marauding northerns that average about 7 pounds and run to over 10. Shooting heads help reach the fish when they are cruising way out. And watch out for muck and quicksand around the inlets. Hit this right, and you can have some very exciting action. Another great target is the smallmouth fishery at the western end of the lake, especially at the mouth of the Musselshell (bass averaging 4.5 pounds). The snakes, cactus, biting insects, and lack of available drinking water add to the experience. Bring a friend.

Highwood Creek: This stream is pretty good fishing for the open country. It pours out of the Highwood Mountains below Highwood Baldy Mountain and flows northwest to the Missouri about 20 miles below Great Falls. It's followed by Forest Service and county roads much of the way, and the upper reaches are fair fishing for brook and rainbow trout to a foot. The lower reaches, especially close to the Missouri, play host to some big rainbows in the spring (before the season opens) and to some even bigger browns in the fall. There are also some decent brook trout in this lower stretch that hold beneath the grassy, brushy, undercut banks and at the bottoms of slow pools. This is good streamer water all the time and nice hopper water from July into September.

Judith River: The Judith flows out of the Little Belt Mountains southwest of Lewistown and runs for about 45 air miles north to the Missouri directly south of the Bears Paw Mountains. The upper reaches are good fishing for wild cutthroats and some rainbows, despite water shortages from irrigation demands. The return of the water also harms the banks. The Lost, Middle, Ross, and South Forks are fun and challenging dry-fly fishing for a very few rainbows to 15 inches, brookies, and a few cutthroats.

The middle sections of the stream flow through farm and ranch land. The stream is characterized by grassy or brushy undercut banks, a rock bottom, and fair numbers of rainbows and browns to perhaps 18 inches. There are also less numbers of brookies. Access is gained from county roads and state highways—take US 87 to Hobson and go up the Judith River Road (which turns into gravel) past Utica.

Not far below the river's confluence with Big Spring Creek, burbot, channel catfish, goldeyes, and sauger take over as the water warms and turns turbid as it slides through arid, barren country. A few large browns are taken in this section, but you need patience and large streamers. Access is not easy either.

Medicine Lake: This is another wildlife refuge with amazing numbers of waterfowl and plenty of other bird, mammal, and reptile species. The fishing found on the 31,000-plus acres of ponds and reservoirs in the northeast corner of the state can be very good for northerns to 8 pounds or so, and for fat largemouth bass that hammer poppers that look like frogs. There are also smallmouth bass in less numbers.

Rhoda Lake: This little hike-in lake is in the Judith River drainage. Go south of Great Falls 70 miles on US 89, along Belt Creek, and then turn left onto the Big Baldy Jeep Road. It's a stiff 3-mile climb from the end of the road up to Rhoda. The lake receives annual plants of Yellowstone cutthroats that survive but don't grow much beyond 15 inches in this 2-acre lake at 9,800 feet in the Little Belts. But this is a shallow body of water, with a maximum depth of 12 feet.

Warm Springs Creek: Warm Springs begins in the Judith Mountains and flows for 25 miles to the Judith River not far from Denton. The upper reaches hold rainbows and smallmouths, while the lower, open-prairie section is mainly smallmouth bass. Both species provide good fishing. Medium-size streamers work for the bass, and general, searching dry flies and nymphs work for the trout. There is fishing access along the highway.

Watt Reservoir: It's way out in the middle of nowhere—and that makes this 10-acre, 20-foot-deep reservoir, located north of Brusett and south of Fort Peck Reservoir, a special stillwater fishery. It's planted annually with rainbows, just like the other prairie reservoirs, but this one is so remote that the fish don't get hammered by strange confections and baits. There are good numbers of two- and three-year survivors that will occasionally top several pounds.

In its upper reaches, the Judith River is a surprisingly scenic jewel of eastern Montana.

If you're planning on fishing the West Poplar, anticipate beautiful solitude and rough roads that turn impassable after a good rainstorm. Four-wheel-drive vehicles are a must.

West Fork Poplar River: The West Fork Poplar flows over the border from Canada north of Scobey and eventually joins the Poplar River, which twists and turns through grassy prairie and badlands country for 50 miles to the Missouri at Poplar. Much of the water is on the Fort Peck Indian Reservation. It has northerns, walleyes, and smallmouths. Access is tough via "roads" that quickly turn impassable at even the hint of a rainstorm. There are a few sizable brookies and browns hiding out in this water, too.

Musselshell River

The Musselshell is another river that offers fly fishers some pleasant action, but should not be considered a "destination" river. True, there are some large brown trout holding here and the country is scenic and uncrowded. But access is poor and there really is not that much water to fish, especially during the height of summer when irrigation demands for adjacent fields suck the poor thing nearly dry. Just the same, if you are driving through the valley and have a few hours to spare, you've nothing to lose casting a streamer for the browns or just working small drys to the rising 9-inchers that are anything but selective.

After the spring runoff and before the Musselshell is drawn down from irrigation, the river here is classic big-brown water, bending and curving through open country, creating untold numbers of holding areas beneath the grassy and brushy banks. Water spills over sand and gravel shelves into deep pools shaded from the persistent sun by alders and cottonwoods. Riffles and silent glides swing lazily in soft arcs as the stream moves gently toward its rendezvous with the Missouri at Fort Peck Reservoir over 150 miles to the northeast. The setting is more agrarian than wild, but for background scenery Local Mountain, Bald Ridge, and the rest of the Crazies run away down south, with the Castle Range showing in the west. From mid-July until mid-September, the fishing is normally poor due to irrigation.

The Musselshell runs for many circuitous miles, but the stretch below Martinsdale, from the confluence of the North and South Forks down to Harlowton, is where you will experience the most "success." This section is perhaps 25 miles and is reached by bridges and county roads that cross and follow the water here and there. The fish population is mostly brown trout in decent but not-close-to-Bighorn-River numbers, with far fewer rainbows and brookies. Mountain whitefish are also present, probably in numbers that exceed the combined totals for all of the trout species put together.

In other words, the Musselshell is not a river to plan a vacation around for those who must travel long distances to reach Montana. Rather, this is a place to fish between trips to locations like Yellowstone or the Missouri River or Glacier National Park, way up by the Canadian border.

The river is easy to wade—not deep and rarely exceeding 20 feet wide—and your entrance is best planned well ahead by cautiously approaching the water to consider the tactical and logistical problems that lie beyond. Usually by late June things have settled

Musselshell River

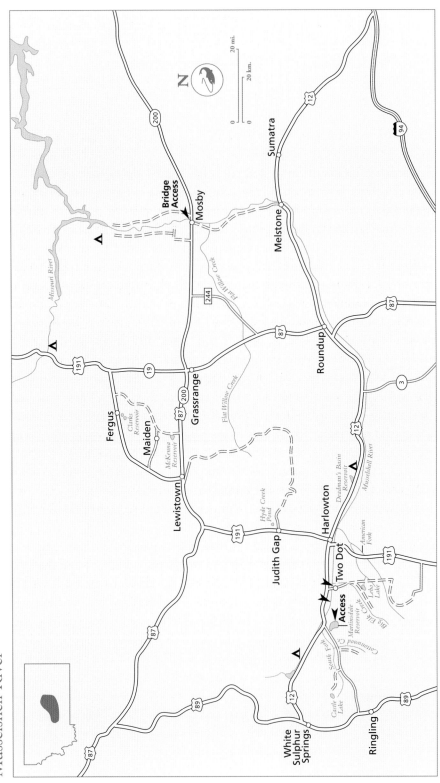

down to the point that some of the browns are visible holding along the bottom, or when they make brief rushes out into the open to take a nymph or unwary minnow.

There are no crowds here, but the trout are spooky, perhaps from the many predators gliding in the air above. Quiet, low-profile movements are in order. The Musselshell is perfect for a 2- or 3-weight rod and a 9-foot (or longer) leader tapered to the absolute maximum of 3X, with 4X or 5X preferred. When hammering streamers, a heavier rod and a shorter leader, to 2X or 3X, are okay, but the drys need the thinner material to do the job properly.

Streamers include Woolly Buggers, Marabou Muddlers, Matukas, and Matuka Sculpins. Nymphs might range from a Hare's Ear to a Prince. A brown-olive or brown Serendipity is effective during emergence. Drys could include Clear Wing Spinners, Goddard Caddis, Humpies, and a range of terrestrials that would include ants, beetles, and hoppers.

The most abundant insect in the river is probably the grannom caddis. You'll crunch the little four-sided cases under your feet when you wade the riffles. The finest hatch of the season on the river occurs in the late spring, from April through early May, when the water is clear and cold and those grannoms fill the air. There are also good hatches of blue-winged olives in April, July, and August, and again in September lasting into October. Sometimes nice browns over 15 inches can be taken on a size 18 or 20 Blue-Winged Olive in the fall. Trico spinners trigger a nice rise on summer mornings. The hoppers are excellent producers from July into September, in part because of the preponderance of hay fields next to the river. The patterns should grow larger as the season progresses—going from size 12 up to 8 or 6.

The Musselshell may be a "hit-or-miss" trout stream in the upper reaches, but in the lower water, from Roundup to Melstone, it is a good and consistent smallmouth bass river. The bass hit the same streamers that the browns hit on the upper river, but it wouldn't hurt to add a crayfish imitation, a bullhead imitation, and a few Slider-style cork bugs to your selection.

POPULAR FLIES

Blue-Winged Olive	Marabou Muddler
Brown Olive	Matuka
Brown Serendipity	Matuka Sculpin
Clear Wing Spinner	Prince Nymph
Goddard Caddis	Trico Spinner
Hare's Ear Nymph	Woolly Bugger
Humpy	

Much of the land in this drainage is posted, but a polite request and a smile often gains access to some of the better water. Offer to pick up any junk you see and close all of the gates you pass through. Then thank the people at the end of the day and send them a bottle of bourbon at Christmas. Maybe they'll let you try your luck again the next season.

You don't need complicated hatches and elaborate pattern-selection dances on the Musselshell. The basics will always take the browns, provided you use extreme caution in your approach and presentation. Use the same care wading the stream. The small-mouths don't see enough anglers to get wise either, but the angler has to understand the association between bass and cover. In this fragile watershed, even with its limited access to visiting fly fishers, the fish demand some finesse.

Fishing Waters in the Musselshell Drainage

American Fork: The American Fork has its beginnings in the Crazy Mountains to the south and flows for 30 miles to the main river east of Harlowton. The lower reaches are good fall fishing, with limited access for good-size browns. The upper section in the mountains is nice pocket water; use Royal Humpies and the like for brookies to 12 inches.

Bair Reservoir: Deep and nearly 300 acres, it's right next to US 12 about 15 minutes east of White Sulphur Springs in windy, open country. There are good numbers of big rainbows that often take streamers and nymphs near shore in the spring. Browns of size and some brook trout are also present. There is a campground and boat launch here. A float tube helps.

Big Elk Creek: This one begins in the Crazy Mountains and joins the Musselshell at Twodot. It's best for brookies, but access is controlled and the surrounding land is heavily posted. This stream, like all of the others on the upper river, can produce superb fishing for big browns in the fall. The fish will hit anything thrown in front of their faces at this time of the year. Use caution wading to avoid damaging the important spawning gravels that also support the insect and forage fish populations.

Cottonwood Creek: Cottonwood is a small Crazy Mountains stream that has decent fishing for little brook and rainbow trout with a few nice browns, especially in the fall. Access is tight, but you can reach the water from the bridge on MT 294 west of Martinsdale.

Grebe Reservoir: Grebe is not too far from Sumatra or Roundup and fair fishing for this part of the prairie for rainbows that average a pound in this 4-acre pond.

Hyde Creek Pond: This one is right by a missile silo, so you know you are safe from Bulgarian attack while you fish for foot-long rainbows in this 3-acre, spring-fed pond just north of Judith Gap.

Martinsdale Reservoir: Heavily planted with Yellowstone cutthroat and rainbow trout, this 985-acre impoundment is reached just south of Martinsdale by dirt road. Lying in a broad dip in open country north of the Crazies, this one is over 100 feet deep with good fishing for rainbows and cutts up to 18 inches. Some very large browns lie near the inlet. Large streamers in the fall take these big boys. Scuds and leeches and damselfly nymphs work on the rest of the salmonids. One hot spot is the little island located just south of the dam; fish between the island and dam and concentrate on the clumps of willows along that south shore. This area of the lake once produced three rainbows over 8 pounds on a single early June weekend (two of those fish were caught with spinning equipment, but the third one was taken and released on a size 6 Red/Black Bristle Leech). Bring a boat or a float tube. The Mint Bar in downtown Martinsdale is a good place to escape the summer sun.

North Fork Musselshell River: Small and brushy but holding some browns over 12 inches, the North Fork is accessed along US 12 and some county roads. Small Buggers and Humpies draw the trout.

South Fork Musselshell River: Beginning a few miles west of Lennep, the South Fork is followed most of the way by county roads to the Musselshell northeast of Martinsdale. Access is gained at bridges along MT 294 or wade up from the main river for fair catches of browns to 18 inches, rainbows to 15 inches, and brook trout that are smaller yet in this very narrow, brushy stream. Getting the fly on the water without scaring the fish or without drag is the problem here, not pattern selection.

Red Rock River

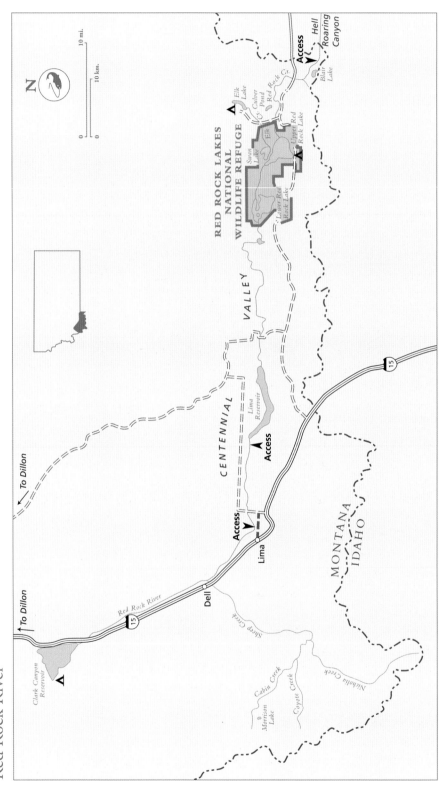

Red Rock River

The headwaters of the Red Rock River eventually find their way into the Gulf of Mexico almost 4,000 miles distant. Formed by waters from streams like Hellroaring Creek and Red Rock Creek in the Centennial Mountains along the Idaho border, this stream offers one of the last riverine refuges for arctic grayling in the Lower 48.

As the Red Rock flows through the Red Rock Lakes National Wildlife Refuge, then Lima Reservoir, and on beneath colorful cliffs to its final destination at Clark Canyon Reservoir, the river is guarded by the Madison, Gravelly, and Snowcrest Ranges in the north and the Tendoys along the southwest.

The upper stretches of the river are excellent dry-fly fishing for grayling that sometimes reach 15 inches and are not all that choosy about the pattern. Cutthroats display similar equanimity. As the Red Rock moves into the Centennial Valley, the stream slows a bit and takes on a marshy character as it wanders between large pools that are treated as lakes in their own right on the refuge. Brook trout, cutthroats, grayling, and even lake trout are taken along this section of the river. Trumpeter swans and large flocks of waterfowl are common sights.

According to officials at Red Rock Lakes National Wildlife Refuge, fisheries on the refuge suffer from low populations. As a result, the refuge has special regulations designed to improve fish numbers. Red Rock Lakes and the creek between them are closed to fishing. Definitely check the US Forest Service regulations regarding what's open and closed. The regs are detailed.

The river from here to Lima Reservoir has suffered from cattle grazing and is too silted in and too warm to sustain a viable trout fishery. Once below Lima, the river returns to a quality environment for trout, running through red-and-ochre-colored rock formations. Rainbow and cutthroat trout are the dominant species, with browns gradually increasing in numbers down to Clark Canyon. Access is severely limited except for some Bureau of Reclamation land just above the reservoir. Wading is the preferred approach, though a few hearty individuals drift downstream in float tubes. Permission on this prime water now comes mainly in the form of daily fee fishing. The angling is excellent on the restricted stretches, but if this is a trend for this river, it is disappointing for local fly fishers.

Blue-winged olives come into play, especially from late August into early October. Pale morning duns are seen from June through September. There is normally some form of caddis activity throughout the summer and into fall, matched by dry flies and emergers in sizes 12 to 18 in tan, gray, and brown. Grannoms are the earliest arrivals, showing up in May, followed by the spotted sedges and then little sister, green, and longhorn sedges in late June. Sizes 12 and 14 for all but the great gray spotted sedge (6 and 8) are adequate. There are also yellow sally stoneflies, sizes 14 and 16, beginning in July.

The browns in the lower river will often top several pounds. Beginning in late September, these fish prefer large streamers like Muddlers, Woolly Buggers, Stub Wing Bucktails, Matukas, and Zonkers cast hard to the willowy, grassy, undercut banks and then pulsed back. Large wet flies in sizes 6 through 10 cast quartering upstream and worked along the current with slight action and then allowed to tail out at the end of the drift can also provoke some serious responses from the trout.

Matching the hatch is not so much the problem as is getting onto the best parts of the lower river. This is a matter of knowing a landowner or being willing and able to pay the daily fee. I find the fee concept antithetical and anathema to fishing in Montana, as well as wealthy yahoos along with guide/outfitting operations buying up stream access. May they enjoy their lot in angling's hell. This is fine country to fish in for good-size browns and rainbows in plentiful supply.

FISHING WATERS IN THE RED ROCK DRAINAGE

Culver Pond (Widow's Pool): Nearly 30 acres and spring-fed several miles east of Upper Red Rock Lake, with plenty of good-size (read: BIG) brook trout that are tough to catch but will bite a Biggs Special worked above the weed beds ever so slowly. There are also cutthroats, grayling, and rainbows. Callibaetis imitations starting at midmorning from July through early September take fish, and brown drakes (*Ephemera simulans*) come off on occasion in the evenings in June and July. No float tubes allowed.

Elk (Elk Springs or Shitepoke) Creek: This is a small stream heading out of Elk Lake. There's good fishing in the beaver-dammed, swampy stretches in the Red Rock Lakes National Wildlife Refuge for brook and rainbow trout up to several pounds. Check the special regulations.

Elk Lake: Elk is one of the best grayling lakes in the state, with fish to 15 inches caught each season. There are also cutthroats and lake trout to 20 inches on this popular water. The gamefish population is threatened by an illegal plant of Utah chub, first discovered in 1986—the number of chub is growing.

Hellroaring Creek: This is a good stream for cutthroats approaching the magic 20-inch barrier, especially in the lower reaches. Cutthroats are cutthroats—don't get a headache trying to figure out what fly you think they will take. Except for the snobs in the

Yellowstone River in Yellowstone National Park, this species is not all that picky. Small brook trout also live here.

McDonald's Pool (Buck Pond): McDonald's is 7 acres below Elk Lake, with rainbows over 20 inches and several pounds. In the summer this place is somewhat crowded.

Morrison Lake: Below Baldy Mountain at over 8,000 feet and 24 acres, Morrison is reached by rough "road" for cutthroat trout that top a couple of pounds.

Red Rock Creek: This is one of the best (among the few) grayling streams in Montana, with fish to 15 inches, along with brook trout and cutthroats. It wanders down from Squaw Pass to Upper Red Rock Lake in the Centennial Valley. Access could be better, but this is a stream worth savoring, at least once. Be sure to check special regulations if you are on the wildlife refuge.

Red Rock Lakes: Closed to fishing in 1996.

Sheep (Big Sheep) Creek: Sheep heads below Eighteenmile Peak in the Beaverhead Mountains along the Idaho border. It enters the Red Rock River just south of Dell and is followed by gravel road for much of its heavily fished length. Rainbows and browns over 20 inches are still taken at times, with the best fish coming as soon as the general season opens, runoff permitting, and in the fall with Buggers and Marabou Muddlers and other ugly stuff worked right up against the brushy, willow-choked, undercut banks.

Widgeon Pond: This one is on the county road between McDonald's Pool and Culver Pond, with good fishing for cutthroats and brookies over 15 inches.

The little town of White Sulfur Springs serves as a point of departure for most Smith River excursions. Mike Cline

Smith River

Ask experienced Montana fly fishers what the most scenic float in the state is, and many will say the Smith River. Throw in sometimes-excellent fishing for browns and rainbows in the isolated 61-mile stretch of canyon river (a four- to five-day float) and you have the ingredients for a quality fishing experience. The quality of the float and the attendant popularity has led to the FWP implementing regulations on using this river. Floating on the Smith River between Camp Baker and Eden Bridge is strictly limited. Mandatory registration, a floater's fee, and other regulations apply. A drawing for launch dates is held in February, with remaining launches filled on a first-come basis.

Formed at the confluence of the North and South Forks in open meadow country west of White Sulphur Springs, the Smith flows for over 100 miles through some of the most spectacular canyon country in Montana. The upper 30 miles of the river wander across an open, rolling-hill mountain valley surrounded by the Castle, Big Belt, and Little Belt mountains. Brown trout to several pounds hide beneath the brushy, willowy banks, as do good numbers of smaller rainbows and brook trout. The pool-to-riffle-to-pool habitat in this gently flowing section is ideal for fishing an Elk Hair Caddis with an Emergent Sparkle Pupa dropper in the evenings, hoppers on a summer afternoon, or streamers, especially in autumn for spawning browns on the move.

The canyon section runs from Camp Baker to Eden Bridge, with no public access in between. Twenty-two designated campsites are scattered along the way, and that's it for amenities. Some private homes and ranches overlook the river in this section. The Smith gets a skwala stonefly hatch, effectively matched with a brown wing/green body Trude or a dark-colored Air Head, in March and April. This is usually before runoff, and the insects can trigger great surface action. Later in the spring, when the river is on the rise from runoff and rain, anglers can expect very slow fishing for browns that will take large Woolly Buggers, especially in brown. Big ugly stuff draws the trout. These fish will be larger on average than fish taken later in the year when the weather warms and the water drops and clears. Perhaps this is because it takes a big fish to handle the swollen flow of the Smith. When the river begins to compress as runoff abates, the angling for browns and rainbows can be superb, again with the streamers, but also with caddis and stoneflies (especially large nymphs). The Smith gets good hatches of salmon flies and golden stoneflies.

Smith River

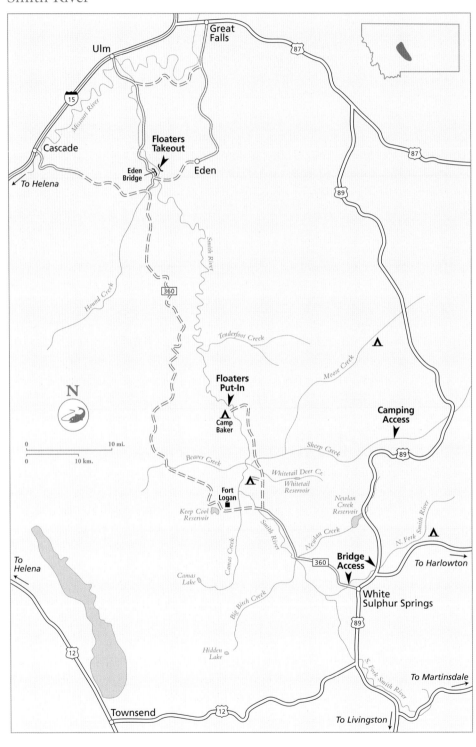

At certain times of the year, the Smith offers fine opportunities for brown trout.

Streamers and nymphs worked bank-tight to grassy pockets or between runs of broken rock and boulders can also be productive. Even after a tough winter, the trout are firm and thick, though lacking the intense shadings attendant with autumn's spawning festivities. Downstream from Camp Baker, rainbow populations can run to more than 1,300 per mile from 6 to 16½ inches.

The peak use period on the Smith runs from late May until levels are too low in mid- to late July (although in drought years floating can become impossible in mid-June). The majority of trout taken at this time will be rainbows, with some browns and a smattering of whitefish that frequently reach a couple of pounds. You may also take an occasional cutthroat.

Below Eden Bridge the river is a slow affair with riprap banks, undercut cottonwood-lined banks, and brushy banks, and trout populations drop off considerably. Large browns and rainbows, both resident and up from the Missouri, will take streamers and terrestrials cast close to the shore. This portion of the Smith is best worked in the spring and again in the fall to take advantage of migrating rainbows and browns.

Notwithstanding its scenic qualities and fishing opportunities, the Smith is not immune to environmental insult. Noxious weeds (in the form of leafy spurge and spotted knapweed), introduced through contaminated hay, have since spread throughout the drainage in epidemic proportions, helped along, in part, by recreational users. Biological controls in the form of weed-eating insects have been introduced.

No less a threat is the proliferation of riverside "ranchettes." The growth of these second-home developments in the canyon have exacerbated landowner disputes in the past few years. Fortunately, one group, the Montana Land Reliance, has embarked on an aggressive program of acquiring conservation easements to limit riverside development. Their efforts have ensured that many miles of private land will not be turned into housing developments.

FISHING WATERS IN THE SMITH DRAINAGE

Big Birch Creek: Big Birch is a few miles west of White Sulphur Springs. It provides solid action for exceptional numbers of brook trout to maybe 12 inches. The marshy, brushy country means hip waders and roll casts with dry flies or nymphs and the like.

Hidden Lake: Go up White Gulch and turn on the "microwave" road to get above Hidden Lake, and then hike down. Or go into the Big Belts, to the end of Big Birch Creek, and hike up to the lake. Either way, with pristine country and nice fishing for fat rainbows to 16 inches, this water is worth the trip. Hidden is deep, even though it's only 5 acres, and a sinking or sink-tip line puts a fly into the prime water at the drop-offs. Try weighted nymphs, such as the A. P. Muskrat, Gold-Ribbed Hare's Ear, or Bead-Head Twist Nymph, fished slowly up the slope.

Hound Creek: Hound Creek enters the Smith not too far above Eden Bridge and winds through open sage country that plays home to rattlesnakes and trophy mosquitoes. Access is poor but the fishing is good for plenty of browns to a foot or more and plenty of little brook trout. A beetle imitation like the Coch-y-Bondhu is a consistent fly, but a hopper pattern brings out the bigger fish.

Moose Creek: A small freestone stream that runs into Sheep Creek with small brookies and cutthroats and an occasional fish to 15 inches. The campground a few miles upstream is a nice place to stay when it's open, also providing a jumping-off spot for nearby Sheep Creek. Reached from US 89 east of White Sulphur Springs then along the Sheep Creek Road.

Newlan Creek Reservoir: Here are 300 acres of water, 12 miles north of White Sulphur Springs, planted each year with thousands of Yellowstone cutthroats that grow to 18 inches. Big fish, easy access, and large water—a combination like that is bound to make this a popular place with anglers of all persuasions. Still, with so many acres a person can usually find his own bit of shoreline to work with a nymph. The cutthroats here do seem to be bottom grubbers. A size 10 to 16 Gold-Ribbed Hare's Ear works.

Moose Creek harbors smaller fish but runs through the middle of some remarkable country.

North Fork Smith River: The North Fork begins in the Little Belts and makes its casual way for more than 20 miles to the Smith not far from White Sulphur Springs. The upper reaches have lots of small brookies and rainbows. The lower sections, below Sutherlin Reservoir, are good fishing for nice browns along with lots of whitefish and some brook trout. Brushy and marshy in places. Much of the land is posted, but access can be gained from county roads.

Rock Creek: Rock Creek comes from the east side of the Big Belts Mountains through private rangeland, and then to the Smith north of the Old Fort Logan Military Reservation. Where you can get on it, it's good fishing for brookies, cutthroats, rainbows, and some fair-size browns that are not all that concerned with what fly is cast upon the water. The roads, such as they are, are not in good shape and they can do a number on your vehicle or your tires. They also turn hazardous with the slightest suggestion of precipitation. When it rains, stay off of these roads. The best fishing is on the Galt property. Good luck there.

The upper stretches of Sheep Creek hold some nice brook trout throughout the year.

Sheep Creek: A good fishing stream with dry flies for a mixed bag of mainly brookies, some browns, and rainbows along with whitefish in its 30-plus-mile journey through forested valleys, canyons, rangeland, and grassy hills to the Smith northwest of White Sulphur Springs, after beginning in the Little Belts north of Porphyry Peak. It is followed by county road much of its length, with Forest Service campgrounds in the upper reaches. In the summer this water can seem barren of all but a few small brook trout. Come late September, a fair number of colorful trout up to 14 inches appear out of nowhere. Small Buggers and attractor drys work at this time.

Sutherlin (Smith River) Reservoir: About 10 miles east of White Sulphur Springs on US 12, at over 270 acres and 80 feet deep with heavy drawdown from irrigation, Sutherlin is planted yearly with thousands of rainbows. This is popular with area anglers. There is a campground and other amenities.

Tenderfoot Creek: Reached by rough road on the east side of the Smith, 20 miles north of the Old Fort Logan Military Reservation, it's followed by both trail and logging road for good fishing for cutthroats, rainbows, and whitefish. The land at its mouth is posted, so if you are going to fish up from the Smith, stay inside the ordinary high-water marks.

Draining straight out of the Beartooths, the Stillwater is clear, cold, and fast.

Stillwater River

The Stillwater River has its wild beginnings in the remote, rugged, and largely inaccessible Beartooth Mountains north of Yellowstone National Park. Wind-scoured plateaus lying thousands of feet above sea level are surrounded by jagged peaks that tower even more thousands of feet above. Snowfields and glaciers carve and crack the rock and provide water that drives the river. Waterfalls offer scenic diversion.

The Stillwater drains hundreds of square miles that hold more than 300 lakes that average less than 10 acres each in surface area. Nearly 40 percent of these waters hold trout of many species, including the rare and beautiful golden trout and Yellowstone cutthroat, rainbow, and brook trout. Grayling also show up in some of these clear, relatively sterile lakes. Many of them are at elevations over 9,000 feet, including an unnamed one at 10,400 feet. Lots of these lakes are unnamed, but a number of them contain trout, usually Yellowstone cutthroats.

The upper section of the Stillwater is a fast-flowing, pocket-water stream holding good numbers of brook, cutthroat, and rainbow trout averaging perhaps 8 inches and occasionally topping 12 inches. Attractor patterns take the eager fish. The middle section of the stream is accessible by road above and below the town of Nye, with good fishing for browns to several pounds along with brookies and rainbows.

The lower section runs out onto private and posted ranchland. This stretch has fair numbers of brook and rainbow trout and some big browns holding the clear riffles, runs, pools, and bank-tight holes. Think Woolly Buggers. There are numerous fishing accesses, and floating the river between Absarokee and the Yellowstone is popular, with the usual suspects for patterns and techniques taking some good fish. Some accesses working upstream are Fireman's Point, Swinging Bridge, and Absaroka.

In the middle and lower sections, nymphing the runs and riffles is a good ploy for catching rainbows. Streamers and large nymphs worked close to the banks always takes browns. Keep an eye out for caddis, especially around dusk as summer progresses. The caddis will bring all of the trout up to the surface as they begin to fall back onto the water during and after mating. Humpies in all colors do the trick.

Stillwater River

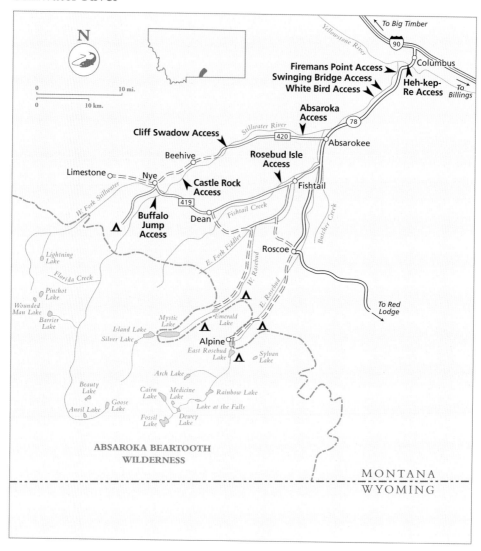

FISHING WATERS IN THE STILLWATER DRAINAGE

Arch Lakes: You can reach these via the East Rosebud Trail above Elk Lake to Little Arch at nearly 10,000 feet below Phantom Glacier. This lake is planted regularly with Yellowstone cutthroats. The other lakes in the basin also have trout, some reaching a couple of pounds.

East Fork Fiddler Creek: This one is followed by road above the West Stillwater–Rosebud Road for nice catches of browns and rainbows in the lower sections and cutthroats in the run below Fishtail Plateau.

East Rosebud Creek: The East Rosebud heads up on the Beartooth Plateau at Cairn Lake and flows for over 50 miles to West Rosebud Creek. To get there, take the road to East Rosebud Lake, and then the trail to the headwaters. You'll find fair fishing in the middle sections for healthy browns and rainbows. Some big fish are taken down below in pastureland country, but permission is required. This valley has turned into one of the most unfriendly places in Montana. Summer and full-time residents look at "outsiders" like they are aliens or worse. The vibe here is so bad that despite the awesome beauty, I'll never go back.

East Rosebud Lake: This is a beautiful lake with mountain vistas all around. It's not a wilderness experience—there are summer homes and it is reached by good road. The fishing is fair at best for cutthroats and rainbows that top 15 inches and a very few browns that reach several pounds. The lake is over 100 acres by 20 feet or more deep. As for the friendly factor, see East Rosebud Creek.

East Rosebud Lake offers alpine habitat with good dry-fly fishing at times along the shoreline.

Emerald Lake: The West Rosebud Road south of Columbus tracks right along the shoreline of this popular lake. It is 28 acres, but very shallow (maximum 7 feet). It is stocked with rainbows each year and, of course, these sacrificial lambs draw the crowds. Some of these fish escape the early slaughter and because of either intelligence or luck, manage to grow larger, to 15 inches within a few months, and get more attuned to the natural environment.

Flood Creek: This outlet of Pinchot Lake flows for several miles to the Stillwater. There is good fishing for goldens (that love Goddard Caddis), rainbows, cutthroats, and all sorts of hybrid combinations.

Fossil Lake: Fossil sits at nearly 10,000 feet and is planted every three years with Yellowstone cutthroats that grow quickly enough, considering the elevation, to 15 inches. The access is from the Clarks Fork of the Yellowstone drainage—find Bald Knob Lake and from there it's a mile hike over to Fossil. The problem on this lake is the bad, almost constant, wind on the exposed plateau. Many anglers wait until evening and hope the cold, steady blasts will go away. When the wind does drop, the fish feed well on the surface, taking any good terrestrial imitation. Ants and beetles are good choices.

Goose Lake: Over 100 acres, deep, and reachable by four-wheel-drive rig south of Grasshopper Glacier out of Cooke City, Goose is good fishing for cutthroats up to a few pounds, but the angling pressure crops off the number of fish here. Sometimes a couple of nice trout are a good day on Goose.

Lake at the Falls: This water is 50 acres of alpine splendor at over 8,000 feet on the East Rosebud Trail above Rainbow Lake. It's good fishing for large cutthroats that may have a slight golden tinge from cross-breeding with the goldens that used to swim here.

Lightning Lake: Over 60 acres and 120 feet deep at 9,340-feet elevation, this one probably holds a golden as big as anyone has ever caught. The big trout are almost impossible to catch unless they are in the connecting flow between Lightning and Little Lightning Lake. At these times a weighted Muddler worked repeatedly in front of the trout as they hold in the flow will provoke territorial strikes. Little Lightning is a nursery for goldens and is easier fishing. After the trout are done spawning, they head back to the deep where reaching them with a small nymph is more than work. Finding your way to this water is not easy, but the best way in is around Chalice Peak from Lake Plateau.

Medicine Lake: Located at almost 10,000 feet in barren country above Dewey Lake, it's 30 acres and deep. Everyone should go to the upper end to see the waterfalls (and the cliffs at the base of the falls aren't a bad place to start fishing). It's planted with cutthroats, but in spite of the long stocking cycle, it always provides consistently good action for fish up to 15 inches. The fish really hug the littoral zone, cruising the edge looking for an easy meal.

Mystic Lake: Mystic is over 400 acres and more than 200 feet deep when full. This reservoir is up West Rosebud Creek. Rainbows greatly outnumber the cutthroats and hybrids. The wind howls on this water, making casting a difficult proposition, but for anyone who can handle the air (remember that British stillwater anglers *prefer* a stiff breeze), the fishing can be exceptional at the upper end for trout up to 16 or 17 inches.

Rosebud River: This is good fishing for browns and rainbows with the landowners' permission. There are some classic deep pools and undercuts here, and this is the water holding the better 2- to 3-pound fish. They can be caught, even during the middle of the day, but the method of choice is deep nymphing. The flies have to be subtle—a size 16 Pheasant Tail and a size 16 Pale Morning Dun Emerger work consistently all summer. The Rosebud is followed by road to the Stillwater River.

Sylvan Lake: Sylvan is in a glacial cirque reached by trail up Spread Creek from East Rosebud Lake. This is one of the better golden trout lakes around, with fishing for trout to 12 inches or a touch bigger. The goldens like small flies (very small flies) hanging motionless 18 to 24 inches below a yarn indicator. The hike into Sylvan is long and steep but worth the effort.

West Fork Stillwater River: The West Fork is followed by road for a few miles, then by trail for 20 miles from the Stillwater at Nye up to the headwaters. It's good fishing in the lower reaches for browns and rainbows to 20 inches, but much of the land is posted. The upper section is good for cutthroats and rainbows.

West Rosebud Creek: It forms just below Grasshopper Glacier, flows through Silver and Mystic Lakes, then courses for 25 miles to the East Rosebud. The lower section is heavily posted but good for browns. The middle portion is good for brookies, browns, cutthroats, and rainbows. The upper run has some small trout.

A freestone river from top to bottom, the character of the Yellowstone varies wildly from season to season.

Yellowstone River

The Yellowstone is spawned in the high mountains of the Yellowstone National Park caldera. It's fed by water melted from snow and ice clinging to jagged rock faces in Wyoming, from steaming geysers and mudpots in the park, and from runoff pouring out of the Gallatin Range and the Absaroka Mountains.

The Yellowstone still flows unsullied for 670 miles to the Missouri in North Dakota. How rare is this? It's the only major river in the Lower 48 that is undammed, if you don't count a number of diversion dams that are death traps to floaters, like the one at Intake. This is a classic western river, ranging from ice-cold headwater runs through deep, fast canyon stretches into wide riffled sections and finally into turbid, warm, meandering flatland flows of deceptive power.

The Yellowstone offers a variety and abundance of water types. Combine this with a complex variety of food forms consisting of hundreds of types of aquatic insects, terrestrial insects, crayfish, and scuds, along with an assortment of forage fish, and consider that the river is a "natural" environment, with flows changing daily, weekly, and monthly, and it's easy to see why "local knowledge" is so important on this big river.

GARDINER TO YANKEE JIM CANYON

The first section of the river in Montana is the 18-mile stretch of water from Gardiner to Yankee Jim Canyon. Browns, cutthroats, and rainbows exist in roughly equal numbers in this big, deep, and powerful water. Look at a topographical map—all the lines are really close right down to both sides of the river. It's a canyon and that limits the amount of wading water, but this is a stretch where the best fishing is often against the banks and in the backwaters anyway.

The great fishing starts in the winter months. A number of hot springs, with LaDuke the most significant, warm up the water and keep the midges hatching even during the nasty spells. On nice days the trout rise well in slower areas to both the pupae and the adults. A Griffith's Gnat on a fine tippet is usually good enough to fool them, but when they get really critical about fly color, try variations in black, brown, and red.

By spring everyone is waiting for the salmon fly hatch, assuming the river hasn't blown out with low-level runoff. The adults emerge in late June, but the nymphs are growing big and restless during the preceding months. It's possible to ignore other

Yellowstone River

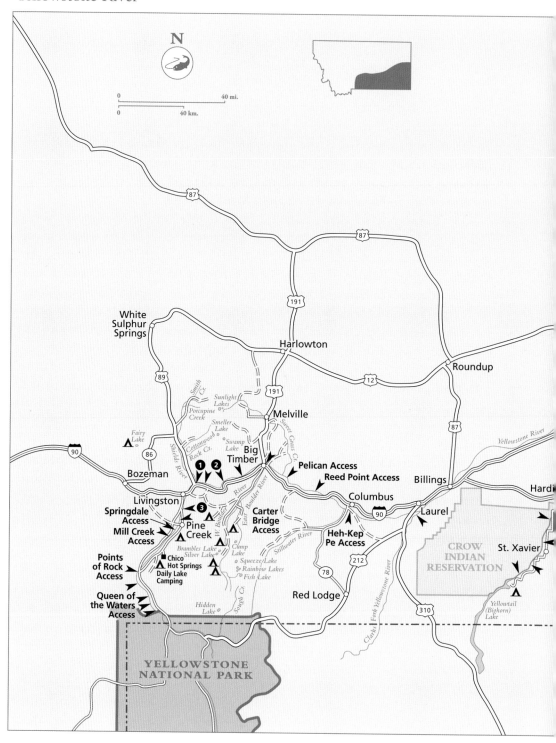

N

0 ———— 40 mi.
0 ———— 40 km.

White Sulphur Springs

Harlowton

Roundup

87

191

89

12

87

Smith Cr.

Sunlight Lakes

Porcupine Creek

Smeller Lake

Melville

Fairy Lake

Swamp Lake

Big Timber

Pelican Access

Reed Point Access

Yellowstone River

90

86

Cottonwood Rock Ct.

Shields River

Bozeman

❶ ❷

Billings

Hardi

Livingston

Springdale Access

Mill Creek Access

❸

Pine Creek

W. Boulder

East Boulder River

Sweet Grass Cr.

Carter Bridge Access

Columbus

Laurel

90

212

Heh-Kep Pe Access

St. Xavier

Points of Rock Access

Chico Hot Springs

Brambles Lake
Silver Lake

Camp Lake

Stillwater River

78

CROW INDIAN RESERVATION

Daily Lake Camping

Squeeze Lake

Rainbow Lakes

Fish Lake

Red Lodge

Clarks Fork Yellowstone River

310

Yellowtail (Bighorn) Lake

Queen of the Waters Access

Hidden Lake

Sough Cr.

YELLOWSTONE NATIONAL PARK

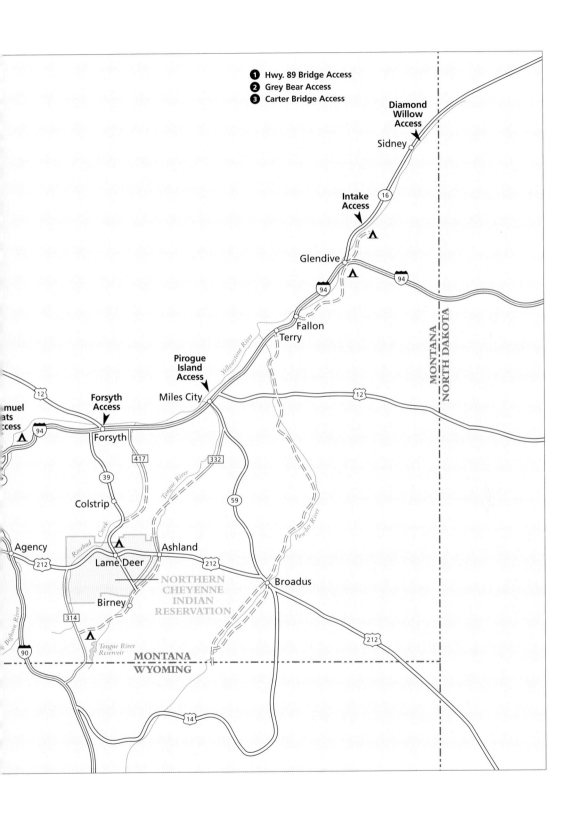

① Hwy. 89 Bridge Access
② Grey Bear Access
③ Carter Bridge Access

Diamond
Willow
Access

Sidney

Intake
Access

16

Glendive

94

94

Fallon
Terry

Pirogue
Island
Access

12

Miles City

muel
ats
ccess

Forsyth
Access

94

Forsyth

12

417

332

39

59

Colstrip

Agency

Ashland

212

212

Lame Deer

Broadus

314

Birney

NORTHERN
CHEYENNE
INDIAN
RESERVATION

212

90

Tongue River
Reservoir

MONTANA
WYOMING

14

Yellowstone River

Tongue River

Powder River

Rosebud Creek

Bighorn River

MONTANA
NORTH DAKOTA

hatches during April and May, even the Mother's Day caddis (the early grannom), because they are spotty in this stretch. Many anglers just concentrate on catching large trout on big nymphs.

The quality of the salmon fly hatch depends on the runoff. A number of upstream tributaries, especially the Lamar in Yellowstone National Park, dump a lot of silt into the main river. Even during a normal year the Yellowstone can be brown soup, and this limits the dry-fly fishing. During the occasional low-water year, however, when the river is somewhat clear, the surface action with size 4 dry flies, including local favorites such as the Elk Hair Salmon Fly, Bird's Stone, Himenator, Tom's Adult Salmon Fly, Muddled Salmon Fly, Improved Sofa Pillow, and Orange Temptation Stone, rivals any salmon fly hatch in the West. For the best shot at big fish, you have to float this stretch and pound the banks, particularly the areas with willows, with cast after cast.

Those willing to work nymphs will always take fish despite water that resembles a chocolate milkshake. Trout feed whenever possible (except for rare periods of satiation). They are opportunists. A large stonefly nymph bounced along the bottom will draw fish, which are not choosy in the fast current and cloudy water. Look for slower water at the end of riffles or along banks, and work a dark pattern (black is best) hard and diligently even during the brightest hours of the day. The big fish are just where you would think they would be, in calm areas where they have shelter from predators. Muddy water turns off anglers far more than it does fish.

Both the salmon fly and the golden stone hatch last until mid-July. A ginger wing and light ginger body in sizes 6 and 8 handles the goldens. There are other stoneflies in this part of the river. For the yellow sally use a wing of light straw with a yellow body. Yellow-bodied Elk Hair Caddis can be a good substitute in a pinch. For the little olive stone, tie a light gray wing and bright green body. Both of these are found in sizes 14 and 16, well into September.

By midsummer the crowds have disappeared from this water. There are summer hatches, but nothing that mesmerizes either fish or fishermen. The usual drill is to pound the banks with large attractors—Wulffs, Trudes, Double Wings, and Humpies, or grasshopper imitations—or slap the edges and creases with streamers such as Flash-A-Buggers, Spuddlers, Marabou Muddlers, and Hornbergs; or keep on working those big nymphs in the runs.

YANKEE JIM CANYON TO TOM MINER CREEK

This is a short piece of water, and everything written about the Gardiner to Yankee Jim stretch applies here. It holds some serious trout, especially in the pockets and eddies found around large rocks and boulders. The water is 60 feet deep in places (use a lot of lead). The canyon has to be floated to cover it properly, but that means running through three Class III rapids. It's no place for amateur boatmen, and wade fishing is limited. It can be a dangerous place to fish.

Tom Miner Creek to Livingston

Browns and rainbows begin to outnumber the cutthroats in this stretch, but the cutthroats in this part of the river tend to run larger than in the upper section. Finding the fish is relatively simple, too—look for the most featureless, currentless, uninspiring bits of river, and that's where the cutthroats will be hanging out. The browns hold near obstructions, and the rainbows use the current edges.

Casting near the mouths of the spring creeks along this part of the Yellowstone is productive (watch for some hatches not important in the main river, such as the pale morning dun, in these microhabitats). The land along the river flattens out, spreading into Paradise Valley. Hay fields along the stream edges give way to sage-and-grass-covered foothills, and they in turn butt up against dark pine forests; and then even the forests yield to the lofty, ice-scoured, snowcapped peaks of the Gallatin and Absaroka mountains. It's a spectacular and humbling setting.

Prior to runoff there is a hatch of grannom caddis that is so predictable, it is called the "Mother's Day hatch" (also found on every major river in the West). "Predictable" is a misleading description, however, for fishing on the Yellowstone. By early May the river is ready to blow out with runoff. Show up on Mother's Day, and you're likely to find a full flood with whole trees bobbing in the current. The best chance of hitting a fishable hatch of grannoms on this river is in late April.

Floating the Yellowstone and camping on islands far from the madding crowd is what it's all about for some of us.

The fly to match the grannom is tied in sizes 12 and 14, with a greenish-brown body and a gray wing shading to brown. Patterns can include a Deep Sparkle Pupa and an Emergent Sparkle Pupa for the hatching stage, and an Olive Elk Hair Caddis, Goddard Caddis, and Fluttering Caddis for the adult, egg-laying female (which conveniently collapses on the surface instead of going underwater).

One other significant hatch on the first 60 miles early in the season is the blue-winged olive, sizes 16 to 20. These mayflies don't draw the largest trout to the surface, but they spark some steady feeding by rainbows and browns and ferocious gorging by whitefish. The blue-wings disappear by early April only to show up again from late July into mid-August, and one more time with feeling from late September through October. This last emergence can trigger some wonderful action for colorful browns. And by October, you'll have much of the best water to yourself.

Various species of mayflies are present on the Yellowstone, but this is not really a mayfly river. The far more abundant caddis and stoneflies make better selections. For working rough water, an Elk Hair size 8 to 12 is a good choice, as is an Orange Bucktail Caddis. Nymphs like the Peeking Caddis in sizes 12 to 18 are nice to have, as are some Montana Stones (for many rivers around here) in 4 to 10, Golden Stones sizes 6 and 8, and George's Brown Stone in 6 to 10. Attractors should include Gray Wulffs (excellent on overcast days), Royal and Grizzly Wulffs, Humpies, and Royal and Coachman Trudes. Add some hoppers. Some red and black ants round out the package.

For general mayfly activity, in addition to Blue-Winged Olives, include some Adams, Quill Gordons, Light Cahills, and Blue Duns, sizes 14 and 16. Also, pack some size 16 and 18 Meloche Duns for the PMDs around those spring creek outlets. A Pheasant Tail Nymph in 16 to 20 and a Hare's Ear from 8 to 16 handle the below-surface action.

When using hoppers, a dead drift still works, but light stretches and some skittering turn big fish with more consistency these days. And don't spend too much time on side channels that have been cut by high water in the past year or so. The fish haven't moved into these places yet.

LIVINGSTON TO REED POINT

As the river passes Livingston, it picks up volume and speed. Wading becomes a bit more sporting, and driftboats are common apparitions. Rainbows of over 13 inches are found in numbers approaching 1,000 fish per mile, along with a few large browns. Working current seams and down through deep holes is the best approach. From Livingston down past Big Timber to Reed Point, the Yellowstone widens and slows, though there are long stretches of riffles flowing over gravel and bouldery streambed. There are also deep runs and pools.

In the broken water, large attractor dry flies produce, as do stonefly nymphs. But the really big browns and rainbows are taken most often on the bottoms of the runs and pools. Think 2/0 sculpins and batting helmets. Casting these things all day is work, and you may feel like someone has been doing a number on your skull with a rigging ax, especially on windy days. But these patterns, worked down deep, will turn some nice trout. The takes are predatory. Trout will rocket downstream with the current once they realize that there are strings attached to their meal.

A survey near Big Timber turned up some trout closing in on 10 pounds. Use heavy leaders. Side channels cut the water down to size here and hold plenty of big trout.

REED POINT TO BILLINGS

A hatch that occurs on the river from Reed Point to the mouth of the Bighorn from late August through September is a mayfly not given a common name in angling literature. The off-white bug covers the flats of the lower river in such numbers that carp, sauger, and catfish join the brown and rainbow trout in a surface feeding frenzy. This large mayfly—best matched with a size 10 or 12 White Humpy (you'll probably have to tie this yourself)—takes fish that are not in a discriminating frame of mind.

There are some heavy hatches of other mayflies on this stretch. The blue-winged olive comes off three times a season—early, middle, and late. The tricos form mating clusters in early-morning clouds during August and September. The yellow drake, a size 16 dun that hatches from late July through September, is very abundant.

There are also steady hatches of caddisflies. The two net-spinning genera, the spotted sedge and the little sister sedge, hatch in heavy numbers on summer evenings. The caddis hatches bring up mainly trout.

The Yellowstone down into Billings gradually turns over to a predominantly warmwater fishery. But there are still some good-size trout in this water that do well feeding on smaller sauger and catfish along with good numbers of other forage fish. Large streamer patterns, such as the Clouser Minnow, worked along brushy, undercut banks, off the ends of gravel shelves, and bounced through riffles are the best bets. Floating is a good but tedious way to probe for these trout.

From downstream of Billings to the confluence with the Missouri River the fishing is almost entirely for warmwater species using primarily bait.

The Yellowstone is a complicated river. The best way to learn something of the water is to invest in a guide for at least a day (several days would be better) and float the section of water you are most interested in. Learn one or maybe two stretches of the river each year and concentrate your efforts. A scattergun approach might initially seem the best way to "have it all." Superficially this may hold true. But in trout fishing, as in many of life's better pursuits, quality is always superior to quantity.

Some anglers focus just on the channels of the river. They discover "little trout streams" that fish much differently than the main Yellowstone. They can wade and cast to individual trout or read the water and fish blind with a nymph or a dry fly.

The secret is knowing the good channels from the poor ones—the ones that have had water flowing through them all winter, and weren't blocked off by ice jams at the mouth or left dry by dropping flow levels, are the best summer fisheries. They have the insect life and the hatches that keep trout in them all the time. From year to year the channels change, with some that were good becoming poor and vice versa. You'll need to retest a number of channels each year to find the best one that season. Focus your attention on small pieces of the Yellowstone to discover what a truly fine trout stream really has to offer.

Fishing Waters in the Yellowstone Drainage

Armstrong Spring Creek: Armstrong is one of several spring creeks in the Paradise Valley south of Livingston on the west side of the Yellowstone River and east of US 89. These spring creeks are considered to be some of the finest water of their kind, anywhere. To fish these streams, you pay a daily fee. From April into autumn, you'll have to make your reservations well in advance. This is one of the few waters I'll pay to fish. This means that there are fantastic numbers of trout living in an exceptionally fertile environment whose temperature and rate of flow remains virtually constant. The banks of these streams are lined with cottonwoods, with thick carpets of long grasses, and some bushes and brush. The creeks themselves are filled with thick beds of bright, emerald aquatic plants. There are smooth, silty stretches, slow slough-like (but cold and pure) runs, riffles running over broken rock, and gravel streambeds. Peacocks and assorted other fowl cackle, squawk, and, in general, proclaim to the world that they are indeed alive as they wander in nearby farmyard pens. Armstrong offers about 2 miles of challenging water.

In spring creeks, food is so abundant that several hatches are often taking place simultaneously. By the time you figure out what species is producing the most action and what particular phase of its life it's in, the trout have switched to another bug. And even if there is only one insect hatching—say, for example, the ubiquitous blue-winged olive—the browns and rainbows and cutthroats are so selective that only a perfect presentation of something size 16 or less will cause the trout to take the imitation. Light tippets (7X is considered a bit heavy at times) make playing a 3- or 4- or 5-pound fish in this water rather sticky. Most of the time when you catch a fish in one of these spring creeks, you have earned it, though there are periods when even these finicky waters yield their trout with ease. Spring creek trout have their weaknesses and, at times, they are especially vulnerable to hoppers. At other times, Pheasant Tails drifted along the edges of current or worked slowly through slack water on the edges of the creeks will take the trout more or less consistently.

Compounding the difficulty of spring creeks is the fact that the trout see anglers covering the complete spectrum of skills nearly every day of the year. And the rainbows and browns have seen every pattern known to the western world many times over. Talk

Armstrong Spring Creek, south of Livingston, offers highly technical, year-round fly fishing. For those unfamiliar with the water, consider hiring a guide for your first excursion. Mike Cline

to those fishing the streams ahead of you—they may have some solid advice. And check the local fly shops—they are always in touch with the current hatching activity.

In addition to the blue-winged olives, there are also pale morning duns. The duns emerge around 10 a.m. Spinners fall in the morning and at dusk. Mid-July through early August, use PMD Thoraxes, Sparkle Duns, PT Emergers, and a PMD Spinner. When caddis are hatching, several patterns seem to have their moments, including the Z-Lon Caddis Emerger, Serendipity, PT Emerger, and the Electric Caddis (in the faster water).

Nymph fishing here can vary from easy to impossible. Ever fish a size 22 or smaller nymph? That's what the fish focus on at times in this water. At other times they'll take a good scud imitation. In the spring, when the rainbows are spawning, a light-colored egg pattern is a winning fly. A little insect net, for seining the flow and sampling the bottom, can provide quick answers on all spring creeks.

Woolly Buggers in sizes 6 and 8 with olive bodies can also turn the fish. Cast the things bank-tight and strip like mad. If nothing takes by the third strip, pick up and cast again. Buggering the banks early in the morning or late in the afternoon can rev up your heart.

One of the most productive (and popular) tailwater fisheries in Montana, the Bighorn receives heavy float pressure. If you don't mind crowds, the fishing here can be truly exceptional. Matt Jeppson/Shutterstock.com

Bighorn River: One of the most fertile rivers in the West, the Bighorn is loaded with aquatic plant and animal life in cold, clear water. It wanders through a gentle valley in the wide, open high plains country way out west. A large mountain range that rolls away into Wyoming adds to the spectacle. There are good numbers of healthy trout here—fish that willingly take a fly. Browns and rainbows weighing a few pounds or more are common. The river flows through a corridor surrounded by the Crow Indian Reservation. While most other waters on the reservation are closed to non-tribal members, the US Supreme Court opened the Bighorn to public access in 1981.

The Bighorn has received extensive coverage from the outdoor press and is very heavily fished from May through October. Literally hundreds of boats and rafts are launched on a typical summer day. Ever since the water below the Yellowtail Dam was opened to fishing, angling writers have raved about the trophy browns and rainbows. When you have a river holding more than twice as many fish exceeding 12 inches in each mile than the Madison, the hype is not all that difficult to understand.

This publicity has translated into incredible fishing pressure on the first 13-mile stretch of water, known as the Upper 13. On a pleasant summer day, you will encounter literally hundreds of anglers fishing from shore and a greater number working the river from driftboats and rafts. There are some things you can do to improve the odds for a pleasant and successful day adrift. For those who have little fly-fishing experience or have never taken a nice trout, the Bighorn is a good river to start out on—this doesn't mean that a beginner will catch a lot of fish, but he'll know that they're there, rising or visibly nymphing right under his nose, and he'll get a lot of chances at them. Many of the articles written in the past claim that fish are taken by the dozens and many of them are in the 5-pound-and-up range. Tales of ninety-fish days with trout averaging 3 pounds or more abound. This can create some unrealistic expectations.

A person who fishes diligently will probably take a half-dozen or more trout that should average around 16 inches in a day's fishing. Experienced anglers have a legitimate chance of catching a large trout. But don't expect 5-pound fish on every cast. Tactics for tailwater that resembles a giant spring creek will work consistently, but there are unique (read: a bit ungainly) setups that work really well at times if an angler is willing to deal with weighted 17-foot leaders that tangle more often than not. Acquiring local information that evolves constantly and rapidly from guides, fly shop owners, and fanatics who congregate in the Fort Smith area is the way to go on this sometimes problematic but beautiful and classy river.

In addition to the Upper 13, there are two other stretches of water of similar length—from Bighorn to Mallard, and from Mallard to Two-Leggins. These places are less crowded, but there are some trade-offs, including low-water and water-quality problems from irrigation practices in the valley. This is often the case for the lower portion of these stretches from Rotten Grass on. Also, access is difficult in spots and many of the outfitters prefer not to float this water. The lower two stretches have fewer fish, but they receive less angling pressure and the trout, on average, are larger.

If you wish to fish the Upper 13 from shore, from a rental boat, or with a guide, hit the water early, say by 6 a.m. This will put you on the river before many other floaters. You'll be fishing over trout who have not been spooked by the casts of several anglers before you, and you will have a much more peaceful experience floating a very pretty river in relatively serene surroundings. As summer gives way to fall, the number of anglers declines slightly to more hard-core types whose main interest is in jumping large fish.

A 9-foot rod with a 6- or 7-weight line will handle all of the water. You want a rod that is light enough to make casting fun, but not so dainty that it lacks the backbone to deal with a stout breeze or to pressure a strong fish in the current. A longer rod will give you better line control.

The only time the Bighorn fishes poorly is in the late spring and early summer during years with high runoff. Normally the first 13 miles of the river are fine even then (a tributary, Soap Creek, can mess up the clarity below that), but when Yellowtail Reservoir fills up and warm water spills over the top of the dam, coming off the top of the lake in the high 60-degree range, it shocks the trout and stops almost all feeding activity.

Early spring, summer, and fall are consistently good fishing. The hatches are heavy and predictable, and the trout seem to ignore the unending stream of boats going over their heads and rise for hours at a time. These fish don't mind someone casting to them, and even sloppy presentations won't put them down, but they won't take a fly that is dragging unnaturally. And they can get pretty critical about the imitation.

You can make pattern selection as complicated as you wish, but you should carry at least a basic selection of flies. The nice contradiction about most tailwaters (and spring creeks) is that the insect populations may be incredibly large, but they aren't particularly diverse. It's a simple equation that means one thing: There may be only a handful of hatches, but they will be really heavy. The hatches include blue-winged olives from April through May and from mid-September through mid-December; pale morning duns from mid-July through late August; yellow sally stoneflies from mid-July through early September; summer grannoms (also called the black caddis here) from mid-August through mid-October; spotted sedges form mid-August into early October; tricos starting in mid-August and lasting into mid-October; summer flier sedges in September; tiny blue-winged olives overwhelming other species during the evenings in September; and midges all winter.

Nymphs are best during non-hatch periods. They may be the primary method—almost every driftboat that goes down the stream with a guide and clients has a couple of strike indicators bobbing on the surface. Popular patterns include the Sow Bug and the Big Horn Shrimp. One fly that may be the best trout-catcher in the bunch is also the most controversial. This is the infamous San Juan Worm, which imitates the red worms found in the river-bottom detritus. I've seen, and at one time used, complicated (read: insane) rigs that were 15 or more feet long with crazy combinations of weight and droppers—a true joy to cast and fish. I'll pass.

Because of the relatively small size of most of these nymph patterns, you will want to use at least 9-foot leaders (12 feet would be better) tapered down to 4X, 5X, and even 6X. Some other nymphs would include a Gold-Ribbed Hare's Ear size 12 to 16, Pheasant Tail size 14 to 22, and Red Squirrel Tail size 14 to 18. These need to be fished right along the bottom, and a twist-on or two of lead will sink them down where they can do their best work.

Streamer fishing demands heavier tippets, 1X or 2X. Woolly Buggers, Zonkers, Muddler Minnows, and Spruce Flies, all in the size 2 to 6 range, work well on the big trout.

Boulder River: This is one of the prettiest trout streams in the state, offering excellent fishing for browns and rainbows to 24 inches in the lower reaches, and brook and rainbow trout in the upper, wilderness reaches. There is one problem, though: The best big-trout water flows almost entirely on heavily posted land owned by celebrities who would prefer to keep the rest of us poor mortals off of "their" water despite the state's stream access law.

Flowing through one of the prettiest valleys in Montana, the main Boulder River is tough to get to, but worth it if you don't mind hiking up- or downstream from one of the few access points.

Wading and floating work well. This lower river flows through ranchland and is characterized by undercut, brushy and grassy banks, good holes, silent runs, and enough riffle water to bring out the rainbows on a sunny summer day to pick off stonefly nymphs and caddisfly pupae. Excellent hatches of caddis take off beginning in midsummer, especially around evening, and hoppers are a superb play from July until the killing frosts of September, as are beetles and ants. Streamers will take the hefty browns; these include Buggers, Matuka Sculpins, Spruce Flies, Hair Suckers, Marabou Muddlers, and the like. Use a 9-foot 5-weight with stout leaders for the streamer action.

The Boulder is followed by state and county roads into the Absaroka Range almost to the base of Mount Rae. From here take a trail past a spectacular 70-foot falls that serves as a natural barrier to the downstream rainbows and browns. Above the falls, brookies and rainbows to 15 inches will come to Royal-anythings in the pocket water. Elk Hair Caddis also take in the pools and glides. Wet flies like Gold-Ribbed Hare's Ears, Royal Coachmans, Black Gnats, and Hendricksons, worked along the edges of current or swung through pools, will take some of the better fish in this wild stretch that heads in the heart of these mountains beneath 10,988-foot Monument Peak. Access on this part of the Boulder is good, since the river runs through national forest 30 miles south of Big Timber.

Runoff until July makes the river a bitch to wade, but after this the work is easy and enjoyable. As for the lower water, put Montana's stream access law to work and strike a blow for fly fishing's proletariat masses.

Bramble Creek Lakes: These four lakes are 3 miles up Bramble Creek from the Boulder River Road below Fourmile Guard Station. Three of the lakes have fish. The best is #3, which is 5 acres at nearly 9,000 feet and planted every eight years with Yellowstone cutthroats that provide good fishing from the second year of the cycle through perhaps the fifth or sixth.

Camp Lake: At 9,000 feet, this one lies east of Contact Mountain and can be reached by trail roughly 4.5 miles east from the Falls Creek Campground on the Boulder River. It grows fair numbers of Yellowstone cutthroats running less than a foot. They take ant imitations from the surface with a satisfying rush and swirl. There's too much competition for food here for the fish to hesitate.

Cottonwood Creek: Cottonwood heads in the Crazies and flows for 17 miles to the Shields River with good fishing for brookies, browns (especially in the lower reaches), cutthroats, and rainbows. Parts of it are dewatered, and if you're not catching anything in one section, it might be smart to move to a new piece. It's followed by county and private roads and then Forest Service trail. Lots of posted land these days.

DePuy Spring Creek: DePuy is another of the famed Paradise Valley spring creeks (see Armstrong discussion for fishing details). This was originally a trout hatchery and is now a well-managed stream with good populations of fat and picky rainbows and browns. Some whitefish, too. A fee fishery, it's 7 miles south of Livingston on US 89.

If you come to the area to fish the Mother's Day caddis hatch and the Yellowstone River is blown out with runoff, try to get a day on DePuy (or Nelson's or Armstrong). The spring creeks also have good hatches of the early grannom, and they fish well in May.

East Boulder River: This one's about 20 miles of 20-foot-wide water running out of the mountains and onto the sere foothills south of the Yellowstone River. There is fair fishing for some decent browns, along with good populations of cutthroats, rainbows, and mountain whitefish that love nymphs, as is their destiny. You'll find access by road here and there.

East Fork Main Boulder River: This one is a little mountain stream with fair fishing in some pretty country several miles above the main river. There are brookies, cutthroats, and rainbows, along with browns in the lower, meadow stretches. The meadow section is good hopper water, but the fish prefer smaller, size 8 to 14, flies.

Fairy Lake receives a lot of pressure from Bozeman. But with a campground and hiking close by, it's a good late-summer destination for families.

Fairy Lake: In the Shields River drainage, it's 35 miles north of Bozeman. You get there on a poor road, and you'll find good numbers of average-size cutthroats. Fairy is 12 acres by 40 feet deep, but there are extensive shallows where the fish love to roam. The lake has a campground and something that looks like a power station. The shoreline trail is full of litter, and the lake is far from pristine.

Fish Lake: This 18-acre lake is up the South Fork of Rainbow Creek, in the Boulder River drainage, in a beautiful setting with naturally reproducing cutthroats that grow to perhaps a foot. The odd thing is that these wilderness fish have a reputation for being tough to catch—they ignore big flies or fast-moving flies, but they'll suck in size 16 or 18 nymphs swimming *slowly* through the water.

In the fall some very big browns move up the Gardner River from the Yellowstone and hold in runs in the Montana section in Yellowstone National Park.

Gardner River: Very little of this beautiful, freestone stream is in Montana, but what is holds some nice Yellowstone cutthroats that love hoppers in the summer and Woolly Buggers in the fall. Some large browns move up into this water in autumn.

Hidden Lake: Hidden lies in the Absaroka Primitive Area north of Yellowstone and offers typical (quite good) wilderness lake fishing for rainbows. You'll want to fish nymphs several feet beneath the surface with the slightest of twitches (this works on cutthroats, too, in these alpine waters). Hare's Ears and small Olive Woolly Worms are easy and obvious selections.

Mill Creek: Mill Creek spills from the Absaroka Mountains west to the Yellowstone, the last stretch across a well-defined alluvial fan about 20 miles south of Livingston. FWP has leased water rights on this stream to provide rearing habitat for cutthroat fry in midsummer. The middle reaches with a nearby campground are popular for brookies, cutthroats, rainbows, and whitefish. The lower stretch is good for browns in the spring and again after the first rains of autumn.

Mission Creek: Mission flows into the Yellowstone 10 miles east of Livingston, and it's followed upstream by road and trail to its origins below Elephanthead Mountain. The lower reaches are good for browns and some rainbows. As you move up the drainage, the browns drop in numbers and size and cutthroats take over. Whitefish are ever-present.

Nelson's Spring Creek: Yet another in the Paradise Valley hit parade of world-class spring creeks (see the discussion on Armstrong Spring Creek), this one is 4 miles south of Livingston and has a mile or so of fishing for lots of browns and rainbows. A few of these fish get very big. It's a fee fishery, and during prime months reservations are locked up a year in advance.

One prominent feature of Nelson's is the pond on the lower end. The currents empty into this deep pool and curl devilishly around. It's almost impossible to get a fly to sit out there drag-free, but that's exactly what the trout demand. These fish, some of the biggest in the stream, cruise leisurely around this slow-water hold. The only way to get a decent presentation to them is to wade upstream to the dam, stand right there, and cast right on the current line.

Porcupine Creek: Porcupine flows to the Shields River north of Wilsall. It's hit by irrigation but there is plenty of brushy bankside cover above as the creek meanders across an open valley. Brookies, browns, cutthroats (in the upper sections), and whitefish take streamers and nymphs and occasionally caddis near evening when the egg-layers drop out of the sky.

Powder River: Not many trout in this muddy often-shallow-to-dry flow, but I love to come here in the spring to try to dredge up channel cats on the largest Bugger I can

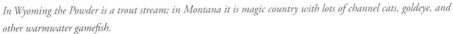

In Wyoming the Powder is a trout stream; in Montana it is magic country with lots of channel cats, goldeye, and other warmwater gamefish.

tie, working the monstrosity along the bottoms of any depressions created by shelving water. Hey! Fishing is fishing for some of us. There are also northerns, crappies, and other panfish here along with some goldeyes.

Rainbow Lakes: This group includes three main lakes and four smaller ones from 2 to 18 acres with rainbow-cutthroat hybrids, rainbows, and cutthroats growing to perhaps 15 inches. They are at the head of Rainbow Creek, in the Boulder River drainage, at over 9,000 feet in unspoiled mountain country with some pines here and there that provide wood for those few still willing to risk the wrath of the environmentally correct and have a small campfire. It's a 6-mile hike, but horse-packing is popular on this water.

Shields River: The Shields has its headwaters in the Crazy Mountains, then flows west, then south for 60 miles to the Yellowstone River east of Livingston. The upper reaches of the river hold fair umbers of Yellowstone cutthroats. The rest of the river, flowing through open ranch and pasture land, is good water for some sizable brown trout, especially those migrating up the river from the Yellowstone in the fall. One consistent plan is to work the brushy, undercut banks or many logjams and brush piles with large streamers like Woolly Buggers, Muddlers, and Spuddlers. Access is from US 89, with

The Shields is a placid, wadeable river, impossible to float and tough to fish for Yellowstone cutthroat and other trout species, along with hordes of mountain whitefish.

an FWP access up the road from the Yellowstone, county roads, and through private land where permission is definitely needed. There are some brook trout in the middle reaches and some good rainbows in the lower runs up from the Yellowstone. The river is often slightly discolored and dark streamers almost always work best, especially with some erratic pulsing action away from the banks and brush piles. The river suffers horribly from irrigation drawdown and by midsummer it is too warm and low to fish, if only for the sake of the fish.

Slough Creek: Slough Creek has its beginnings high in the Absaroka Range and flows for 15 miles south to Yellowstone National Park, where it is one of the best big-trout waters in the park. You can reach the meadow section north of the park by a Forest Service trail. There is some good fishing for truly large cutthroats in the sapphire pools and beneath the undercut banks protected by thick mats of grass. Hoppers come into play about mid-July, as do ants. Look for caddis activity, especially toward evening.

Sweet Grass Creek: Sweet Grass heads in the Crazies and is followed by trail, private road, and county road for 50 miles to the Yellowstone east of Big Timber. The upper reaches are good for small brookies and some rainbows. The lower reaches get hurt by irrigation, but can be good for nice browns later in the fall after the rains return. Whitefish swim here, too.

Tongue River: The headwaters lie in Wyoming, then it flows through the Tongue Reservoir in Montana just north of Sheridan, Wyoming, and on to the Yellowstone near Miles City. Some browns and rainbows are taken with heavy streamers down deep in the first 9 miles below the dam, especially right below it. After this, smallmouths are found in the river and they like large drys and minnow patterns. Catfish, sauger, bullheads, walleyes, and other warmwater species take complete control on the final stretches to the Yellowstone. Not a destination river for fly fishers.

Tongue River Reservoir: Northern pike, koi, walleye, sauger, crappie, smallmouth bass, great whites. The peak for crappie (great eating) is in late May and early June during the spawn, and they love the jigging action of a Clouser Minnow on a slow retrieve. The best smallmouth action is in late June and early July along the shoreline in the brush.

West Boulder River: Formed by the junction of the East and West Forks above Beaver Meadows, it flows 25 miles to the Boulder River in the north. The stream is followed by state and county roads and then trail. Browns and rainbows are in the lower reaches, but there's only limited access. There are cutthroats up above in the pocket water. It's

Depending on where you fish along the Tongue's length, it's possible to catch brown or rainbow trout as well as smallmouths on drys and minnow patterns. T. Bennert

A 3-plus-mile hike into the West Boulder meadows takes you into burned-over mountains to fish for native Yellowstone cutts.

a good stream to hit early in the season. Usually it is fishable when the main river is blown out with runoff. Hiking several miles upstream from the campground at the end of the road into the wilderness brings you to some crystalline water with large, deep pools sliding through burned-over country. There are some 15-inch and larger Yellowstone cutthroats here. Above this stretch the stream runs through timber with pocket water holding smaller cutthroats.

Almost as fun as fishing a river, creek, or lake in Montana is figuring out where in Montana you're going to go fishing next.

Travel in Montana

Negotiating your way around Montana is easy. Routes from interstate highways all the way down to some gravel roads are marked on the state road map. Adequate signs make navigation a straightforward proposition.

Gravel roads are accorded the status of main thoroughfares in much of the state, but once you leave the unmarked systems, you enter the exciting world of "Where in the hell are we?" Topographic maps help and so does asking directions. Montanans, for the most part, are friendly and helpful. They are used to misguided souls, so they know how to give good directions. You just have to know how to listen. If you run out of gas, they will normally offer you a gallon or two and frequently seem offended at the concept of payment. This is still honest country. May it always be so.

For those new to the state, a little pretravel preparation will make the adventure run quite smoothly.First, contact Visit Montana at (800) 847-4868 connect to visitmt .com.

Next, check out Montana Department of Fish, Wildlife & Parks (FWP) website at fwp.mt.gov.

When you purchase your fishing license, be sure and pick up a copy of the current fishing regulations (or get it in advance from FWP).

Be especially careful when sailing around that Winnebago on the two-lane—vehicles coming the other way may be traveling as fast as you are. During spring and fall, all-weather tires or four-wheel drive are good ideas for the mountain passes. And when the highway department states that a certain pass is closed due to rough weather, believe it. You will be risking your life on a grand scale if you ignore the warnings. And keeping your gas tank topped up is prudent. Off the main roads, stations often close early or do not open some days. The boys at the local Cenex like to go fishing, too.

Additional Indian Reservations

There are five other reservations in Montana east of the Continental Divide in addition to Blackfeet: Rocky Boy's (south of Havre), Fort Belknap (west of Malta), Fort Peck (northeastern corner), Crow (south of Billings), and Northern Cheyenne (east of Crow).

The first three are located along the Hi-Line near the Canadian border and offer limited angling potential and serious access problems because of tribal regulations and restrictions. The only fishing of note is provided by ranch ponds and these are private, for the most part, and off-limits. There are some on the Fort Peck Reservation that are managed by the Montana Department of Fish, Wildlife & Parks and open to fishing. There is so much other prime water in Montana that to risk a hassle or ticket to catch a ling or sauger or catfish approaches folly or worse.

The Northern Cheyenne Reservation has similar access limitations, but access to the Tongue River can be gained along the river's eastern shore, which is off the reservation.

As for the Crow Reservation, there are reports of ponds, reservoirs, and lakes with tremendous trout in them, but they are currently closed to all but tribal members, unfortunately. The only waters available to non-tribal members are Bighorn Lake and the Bighorn River in the Bighorn Canyon National Recreation Area. Everything else is out-of-bounds. Perhaps someday the tribe will recognize the potential of this resource in terms of their own financial welfare. But when we feel excluded, we must remember that we have not exactly done these people (or the other tribes) any favors in the past.

The bottom line is that there is some wonderful fishing for trophy trout that is available to only a lucky few on these eastern reservations.

Real and Perceived Dangers

Marauding, red-eyed bears lusting for a taste of human flesh and 18-foot-long rattle-snakes as thick as your hip with 6-inch fangs dripping milky venom are the deluded creations of Hollywood and not the stuff of everyday Montana reality.

Yes, bears do attack us and snakes do bite us, but these rare encounters are even more rarely fatal. Far more dangerous are threats from lightning, wind, and cold.

Lightning kills more people each year than rap concerts, and a fly fisher waving a graphite rod is a superb conductor of this static electricity. When heavy electrical weather looks imminent, get off the water, look for low ground, discard your rod, and wait for the storm to pass. Undercut banks, caves, and isolated trees are not safe locations. Nor are overturned aluminum boats. When lightning shows up, always think invisible. Try to become the lowest-profile object in the immediate area.

The combination of cold, wind, and moisture can quickly lead to hypothermia, a deadly condition in which the body's core temperature drops low enough to cause blood to rush from the extremities to the vital organs. Numbness in the toes and fingers progressing into the arms and legs is an obvious symptom, as are shaky fingers. Shivering is another early warning sign. The real danger is the loss of reasoning (in many of us, this may be extremely difficult to detect) and the ability to make rational decisions. Paddling around in an ice-cold lake in a float tube is an easy way to become hypothermic, and if early warnings are not heeded, an angler could just stop moving and die. If you start to get cold, head to shelter—tent, car, cabin, etc.—and get warm and dry. Don't try to tough it out. Pay attention to your fishing partners. If they show any signs of hypothermia, get them off the water, to shelter, and warm them up.

Insects are another problem. Mosquitoes, blackflies, and deerflies can make life hell. Repellent works well against the first two, and a .28-gauge handles the third. Taking B-complex vitamins each day for a couple of weeks also works. Afterwards the body secretes a compound that insects find offensive. Ticks are another matter, and Lyme disease and Rocky Mountain spotted fever can cause acute illness or death. Tick patrol at the end of each day during tick season is mandatory. Be sure to remove the head. This may require tweezers.

Most spider bites are locally painful but not life-threatening. Treat with cold compresses and perhaps aspirin. If the victim exhibits nausea, vomiting, or diarrhea followed by weakness and disorientation, a systemic reaction is under way and you need to get immediate treatment by a doctor, unless you are capable of injecting a syringe of epinephrine (synthetic version of adrenaline). An antihistamine such as Benadryl can help prevent further reaction to histamine and rebound effect.

Rattlesnakes really do try to stay out of our way. The most common places to encounter these gentle reptiles is in rock piles, cliffs, and walls, and in the dry grasses of eastern Montana. The sound of a rattle will turn even the most graceful among us into a world-class spastic whirling from toe to toe in a desperate attempt to reverse direction.

If bitten, one or two puncture marks will be visible. If venom has been injected, swelling and pain will be immediate. Transport the victim as quickly as possible for antivenin treatment. Pain may be severe, but the victim can usually walk to transportation. Splint the affected part if possible. Remove any constricting items such as rings and clothing from the bitten extremity before swelling makes it difficult. The sooner a person reaches medical help, the better. Bites are rarely fatal in healthy adults, but the symptoms can be awful.

Most medical experts agree that traditional field treatments, such as tourniquets, pressure dressings, ice packs, and "cut and suck" snakebite kits, are ineffective and often dangerous. Treatment in the field is a waste of time.

The almighty Montana sun can cook your brains and fry your hide in a hurry. Wear a hat, sunglasses, and plenty of sunscreen. Drink cool liquids constantly. A gallon of water per person is the minimum, and a cooler full of ice and preferred beverages is a godsend. If dizziness, weakness, or a rapid pulse occur, seek shelter. If you stop sweating and get flushed, cool down fast. You may have heatstroke.

Another problem, especially in the backcountry, is avalanches. Even in July, tons and tons of snow and ice remain on steep rock walls and packed into bowls. Avoid crossing these areas of exposure. A peaceful-looking snow bowl with well-defined cornices is an invitation to disaster. If you absolutely must cross such an area, do it one at a time. If caught in an avalanche, try to swim with the flow and, as the avalanche starts to slow and the snow starts to pile up, ball up and get one hand in front of your face to create an air pocket and thrust the other hand as high as possible.

Wading swift rivers can also be deadly. Losing your footing can mean being swept under a logjam or into midstream boulders. On slippery, freestone streams, wear stream cleats and even carry a wading staff. Always look ahead and choose footing carefully.

As for bears and other wild animals (read the first part of the chapter on Glacier National Park), make noise to alert animals of your presence. Keep your eyes open and always leave an area immediately whenever a bear or bison or moose is spotted. Yelling, eye contact, and bluffing often provoke attacks and are last-resort (like when a charging grizzly is 10 feet away) measures. Most big-game animals avoid humans like the plague. Attacks are almost always a result of moving into an animal's territory unannounced or threatening its food supply, such as a buried carcass.

The number of anglers injured or killed by these real and perceived dangers is insignificant compared to those that suffer at the hands of car crashes and heart attacks. So do not fear the natural world, just give it a good deal of respect.

Suggested Gear

Successfully fishing in Montana does not require truckloads of equipment, although most fly fishers are collectors, hoarders, and gadget freaks, often forgoing the monthly house payment in favor of purchasing a new rod. Most experienced anglers have their own preferences, but for those who have never fished Montana or are new to the pursuit, the following, while subjective, is representative of tackle and related gear needed to enjoy fishing in the state.

Rods: If you bring just one, pick a 5- or 6-weight. These have enough strength to handle some wind and big water and still fish smaller streams halfway decently. If you bring two, an ideal combination would be a 9-foot 7-weight and an 8-foot 4-weight. The 7-weight will fight the wind that blows crazily along the Rocky Mountain Front and out onto the plains and also will work well nymphing and fishing heavy streamers. The 4-weight will fish smaller rivers and streams along with quiet ponds quite nicely. Others might include a 2-weight for spring creeks, a 5-weight for medium rivers, and an 8-weight for the hurricane conditions often found around places like the Blackfeet Indian Reservation.

Reels: While the current cliché is that reels are now much more than a contrivance for holding line, the need for disk drag is almost nonexistent. So if you cannot afford one, do not despair. The chances that a trout will smoke your reel are unlikely. On the other hand, purchase the best equipment you can afford. It can't hurt.

Lines: Use either double-taper or weight-forward lines and match them to your rods, or go maybe one step up in weight (say a 7-weight line for a 6-weight rod) to cheat the wind a bit. Definitely bring at least a 6-foot sink-tip for nymphing, streamers, and lake action. A 10-foot sink-tip is nice, too. Stick with floaters for 2-weights and 3-weights. A little weight above the fly works fine. Optional lines would include intermediate and fast-sinking lines for working deep in lakes. Shooting heads are nice and will give you a few more feet, but this is trout, not tarpon, fishing we're talking about. Backing of 12 pounds is adequate.

Patterns and leaders: A few suggestions are: Blue-Winged Olives, Tricos, and Pale Morning Duns in emergers, duns, and spinners; Stonefly Nymph, Pheasant Tail Nymph, Hare's Ear Nymph, Zug Bug, Sheep Creek, Scud, Kaufmann's Damsel Nymph, LaFontaine Antron, Prince Nymph, Partridge and Peacock; Muddler Minnow, Woolly Bugger, Zonker, Spruce Fly, Marabou Leech; Elk Hair Caddis, Royal Wulff, Adams, Humpy, Goddard Caddis, Royal Trude, Hopper Sofa Pillow, Girdle Bug, and Bitch Creek. A fair investment to be sure, but also a pretty good all-around selection for the rest of the country.

Whatever you have, bring, but be sure to stop at the nearest fly shop or sporting goods store to stock up on a few recommended patterns. The days of proprietors selling you everything in the store are pretty much over. You can buy with confidence in Montana.

Nine-foot leaders tapering to 3X or 4X are basic tools. You can add tippet material for finer work or cut the leaders back for heavy-water nymphing. Or, best of all, you can tie your own.

Clothing: Even in summer, bring clothes for cold weather. Snow and sleet, especially in the high country, is a twelve-months-a-year situation. Rain gear is a must, as is a hat to protect you from the sun. Boots are helpful. For fall, winter, and spring fishing, be prepared for anything weather-wise. This can be very cold country.

Miscellaneous accouterments: Obviously, bring your vest. Hip and chest waders will give you added versatility and comfort. If bringing only one pair, bring chest waders. Stream cleats are great for freestone streams. You need sunglasses and sunscreen, as well as insect repellent. A small camera for trophy photographs is handy. If you have room, bring a landing net, float tube and fins, and a fly-tying kit.

Stream Etiquette

Stream etiquette involves many things but boils down to treating all waters, land, and other anglers the way you would like to be treated.

Catching the largest or the most fish should be far down the list of fly-fishing priorities. Certainly, it is more fun catching fish than not catching them, and most of the time taking big fish is more exciting than hooking little ones. Unfortunately, the drive to take the most or largest has led directly to some boorish if not downright obnoxious behavior on Montana's rivers, creeks, and lakes.

It has become all too common to have some inconsiderate jerk walk right in next to someone who has been carefully working a pool, and begin casting to the same pod of fish. Others throw rocks into pools to drive away anglers from "chosen" spots. Still others float over and in front of wading anglers. Obscene language, gestures, and even fist fights seem to be on the rise. The growing lack of consideration is ruining fly fishing for many of us on a number of rivers. The observation of a few basic rules would go a long way toward eliminating some contentious scenes.

Perhaps most importantly, respect another angler's desire for space and privacy. Don't plunge right into water another person is working and crowd the poor soul. If this is your idea of pleasure, take up tournament bass fishing. Enter the water as far below and behind as possible—out of sight is best—of an angler working upstream. Do the opposite (above and behind) for an angler working downstream. Just don't step into the stream ahead of someone else. Avoid crowding those in canoes or float tubes on lakes and keep your voice down. Sound travels quite well over water.

On busy waters, wait until an angler finishes a stretch of water before entering. On opening day in some parts of Montana, the crowding may be excessive on popular waters, but, like New Year's Eve, this date is reserved for amateurs. While you wait, observing another's technique can have its own pleasures, but many of us are uncomfortable with being watched. Try to play the invisible man while waiting—out of sight, out of mind.

All good guides, when floating a river, will steer well clear of other boats on the water. They will also pull far away from wading anglers, leaving them the water they are fishing. This sometimes means that the clients in the boat have to stop casting for a minute or so, but the floaters have the whole river and can afford to pass up a short stretch. A nod, a friendly word, or even an exchange of information on the day's fishing is the norm between floaters and waders on Montana's rivers when both parties respect each other's rights.

In some parts of the country in the past few years, the concept of fellowship among anglers has taken an awful beating. Just saying "Hello" and receiving a friendly response is now an occasion worthy of log-book notation. One of the true virtues and assets of fly fishing is (or was) the friendliness and willingness of anglers to share information and a little small talk. Who cares if another manages to connect with a trout you were unable to fool? Competition in fly fishing is an obscenity.

If you're crossing private land, treat it with respect. Close any gates you open; don't harass the livestock; and if you take your dog, keep it under control. If you can't control it, leave it home.

In Montana the penalty for littering can be a good thumping if the wrong person catches you in the act (and few juries, in spite of all the DNA evidence, are going to convict the attacker). But with the growing number of slobs in our midst, it's no longer enough to simply not litter. If you find other people's leavings in the form of cans and candy wrappers, pick them up and stow them in your vest. This concept of littering also applies to throwing "trash" fish up on the bank to die—don't. Most of those "trash" fish are natives to our rivers, and don't deserve that kind of treatment.

Finally, catch-and-release has done more for preserving and improving trout fishing in Montana than anything else. It may be more important in Montana than anywhere else because of our state's reliance on wild fish populations in our creeks and rivers. Catch-and-release is the ultimate form of etiquette—preserving the resource for others to enjoy. It's not the end-all and be-all for every water (in many lonely places, it doesn't hurt to keep a few), but on our best-known and hardest-hit fisheries, it is the last hope for quality angling. For this concept to be successful, trout must be played fairly but quickly. Work a fish too long and lactic acid builds up in its muscle tissues. Even an apparently successful release will eventually result in death. Releasing that first 20-inch trout is tough, but after a season or two, watching them swim off to cover is reward enough.

All stream etiquette amounts to is the Golden Rule: Do unto others as you would have them do unto you. (As Jimmy Buffett once said regarding another matter, "The concept was so simple, it plum evaded me.")

Whirling Disease

A little-known parasite that infects members of the salmonid family may have a devastating impact on Montana's rainbow trout fishery, and apparently there is no cure in sight.

Myxobolus cerebralis, the parasite that causes whirling disease, was first discovered in 1994 in the 50-mile stretch of the Madison River above Ennis Lake, and the first reports are frightening. The rainbow population in this world-famous stretch of water has declined by more than 90 percent since 1991, from approximately 3,400 fish per mile to less than 300, according to the Montana Department of Fish, Wildlife & Parks (FWP). Since then, it has been found in twenty-two other locations within the Clark Fork, Jefferson, Madison, Beaverhead, and Swan river drainages. State officials predict that eventually it will spread into every major watershed in the state where both salmonids and the parasite's alternative host, tubificid worms, are found. Nonetheless, the potential effects of the disease in watersheds other than the Madison remain uncertain.

According to Marshall Bloom of Montana Trout Unlimited, whirling disease endangers Montana's wild trout populations: "Montana is the only state in the Lower 48 that relies nearly exclusively on natural reproduction rather than hatcheries to populate its rivers and streams with catchable trout." While hatcheries are able to grow fish through the disease—food is provided and there are no predators in hatcheries—some wild trout populations have been decimated.

The threat is especially great to Montana's native trout species such as redband rainbows, westslope cutthroats, arctic grayling, and bull trout. Populations of these species are greatly diminished from habitat loss and hybridization. While the effects of whirling disease on native trout species is still unknown, 90 percent population declines such as happened on the Madison could drive these species to extinction.

Myxobolus cerebralis has a complex life history. Trout are infected by the parasite when the Triactinomyon (TAM) form of the parasite is released into the water column by tubificid worms. In the few days of their life, TAMS can attach to a trout's mucus cells or on its skin. Once attached, they can inject a pre-spore material which migrates to the trout's cartilage. Once in the cartilage, spores that consume cartilage develop. In Colorado, researchers have found some heavily infected fish with as many as 500,000 spores.

The most common signs of infection are cranial deformities, black tails in young fish, "bug-eyes," and spinal deformities. Only occasionally is the tail-chasing swimming motion that gives the disease its name ever witnessed in wild trout. These symptoms are caused by the destruction of cartilaginous tissues and subsequent deformities of the skeleton. The black tail results from inflammatory pressure on the nerves controlling the pigment cells. In the wild, these stresses may cause direct mortality and most certainly cause secondary mortality by increasing the trout's susceptibility to predation and by inhibiting its ability to feed.

The spores remain in the fish until it either dies or is consumed by a predator. When the fish dies, more spores are released into the environment. The spores are especially hearty. They can survive in frozen fish at –20 degrees Fahrenheit, and for up to twenty years in dried mud. Once released into the water, the spore is consumed by tubificid worms. The spore then attaches to the worm's gut, where it metamorphoses into a TAM and the life cycle begins again.

Nobody knows how whirling disease spread to Montana. The primary cause of its spread across the nation has been through the transportation and stocking of live infected fish—often by state fish and wildlife agencies. In 1995, however, all federal, state, and private fish hatcheries in Montana tested negative for whirling disease. Other possible vectors for its spread include escaped fish from private fish ponds, illegal stocking by "bucket biologists," and the disposal of whirling disease–contaminated fish in a kitchen disposal (conventional sewage treatment will not kill whirling disease). "Once it's there, it's there," said state fisheries biologist Mark Lere.

Biologists first noticed a decline in rainbow trout numbers in the Madison near the West Fork in 1991. By 1993 the reduction in rainbows had reached Varney Bridge.

Brown trout are not as severely affected by whirling disease, perhaps because North America's original brown trout stocks came from Europe, where the disease originated. It was first reported in central Europe in 1903, but the complete life cycle was not described until the early 1980s. Whirling disease now occurs across Europe and was accidentally introduced into the United States around 1955, when its presence was found in Pennsylvania and Nevada. To date it has been detected in seventeen additional states: Alabama, Colorado, California, Connecticut, Idaho, Massachusetts, Michigan, Montana, New Hampshire, New Jersey, New York, Ohio, Oregon, Virginia, Washington, West Virginia, and Wyoming.

The Madison River is one of the world's best wild-trout fisheries, with a significant rainbow population, particularly in its upper reaches from the West Fork upstream to Quake Lake. Once the elimination of stocking took place (in 1973), the number and size of wild trout rose dramatically on the Madison, to the point where the river could provide a sustained quality fishery despite experiencing 140,000 angler fishing days per year, with summer catch rates of rainbows on some upper Madison stretches running as high as four fish per hour.

Rainbows used to make up 80 percent of the Madison below Quake Lake. Browns were the next largest population. Should the rainbows be wiped out in this section of the river, biologists do not look for a dramatic rise in the number of brown trout.

I'm an alarmist by nature. I asked several biologists and guides what they thought were the chances for a worst-case scenario. None wanted to be quoted by name, but all but one felt the chances for such a disaster were greater than fifty-fifty. One guide said the outbreak could seriously harm his business.

Despite the bleak outlook, Montana officials say all is not lost and there are several signs of hope. First, brown trout populations on the Madison have not been affected, and the Madison still offers world-class fishing for brown trout. This may hold true for other rivers as well.

Second, FWP biologists are not certain that trout in all rivers will suffer the same declines as the Madison rainbows. The states of California and Idaho, for reasons that no one understands, say they have some streams where whirling disease is present and the impacts on fish populations are minimal.

Third, Dick Vincent, FWP fisheries manager in Bozeman, believes that the Madison rainbows will eventually develop a disease-resistant strain. Currently he has found about a 5 percent survival rate among rainbows subjected to the disease in the infected area. "That's not much, but it's better than nothing. It may take a decade or as long as a century for resistant strains to develop. We don't know." If these fish are surviving because of a behavioral trait such as spawning time or location, there will be strong selective pressure for a population of fish with these characteristics.

Fourth, little is currently known about tubificid worms. As more is learned about their distribution, life history, and interaction with *Myxobolus cerebralis*, more management options may emerge.

Finally, researchers are looking for species and strains of trout that are immune to the disease. If one can be found, then infected streams may be repopulated with resistant fish.

In 1995, to underscore the state's commitment to dealing with whirling disease, Governor Mark Racicot convened a multidisciplinary Whirling Disease Task Force to try to identify immediate research needs and available resources to meet those needs. Since that time, angler awareness and management initiatives have helped to control the disease though continued vigilance will be necessary.

Stream Access

By Stan Bradshaw

(Stan wrote this for the original two *Montana Fly-Fishing Guides* that appeared nearly twenty years ago, but it is still applicable today. The stream access issue was upheld by the Montana State Supreme Court in January 2014 despite a nuisance appeal.)

Imagine that you're floating one of Montana's blue-ribbon trout streams, like the Beaverhead. It's a perfect day for fishing, cool, slightly overcast, and bugs are up on the surface. Even better, you're in your brand-new customized fishing raft with all the latest doodads. As you come around a bend, a low bridge looms up. Low, but not too low to clear. But, as you start under it, and too late to respond, you spot the strands of barbed wire, hidden in the shadows of the bridge, strung taut across the entire river at raft height. Before you can react, your boat is swept into it, the tubes are torn, and the boat sinks. Within seconds, you and most of your fishing gear are strewn downstream. Question: Do you have any recourse against the jerk who strung the barbed wire?

Or imagine another day on Little Piddly Creek. It's a small creek, too small for floating, but, with runs, ruffles, and undercut banks, a good small stream fishery. You get on the creek where it goes under a state highway and wade upstream, staying in the water all the way. A half mile upstream from the highway, a pickup roars across an adjacent hay meadow, pulls up opposite where you are fishing, and a big beefy fellow jumps out, veins popping out of his neck, and proceeds to read you the riot act for trespassing and tells you that you have to get the hell off the creek. Question: Just what are your rights to fish the Little Piddly?

Both of these hypotheticals occur, in one form or the other, each year in Montana. Prior to 1984, the answers to these questions were anybody's guess. In 1984, two Montana Supreme Court rulings went a long way toward answering these questions. In 1985, legislation enacted to clarify the court rulings further defined the rights of recreationists to use Montana's rivers and streams. At the end of this chapter, we'll revisit those examples and apply the current law to them to provide some answers.

In the early 1980s, a coalition of recreationists and sportsmen's groups, the Montana Coalition for Stream Access, filed lawsuits against landowners on two rivers, the Beaverhead and the Dearborn, to establish the right of recreationists to use them.

While there were some differences in the historic uses of these two rivers (the Dearborn had been used to float logs to market; the Beaverhead had not), the issue was the same in both cases—whether recreationists had the right to float, wade, and fish on these rivers. The Supreme Court decided both cases within months of each other, and the basic ruling was the same in each.

The court said that any surface waters capable of recreational use may be used by the public regardless of who owns the streambed, and regardless of whether the river is navigable. This ruling marked a dramatic departure from the law in most other states. With the exception of Wyoming, in every other state the right of public use hinges on whether a waterway is navigable by some kind of craft ("navigable" is one of those chameleon terms in the law that changes meaning according to how it's used, so take care to know in your home state what the term means). After 1984, in Montana, if a stream held some recreational value, landowners could not keep recreationists out of the stream.

The court, and later the legislature, placed some limits on this right of access, however. First, the law limits your right to use a stream to the land between the "ordinary high water marks." What is the ordinary high water mark? It is:

> *The line that water impresses on land by covering it for sufficient periods to cause physical characteristics that distinguish the area below the line from the area above it. Characteristics of the area below the line include, when appropriate, but are not limited to deprivation of the soil of substantially all terrestrial vegetation and destruction of its agricultural vegetative value.*

The legislature was careful to caution that a floodplain is not considered to be within a stream's ordinary high water mark. Is that clear as mud now?

Actually, the ordinary high water mark is pretty clear most of the time. If you stay below any visible shoreline vegetation, you're probably okay. Otherwise, if you are in doubt about where the mark is, err to the narrowest possible interpretation. Better to narrow your range of movement some than to risk a trespass charge.

The second major limitation to public use is that it does not include a right to cross private lands. You can enter a waterway at some point of public access, such as a highway right-of-way or a fishing access site, but a landowner may post his land against trespass (more about trespass below) above the ordinary high water mark.

The statute also allows landowners to petition the Fish, Wildlife & Parks Commission to close or restrict waters to public use if the stream does not support any recreational use, the public use is damaging the banks and land adjacent to the stream, the public use is damaging the landowner's property under or next to the stream, or if the public use is causing other environmental damage. In the year after passage of the law, there was a spate of closure petitions. Most of these were denied. Only two, one on Nelson's Spring Creek and one on a part of the Musselshell River, were granted.

On Nelson's Spring Creek, the commission simply prohibited wading in the stream during cutthroat spawning (June 15 to September 15) to protect spawning beds. Since the landowner on this stream charges a fee, this has the practical effect of keeping uninvited people off the stream during that period.

On the Musselshell, the Fish, Wildlife & Parks Commission closed the river to public use through the landowner's bison pasture for safety reasons. In both cases, the closures are marked by signs.

An Infestation of Orange

Anywhere you go in Montana, you are likely to be struck by the profusion of fluorescent-orange-topped fenceposts. Those orange monuments are the equivalent of trespassing signs in Montana. They're an offshoot of the stream-access battles of the mid-eighties. One concession to landowners was the simplification of a previously obscure posting requirement by allowing the use of fluorescent orange paint to signify that land is posted, and describing what constitutes adequate posting (a landowner simply has to post his land at gates going into his land and on stream banks where they pass into his land).

Orange paint aside, however, Montana law requires some specific notice that land is closed to trespass before you can be cited for criminal trespass. (The one exception to this is big-game hunting—if you plan to hunt big game on private land, you need the landowner's permission even if the land is not posted.) This notice can be made by use of signs, orange paint, or even verbally ("Get the hell off my land" will do), but the burden is nonetheless on the landowner to notify you that you are not welcome on his land. If you pass onto land that is not posted and you haven't otherwise been notified that you are not welcome, you can go above the ordinary high water mark. Use this right judiciously, however; landowners have been quite rightly outraged by careless recreationists who have abused the land, and in some instances have simply closed their land off to public use.

When the legislature first amended the law to allow orange paint for posting, word quickly circulated that anyone who posted their land with orange paint couldn't let anybody—even their relatives—on it. Wrong. Just because land is posted does not mean that you can't ask permission. The orange paint simply means that you cannot use the land without express permission. (On the other hand, if the landowner posts a sign that says "No trespassing, don't ask," you can take that as a hint about the value of asking permission.) If you're not sure about whether you can cross private land to get to a reach of stream, find the landowner and ask permission. The worst you can get from the landowner is a "no."

Now back to those hypothetical problems.

As to the jerk whose barbed wire destroyed our raft, a number of possibilities exist. First, it is not illegal to run boundary fences or stock fences across rivers and streams.

But Montana law does make it a criminal misdemeanor to impede navigation on a public stream (Section 45-8-111 MCA). This carries with it a possible fine of $500 and possible jail time. Not exactly a capital crime, but a clear statement of public policy against this kind of shenanigan. The trick here may be in determining whether the fence is a legitimate boundary or stock fence, or whether it is a spite fence. As a practical matter, the criminal statute has rarely, if ever, been used in Montana, perhaps because most people, including county attorneys (who would have to prosecute any violations under it), are unaware of it.

A second possibility would be a civil suit. While civil liability in a case like this always requires close scrutiny of the specific facts, the law generally does not countenance the deliberate placement of hazards such as this. In fact, the stream access statute says that a landowner is liable to a recreationist only for "willful or wanton misconduct"—basically intentional acts. If this happens to you, and you and your camera survive it, get pictures—not only of the damage, but also shots of the hazard from every angle, especially the upstream side.

A couple of other observations about this situation are in order. First, if you are able to see the hazard before you get to it, Montana law allows you to leave the ordinary high water marks and portage around it "in the least intrusive manner possible." This does not mean that you can leave the river at the slightest excuse and call it a "portage," but where an obstacle makes the river genuinely unpassable, you may get out and go around it. Curiously, the legislature has specifically allowed you to portage around artificial obstacles, but is silent as to natural obstacles. So if you come to a waterfall or some other natural obstacle and the adjacent land is posted, you are on your own.

Hypothetical number two: The answer to this one is simple. As long as you keep inside the ordinary high water mark, you may lawfully fish Little Piddly. Whether you want to brave the wrath of a big brute who seems dangerously close to committing mayhem is a judgment call that you have to make. But let's embellish the facts a little.

What if, when you got out of your car on the state highway, you could see no orange paint or other indications of "no trespassing" on the land adjacent to the creek? Then, you could cross the field to get to the creek, at least *until* the landowner came out and yelled at you and told you to get off. At that point, you either have to leave his land or stay inside the ordinary high water mark.

Despite the variations described above, staying legal under Montana's stream access law is not all that difficult. Likewise, staying on an amicable footing with landowners and your fellow anglers is fairly easy. If you follow the basic rules below, you should have no trouble using our rivers and streams with a minimum of hassle. Just use a little common sense and courtesy.

RULES OF THE RIVER

1. If in doubt about your right to get onto a given stream, ask permission.

2. Make sure you know the current regulations for the water you are fishing.

3. Don't litter. If you see litter, pick it up and take it out. Leave the river cleaner than you found it.

4. If you take a dog, keep it under control. If you can't control it, leave it home. If you want it to survive your trip, don't let it harass livestock.

5. If you are camping, don't leave a trace.

6. Take extreme care with fire. If things feel dry to you, don't build one.

7. If there are other anglers on the stream, give them a wide berth.

8. If you're crossing private land, leave all gates as you find them, and leave all fences intact.

HATCH CHARTS

Fly fishers have basically three choices with insect hatches: ignore them, accept them, or hunt them. The hatch charts are designed to help all of these strategies (even "ignoring them" works best when it isn't practiced in ignorance). These charts are not complete. The expanse of the state, with its diverse terrestrial and aquatic environments, makes that impossible. The charts identify the major insect hatches, the ones heavy enough to trigger consistent and often selective trout feeding. The dates for these hatches, covering a number of waters, are broad, too, but the references in the write-ups to individual rivers or lakes give more specific time periods.

Western Montana

The waters mentioned in the hatch chart are rivers unless otherwise noted.

CADDISFLIES	JAN	FEB	MAR	APR	MAY	JUNE
Grannom				•	••	

Brachycentrus sp. size 12–16, wings=dark gray to almost black, body=medium to very dark green
> The early grannom (*B. occidentalis*) is also known as the Mother's Day hatch. The summer grannom is *B. americanus*.
> Bitterroot, Kootenai, Little Blackfoot, lower Clark Fork, Swan, Thompson

	JAN	FEB	MAR	APR	MAY	JUNE
Green Sedge				•	••••	••••

Ryacophila sp. size 12–16, wings=mottled brown or gray, body=bright green
> Many important species hatch throughout the summer months on fast-water streams and rivers.
> Blackfoot, Rock Creek

	JAN	FEB	MAR	APR	MAY	JUNE
Traveler Sedge				•	••••	••••

Banksiola crotchi size 6–10, wings=tan to brown, body=tan to brown
> Appears on lakes two to three weeks after ice-out.
> Browns Lake, Georgetown Lake

	JAN	FEB	MAR	APR	MAY	JUNE
Great Gray Spotted Sedge					•	••••

Arctopsyche grandis size 8–10, wings=mottled dark gray, body=green
> Rock Creek

	JAN	FEB	MAR	APR	MAY	JUNE
Spotted Sedge						••

Hydropsyche sp. size 12–14, wings=spotted brown, body=dirty yellow
> Major species include H. *vera*, H. *oslari*, H. *occidentalis*, and H. *cockerelli*.
> Bitterroot, Lolo Creek, Kootenai, Rock Creek, Swan, Thompson, upper Clark Fork, West Fork Bitterroot

	JAN	FEB	MAR	APR	MAY	JUNE
Little Sister Sedge						•

Cheumatopsyche campyla size 16–18, wing=tan, body=ginger
> Bitterroot, lower Clark Fork, Kootenai, Swan, upper Clark Fork

Longhorn Sedge

Oecetis avara size 12–14, wings=ginger, body=ginger
> Bunyan Lake

Giant Orange Sedge

Discosmoecus sp. size 8, wings=mottled dark brown, body=burnt orange
> Also known as October caddis, which is misleading because it is more important during September in Montana.
> Bitterroot, Blackfoot, Rock Creek, Swan, West Fork Bitterroot

JULY	AUG	SEPT	OCT	NOV	DEC
•	••••	••			
••••	••••	••••	••		
••••	•••				
••••	•				
••••	••••	••••	••		
••••	••••	•••			
•••	•••				
		••••	•••		

347

CRANEFLIES	JAN	FEB	MAR	APR	MAY	JUNE

Orange Cranefly
Tipula sp. size 6–10, wings=light veined, body=orange
    Upper Clark Fork

DAMSELFLIES

	JAN	FEB	MAR	APR	MAY	JUNE
Various species						••

size 12–16, size 8–12, wings=clear in most species, body=bright blue or green in most common species. Often hatch at the same time as mosquitoes.
    Lakes: Brown's, Burnt Fork, Echo, Frank, Georgetown, Gleason, Horseshoe, Hubbart Reservoir, Medicine, Metcalf, Moore, Willow, Woods

MAYFLIES

	JAN	FEB	MAR	APR	MAY	JUNE
Blue-Winged Olive			••••	••		

Baetis parvus and *Baetis tricaudatus* size 16, wings=slate gray, body=olive
Also called iron dun on some Montana rivers.
    Bitterroot, Bitterroot Irrigation Ditch, Blackfoot, Kootenai, Little Blackfoot, lower Clark Fork, Rock Creek, Thompson, upper Clark Fork

	JAN	FEB	MAR	APR	MAY	JUNE
Red Quill			•	••••	•	

Rhithrogena morrisoni size 14, wings=medium gray, body=light reddish brown
Also known as western march brown.
    Lower Clark Fork

	JAN	FEB	MAR	APR	MAY	JUNE
Green Drake					•	••••

Drunella grandis size 6–8, wings=gray, body=dark olive
Formerly was genus *Ephemerella*.
    Bitterroot, Thompson, upper Clark Fork, West Fork Bitterroot

	JAN	FEB	MAR	APR	MAY	JUNE
Brown Drake					•	••••

Ephemera simulans size 10–12, wings=brown, body=yellowish brown
Bitterroot, Thompson, upper Clark Fork, West Fork Bitterroot

	JAN	FEB	MAR	APR	MAY	JUNE
Light Cahill						••

Cinygma dimicki size 12–14, wings=cream, body=cream
Also known as western light cahill.
    Lower Clark Fork

Gray Drake
Siphlonurus occidentalis size 10–12, wings=medium gray, body=gray
    Bitterroot, Bitterroot Irrigation Ditch, lower Clark Fork, Thompson

JULY	AUG	SEPT	OCT	NOV	DEC
•••	••••	•			
••••	••••	••			
••••		•	••••	•	
•••					
•••					
•••					
•••	••				

MAYFLIES	JAN	FEB	MAR	APR	MAY	JUNE

Ginger Quill
  Heptagenia simplicoides size 12–14, wings=ginger, body=ginger
    Lolo Creek, lower Clark Fork

Callibaetis
  Callibaetis americanus size 14–16, wings=gray, body=gray
    Blackfoot, Cottonwood Lakes, Elk Lake, Georgetown Lake, Horseshoe Lake, Job Corps Ponds

Pale Morning Dun
  Ephemerella infrequens and *Ephemerella inermis* size 14–18, wings=pale gray, body=pale yellow
    Bitterroot, Blackfoot, Kootenai, lower Clark Fork, Frock Creek, upper Clark Fork

Trico
  Tricorythodes minutus size 18–20, wings=dark gray, body=very dark olive (appears black)
    Bitterroot, Bitterroot Irrigation Ditch, Blackfoot, Georgetown Lake, Kootenai, lower
    Clark Fork Rock Creek, Thompson, upper Clark Fork

Blue-Winged Red Quill
  Rhithrogena undulata size 16, wings=brownish gray, body=reddish brown
    Also known as small western red quill.
    Bitterroot, West Fork Bitterroot

Slate-Winged Mahogany Dun
  Paraleptophlebia bicornuta size 12–14, wings=dark gray, body-blackish brown
    Lower Clark Fork

STONEFLIES

Winter Stone ••••   •••
  Capnia sp. size 16–18, wings=dark veined, body=very dark olive (appears black)
    Little Blackfoot

Skwala   •••   •••
  Skwala parallela size 10–12, wings=dark veined, body=olive
    Bitterroot, lower Clark Fork, West Fork Bitterroot

Brown Stone   •   ••••   •
  Nemoura sp. size 10–14, wings=dark veined, body=brown
    Lower Clark Fork

Salmon Fly   •••
  Pteronarcys californica size 4–6, wings=dark veined, body=dark orange
    Bitterroot, Blackfoot, lower Clark Fork, Rock Creek, Thompson, upper Clark Fork

JULY	AUG	SEPT	OCT	NOV	DEC
•••	•••				
••	••••	••••	•		
	••	••••	•••		
	••	•••			
	•	••			
		••	••		
••					

STONEFLIES	JAN	FEB	MAR	APR	MAY	JUNE
Little Olive Stone					•••	

Alloperla sp. size 14–16, wings=dark veined, body=bright olive
    Blackfoot

Golden Stone					•••	

Calineuria californica size 6–8, wings=ginger veined, body=golden
    Big Salmon, Bitterroot, Blackfoot, Clearwater, Rock Creek, upper Clark Fork,
    West Fork Bitterroot

Yellow Sally

Isoperla sp. size 14–16, wings=yellow veined, body=bright yellow
    Nez Perce Fork, West Fork Bitterroot

TWO-WINGED FLIES

Midges	••••	••••	••••	••••	••••	••••

Diptera sizes 14–28, midges come in most colors
    Hatch everywhere and all year. Midges are especially important on rivers during the winter
    months and on high-mountain lakes all summer.

JULY	AUG	SEPT	OCT	NOV	DEC
••••	••				
••••	••				
••	••••	••••	•		
••••	••••	••••	••••	••••	••••

Eastern Montana

The waters mentioned in the hatch chart are rivers unless otherwise noted.

CADDISFLIES	JAN	FEB	MAR	APR	MAY	JUNE
Grannom				• •	• •	

Brachycentrus sp. size 12–16, wings=dark gray to almost black, body=medium to very dark green
The early grannom (*B. occidentalis*) is also known as the Mother's Day hatch. The summer grannom is *B. americanus*.
Beaverhead, Big Hole, Bighorn, DePuy Spring Creek, Grasshopper Creek, Madison, Marias, McClellan Creek, Missouri, Musselshell, Nelson's Spring Creek, Poindexter Slough, Red Rock, Yellowstone

	JAN	FEB	MAR	APR	MAY	JUNE
Green Sedge				• •	• • • •	• • • •

Ryacophila sp. size 12–16, wings=mottled brown or gray, body=bright green
Many important species hatch throughout the summer months on fast-water streams and rivers.
Madison, Red Rock

	JAN	FEB	MAR	APR	MAY	JUNE
Little Tan Short Horn Sedge						• • • •

Glossosoma sp. size 14–18, wings=tan, body=greenish brown
The larvae make the turtle-shell cases found on rocks in riffles.
Madison

	JAN	FEB	MAR	APR	MAY	JUNE
Ring Horn Microcaddis						• • •

Leucotrichia pictipes size 20–24, wings=spotted black, body=brown
This is a tiny insect, but there are larval densities of 5,000 per square foot on the Madison.
Madison

	JAN	FEB	MAR	APR	MAY	JUNE
Spotted Sedge						

Hydropsyche sp. size 12–14, wings=spotted brown, body=dirty yellow
Major species include H. *oslari*, H. *occidentalis*, and H. *cockerelli*.
Beaverhead, Big Hole, Bighorn, Grasshopper Creek, Madison, Missouri, Red Rock, Ruby, Yellowstone

	JAN	FEB	MAR	APR	MAY	JUNE
Little Sister Sedge						• •

Cheumatopsyche campyla size 16–18, wing=tan, body=ginger
There are massive evening hatches on major, rich rivers.
Beaverhead, Big Hole, Grasshopper Creek, Missouri, Poindexter Slough, Red Rock, Ruby, Yellowstone

	JAN	FEB	MAR	APR	MAY	JUNE
Little Plain Brown Sedge						• •

Lepidostoma pluviale size 14–16, wings=brown, body=light brown
Madison

JULY	AUG	SEPT	OCT	NOV	DEC
••••	••••	••••	••		
••••	•				
••					
•••	••••	••••	••		
••••	••••	•••			
••••	••				

CRANEFLIES	JAN	FEB	MAR	APR	MAY	JUNE

Varicolored Microcaddis
    Hydroptila sp. size 18–22, wings=gray to brown, body=yellow to brown
        Abundant in spring creek environments.
        Poindexter Slough

Long Horn Sedge
    Oecetis avara size 12–14, wings=ginger, body=ginger
        Beaverhead, Red Rock

Little Western Weedy Water Sedge
    Amiocentrus aspilus size 16–18, wings=very dark brown, body=dark green
        An especially important midsummer hatch on the Bighorn (mixes with the summer
        grannom in a black caddis hatch).
        Bighorn, Poindexter Slough

Summer Flier Sedge
    Limnephilus sp. size 8–10, wings=cinnamon, body=dark ginger
        Bighorn

Giant Orange Sedge
    Dicosmoecus sp. size 8, wings=mottled dark brown, body=burnt orange
    Big Hole, Smith

Orange Cranefly
    Tipula size 6–10, wings=light veined, body=orange
        Beaverhead

DAMSELFLIES

Various species
    size 12–16, size 8–12, wings=clear in most species, body=bright blue or green in
    most species
        Bailey's Reservoir, Bean Lake, Bighorn Reservoir, Carter's Pond, Deerhead
        Lake, Dickens Lake, Faber Reservoir, Grasshopper Reservoir, Lisk Creek
        Reservoir, Martinsdale Reservoir, Mission Lake, Missouri, Pintlar Lake,
        Rat Lake, Wade Lake, Willow Creek Reservoir

JULY	AUG	SEPT	OCT	NOV	DEC
••••	••••				
••••	•••				
•••	••••	••			
••	•••				
		••••			
••••	••••				
••••	••••	••			

MAYFLIES	JAN	FEB	MAR	APR	MAY	JUNE
Blue-Winged Olive			••••	••		

Baetis parvus and *Baetis tricaudatus* size 16, wings=slate gray, body=olive

    Armstrong Spring Creek, Beaverhead, Benhart Creek, Big Hole, Bighorn, Big Spring Creek, Blaine Spring Creek, East Fork Gallatin, Gallatin, Grasshopper Creek, Madison, Marias, Missouri, Musselshell, Poindexter Slough, Red Rock, Ruby, Yellowstone

MAYFLIES	JAN	FEB	MAR	APR	MAY	JUNE
Red Quill		••	••••	•		

Rhithrogena morrisoni size 14, wings=medium gray, body=light reddish brown

    Also known as the western march brown.

    Madison

MAYFLIES	JAN	FEB	MAR	APR	MAY	JUNE
Green Drake					••	••••

Drunella grandis size 6–8, wings=gray, body=dark olive

    Often hatches on the same rivers and at the same times as the brown drake.

    Big Hole

MAYFLIES	JAN	FEB	MAR	APR	MAY	JUNE
Brown Drake					••	••••

Ephemera simulans size 10–12, wings=brown, body=yellowish brown

    Big Hole, Culver Pond

Small Western Green Drake

Ephemerella flavinea size 14, wings=slate gray, body=olive

    Also commonly called the flav.

    Madison

Callibaetis

Callibaetis americanus size 14–16, wings=gray, body=gray

    Alder Gulch Creek, Beaver Creek Reservoir, Beaverhead, Carter's Pond, Clark Canyon Reservoir, Cliff Lake, Culver Pond, Dickens Lake, Goose Lake, Hebgen Lake, Lisk Creek Reservoir, Madison, Wade Lake, Willow Creek Reservoir

Yellow Drake

Heptagenia elegantula size 14–16, wings=straw yellow, body=yellow

    Yellowstone

Pale Morning Dun

Ephemerella infrequens and *Ephemerella inermis* size 14–18, wings=pale gray, body=pale yellow

    Armstrong Spring Creek, Beaverhead, Benhart Creek, Big Hole, Bighorn, Big Spring Creek, Blaine Spring Creek, Cliff Lake, Gallatin, Grasshopper Creek, Madison, Missouri, Poindexter Slough, Red Rock, Wade Lake, Yellowstone

Ghost Fly

Traverella albertana size 10–12, wings=cream, body=light cream

    Yellowstone

JULY	AUG	SEPT	OCT	NOV	DEC
••••	•	••	••••	•	
		•••			
•••					
•••					
••••	••••				
•••	••••	••••	•		
	••••	•••			
	••••	••••	••		
	•••	••			

MAYFLIES	JAN	FEB	MAR	APR	MAY	JUNE

Trico
    Tricorythodes minutus size 18–20, wings=dark gray, body=very dark olive (appears black)
        Beaverhead, Benhart Creek, Big Hole, Bighorn, Blaine Spring Creek, Clark Canyon
        Reservoir, Gallatin, Grasshopper Creek, Hebgen Lake, Madison, Missouri, Musselshell,
        Poindexter Slough, Yellowstone

White Fly
    Ephoron album size 12–14, wings=white, body=white
        Yellowstone

Tiny Blue-Winged Olive
    Pseudocloeon sp. size 22–24, wings=gray, body=olive
        Beaverhead, Benhart Creek, Big Hole, Bighorn, Blaine Spring Creek, Poindexter Slough

STONEFLIES

	JAN	FEB	MAR	APR	MAY	JUNE
Skwala			••••	•••		

    Skwala parallela size 10–12, wings=dark veined, body=olive
        Dearborn, Smith

| Salmon Fly | | | | | | •••• |

    Pteronarcys californica size 4–6, wings=dark veined, body=orange
        Big Hole, Gallatin, Madison, Yellowstone

| Little Olive Stone | | | | | | •••• |

    Alloperla sp. size 14–16, wings=dark veined, body=bright olive
        Beaverhead, Madison, Yellowstone

| Golden Stone | | | | | | •••• |

    Calineuria californica size 6–8, wings=ginger veined, body=golden
        Big Hole, Madison, Yellowstone

Yellow Stone
    Isoperla sp. size 14–16, wings=yellow veined, body=bright yellow
        Also known as the little yellow stone.
        Beaverhead, Bighorn, Madison, Red Rock, Yellowstone

TWO-WINGED FLIES

	JAN	FEB	MAR	APR	MAY	JUNE
Midges	••••	••••	••••	••••	••••	••••

    Diptera sizes 14–28, midges come in most colors
        Hatch everywhere and all year. Midges are especially important on rivers during the winter
        months and on high-mountain lakes all summer.

	JULY	AUG	SEPT	OCT	NOV	DEC
		•••	•••			
		••	••••	••		
			••	••••	•	
	••					
	••••	••				
	••••	••				
	•••	••••	•			
	••••	••••	••••	••••	••••	••••

Further Information

Many fly fishers think of Yellowstone National Park as being mostly in Montana, but, in fact, very little of the land is in the state. The Gardner is the only river that comes to mind, as it flows out of the Montana portion of the park and into the Yellowstone. For those wishing to fish the many varied and classic waters here, I recommend *Fishing Yellowstone Waters* by Charles Brooks. It's an oldie but a goodie and nearly as timely today as when it was first released by Nick Lyons Books in 1984. *The Lakes of Yellowstone* by Steve Pierce and published by The Mountaineers is another good source of information.

Pat Marcuson's *Fishing the Beartooths* is still the definitive book for the many alpine lakes and streams in the spectacular Beartooth Mountains. It was released by Falcon Press in 1997 and a second edition was published in 2008 under Lyons Press.

Fishing Glacier National Park by Paul M. Hintzen from 1982 is a fun pamphlet on fly-fishing opportunities in Glacier. Used copies can be found at abebooks.com.

My original *Montana Fly-Fishing Guides, East and West,* contain hundreds of small and lesser waters in the back of each river section that have not been included in this book. Copies can be found at Amazon, among others.

For up-to-date stream flows in Montana, I recommend the USGS site at http://waterdata.usgs.gov/MT/nwis/current/?type=flow and for current road conditions the Montana Road Report Map at www.mdt.mt.gov/travinfo/map/mtmap_frame.html.

The Montana Department of Fish, Wildlife & Parks website is an excellent source of information and is found at http://fwp.mt.gov.

The *DeLorme Montana Atlas & Gazetteer* provides accurate large-scale maps of Montana in book form. The waters mentioned in this book can all be located here. It is available at http://shop.delorme.com.

For a more detailed mapping of Montana, USGS topographical maps for the state are available at http://topographicalmaps.com/250k.mgi?state=mt.

The Montana Official Travel Site is an excellent site for gathering travel information, including food and lodging. It is found at http://visitmt.com.

INDEX

A

access, stream, 339–43
Ackley Lake, 272
Ajax Lake, 188
Akokala (Indian) Creek and Lake, 130
Alberton Gorge, 65
Albicaulis Lake, 43
Albino Lake, 206
Alder Creek, 43
Alice Creek, 28
American Fork, 284
Anaconda Settling Ponds, 38–40, 43–44
Arch Lakes, 300
Armstrong Spring Creek, 312–13
Arrastra Creek, 28
Arrow Lake, 130
Arrowhead Lake, 67
Ashley Creek, 91
Ashley Lake, 91
Avalanche Lake, 130
Axolotl (Twin or Crater) Lakes, 238

B

Badger Creek, 246
Bair Reservoir, 284
Baker Creek, 217
Baker Lake, 9
Baldy Lake, 67, 188
Bartlett Creek, 112
Bass Creek, 9–10
Bass Lake, 10
Bear Creek, 99
Bearpaw Lake, 249
Beartrap Canyon, 237–38
Beaver Creek, 68
Beaver Creek (Bears Paw Mountains), 250
Beaver Creek (below Hauser), 263
Beaver Creek Reservoir, 250–51
Beaver Lake, 91

Beaverhead River, 163–79
    about: overview of, 163–70
    Barrett's Diversion to Dillon, 172
    Blacktail Deer Creek, 173
    Clark Canyon Dam to Barrett's Diversion,
        170–71
    drainage fishing waters, 173–79
    map, 164–65
    popular dry flies, 168
    popular nymphs, 166
    Ruby River mouth to Big Hole River, 172
Belly River, 125
Belt Creek, 272–73
Benhart Creek, 217
Bergsicker Creek, 101
Berry Lake, 188
Big Beaver Creek, 68
Big Birch Creek, 294
Big Creek, 10, 139
Big Creek Lakes, 10
Big Elk Creek, 284
Big Hawk Lakes, 112
Big Hole River, 172, 181–92
    about: overview of, 181–85
    drainage fishing waters, 188–92
    Glen to Beaverhead confluence, 187–88
    headwaters to Wise River, 185–86
    Maiden Rock to Melrose Bridge, 187
    map, 182–83
    popular flies, 185
    Wise River to Maiden Rock, 186
Big Horn (Brockton) Reservoir, 273
Big Moose Lake, 206
Big Otter Creek, 275
Big Pipestone Creek, 225
Big Pozega (Deep) Lake, 44
Big Salmon Creek, 112
Big Salmon Lake, 112
Big Sandy Creek, 251–52
Big Sheep (Sheep) Creek, 289

Big Spring Creek, 275–76
Bighorn River, 314–16
Bighorn (Sheep) Lake, 29
Bison Creek, 225
Bitterroot Blackfoot, 3–19
    about: overview of, 3
    Connor to Hamilton, 3
    drainage fishing waters, 9–19
    Florence to Clark Fork confluence, 7–9
    Hamilton to Victor, 6–7
    map, 4–5
    popular flies, 9
Bitterroot Irrigation Ditch, 10–11
Black Bear Creek, 112
Black Canyon Lake, 206
Blackfeet Reservation, 193–201
    about: overview of, 193–97
    fishing waters, 197–201
    map, 194
    popular flies, 200
Blackfoot Lake, 113
Blackfoot River, 21–35
    about: overview of, 21–24
    Clearwater Junction to Johnsrud Park, 26
    drainage fishing waters, 28–35
    headwaters to Lincoln, 24
    Johnsrud Park to Bonner, 27–28
    Lincoln to Helmville Bridge, 24
    map, 22–23
    mines, 21–24
    mouth to Kelly Island, 61
    North Fork mouth to Clearwater Junction, 25–26
    popular flies, 27
Blacktail Deer Creek, 173
Blankenship Bridge, 85–88
Blodgett Creek, 11
Bloody Dick Creek, 173
Blue Joint Creek, 11
Blue Sky Creek, 139
Bluebird Lake, 140
Bluewater Creek, 206
Bobcat Lakes, 188
Bohn Lake, 44
Bonanza Lakes, 68
Bootjack Lake, 91
Boulder Creek, 12
Boulder Lake (Bitterroot drainage), 12

Boulder Lakes (upper Clark Fork drainage), 45
Boulder River (Jefferson drainage), 225–26
Boulder River (Yellowstone drainage), 316–18.
    See also East Boulder River; East Fork
    Main Boulder River; South Boulder
    River; West Boulder River
Bowdoin Lake, 252
Bowl Creek, 101
Bowman Lake, 130
Bramble Creek Lakes, 318
Branham Lakes, 226
Brewster Creek, 45
Browns Lake, 29
Buck Pond (McDonald's Pool), 289
Bull River, 68
    East Fork, 69–70
Bunker Creek, 113
Burdette Creek, 68
Burns Slough, 45
Burnt Fork Bitterroot River, 12
Burnt Fork Lake, 12
Burnt Lake, 91
Butte to Warm Springs (upper Clark Fork), 38

C
Cabin Lake, 68
Cabinet Gorge Reservoir, 69
Cache Creek, 69
Callahan Creek, 140
Camas Lake and Creek (Glacier National Park), 131
Camas Lakes (Bitterroot drainage), 12
Cameron Creek, 12
Cameron Lake, 239
Camp Lake (Blackfoot drainage), 29
Camp Lake (Yellowstone drainage), 318
Canyon (Crazy) Lake, 206
Canyon Creek (Big Hole drainage), 188–89
Canyon Creek (North Fork drainage), 105
Canyon Creek (Upper Missouri waters), 263
Canyon Ferry Reservoir, 256–57, 263–66
Canyon Lake, 189
Carlton Lake, 13
Carruthers Lake, 45
Carter's Ponds, 276
Castle Lake, 101
Cat Lake, 154

Cataract Creek, 69

Cedar Creek, 154

Cedar Lakes, 140

Cedar Log Lakes, 69

Cerulean Lake, 131

Chain Lakes, 105

Cherry Creek, 239

Cherry Lake, 239

Cirque (Upper Wanless) Lakes, 69

Clark Canyon Reservoir, 173–74

Clark Fork. *See* lower Clark Fork; upper
    Clark Fork

Clarks Fork of the Yellowstone, 203–10
    about: overview of, 203–5
    drainage fishing waters, 206–10
    map, 204
    popular flies, 205

Clayton Lake, 113

Clear Creek, 252

Clearwater Junction, 25–26

Clearwater Lake, 29–30

Clearwater River, 30. *See also* West Fork
    Clearwater River

Cliff Lake (lower Clark Fork drainage), 69

Cliff Lake (Madison drainage), 239

Cliff Lake (South Fork of Flathead River
    drainage), 113

clothing, 332

Coal Creek, 105

Cold Lakes, 154

Como Lake, 13

Cooper Creek, 30

Copper Creek (Blackfoot drainage), 30

Copper Creek (upper Clark Fork drainage), 45

Coppers Lake, 30

Cottonwood Creek (Blackfoot drainage),
    30–31

Cottonwood Creek (Musselshell drainage), 284

Cottonwood Creek (upper Clark Fork
    drainage), 45–46

Cottonwood Creek (Yellowstone drainage), 318

Cottonwood Lakes, 31

Cougar Creek, 239

Crescent Lake, 154

Crow Creek, 266

Crow Indian Reservation, 328

Crystal Lake (Kootenai drainage), 140

Crystal Lake (Lower Missouri waters), 277

Culver Pond (Widow's Pool), 288

Cut Bank Creek (Glacier National Park), 126

Cut Bank Creek (Marias drainage), 246

D

Daly Creek, 13

Danaher Creek, 113

dangers, real and perceived, 329–30

Dark Horse Lake, 189

Darlington Creek, 239

Dead Man's (Dead) Lake, 46

Dearborn River, 266–67

Deep Creek, 267

Deer Lake, 217

Deer Lodge
    Anaconda Settling Ponds (Warm Springs)
        to, 38–40
    to Drummond, 40

Deerhead Lake, 189

DePuy Spring Creek, 318

Diamond Lake, 217

Dickey Lake, 140

Doctor Lake, 113

Dolus Lakes, 46

Drummond, 40–42

Dry Fork of North Fork of Blackfoot
    River, 31

Duck Creek, 239–40

Duck Lake, 197

Duckhead Lake, 69

Dutchman Creek, 46

E

East Boulder River, 318

East Fisher River, 140–41

East Fork Bitterroot River, 13–14

East Fork Bull River, 69–70

East Fork Fiddler Creek, 300

East Fork Lee Creek, 198

East Fork Main Boulder River, 318

East Fork of North Fork of Blackfoot
    River, 31

East Fork Reservoir, 46

East Fork Rock Creek, 46, 70

East Fork Yaak River, 141

East Gallatin River, 217–18

East Rosebud Creek, 301
East Rosebud Lake, 301
Echo Lake, 46
El Capitan Lake, 14
Elaine Lake, 207
Elizabeth Lake, 126
Elk (Elk Springs or Shitepoke) Creek, 288
Elk Lake, 288
Elk (Sims) Lake, 70
Emerald Lake, 302
Emery Creek, 113–14
Ennis Lake, 237, 240
Essex Creek, 101
Estelle Lake, 207
etiquette, 333–34

F
Fairy Lake, 319
Fatty Lake, 154
Ferguson Lake, 189
Finley Lakes, 118
First Lake, 118
Fish Creek, 70
Fish Lake (Glacier National Park), 131
Fish Lake (Yellowstone drainage), 319
Fish Lakes (Kootenai drainage), 141
Fisher River, 142
fishing
    clothing, 332
    dangers (real and perceived), 329–30
    patterns and leaders, 332. *See also* flies,
        popular
    rods, reels, lines, 331
    stream access, 339–43
    stream etiquette, 333–34
    suggested gear, 331–32
    whirling disease and, 234, 335–37
Fishtrap Creek, 72
Fishtrap Lake, 72
Five Mile Creek, 142
Flat Creek, 267
Flat Rock Lake, 207
Flathead, 81–120
    Flathead Indian Reservation, 117–20
    Flathead Lake, 81–84
    Flathead River, 85–97; below Kerr Dam,
        88–90; Blankenship Bridge, 85–88;
        drainage fishing waters, 91–97

maps, 82, 86–87, 100, 104, 110–11
    Middle Fork of Flathead River, 97–102
    North Fork of Flathead River, 102–7
    South Fork of Flathead River, 108–17;
        drainage fishing waters, 112–17; map,
        110–11; wilderness in upper river,
        109–12
flies, popular
    about: author's top nine, ix; suggested
        patterns and leaders, 332
    Beaverhead River (dry flies), 168
    Big Hole River, 185
    Bitterroot Blackfoot, 9
    Blackfeet Reservation, 200
    Blackfoot River, 27
    Clarks Fork of the Yellowstone, 205
    Gallatin River, 216
    Glacier National Park, 125
    Jefferson River, 224
    lower Clark Fork, 67
    Missouri River, 257
    Missouri River (sub-surface patterns), 258
    Musselshell River, 283
    nymphs, 166
    upper Clark Fork, 42
Flint Creek, 46–47
Flood Creek, 302
Flotilla Lake, 101–2
Forest Grove, 65
Fort Belknap, 328
Fort Peck reservation, 328
Fort Peck Reservoir, 262–63, 277
Fortine Creek, 142
Four Horns Lake, 198
Four Mile Basin Lakes, 47–48
Fox Lake, 207
Fran Lake, 154–55
Frances Lake (Lake Frances), 246
Francis Creek, 189
Francis Lake, 126
Frank Lake, 142
French Lake, 72
Fresno Reservoir, 252
Frozen Lake, 105, 142

G
Gallatin River, 211–19
    about: overview of, 211

drainage fishing waters, 217–19
Gallatin Forks to Missouri River, 214–17
Gallatin Gateway to Gallatin Forks, 214
map, 212
popular flies, 216
Taylor Fork to Gallatin Gateway, 213
Yellowstone Park boundary to Taylor Fork, 211–13
Gardner River, 320
gear, suggested, 331–32
George Lake, 114
Georgetown Lake, 48–49
Gibson Reservoir, 267
Glacier Creek, 155
Glacier Lake (Clarks Fork drainage), 207
Glacier Lake (Swan drainage), 155
Glacier National Park, 121–32
about: overview of, 121–25
eastern waters, 125–29
map, 122–23
popular flies, 125
western waters, 129–32
Gleason Lake, 14
Glen Lake, 142–43
Glenn's Lake, 126
Goat Mountain Lakes, 49
Gold Creek, 49
Gold Creek Dredge Ponds, 49
Good Creek, 91
Goose Lake (Madison drainage), 240
Goose Lake (Stillwater drainage), 302
Gordon Creek, 114
Gorge Creek, 114
Grace Lake, 131
Granite Lake, 207
Grasshopper Creek, 174
Grasshopper Reservoir, 252
Grave Creek, 143
Graves Creek, 114
Gray Wolf Lake, 155
Grayling Creek, 240
Grebe Reservoir, 284
Green Canyon Lake, 49
Green Lake, 207
Griffin Creek, 91–92
Grinnell Lake, 126
Gunsight Lake, 126

H
Hall Lake, 155
Hamby Lake, 189
Handkerchief Lake, 114
Harper's Lakes, 31
Harrison Lake and Creek, 131
Hart (or Heart) Lake, 155
hatches, important, 8
Hauser Lake/Dam, 257–58, 267–68
Hawkins Lakes, 144
Hay Lake, 105
Hearst Lake, 49
Heart Lake (Blackfoot drainage), 31
Heart Lake (lower Clark Fork drainage), 72
Hebgen Lake, 233, 240–41
Hellroaring Creek, 288–89
Hellroaring Lakes, 207
Helmville Bridge, 24–25
Hemlock Lake, 155
Herat (or Hart) Lake, 155
Hidden Lake (Big Creek drainage), 14
Hidden Lake (Glacier National Park, eastern waters), 126
Hidden Lake (Glacier National Park, western waters), 131
Hidden Lake (Madison drainage), 241
Hidden Lake (Marias drainage), 246
Hidden Lake (Smith drainage), 294
Hidden Lake (Yellowstone drainage), 320
Hidden Lakes (Gallatin drainage), 218
Hidden Lakes (Rock Creek drainage), 49
High Park Lake, 156
Highwood Creek, 277
Holland Lake, 156
Holter Lake, 258–59, 268
Horseshoe Lake, 156–57
Hoskin Lake, 144
Hound Creek, 294
Howard Lake, 144
Hubbart Reservoir, 92
Hughes Creek, 14
Hungry Horse Reservoir, 114
Huntsberger Lake, 107
Hyalite Creek, 218
Hyalite Reservoir, 218
Hyde Creek Pond, 285

I

Indian reservations
    Blackfeet Reservation, 193–201
    Crow, 328
    Flathead Indian Reservation, 117–20
    Fort Belknap, 328
    Fort Peck, 328
    Northern Cheyenne, 328
    Rocky Boy's, 328
International Creek, 226
Isabel Lake, 131
Island Lake, 157

J

Jackson (Rocky) Creek, 218
Jasper Lake, 208
Jefferson River, 221–27
    about: overview of, 221–25
    drainage fishing waters, 225–27
    map, 222
    popular flies, 224
Jewel Lakes, North and South, 115
Jim Creek, 157
Jim Lake, 157
Job Corps (Duck) Ponds, 49–50
Jocko River, 92
Johnsrud Park, 26–27
Judith River, 277–79

K

Keep Cool Creek, 32
Keep Cool Lakes, 32
Kelly Reservoir, 175
Kennedy Creek, 126
Kersey Lake, 208
Kicking Horse Reservoir, 118
Kilbrennan Lake, 144
Kintla Lake and Creek, 131
Kipp Lake, 198
Koessler Lake, 115
Kootenai, 133–50
    about: overview of, 133–36
    below Libby Dam, 136–37
    big water country, 137–38
    drainage fishing waters, 139–50
    map, 134–35
    warm weather action, 138–39
Kootenai Creek, 14

Kootenai Lakes, 14, 126

L

Lace Lake, 157
Lagoni Lake, 92
Lake Agnes, 189
Lake Alva, 32
Lake at the Falls, 302
Lake Creek (Clarks Fork drainage), 208
Lake Creek (Kootenai drainage), 144
Lake Ellen Wilson, 131
Lake Frances (Frances Lake), 246
Lake Helena, 268
Lake Inez, 32
Lake Koocanusa, 145
Lake Mary Ronan, 92
Lake of the Winds, 208
Landers Fork of Blackfoot River, 32
Lawn Lake, 72
leaders, suggested patterns and, 332. *See also*
    flies, popular
Leigh Creek, 144
Leigh Lake, 145
Lena Lake, 115
Leon Lake, 145
Leslie Lake, 226
Libby Creek, 145
Libby Dam, Kootenai below, 136–37
Lightning Lake, 302
Lily Lake, 190
Lincoln Lake, 131
Line Lake, 208
lines, suggested, 331
Little Bitterroot Lake, 92
Little Blackfoot River, 50–51
Little Boulder River, 226–27
Little McGregor Lake, 72, 145
Little Prickly Pear Creek, 268–69
Little Rock Creek, 14–15
Little Salmon River, 116
Little Thompson River, 72, 145
Logan Creek, 92
Logging Lake and Creek, 131
Lolo Creek, 15. *See also* South Fork Lolo Creek
Lone Elk Lake, 208
Long Lake, 208–9
Loon Lake, 145, 157–58

Lost Creek, 51
Lost Horse Lake, 15
Lost (Morigeau) Lakes, 118
Lowell Lake, 72
lower Clark Fork, 61–79
  about: overview of, 61
  Blackfoot River mouth to Kelly Island, 61
  drainage fishing waters, 67–79
  Forest Grove to Paradise, 65–66
  Kelly Island to Petty Creek, 61–63
  map, 62–63
  Paradise to Thompson Falls, 66
  Petty Creek to Forest Grove (Alberton Gorge), 65
  popular flies, 67
  Thompson Falls to Idaho, 67
Lower (Little) Barker Lake, 51
Lower Quartz Lake, 132
Lower Stillwater Lake, 92–93
Lower Thompson River, 72–73
Lower Willow Creek Reservoir, 52
Lucifer Lake, 118
Lupine Lake, 93

M
Madison River, 229–42
  about: overview of, 229
  Beartrap Canyon mouth to Three Forks, 238
  drainage fishing waters, 238–42
  Ennis Lake to Bear Trap Canyon, 237–38
  Hebgen Lake to Quake Lake, 233
  junction to Hebgen Lake, 229–33
  map, 230–31
  Quake Lake to Slide Inn, 234
  Slide Inn to Varney Bridge, 234–37
  Varney Bridge to Ennis Lake, 237
Margaret Lake, 116
Marias River, 243–47
Marion Lake, 102
Marl Lake, 145
Martin Creek, 16
Martinsdale Reservoir, 285
Mason Lakes, 227
McDonald Creek, 132
McDonald Lake, 132
McDonald's Pool (Buck Pond), 289
McGregor Lake, 73
Meadow Creek, 32

Meadow Lakes, 52
Medicine Grizzly Lake, 126
Medicine Lake (Lower Missouri waters), 279
Medicine Lake (Stillwater drainage), 302–3
Medicine Lake (upper Rock Creek drainage), 52
Metcalf Lake, 158
Middle Fork Dearborn River, 269
Middle Fork Flathead River, 97–102
Middle Fork Milk River, 253
Middle Fork Rock Creek, 52
Middle Quartz Lake, 132
Middle Thompson Lake, 73
Milk River, 249–53
Mill Creek, 320
Milltown Dam, removal of, 41
Miner Lake, 190
Mission Creek, 320
Mission Lake, 198
Missouri River, 255–80
  about: overview of, 255
  Canyon Ferry Dam to Hauser Lake, 257
  Cascade to Fort Peck Reservoir, 262–63
  Hauser Dam to Holter Lake, 258
  Holter Dam to Cascade, 259–61
  Lower Missouri fishing waters, 272–80
  maps, 264–65, 274
  popular flies, 257
  popular sub-surface patterns, 258
  Three Forks to Toston Dam, 256
  Toston Dam to Canyon Ferry Reservoir, 256–57
  Upper Missouri fishing waters, 263–72
Mitten Lake, 198
Mollman Lakes, 158
Monture Creek, 32–33
Moon Lake, 209
Moore Lake, 73
Moose Creek, 107, 294
Moose Lake, 107
Moran Lake, 146
Morrell Creek, 33
Morrison Lake, 289
Mount Henry Lake, 146
Mud Lake, 52
Mud Lakes, 118–19
Murphy Lake, 146
Murray Lake, 93
Musselshell River, 281–85

Mystic Lake (Big Hole drainage), 190
Mystic Lake (Stillwater drainage), 303
Myxobolus cerebralis. See whirling disease

N
Nasukoin Lake, 107
Necklace Lakes, 116
Nelson Reservoir, 253
Nelson's Spring Creek, 321
Nevada Creek, 33
Nevada Creek Lake, 33
Newlan Creek Reservoir, 294
Nez Perce Fork, 16
Nilan Reservoir, 269
Ninemile Creek, 74
Ninepipe and Pablo Reservoirs, 93
North Fish Lake, 158
North Fork Big Hole River, 190
North Fork Hilgard Lakes, 241
North Fork Musselshell River, 285
North Fork of Blackfoot River, 33–34
North Fork of Flathead River, 102–7
North Fork Smith River, 296
North Fork Sun River, 269
Northern Cheyenne Indian Reservation, 328
Norwegian Creek, 227
Notlimah Lake, 158
Noxon Reservoir, 74. *See also* Trout Creek
    (Noxon Reservoir); West Fork Trout
    Creek (Noxon Reservoir)
nymphs, popular, 166

O
O'Dell Creek, 190
O'Dell Lake, 190
Oldman Lake, 126
orange paint, stream access and, 341–43
Otatsy Lake, 34
Otokomi Lake, 129
Ovis Lake, 209

P
Pablo Reservoir, 93
Painted Rocks Lake, 16
Paradise, 65–66
patterns, suggested leaders and, 332. *See also*
    flies, popular

Peterson Lake, 16
Petty Creek, 74
Phyllis Lakes, 52
Pintler Lake, 190
Pipe Creek, 146
Pishkun Reservoir, 269
Placid Lake, 34
Pleasant Valley Fisher River, 146
Poindexter Slough, 175–76
Polaris Lake, 176
Porcupine Creek, 321
Post Creek, 93
Powder River, 321–22
Prickly Pear Creek, 270
Prospect Creek, 74
Ptarmigan Lake, 129

Q
Quake Lake, 233–34, 241–42
Quartz Creek and Lower Quartz, Middle
    Quartz, and Quartz Lakes, 132
Quintonkon Creek, 116

R
Racetrack Creek, 52–53
Racetrack Lake, 53
Rainbow Lake (Flathead River drainage), 93
Rainbow Lake (upper Clark Fork drainage), 53
Rainbow Lakes (Yellowstone drainage), 322
Rainy Lake, 34
Ranch Creek, 53
Rat Lake, 218–19
Rattlesnake Creek, 74–75
Red Eagle Lake, 129
Red Lodge Creek, 209
Red Meadow Lake, 107
Red Rock Creek, 289
Red Rock Lakes, 289
Red Rock River, 287–89
reels, suggested, 331
Reservoir Lake, 176–77
Rhoda Lake, 279
Ridge Lake, 190
Ripple Lake, 16
A River Runs Through It (film), 21
A River Runs Through It (Maclean), 21
Roaring Lion Creek, 16

Rock Creek (Bitterroot drainage), 16
Rock Creek (Clarks Fork drainage), 209
Rock Creek (Garrison), 53–54
Rock Creek (lower Clark Fork drainage), 75
Rock Creek (Smith drainage), 296
Rock Creek (upper Clark Fork drainage), 54–58
Rock Creek Lake (Rock Lake), 75
Rock Island Lake (Clarks Fork drainage), 209
Rock Island Lakes (Big Hole drainage), 191
Rock Lake (Rock Creek Lake), 75
Rocky Boy's reservation, 328
Rocky (Jackson) Creek, 218
rods, suggested, 331
Rogers Lake, 93
Rosebud River, 303
Ross Fork Rock Creek, 58
Rough Lake, 209
Ruby Reservoir, 177
Ruby River, 177–79
rules stream access, 343
Rumble Creek Lakes, 158–59
Russ Lake, 159

S
St. Mary Lake, 129
St. Mary River, 198–200
St. Paul Lake, 75
St. Regis River, 75
Salmon Lake, 34
Sawtooth Lake, 179
Schwartz Creek, 58
Scott Lake, 179
Seeley Lake, 34
Seventeenmile Creek, 146
Shay Lake, 159
Sheafman Lakes, 16
Sheep (Big Sheep) Creek (Red Rock drainage), 289
Sheep Creek (Smith drainage), 297
Shelf Lake (Bitterroot drainage), 17
Shelf Lake (South Fork of Flathead River drainage), 116
Shields River, 322–23
Shitepoke (Elk or Elk Springs) Creek, 288
Siamese Lakes, 75
Silver Lake (Clarks Fork drainage), 210

Silver Lake (lower Clark Fork drainage), 75
Sixteen Mile Creek, 270
Skalkaho Creek, 17. *See also* South Fork Skalkaho Creek
Sleeping Child Creek, 17
Slide Inn, 234
Slough Creek, 323
Smith Lake, 93
Smith River, 291–97
    about: overview of, 291–94
    drainage fishing waters, 294–97
    map, 292
Snowbank Lake, 35
Sodalite Lake, 210
Sophie Lake, 146
South Boulder River, 227
South Crow Creek (and Terrace) Lakes, 119–20
South Fork Big Hole River, 191
South Fork Birch Creek, 246
South Fork Cold Creek Lakes, 159
South Fork Dearborn River, 270
South Fork Flathead River, 108–17
South Fork Lolo Creek, 17
South Fork Madison River, 242
South Fork Milk River, 253
South Fork Musselshell River, 285
South Fork Skalkaho Creek, 17
South Fork Spanish Creek, 219
South Fork Sun River, 270
Spanish Lakes, 219
Spar Lake, 146
Spencer Lake, 94
Spotted Bear River, 116
Spring Creek (Flathead River drainage), 94
Spring Creek (upper Clark Fork drainage), 58
Square Lake, 159
Squaw Creek, 219
Stanton Lake, 102
Steel Creek, 191
Stewart Lake, 58
Stillwater River, 94, 299–303
Stone Lakes, 191
Stony Lake, 75
Storm Lake, 58
Strawberry Lake, 94
stream access, 339–43

stream etiquette, 333–34
Stryker Lake, 94
Summit Lake (Blackfoot drainage), 35
Summit Lake (Gallatin drainage), 219
Sun River, 270–71
Sunrise Lake, 227
Sutherlin (Smith River) Reservoir, 297
Swamp Creek, 77
Swan Lake, 154, 159–60
Swan River, 151–60
  about: overview of, 151
  drainage fishing waters, 154–60
  headwater tributaries to Lindbergh
    Lake, 151
  Lindbergh Lake mouth to Swan
    Lake, 153–54
  map, 152
Sweet Grass Creek, 323
Swiftcurrent Lake, 129
Sylvan Lake, 303

T
Tahepia Lake, 191
Tally Lake, 94
Taylor Fork Gallatin River, 211–13, 219
Ten Lakes, 147
Ten Mile Creek, 271–72
Ten Mile Lakes, 191
Tenderfoot Creek, 297
Tendoy Lake, 191
Terrace Lake, 77
Teton River, 246–47
Therriault Lakes (Big and Little), 147
Thompson Falls, 65–66
Thompson Lake, 219
Thompson River, 77–78
Thornton Lake, 58
Three Forks, 238, 256
Threemile Creek, 17
Timber Lake, 147
Tin Cup Creek, 18
Tin Cup Lake, 18
Tobacco River, 148
Tom Poole Lake, 148
Tongue River, 323
Tongue River Reservoir, 323
Topless Lake, 148
Toston Dam, 256

Tranquil Basin Lake, 102
Trask Lake, 59
travel in Montana, 327. *See also* stream access
Triangle Lake, 210
Trio Lakes, 78
Trout Creek, 78
Trout Creek (Noxon Reservoir), 78
Trout Lake, 132
Tuchuck Lake, 107
Tunnel Creek, 102
Turquoise Lake, 160
Twin Lakes (Big Hole drainage), 191
Twin Lakes (Blackfeet Reservation), 201
Twin Lakes (Blackfoot drainage), 35
Twin Lakes (upper Clark Fork drainage), 59
Two Medicine River, 129

U
upper Clark Fork, 37–59
  about: overview of, 37–38
  Anaconda Settling Ponds (Warm Springs) to
    Deer Lodge, 38–40
  Butte to Warm Springs, 38
  Deer Lodge to Drummond, 40
  drainage fishing waters, 43–59
  Drummond to Rock Creek mouth, 40–42
  Milltown Dam removal, 41
  popular flies, 42
  Rock Creek mouth to Milltown Dam,
    42–43
Upper Holland Lake, 160
Upper Stillwater Lake, 94
Upper Thompson Lake, 78–79
Upper Two Medicine River, 129
Upper Whitefish Lake, 94
Upsata Lake, 35

V
Valley Creek, 96
Van Lake, 160
Varney Bridge, 234–37
Vermilion River, 79
Vinal Lake, 148

W
Wade Lake, 242
Wallace Reservoir, 59
Wanless Lake, 79

Warm Spring Creek (Warm Springs), 59

Warm Springs, Anaconda Settling Ponds, 38–40

Warm Springs Creek (Big Hole drainage), 191

Warm Springs Creek (Bitterroot drainage), 18

Warm Springs Creek (Lower Missouri waters), 279

Warren Creek, 35

Warren Lake, 192

Watt Reservoir, 279

Weasel Lake, 148

West Boulder River, 323–25

West Fork Bitterroot River, 18–19

West Fork Clearwater River, 35

West Fork Gallatin River, 219

West Fork of South Fork of Sun River, 272

West Fork Poplar River, 280

West Fork Rock Creek, 59

West Fork Stillwater River, 303

West Fork Thompson River, 79

West Fork Trout Creek (Noxon Reservoir), 79

West Fork Yaak River, 148

West Rosebud Creek, 303

Whale Creek, 107

Whale Lake, 107

whirling disease, 234, 335–37

White River, 116

Whitefish Lake, 96

Whitefish River, 96–97

Whitetail Creek, 227

Widewater Lake, 210

Widgeon Pond, 289

Widow's Pool (Culver Pond), 288

Wigwam River, 148

Wildcat Lake, 116

Willow Creek (Big Hole drainage), 192

Willow Creek (Harrison) Reservoir, 227

Willow Creek (Jefferson drainage), 227

Willow Creek Reservoir, 272

Willow (Fool or Sage Hen) Lake, 19

Wise River, 185–86, 192

Wolf Creek, 148

Wolverine Lakes, 149

Woodward Creek Lakes, 160

Woodward Lake, 117

Y

Yaak River, 149–50. *See also* East Fork Yaak River; West Fork Yaak River

Yakinikak Creek, 107

Yellowstone Park boundary to Taylor Fork, 211–13

Yellowstone River, 305–25

    about: overview of, 305

    drainage fishing waters, 312–25

    Gardiner to Yankee Jim Canyon, 305–8

    Livingston to Reed Point, 310–11

    map, 306–7

    Reed Point to Billings, 311–12

    Tom Miner Creek to Livingston, 309–10

    Yankee Jim Canyon to Tom Miner Creek, 308

Young Creek, 150

Youngs Creek, 117

Z

Zimmer Lake, 210

ABOUT THE AUTHOR AND PHOTOGRAPHER

Ginny and John Holt live in Livingston, Montana. They have completed a number of books and magazine stories together with Ginny's photographs illustrating John's words. Books include *Coyote Nowhere, Stalking Trophy Browns,* and *Arctic Aurora.* Their work has appeared in *Fly Rod & Reel, Men's Journal, American Cowboy, The Fly Fish Journal* and the late, great *Crossroads Magazine.* They spend a good deal of time on the road camping and fishing in isolated Montana locations along with trips to Alberta, British Columbia, the Yukon, and the Northwest Territories.

Ginny and John Holt donate ten percent of their royalties to benefit Livingston's Loaves and Fishes, an operation that provides meals for those in need.